Atlantic Canadian Imprints,

1801–1820

A BIBLIOGRAPHY

The first comprehensive analytical bibliography of Atlantic Canadian imprints, this volume covers some 320 books, pamphlets, broadsides, government publications, and serials. Most have not been listed before in any bibliography or catalogue. They represent the holdings of more than thirty libraries and archives in the four Atlantic provinces and in Ontario, Quebec, the United States, and England.

Each entry follows the principles of descriptive bibliography and includes full collation, contents, record of paper, type, and binding, analysis of issue and state, and location of every copy examined. Historical notes deal with authorship, printing, publishing, distribution and sales, and with the content of important works and the relationship between items. Arrangement is by province, then by year of publication.

The material catalogued encompasses a wide range of subjects. God and government are two of the most common, but there are many others: education, municipal organization, history, elections, transportation, agriculture, legal trials, and a number of societies – benevolent, national, religious, and masonic. There are also many almanacs, including one in German, several satires and addresses in verse, and a French *abécédaire*. Not surprisingly in a nineteenth-century Maritime bibliography, signal books and decisions about privateers and piracy abound.

Six indexes provide access by author, title, genre, trades, place of publication, and language.

Patricia Fleming's work continues Marie Tremaine's *A Bibliography of Canadian Imprints, 1751–1800*. It adds an essential element to our understanding of print communication in Atlantic Canada.

PATRICIA LOCKHART FLEMING is Associate Professor in the Faculty of Library and Information Science, University of Toronto. She is the compiler of *Upper Canadian Imprints, 1801–1841: A Bibliography*.

Atlantic Canadian Imprints, 1801–1820: A Bibliography

PATRICIA LOCKHART FLEMING

University of Toronto Press
Toronto Buffalo London

Toronto Buffalo London
Printed in paperback 2014

ISBN 978-0-8020-5872-0 (cloth)
ISBN 978-1-4426-2373-6 (paper)

Printed on acid-free paper

Canadian Cataloguing in Publication Data

Fleming, Patricia, 1939–
Atlantic Canadian Imprints, 1801–1820

Includes indexes.
ISBN 978-0-8020-5872-0 (bound)
ISBN 978-0-4426-2373-6 (pbk.)

1. Atlantic Provinces – Imprints – Union lists.
2. Maritime Provinces – History – To 1867 – Bibliography – Union lists. 3. Newfoundland – History – 1763–1855 – Bibliography – Union lists.
4. Catalogs, Union – Canada. I. Title.

Z1392.A8F5 1991 015.715 C91-093339-1

Contents

Acknowledgments vii
Introduction ix
Illustrations xiii
Symbols xv
Other Sources xvii

New Brunswick 3

Newfoundland 47

Nova Scotia 56

Prince Edward Island 140

Appendix: Imprints Not Located 157
Name Index 163
Title Index 171
Genre and Subject Index 180
Language Index 186
Trades Index 187
Place of Publication Index 189

Acknowledgments

It was for the National Library of Canada that I began in 1987 to search out and examine Atlantic Canadian imprints to be included in *Canadiana*, the retrospective national bibliography. For that original support and for permission to expand and publish the work I thank Marianne Scott, the National Librarian, and Tom Delsey, director Acquisitions and Bibliographic Services Branch. David Murrell-Wright, chief, Monographs Cataloguing Division, encouraged me through the first phase.

Colleagues in each of the Atlantic provinces offered advice and generous access to their collections. From the very outset I have depended on Shirley Elliott and Karen Smith in Halifax and Eric Swanick in Fredericton. David Bell provided expert guidance to New Brunswick imprints in several institutions. I also wish to thank Burton Glendenning, Carol Rosevear, and Tom Vincent for their help in New Brunswick; Anne Hart and Agnes O'Dea for Newfoundland; Wendy Duff, Sandra Haycock, and John MacLeod at the Public Archives of Nova Scotia; and Edith Haliburton and Pat Townsend at Acadia University. For assistance at the American Antiquarian Society I thank Joanne Chaison, Vincent Kinane, and Marcus McCorison.

It is a pleasure to acknowledge the continuing support of Duncan Chalmers at the Public Record Office, Nellie Reiss and Bruce Whiteman at McGill, Patricia Kennedy and Dawn Monroe at the National Archives, Liana Van der Bellen at the National Library, Robert Montague of the Canadian Institute for Historical Microreproductions, Robert Cupido at the Metropolitan Toronto Reference Library, Sandra Alston and Philip Oldfield at the University of Toronto, and my almanac colleagues, Anne Dondertman and Judith Donnelly.

Before the work could begin Richard Simpson and Lynn Murphy searched bibliographies, newspapers, and primary sources for information about imprints and publishing. Lynn Murphy also completed a survey of collections at the Public Archives of Nova Scotia. I am grateful for their expert help.

Gerald Hallowell got the project started at the University of Toronto Press. When he became an Atlantic Canadian himself, Laura Macleod took over in Toronto. My thanks to both.

Once again, I am greatly indebted to Gwen Peroni for all aspects of the production of the text and to John Fleming for his interest and encouragement.

Introduction

Printing began in Canada at Halifax in 1751 when Bartholomew Green moved his shop from Boston to Nova Scotia. In New Brunswick the first press was established in 1783 by William Lewis and John Ryan. During that same year the loyalist printers James and Alexander Robertson arrived in Shelburne, Nova Scotia. By 1787 James Robertson had set up his press in Charlottetown, Island of St John. Beyond the Atlantic provinces presses were founded in Quebec in 1764 by William Brown and Thomas Gilmore and in Montreal by Fleury Mesplet in 1776. A printer from Quebec and Montreal, Louis Roy, started printing at Niagara in Upper Canada in 1793.

Almost forty years ago Marie Tremaine recorded this first half-century of printing in *A Bibliography of Canadian Imprints, 1751–1800*. The present work deals with printing in New Brunswick, Nova Scotia, and Prince Edward Island during the first two decades of the nineteenth century. For Newfoundland where a press was not established until John Ryan's arrival in 1807 it records imprints of the first fourteen years. Since a supplement to Tremaine is being prepared for the Bibliographical Society of Canada/Société bibliographique du Canada imprints from the period covered by Tremaine have been excluded apart from three almanacs printed late in 1800 and titled for the year 1801. One of them (**NS1**) is in Tremaine; the others (**NS2, NS3**) are additions to the record.

For each of the four Atlantic provinces I have used a numbered sequence which includes books, pamphlets, government publications, broadsides, and serials examined in thirty-five libraries and archives. Newspapers do not form part of this bibliography since provincial directories are in preparation or have been published recently as part of the National Library's Decentralized Program for Canadian Newspapers. Although newspaper supplements and extraordinary issues have also been excluded, carrier's addresses written and printed for presentation as a New Year's greeting from an apprentice to patrons of the newspaper are recorded as a distinct genre. Separately published maps and illustrations have been omitted along with tickets and forms printed for completion in manuscript as part of official transactions such as contracts and land grants.

BIBLIOGRAPHICAL METHOD

This is a descriptive and historical bibliography based on analytical principles derived from the concept of ideal copy. Standards for description have been developed from Fredson Bowers's *Principles of Bibliographical Description* extended by Thomas Tanselle whose paper 'A Sample Bibliographical Description, with Commentary' reviews the literature leading up to Bowers as well as work published since 1949. An earlier study, *Upper Canadian Imprints, 1801–1841: A Bibliography* published in 1988, has served as a model for this bibliography.

Imprints are arranged chronologically by year of publication with undated items assigned to the most probable or the earliest possible year on the basis of content and physical evidence. Such attributions are discussed in the notes. Since almanacs were intended for publication before the New Year I have assumed, except where primary evidence indicates a delay in publication, that Atlantic almanacs appeared late in the autumn before the year for which they were calculated.

Heading Each imprint has been assigned a provincial code (NB, NS, Nfld, PEI) and an item number. Headings and cross references are intended to be compatible with *Anglo-American Cataloguing Rules* (2d ed). Personal names are consistent with usage established by the *Dictionary of Canadian Biography*.

Title page transcription Quasi-facsimile transcription records the full text of each title page with line endings (|), rules, and typographic identification. LARGE and SMALL capitals are reproduced along with DROP letters and *italic* type. The lower-case long s is printed as ſ. Black letter founts, both the fraktur used by Anthony Henry and the English display face, are printed in ***bold italic*** with bold roman punctuation. Square brackets mark off [interjections by the author]; bold square brackets **[ ]** are transcriptions of the original. For works without a title page the caption title, half title, wrapper title, or opening lines of text have been transcribed. An imprint or printer's note added to the text is noted in the contents and transcribed below the title page as IMPRINT (**NS144**).

In the case of broadsides, a full transcription of the opening lines is followed by selective transcription from the text to provide a title page substitute with author, content, imprint, and date. The use of an ellipsis within a line of text indicates omission of part of that line; an ellipsis between line endings (| ... |) shows that one or more lines have been omitted. The second line ending is dropped when the text continues beyond the final line of transcripton (| ...).

Collation Format and dimension precede the statement of signature collation. Since the 23-letter alphabet was not consistently used in Atlantic printing the record of signatures sets down precisely what is there. Italic is used for unsigned gatherings in a regularly signed sequence (A^8 B–E^8). An unsigned sequence is numbered in italic (1–5^8) while π and χ designate unsigned preliminary and inserted gatherings (π^4 A^8 B–C^8 χ^2 D–E^8). The convention of indicating double and multiple signing by writing 3A in place of AAA or Aaa has not been followed for Nova Scotia's annual laws which were published without caption title or half title. Signing which was continued on from year to year has been recorded as it was printed to aid in the identification of these confusing items (**NS7**). Italic is used to supply numbers for pages which are part of a regular sequence but are not numbered (*1–3* 4–21 *22–24*). Pages which cannot be inferred as part of a sequence are recorded by total in italic within square brackets ([*4*] *1–3* 4–21 *22–24*).

Contents The contents note that follows collation accounts for every leaf recorded in the signature collation and total, and in the statement of pagination. Every page which went through the press, whether printed or blank, is enumerated in a summary statement of contents.

Paper Watermarks and papermakers' names have been verified in sources such as Churchill, Gravell and Miller, and Shorter. The method of fabrication of the wove paper, hand or machine-made, is not recorded since all of the wove paper used in these imprints appears to be handmade. A native paper industry was not established in the Atlantic provinces until the end of this period when Anthony Holland's Acadian Paper Mill at Hammond Plains near Halifax began production of wrapping paper in November of 1819 and of printing paper early in 1820 (**NS183**).

Illustrations Apart from the astrological man of signs figure used in many of the Nova Scotia almanacs and the two cuts, one scenic and the other veterinary, taken over by Archibald and Elizabeth Gay with Anthony Henry's print shop (**NS4, NS20, NS34**), there are only two original illustrations in the imprints listed, a woodcut of weapons (**NS121**) and a topographic engraving (**NS170**). Another plate in a false Halifax imprint is probably English (**NS172**). The man of signs cuts are described using illustrations in specimen books and Reilly's *Dictionary of Colonial American Printers' Ornaments & Illustrations.*

Typography Text types are identified by size and design. Display faces and ornaments have been described in conventional decorative terms and cited visually by reference to published specimens of contemporary type founders. Precise attribution to one specimen is difficult since similar letters and flowers were available from several foundries at the same time. The specimens are listed with other symbols.

The type measurement is standard consisting of the number of lines on a page followed by the dimension of the type page (extended) and concluding with a measurement of 20 lines of text.

Binding The simplest binding operation is stitching, passing a thread through all the leaves of a pamphlet or even a substantial book. Wrapping the stitched gatherings in paper, coloured, marbled, or printed like the title page, was a common finish for almanacs and popular works (**Nfld15, NS121**). The addition of a paper spine strengthened the wrapper (**NS69**). Still humble but more durable was a paper spine and paper covered boards over gatherings sewn through the fold (**NS119**); the paper for the upper board was sometimes printed to identify the work (**NS139**) or a label could be printed and pasted to the spine (**NB85**). For laws and legislative journals bindings of leather (**NB64, NS37**) or leather and paper covered boards were traditional. A series of half leather and marbled paper bindings from New Brunswick dated 1810 to 1816 has a distinctive trapezoidal leather label on the upper board.

Bindings have been described using Middleton for marbled paper and the ISCC-NBS *Centroid Color Charts* for a vocabulary of colour. This section has been omitted from the entry for broadsides and rebound materials.

Notes The notes dealing with authorship, printing, publishing, distribution, and sales have been compiled largely from primary sources: newspapers, manuscripts, and government records.

Copies examined All copies cited here have been examined by the author. Standard symbols for the collections are listed following this introduction.

References Catalogues and bibliographies which include these imprints are noted in abbreviated form. Full entries are found in the symbols list.

Appendix Conjectural entries for imprints which are documented in contemporary sources or in bibliographies but have not been located comprise the appendix. A paragraph quoting primary evidence or citing the bibliographic source follows each entry. In addition to these documented imprints there were scores, perhaps hundreds, of handbills or broadsides printed to disseminate official notices and regulations, announce community events and entertainments, and advertise sales of every possible commodity. As a visitor to Halifax remarked in 1817, 'Nothing is more apt to strike an Englishman with wonder on his first arrival here, than the very marked difference, which obtains in the general management of business, and the handbills, which meet his eye every where, announcing the Public Auctions of the day' (*Free Press*, 2 September 1817).

Name Index Personal and corporate names have been taken from the main imprint file along with pseudonyms, attributions of authorship, and added entries such as the names of ships tried in prize cases.

Title Index Title entries have been extended to accommodate broadsides and to group related imprints under a uniform heading.

Genre and Subject Index Genre terms and subjects come from published lists and from established usage in catalogues and bibliographies of Canadian materials. Detailed contents notes in the entry for each almanac provide access to lists such as local officials, organizations, army and militia, clergy, schools, roads, and miscellaneous information. For prose selections and poetry in almanacs I have quoted titles along with a sample of opening lines from seasonal verses added to the calendars.

Language Index Although French, German, Irish, and Gaelic were spoken and read in the Atlantic provinces (**PEI1, PEI3, NS117**) only two imprints in languages other than English have been located, Anthony Henry's last German almanac (**NS3**), and an incomplete copy of an *Abécédaire* (**NS138**).

Trades Index The two bookbinders whose work is documented in primary sources lead off the list followed by printers, publishers, and printing offices identified by name in the imprints. Attribution of work published without a printer's name has been suggested only when there is primary evidence for the claim. The Nova Scotia laws and journals for example can be attributed to John Howe, the king's printer, on the basis of payments made in some years and copies offered for sale in others. In Charlottetown where James Bagnall was the only printer it can be assumed that all the work came from his shop, but in St John's where several printers were working at the same time attribution is not possible.

Place of Publication Index In Newfoundland and Prince Edward Island printing was limited during this period to one city as it was in Nova Scotia after the second press established at Shelburne in the eighteenth century was removed to Charlottetown. New Brunswick had presses in both Fredericton and Saint John as well as a third press founded in St Andrews late in 1819 but seized and offered at auction in April of the following year 'for a breach of the Revenue Laws' (*New Brunswick Royal Gazette*, 17 August 1819; *New Brunswick Courier*, 20 April 1820).

Illustrations

NB5 New Brunswick. Parliament (3rd, 5th session: 1801). House of Assembly. *Journal*. 1801 5
NB11 Job Creon. *A Statement of Facts Relative to The Standfasts and The Runaways*. 1802 9
NB25 *The News-Carrier's Address*. 1805 15
NB55 George J. Mountain. *A Sermon Preached in the Parish Church of Fredericton*. 1816 29
NB57 New Brunswick. Parliament (5th, 5th session: 1816). House of Assembly. *Journal*. 1816 31
NB60 *An Almanack for the Year of Our Lord, 1818* 33
Nfld1 Benevolent Irish Society (St John's). *A Report*. 1807 48
Nfld15 James Sabine. *A Sermon in Commemoration of the Benevolence of the Citizens of Boston*. 1818 55
NS3 *Der-Neu-Schottländische Calender*. 1801 57
NS7 Nova Scotia. Laws (8th Parliament, 2nd session: 1801). 1801 61
NS26 University of King's College (Windsor). *The Statutes, Rules, and Ordinances*. 1803 67
NS34 *View of Halifax* 73
An Almanack for the Year of Our Lord, 1806 74
NS47 John Wilson, defendant. *The Trial of John Wilson alias Jenkin Ratford*. 1807 81
NS95 John Inglefield. *Captain Inglefield's Narrative of the Loss of the Centaur*. 1813 99
NS119 *A Poetical Account of the American Campaigns*. 1815 109
NS121 William James. *An Inquiry into the Merits of the Principal Naval Actions between Great Britain and the United States*. 1816 111
NS136 *The Nova-Scotia Calendar for 1818* 119
NS158 Lunenburg Farmer Society. *Articles or Rules for the Government*. 1819 127
PEI19 Prince Edward Island. Laws (6th Parliament, 7th session: 1798 to 9th Parliament, 2nd session: 1814). *Acts*. 1814 145
PEI33 Robert Alder. *Vastator Perditus: The Substance of a Sermon Delivered February 21st, 1819, at the Wesleyan Methodist Chapel, Charlotte-Town*. 1819 151

Symbols

COPIES EXAMINED

NBFA Provincial Archives of New Brunswick, Fredericton
NBFL Legislative Library, Fredericton
NBFU University of New Brunswick, Fredericton
NBS Saint John Regional Library
NBSAM Mount Allison University, Sackville
NBSM New Brunswick Museum, Saint John
NFSA Provincial Archives of Newfoundland and Labrador, St John's
NFSM Queen Elizabeth II Library, Memorial University of Newfoundland, St John's
NFSPR Provincial Reference and Resource Library, St John's
NSHD Dalhousie University, Halifax
NSHK University of King's College, Halifax
NSHL Legislative Library, Halifax
NSHP Nova Scotia Public Archives, Halifax
NSWA Acadia University, Wolfville
OOA National Archives, Ottawa
OONL National Library of Canada, Ottawa
OTAR Archives of Ontario, Toronto
OTCC United Church of Canada Archives, Toronto
OTMCL Metropolitan Reference Library, Toronto
OTUTF Thomas Fisher Rare Book Library, University of Toronto
PCA Public Archives, Charlottetown
PCL Confederation Centre Library, Charlottetown
PCU University of Prince Edward Island, Charlottetown
QMBM Bibliothèque de la ville de Montréal
QMM McLennan Library, McGill University, Montreal
QMMRB Rare Books and Special Collections, McGill University, Montreal
QQAA Archives de l'Archevêché de Québec

GBL British Library, London
GBPRO Public Record Office, Kew

USICRL Center for Research Libraries, Chicago
USMBAt Boston Athenaeum
USMH-H Harvard University, Houghton Library, Cambridge, Mass.
USMH-L Harvard University, Law School, Cambridge, Mass.
USMHi Massachusetts Historical Society, Boston
USMWA American Antiquarian Society, Worcester, Mass.

From *Symbols of Canadian Libraries*, 12th ed. Ottawa: National Library of Canada, 1987; *Symbols of American Libraries*, 13th ed. Washington, DC: Library of Congress, 1985

REFERENCES, CATALOGUES, AND TYPE SPECIMENS

Akins — *A Catalogue of the Akins Collection of Books and Pamphlets.* Publications of the Public Archives of Nova Scotia, No 1. Halifax: Imperial Publishing, 1933

Binny and Ronaldson — Binny and Ronaldson (Philadelphia). *The Specimen Books of Binny and Ronaldson, 1809–1812, in Facsimile.* Connecticut: Columbiad Club, 1936

Bishop — Bishop, Olga Bernice. *Publications of the Governments of Nova Scotia, Prince Edward Island, New Brunswick, 1758–1952.* Ottawa: National Library of Canada, 1957

Casey — Casey, Magdalen. *Catalogue of Pamphlets in the Public Archives of Canada, 1493–1877.* Ottawa: King's Printer, 1931

Caslon 1785 — 'A Specimen of Printing Types by William Caslon, London, 1766.' Edited by James Mosley. *Journal of the Printing Historical Society* 16 (1981/82)

Dennis — *A Catalogue of the Eric R. Dennis Collection of Canadiana in the Library of Acadia University.* Wolfville: 1938

Figgins 1815 — *Vincent Figgins Type Specimens, 1801 and 1815.* Edited by Bernard Wolpe. London: Printing Historical Society, 1967

Fry and Steele 1790 — Berry, W.T. and A.F. Johnson. *Catalogue of Specimens of Printing Types by English and Scottish Printers and Founders, 1665–1830.* London: Oxford University Press, 1935

Fry and Steele catalogue — undated catalogue of ornaments 'formerly the property of Hon John Neilson' now at the University of Western Ontario. James Mosley has suggested a date in the second half of the first decade of the nineteenth century.

Fry and Steele in Stower — Stower, Caleb. *The Printer's Grammar; or, Introduction to the Art of Printing.* London: Crosby, 1808; reprint, London: Gregg, 1965

Gagnon — Gagnon, Philéas. *Essai de bibliographie canadienne.* Québec: 1895, 1913

Gravell and Miller, *Foreign* — Gravell, Thomas L. and George Miller. *A Catalogue of Foreign Watermarks Found on Paper Used in America, 1700–1835.* New York, London: Garland, 1983

Lande — *The Lawrence Lande Collection of Canadiana in the Redpath Library of McGill University.* Montreal: Lawrence Lande Foundation, 1965; *First Supplement.*Montreal: McGill University, 1971

MTL — *A Bibliography of Canadiana, Second Supplement, Volume 2, 1801–1849.* Toronto: Metropolitan Toronto Library Board, 1985

MacFarlane — MacFarlane, W.G. *New Brunswick Bibliography: The Books and Writers of the Province.* Saint John: Sun Printing, 1895

O'Dea — O'Dea, Agnes C. *Bibliography of Newfoundland*, 2 vols. Toronto: University of Toronto Press, 1986

Reilly — Reilly, Elizabeth Carroll. *A Dictionary of Colonial American Printers' Ornaments & Illustrations.* Worcester, Mass.: American Antiquarian Society, 1975

TPL — *A Bibliography of Canadiana.* Toronto: Toronto Public Library, 1934; *First Supplement*, 1959

Tremaine — Tremaine, Marie. *A Bibliography of Canadian Imprints, 1751–1800.* Toronto: University of Toronto Press, 1952

Other Sources

Acadiensis 1971–

Bell, David Graham. *Early Loyalist Saint John: The Origin of New Brunswick Politics, 1783–1786*. Fredericton: New Ireland Press, 1983

Bowers, Fredson. *Principles of Bibliographical Description*. Princeton, NJ: Princeton University Press, 1949

Bumsted, J.M. 'The Origins of the Land Question on Prince Edward Island.' *Acadiensis* 11, no 1 (Autumn 1981): 43–56

Canada's Smallest Province: A History of P.E.I. Edited by Francis W.P. Bolger. Charlottetown: Prince Edward Island 1973 Centennial Commission, 1973

Checklist and Historical Directory of Prince Edward Island Newspapers, 1787–1986. Compiled by Heather Boylan. Charlottetown: Public Archives of Prince Edward Island, 1987

Churchill, W.A. *Watermarks in Paper*. Amsterdam: Hertzberger, 1935

Condon, Ann Gorman. *The Envy of the American States: The Loyalist Dream for New Brunswick*. Fredericton: New Ireland Press, 1984

Craig, Helen C. *New Brunswick Newspaper Diretory, 1783–1988/Répertoire des journaux du Nouveau-Brunswick, 1783–1988*. Fredericton: Council of Head Librarians of New Brunswick, 1989

Cuthbertson, Brian C. *The First Bishop: A Biography of Charles Inglis*. Halifax: Waegwoltic Press, 1987

—*The Loyalist Governor: A Biography of Sir John Wentworth*. Halifax: Petheric Press, 1983

—*The Old Attorney General: A Biography of Richard John Uniacke, 1753–1830*. Halifax: Nimbus Publishing, 1980

The Dalhousie Journals. Vol 1. Edited by Marjorie Whitelaw. Ottawa: Oberon Press, 1978

Dictionary of Canadian Biography. Toronto: University of Toronto Press, 1966–

Ellison, Suzanne. *Historical Directory of Newfoundland and Labrador Newspapers, 1807– 1987*. St John's: Memorial University of Newfoundland, 1988

Fingard, Judith. *The Anglican Design in Loyalist Nova Scotia, 1783–1816*. London: S.P.C.K., 1972

Genre Terms: A Thesaurus for Use in Rare Book and Special Collections Cataloguing. Chicago: ACRL, 1983

Graham, Gerald S. *Sea Power and British North America, 1783–1820: A Study in British Colonial Policy*. Cambridge: Harvard University Press, 1941

Gravell, Thomas L. and George Miller. *A Catalogue of American Watermarks 1690–1835*. New York: Garland, 1979

Gray, Nicolete. *Nineteenth Century Ornamented Typefaces*. With a chapter by Ray Nash. 2d ed. London: Faber and Faber, 1976

Harper, J. Russell. *Historical Directory of New Brunswick Newspapers and Periodicals*. Fredericton: University of New Brunswick, 1961

Head, C. Grant. *Eighteenth Century Newfoundland: A Geographer's Perspective*. Toronto: McClelland and Stewart, 1976

Heawood, Edward. *Watermarks*. Hilversum: Paper Publications Society, 1950

ISCC-NBS *Centroid Color Charts*. Washington, DC: National Bureau of Standards, 1965
Laing, Lionel H. 'Nova Scotia's Admiralty Court as a Problem of Colonial Administration.' *Canadian Historical Review* 16, no 2 (1935): 151–61
The Legislative Assembly of Nova Scotia, 1758–1983: A Biographical Directory. Edited by Shirley B. Elliott. Halifax: House of Assembly, 1984
Lewis, Philippa and Gillian Darley. *Dictionary of Ornament*. New York: Pantheon, 1986
MacNutt, W.S. *The Atlantic Provinces: The Emergence of Colonial Society, 1712–1857*. Toronto: McClelland and Stewart, 1965
—*New Brunswick: A History: 1784–1867*. Toronto: Macmillan, 1963
Middleton, Bernard. *A History of English Craft Bookbinding Technique*. London: Hafner, 1963
Murdoch, Beamish. *A History of Nova-Scotia, or Acadie*. Vol III. Halifax: James Barnes, 1867
National Library of Canada. *Canadian Subject Headings*. 2d ed. Ottawa: The Library, 1985
Newfoundland in the Nineteenth and Twentieth Centuries: Essays in Interpretation. Edited by James Hiller and Peter Neary. Toronto: University of Toronto Press, 1980
The Newfoundland Quarterly 1901–
Nova Scotia Historical Quarterly 1971–
Nova Scotia Historical Review 1981–
O'Flaherty, Patrick. 'The Seeds of Reform: Newfoundland, 1800–18.' *Journal of Canadian Studies* 23, no 3 (Fall 1988): 39–59
Pedley, Charles. *The History of Newfoundland from the Earliest Times to the Year 1860*. London: Longman, Green, Longman, Roberts, & Green, 1863
Prowse, D.W. *A History of Newfoundland from the English, Colonial, and Foreign Records*. 2d ed. London: Eyre and Spottiswoode, 1896
Pullen, Hugh F. *The Sea Road to Halifax: Being an Account of the Lights and Buoys of Halifax Harbour*. Halifax: Nova Scotia Museum, 1980
Rowe, Frederick W. *A History of Newfoundland and Labrador*. Toronto: McGraw-Hill Ryerson, 1980
Shorter, Alfred H. *Paper Mills and Paper Makers in England 1495–1800*. Hilversum: Paper Publications Society, 1957
Snider, C.H.J. *Under the Red Jack: Privateers of the Maritime Provinces of Canada in the War of 1812*. Toronto: Musson, 1928
Tanselle, G. Thomas. 'A Sample Bibliographical Description, with Commentary,' *Studies in Bibliography*, 40 (1987): 1–30
Whitelaw, Marjorie. *First Impressions: Early Printing in Nova Scotia*. Halifax: Nova Scotia Museum, 1987
Winslow Papers, A.D. 1776–1826. Edited by W.O. Raymond. Saint John: New Brunswick Historical Society, 1901
Woolnough, C.W. *The Whole Art of Marbling*. 2d ed. London: Bell, 1881

ATLANTIC CANADIAN IMPRINTS, 1801–1820

New Brunswick

1801

NB1 Andrews, Samuel, 1737–1818
THE | NECESSITY, THE CERTAINTY, AND THE SUFFICIENCY OF | REVEALED RELIGION, | PROVED IN | TWO SERMONS, | DELIVERED BY THE AUTHOR TO HIS CONGREGATION | AT SAINT ANDREWS, JUNE 7th, 1801, | AND NOW PUBLISHED, | Principally for the Benefit of the Candid, but yet Inquiſitive, | who however want Leiſure to examine more voluminous, | although more perfect Treatiſes upon the Subject. | By Samuel Andrews, A.M. [script] | Rector of SAINT ANDREW's CHURCH, in the Pariſh of | SAINT ANDREWS, and Miſſionary from the Society, &c. | [dot and arrow rule 106 mm] | "*Whoſoever ſhall deny me before Men, him will I alſo deny be- | fore my Father which is in Heaven.*" JESUS CHRIST. | [dot and arrow rule 106 mm] | ST. JOHN, NEW-BRUNSWICK: | PRINTED BY JOHN RYAN, PRINTER TO THE KING'S MOST | EXCELLENT MAJESTY, AT HIS OFFICE, NO. 58, | PRINCE-WILLIAM STREET. | MDCCCI.
COLLATION: 8° (22.5 x 14.3 cm), *1–4*[4] *5*[1], 17 leaves, pp *1–3* 4–15 *16*, [2]*1–2* 3–17 *18* (pagination underlined)
CONTENTS: *1* title; 2 dedication to Charles, Bishop of Nova Scotia; *3*–15 sermon, text: Habakkuk 2d, 14th; *16* blank; [2]*1* half-title [between dot and arrow rules with central ornament 106 mm] | SERMON II. |; [2]2–17 sermon, text: Acts 18th, 28th; [2]*18* blank
PAPER: Laid, unmarked except *1* marked 1799 | (NSHL); chains vertical 28 mm
TYPOGRAPHY: *Text*: english, transitional. *Display*: dot and arrow rule with ornament (brevier 28 of Fry and Steele 1790 specimen)
36 ll., 171 (184) x 107; 93 mm for 20 ll.
BINDING: Stitched (NSHL, USMWA); USMWA copy inscribed 'Joseph Pierpont Eſquire, from his Friend, the Author'
NOTES: A native of Connecticut and a graduate of Yale, Andrews served Charlotte County as a missionary of the Society for the Propagation of the Gospel from 1786 until his death.
Like Andrews John Ryan was an American. He had come with a group of fellow loyalists to the Saint John River settlement in the autumn of 1783. With William Lewis, his partner from New York, he started the *Royal St. John's Gazette* later that year. In 1799 he succeeded Christopher Sower as king's printer, an appointment he held until his move to Newfoundland in 1807 (**Nfld1**).
COPIES EXAMINED: NSHL, QMMRB, USMWA
REFERENCES: Lande S48, MacFarlane

NB2 New Brunswick. Parliament (3rd, 3rd session: 1798). House of Assembly
[within 6 mm ribbon and stick rules 257 x 133 mm] JOURNAL | OF THE | VOTES *and* PROCEEDINGS | OF THE | HOUSE OF ASSEMBLY | OF THE | PROVINCE OF NEW BRUNSWICK: | From TUESDAY the 16th of JANUARY, to FRIDAY the 9th | of FEBRUARY, 1798. | [dot and arrow rule 120 mm] | [royal arms 62 x 118 mm] | [dot and arrow rule 121 mm] | SAINT JOHN: | Printed by JOHN RYAN, N°. 58, Prince William-Street, | PRINTER to the KING'S MOST EXCELLENT MAJESTY. | [dot and arrow rule 22 mm] | 1801.
COLLATION: 2° (32.8 x 20.5 cm), π^1 *A*[2] B–E[2] [$1 signed], 11 leaves, pp *582–584* 585–603
CONTENTS: *582* title; *583* blank; *584*–603 text

PAPER: Laid, marked Vryheyt except π marked Britannia; NBFU copy with π marked EDWARD MUNN | 1800; *A*–E marked Britannia; chains vertical 26 mm
TYPOGRAPHY: *Text*: english, old face. *Display*: title page with frame of great primer 11 of 1785 Caslon specimen and dot and arrow rule (brevier 28 of Fry and Steele, 1790). Text with bead and reel, fret, and snowflake flowers (pica 2 and 5, english 5 of Caslon, 1785)
50 ll., 255 (268) x 143; 94 mm for 20 ll.
NOTES: The laws for 1798 were printed by Christopher Sower in that year but not the Journals although the Assembly had authorized printing of the latter for both 1798 and 1799. A deadlock over the Appropriations Bill between the Assembly and the Council delayed publication until 1801 when Sower's successor John Ryan printed Journals of the third, fourth, and fifth sessions of the third parliament in that same year (**NB3, 4, 5**).
COPIES EXAMINED: NBFU, NBSM (3 copies), OOA
REFERENCE: Tremaine 1096, p 559

NB3 New Brunswick. Laws (3rd Parliament, 5th session: 1801)
[within 6 mm snowflake and berry rules 255 x 129 mm] ACTS | OF THE | GENERAL ASSEMBLY | OF | HIS MAJESTY'S PROVINCE | OF | NEW-BRUNSWICK, | PASSED IN THE YEAR 1801. | [dot and arrow rule 122 mm] | [royal arms 63 x 119 mm] | [dot and arrow rule 122 mm] | SAINT JOHN: | Printed by JOHN RYAN, N°. 58, Prince William-Street, | PRINTER to the KING'S MOST EXCELLENT MAJESTY. | [dot and arrow rule 22 mm] | 1801.
COLLATION: 2° (33.2 x 20 cm), π^2 $2\pi^1$ A^2 B–F^2 [$1 signed], 15 leaves, pp [*6*] *423* 424–445 *446*
CONTENTS: [*1*] title; [*2*] errata (11 ll.); [*3*] session title; [*4*] blank; [*5*] titles of acts; [*6*] blank; *423–445* text; *446* blank
PAPER: Laid, mixed lot with many sheets watermark Britannia; π countermark 1796; 2π marked S LAY | 1799; B, D, F marked GOLDING | & | SNELGROVE | 1799 (NBSM); F marked crown | GR | 1797 in USMH-L copy; chains vertical, varied
TYPOGRAPHY: *Text*: english, old face; script. *Display*: title page with frame of english flowers 5 and 6 of 1785 Caslon specimen and rule (brevier 28 of Fry and Steele 1790). Five more flowers from the 1785 Caslon specimen in text (pica 2 and 10; long primer 11, 14, and 15) with lattice and bead flowers for a head-piece and bead and reel and foliage rules
54 ll., 252 (268) x 115 (142); 93 mm for 20 ll.
NOTES: Christopher Sower, a third generation printer who had apprenticed in the family shop at Germantown, Pennsylvania, printed the Journal and Acts of New Brunswick's first parliament in 1786. His title pages with text framed by printer's flowers established the image of New Brunswick documents which prevailed, with few exceptions, for more than three decades. Perhaps to distinguish his shop from Sower's when the two were competing for government work, John Ryan composed austere titles for the 1787 and 1788 Journals and Acts. Christopher Sower then won back the contract, which was rightly his as king's printer, for 1790 and consolidated his style during the decade before his departure from the province in 1799. When Ryan took over as king's printer after Sower's death in that same year he composed title pages consistent with the Sower model, as did his successors (**NB73**).
Ryan's accounts show that he printed three hundred copies of the Acts at a charge of £27 with £3 2s 6d for folding, stitching, and pressing (NBFA: RS24/S16/R2). A copy was sent along with the Journal (**NB5**) from Fredericton to the Colonial Office on 12 September 1801.
COPIES EXAMINED: NBSM, GBPRO: CO 188, vol 11, ff 81–109, USMH-L

NB4 New Brunswick. Parliament (3rd, 4th session: 1799). House of Assembly
[within 6 mm ribbon and stick rules 256 x 133 mm] JOURNAL | OF THE | VOTES *and* PROCEEDINGS | OF THE | HOUSE OF ASSEMBLY | OF THE | PROVINCE OF NEW-BRUNSWICK: | From TUESDAY the 15th of JANUARY, to FRIDAY the 8th | of FEBRUARY, 1799. | [dot and arrow rule 121 mm] | [royal arms 62 x 118 mm] | [dot and arrow rule 121 mm] | SAINT JOHN: | Printed by JOHN RYAN, N°. 58, Prince William-Street, | PRINTER to the KING'S MOST EXCELLENT MAJESTY. | [dot and arrow rule 22 mm] | 1801.
COLLATION: 2° (32.5 x 20.2 cm), π^1 A^2 B–F^2 [$1 signed], 13 leaves, pp *604–606* 607–629
CONTENTS: *604* title; *605* blank; *606*–629 text
PAPER: Laid, marked Britannia; chains vertical 26 mm
TYPOGRAPHY: *Text*: english, old face. *Display*: title page with frame of great primer 11 of 1785 Caslon specimen and dot and arrow rule (brevier 28 of Fry and Steele, 1790). Text with head-piece of bracket flowers composed as circles and rosebud tail-piece (small pica 17 and double pica 3 of Caslon, 1785)

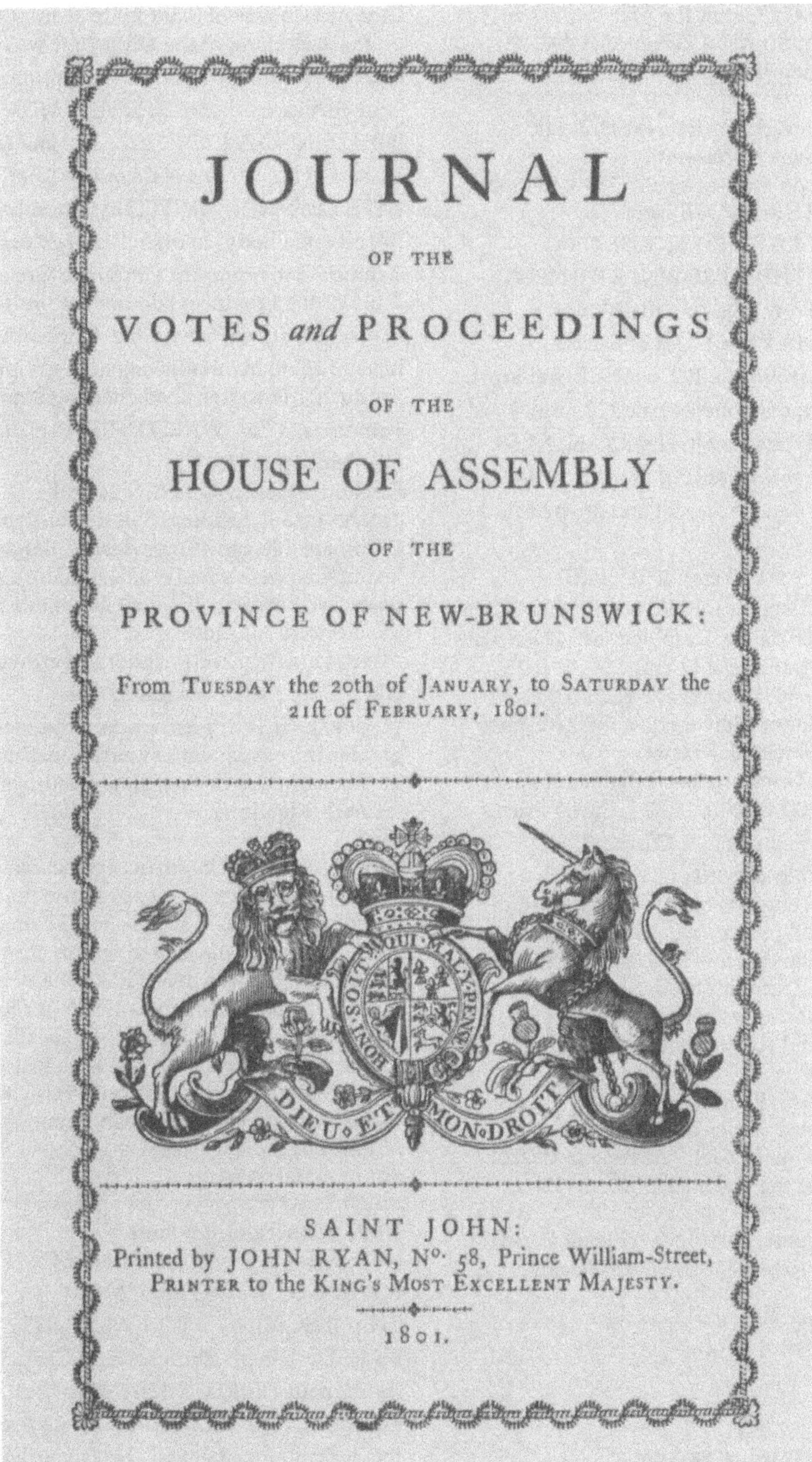

JOURNAL

OF THE

VOTES *and* PROCEEDINGS

OF THE

HOUSE OF ASSEMBLY

OF THE

PROVINCE OF NEW-BRUNSWICK:

From TUESDAY the 20th of JANUARY, to SATURDAY the 21ſt of FEBRUARY, 1801.

SAINT JOHN:
Printed by JOHN RYAN, N°. 58, Prince William-Street,
PRINTER to the KING'S MOST EXCELLENT MAJESTY.

1801.

NB5 Courtesy Legislative Library, Fredericton

53 ll., 249 (266) x 141; 93 mm for 20 ll.
COPIES EXAMINED: NBFU, NBSM (3 copies), OOA
REFERENCE: Tremaine 1096, p 559

NB5 New Brunswick. Parliament (3rd, 5th session: 1801). House of Assembly
[within 6 mm ribbon and stick rules 258 x 134 mm] JOURNAL | OF THE | VOTES *and* PROCEEDINGS | OF THE | HOUSE OF ASSEMBLY | OF THE | PROVINCE OF NEW-BRUNSWICK: | From TUESDAY the 20th of JANUARY, to SATURDAY the | 21*ſt* of FEBRUARY, 1801. | [dot and arrow rule 122 mm] | [royal arms 63 x 119 mm] | [dot and arrow rule 122 mm] | SAINT JOHN: | Printed by JOHN RYAN, N°. 58, Prince William-Street, | PRINTER to the KING'S MOST EXCELLENT MAJESTY. | [dot and arrow rule 23 mm] | 1801.
COLLATION: 2° (31.9 x 19.8 cm), π^1 A^2 B^2 (B1 + χ1,2χ1) C–F^2 G^1 [$1 signed], 16 leaves, pp *630–632* 633–637 [*4*] 638–656 *657* [χ1 is folded leaf 42.3 x 51 cm; 2χ1 is folded leaf 26.5 x 42 cm]
CONTENTS: *630* title; *631* blank; *632*–637 text; [*1–3*] 'A General Account of Merchandize'; [*4*] 'Abstract of Duties'; 638–656 text; *657* blank
PAPER: Laid, π, *A*–G watermark Britannia; *A*–G countermark LEWIS MUNN | 1800; χ, 2χwatermark post horn in crowned shield | C [script]; countermark CURTEIS & SONS
TYPOGRAPHY: *Text*: english, old face. *Display*: title page with frame of great primer 11 of 1785 Caslon specimen and dot and arrow rule (brevier 28 of Fry and Steele, 1790). Text with head-piece of berry and foliage frame enclosing snowflakes (english 6, 7, 5 of Caslon, 1785) and rosebud tail-piece (double pica 3 of Caslon, 1785)
52 ll., 251 (269) x 142; 94 mm for 20 ll.
NOTES: Two hundred copies of the Journal were ordered to be printed (p 645). The copy in GBPRO was transmitted to the Colonial Office on 12 September 1801.
COPIES EXAMINED: NBFL, NBFU, NBSM (2 copies), OOA, OTMCL, GBPRO: CO 188, vol 11, ff 96–109 (lacking χ1, 2χ1)

1802

NB6 Chipman, Ward, 1754–1824
Saint John, (N.B.) 5th October, 1802. | *To WARD CHIPMAN, Esquire*, | SIR, | AT a MEETING of a re*ſ*pectable number of the Electors, | both for the City and County of Saint John, at the Coffee-Hou*ſ*e on the | Evening of the 4th in*ſ*t. it was proposed and agreed that you *ſ*hould be | reque*ſ*ted to offer your *ſ*ervices ... | ... | STEPHEN HUMBERT, | JOHN SINNOT. | ... | *To the Free and Independent Electors of the* | *City and County of Saint John*, | GENTLEMEN, | INVITED by a number of your Re*ſ*pectable Body, to offer | my*ſ*elf once more as a Candidate to repre*ſ*ent you in the General A*ſſ*em- | bly of the Province, I do not feel my*ſ*elf at liberty, con*ſ*i*ſ*tently with the | principles, which have hitherto invariably actuated my public conduct, | to refu*ſ*e obedience to *ſ*o honorable a *ſ*ummons. | ... | WARD CHIPMAN. | Saint John, 5th October, 1802.
Election notice: 1/2 ° (39.3 x 24 cm)
CONTENTS: 3 ll. heading; 8 ll. text of letter to Chipman; 3 ll. signatures; dash; 2 ll. heading; 10 ll. text of Chipman's reply; 3 ll. signature and address; dash; 3 ll. heading; 15 ll. of Chipman's address to the electors; 2 ll. closing
PAPER: Laid, marked post horn in crowned shield | GR | 1795; chains vertical 25 mm
TYPOGRAPHY: *Text*: great primer, old face; two-line great primer italic with swash tendrils. *Display*: long ornamental dash of shadowed ovals with tapered side pieces
345 x 173 mm
NOTES: Although Chipman represented Saint John in New Brunswick's first assembly, his victory was tainted by charges that the sheriff had stolen the election for him and five other government candidates. He was defeated by the voters of Saint John in the next election in 1793 but returned for Northumberland. In 1795 he was beaten in Saint John for the second time and then lost his third election there in this 1802 contest (*Dictionary of Canadian Biography* VI, s.v. 'Chipman, Ward,' by Phillip Buckner).
COPY EXAMINED: NBSM

NB7 Church of England
[within frame of section marks 166 x 102 mm] A | FORM | OF | PRAYER | AND | THANKSGIVING | TO | ALMIGHTY GOD; | TO BE USED | In all Churches and Chapels throughout His MA- | JESTY'S Province of *New-Brunswick*, on TUESDAY | the Twenty-seventh of this in*ſ*tant, *July*, being | the Day appointed by Proclamation for a General | THANKSGIVING to Almighty GOD, for | putting an End to the late

bloody, extended, and | expen*f*ive War in which we were engaged. | [rule 95 mm] | *By Defire of His Excellency the* Lieutenant-Governor. | [rule 95 mm] | City of Saint John: [script] | Printed by JOHN RYAN, at his Office, No. 9, Long-Wharf, South | *f*ide Market Slip, Printer to KING's mo*f*t | Excellent MAJESTY. 1802.
COLLATION: 8° (22.8 x 14 cm uncut), 1^4 2^2, 6 leaves, pp *1–3* 4–12
CONTENTS: *1* title; 2 blank; *3*–12 text
PAPER: Laid, unmarked; chains vertical 26 mm
TYPOGRAPHY: *Text*: english, old face; Caslon double pica on title. *Display*: two-line great primer drop letter
32 ll., 150 (164) x 95; 94 mm for 20 ll.
NOTES: Since the province of New Brunswick had stagnated while its rival Nova Scotia, and particularly the busy port of Halifax, had prospered from military and commercial activity during a decade of the Napoleonic wars, there was good reason to celebrate news of the peace concluded at Amiens in March. 'A Few Copies' priced at nine pence were offered for sale at Ryan's office (*Royal Gazette*, 21 July 1802).
COPY EXAMINED: NBSM: Jarvis Family Collection, Box 25

NB8 Creon

A | ***Statement of Facts*** | RELATIVE TO THE PROCEEDINGS | OF THE | HOUSE OF ASSEMBLY | ON WEDNESDAY THE THIRD, AND THURSDAY THE FOURTH | OF MARCH, 1802, AT THE CLOSE OF THE LAST SESSION. | ADDRESSED TO | THE INHABITANTS OF NEW-BRUNSWICK. | [thick-thin rule 44 mm] | READ AND RECEIVE LIGHT. | [thin-thick rule 52 mm] | PUBLISHED BY DESIRE. | [thin-thick rule 57 mm] | PRINTED FOR THE AUTHOR. | [dotted rule 15 mm] | 1802.
COLLATION: 8° (20.2 x 13.7 cm), A^4 B^4 [B1 signed], 8 leaves, pp *1–3* 4–15 *16*
CONTENTS: *1* title; 2 blank; *3*–15 text signed Creon; *16* blank
PAPER: Laid, marked possibly Strasbourg lily; chains vertical 28 mm (NBSM); unmarked (OTMCL)
TYPOGRAPHY: *Text*: pica, transitional face. *Display*: tail piece with FINIS in panel surmounted by urn and palm leaves, swag beneath (86 in Fry and Steele catalogue)
31 ll., 156 (165) x 91; 101 mm for 20 ll.
NOTES: Undoubtedly the work of Samuel Denny Street this pamphlet is part of a political dispute which began in the House of Assembly early in 1802, erupted into a pamphlet and paper war in the spring and summer, and ended at the polls in the autumn. It was the culmination of a struggle between certain members elected to the House of Assembly for the third legislature (1795–1802) on one side and the lieutenant governor, the Executive Council, and their allies in the Assembly on the other. James Glenie, a Scot representing Sunbury, led the opposition to Lieutenant Governor Carleton in a contest for financial and political control. In 1796, 1797, and 1798, Carleton and his Council had rejected the House of Assembly's Appropriations Bill because of a clause instituting payment for members of the Assembly. After four years without appropriations to run the province a compromise worked out by the British government was accepted in 1799. However in 1802 the conflict was revived, first over the appointment of Glenie's ally, Samuel Denny Street, to the position of clerk of the House of Assembly, and then over payment accorded to Street in the Appropriations Bill. When Council once again returned the Bill demanding that Street's name and salary be removed Glenie and his followers boycotted the House of Assembly leaving it without a quorum. Undeterred, the remaining members continued the business of the House which included the deletion of Street's payment and subsequent passage of the contentious Bill. Soon afterwards the lieutenant governor dissolved the Legislature and in May called an election for October.

Street who was standing for re-election in Sunbury launched the pamphlet war with this *Statement of Facts*. His version of the proceedings was disputed in three pamphlets (**NB10, 11, 15**) and in the *Royal Gazette* throughout the summer. A bare majority of the electors of Sunbury returned Street to the House of Assembly but his victory was challenged then overturned. In the next election in 1809 he was successful. Several times a candidate for a position in the Supreme Court he came close enough in 1808 to prompt Ward Chipman, one of his 1802 adversaries to write to another, Edward Winslow then president, 'How mortifying to us all must it be if the Creeper Cock, the insignificant "Creon," should by any unexpected interest, in case of Judge Upham's death, obtain his seat upon the Bench' (*Winslow Papers, A.D. 1776–1826*, ed. by W.O. Raymond. Saint John: New Brunswick Historical Society, 1901, 606).

Creon's text was also published in verse form, probably by Street, in the *Saint John Gazette* in October and November 1802. It has been reprinted

twice with an introduction by Thomas B. Vincent (*Acadiensis* 3, no 2 (Spring 1974): 80–98; *Narrative Verse Satire in Maritime Canada, 1779–1814*. Ottawa: Tecumseh Press, 1978, 117–42).
COPIES EXAMINED: NBS, NBSM, OTMCL

NB9 A Dissertation on the Thirteenth and Seventeenth Chapters of the Book of St John's Revelation
A | DISSERTATION [open] | ON THE | *THIRTEENTH and SEVENTEENTH* | CHAPTERS OF THE BOOK | OF | ST. JOHN's REVELATION, | OR, | AN ATTEMPT TO PROVE THAT | *JACOBINISM is the Eighth Head of the BEAST,* | AND | *VOLTAIRE the Number of the BEAST.* | [double rule 98 mm] | REV. XIII. 8. *Here is wisdom. Let him that hath understand- | ing count the number of the Beaſt. For it is the number | of a Man: And his number is Six hundred, three-score | and six.* | REV. XVIII. 11. *The Beast that was, and is not, even he is the | Eighth, and is of the Seven, and goeth into perdition.* | DANIEL VII. 25. *He shall speak great words against the Most | High, and shall wear out the Saints of the Most High, and | think to change times and laws.* | [double rule 98 mm] | *St. John, New-Brunswick:* | PRINTED BY JOHN RYAN, PRINTER TO THE KING'S MOST | EXCELLENT MAJESTY, AT HIS OFFICE, No. 9, | LONG-WHARF, SOUTH SIDE *Market-Slip.* | [leaf ornaments 14 and 14 mm] | 1802.
COLLATION: 8° (20.6 x 13 cm), *A*[4] B–C[4] D[2] [$1 signed], 14 leaves, pp *1–5* 6–28 (pagination in ( ))
CONTENTS: *1* title; *2* blank; *3* 'Proem'; *4* blank; *5*–18 text; 19–26 notes; 27–28 appendix
PAPER: Laid, unmarked; chains vertical 27 mm
TYPOGRAPHY: *Text*: small pica, old face. *Display*: ornamental dashes and rules of bead and reel, snowflake, and foliage ornaments from 1785 Caslon specimen (pica 2, english 5 and 1); dot and arrow rule (brevier 28 of Fry and Steele, 1790)
46 ll., 161 (172) x 99; 71 mm for 20 ll.
NOTES: First advertised as a proposal in 1800 the dissertation was offered at one shilling with subscriptions taken by the printer and Church of England clergymen Jacob Bailey, Robert Stanser, Roger Viets, John Wiswall, and George Pidgeon who were serving in New Brunswick and Nova Scotia. On 29 December 1802 John Ryan announced that the books would be ready for delivery to subscribers on the following day. He changed the notice to 'now ready' with a price of 'Quarter Dollar' for the early issues of 1803 (*Royal Gazette*).
COPY EXAMINED: QMBM
REFERENCES: Gagnon II 13, Tremaine 1172A

NB10 The Elector's Mirror
THE | ELECTOR's MIRROR; | OR, | TRUTH UNVEILED, | IN A | BRIEF REPLY TO CREON, | AUTHOR OF A | STATEMENT OF FACTS. | WITH | HINTS ON THE TRUE POLITICS OF THE PROVINCE, COMPARED WITH | A CONCISE HISTORY OF THE PROCEEDINGS OF THE | LATE HOUSE OF ASSEMBLY. | [ornamental dash 25 mm] | INSCRIBED WITH RESPECT | TO THE | GOVERNMENT AND FREEHOLDERS | OF | *NEW-BRUNSWICK.* | [leaf ornaments 20 mm] | WITH AN APPENDIX. | [thick-thin rule 96 mm] | Truth would you teach, to ſave a ſinking land, | All fear, none aid you, and few underſtand. POPE. | [thin-thick rule 96 mm] | PRINTED FOR THE BENEFIT OF THE PUBLIC. | 1802.
COLLATION: 8° (20.2 x 13 cm), *A*[4] B[4] C[2] [$1 signed], 10 leaves, pp *1–5* 6–20 (pagination underlined with thin-thick rule)
CONTENTS: *1* title; *2* blank; *3* note 'To the unprejudiced Reader'; *4* blank; *5*–16 text headed 'To CREON, *Author of a Statement of Facts, &c.*'; 16 'P.S.' (6 ll.); *17*–20 appendix: *17* members of the House of Assembly and Council; 18–20 extracts of letters from the Duke of Portland to Lieutenant Governor Carleton dated 1795 to 1798
PAPER: Laid, unmarked; chains vertical 26 mm
TYPOGRAPHY: *Text*: pica, old face
40 ll., 170 (179) x 102; 84 mm for 20 ll.
NOTES: In his note to the Reader the author claims 'I have met every thing which had the appearance of argument' (p 3). To Creon (**NB8**) he said 'Had you fulfilled what the title of your book profeſſes, you would have prevented the neceſſity of this, and perhaps taken one ſtep towards gaining the reputation of an honeſt man' (p 5). The author or Mirror may himself have been one of the members subsequently re-elected who had 'remained faithful' at the time of the 'memorable retreat' from the House of Assembly (p 17). A satire on the results of the autumn election titled 'Ship News since the Storm' by 'An Old Tar' reported on two of the pamphlet warriors: 'The *Fair Review* and the *Mirror* are at sea – they have been spoken with. – All well.' The *Spectator* (**NB15**) he characterized as 'a great North-Country-built Cat' with wooden guns and damaged gunpowder 'the old ſtuff which was imported into America during the laſt Rebellion.' As for Samuel Denny Street: 'The *Creon* spew'd her oakum, ſtrain'd her upper works, is

A

STATEMENT OF FACTS

RELATIVE TO

The Standfasts and The Runaways,

OR,

SAMMY CREON's PAMPHLET TURN'D RIGHT SIDE OUTWARDS,

BY

JOB CREON, A TAYLOR;

ADDRESSED TO

THE MECHANICS AND FARMERS OF NEW-BRUNSWICK.

A STITCH IN TIME
SAVES NINE.

PUBLISHED FOR FUN.

PRINTED FOR THE AUTHOR.

1802.

NB11 Courtesy Lande Canadiana Collection, Rare Books and Special Collections, McGill University, Montreal

hog'd [with keel arched upwards] and crazy, and will probably never make another trip' (*Royal Gazette*, 27 October 1802).
COPY EXAMINED: NBS
REFERENCE: MacFarlane

NB11 Job Creon
A | STATEMENT OF FACTS | RELATIVE TO | The Standfasts and The Runaways, | OR, | SAMMY CREON's PAMPHLET TURN'D | RIGHT SIDE OUTWARDS, | BY | *JOB CREON, A TAYLOR*; | ADDRESSED TO | THE MECHANICS AND FARMERS OF | NEW-BRUNSWICK. | [thick-thin rule 71 mm] | A STITCH IN TIME | SAVES NINE. | [thin-thick rule 71 mm] | PUBLISHED FOR FUN. | [thick-thin rule 74 mm] | PRINTED FOR THE AUTHOR. | [dotted rule 16 mm] | 1802.
COLLATION: 8° (18.8 x 12.1 cm), *1–2*⁴, 8 leaves, pp *1–3* 4–16 (pagination in [ ])
CONTENTS: *1* title; 2 blank; *3*–16 text signed JOB CREON
PAPER: Laid, chains horizontal 30 mm; dark with blue fibres
TYPOGRAPHY: *Text*: english, modern face
34 ll., 159 (167) x 95; 93 mm for 20 ll.
BINDING: Disbound, stab holes
NOTES: Attributed by Thomas B. Vincent (**NB8**) to Edward Winslow, judge, executive councillor, and loyalist leader, Job Creon's reply to Creon was heralded by 'Mungo' in the *Royal Gazette* of 15 September:

Poor Creon! alaſs,
  Is it come to the paſs?
By a *Taylor* so
  turn'd outſide in!
...
Creon here, Creon there,
Creon every where;
What a fidgeting life have you led,
From the Gallery peeping
Then ſtrutting, then creeping;
...

COPIES EXAMINED: NBS, QMMRB
REFERENCE: Lande S2137

NB12 New Brunswick. Laws (3rd Parliament, 6th session: 1802)
[within 6 mm ribbon and stick rules 269 x 144 mm] ACTS | OF THE | GENERAL ASSEMBLY | OF | HIS MAJESTY's PROVINCE | OF | NEW-BRUNSWICK, | PASSED IN THE YEAR 1802. | [dot and arrow rule 128 mm] | [royal arms 63 x 119 mm] | [dot and arrow rule 128 mm] | SAINT JOHN: | PRINTED BY JOHN RYAN, NO. 9, LONG-WHARF, SOUTH SIDE | MARKET SLIP, PRINTER TO THE KING'S | MOST EXCELLENT MAJESTY. | [dot and arrow rule 23 mm] | 1802.
COLLATION: 2° (30.2 x 18.7 cm), π^2 $2\pi^1$ A–D² χ^1 [$1 signed], 12 leaves, pp *[6]* *452* 453–468 *469*
CONTENTS: *[1]* title; *[2]* blank; *[3]* session title; *[4]* blank; *[5]* titles of the acts; *[6]* blank; *452*–468 text; *469* blank
PAPER: Laid, unmarked; chains vertical 27 mm
TYPOGRAPHY: *Text*: english, old face. *Display*: title page with frame of great primer 11 of 1785 Caslon specimen and dot and arrow rule (brevier 28 of Fry and Steele, 1790). Text with rules of foliage and bead and reel; foliage head-piece (pica 10 and 2, long primer 15 of Caslon, 1785)
33 ll., 251 (266) x 115 (142); 94 mm for 20 ll.
NOTES: Three hundred copies were printed at a charge of £27 with £2 10s for folding, stitching, and pressing the six sheets (NBFA: RS24/S16/R2).
COPY EXAMINED: USMH-L

NB13 New Brunswick. Parliament (3rd, 6th session: 1802). House of Assembly
[within 6 mm ribbon and stick rules 279 x 145 mm] JOURNAL | OF THE | VOTES AND PROCEEDINGS | OF THE | HOUSE OF ASSEMBLY | OF THE | PROVINCE OF NEW-BRUNSWICK: | From TUESDAY the 26th of JANUARY, to FRIDAY the 5th of | MARCH, 1802. | [dot and arrow rule 129 mm] | [royal arms 63 x 119 mm] | [dot and arrow rule 129 mm] | SAINT JOHN: | PRINTED BY JOHN RYAN, NO. 9, LONG-WHARF, SOUTH SIDE | MARKET SLIP, PRINTER TO THE KING'S | MOST EXCELLENT MAJESTY. | [dot and arrow rule 23 mm] | 1802.
COLLATION: 2° (30 x 18.2 cm), π^1 *A*² B–H² I¹ [$1 signed], 18 leaves, pp *658–660* 661–693
CONTENTS: *658* title; *659* blank; *660*–693 text
PAPER: Laid, unmarked; chains vertical 27 mm
TYPOGRAPHY: *Text*: english, old face. *Display*: title page with frame of great primer 11 of 1785 Caslon specimen and dot and arrow rule (brevier 28 of Fry and Steele, 1790). Text with head-piece of bracket flowers composed as circles and rosebud tail-piece (small pica 17 and double pica 3 of Caslon, 1785)
55 ll., 258 (276) x 145; 94 mm for 20 ll.
BINDING: Half sprinkled calf edged in blind with rope roll and pasteboard, pieced and coloured grayish blue. Spine divided by blind and gilt rules with black lettering piece edged in gilt with thick-

thin and rope rules, lettered JOURNALS | H. OF A. | N. BRUNSWICK | 1793–1802 | . Endpapers laid, marked arms of England (Ward Chipman copy at NBFU)
NOTES: John Ryan's account for 20 August 1802, records a charge of £33 15s for printing two hundred copies of nine sheets and £2 1s 2d for folding, stitching, and pressing (NBFA: RS24/S16/R2). The *Royal Gazette* announced on 1 September that the Journals would be ready for delivery on the fourth.
COPIES EXAMINED: NBFL, NBFU, NBSM

NB14 Opinions of Several Gentlemen of the Law

OPINIONS | OF SEVERAL | GENTLEMEN OF THE LAW, | ON THE SUBJECT OF | NEGRO SERVITUDE, | IN THE PROVINCE OF | NOVA-SCOTIA. | [dot and arrow rule 102 mm] | ST. JOHN: | PRINTED BY JOHN RYAN, NO. 9, LONG-WHARF: | SOUTH SIDE MARKET SLIP, PRINTER TO | THE KING'S MOST EXCELLENT | MAJESTY. | [dot and arrow rule 15 mm] | 1802.
COLLATION: 8° (22.3 x 13.5 cm), *A*[4] B–C[4] *D*[1] [$1 signed], 13 leaves, pp *1–2* 3–25 *26* (pagination underlined)
CONTENTS: *1* title; 2–4 preface; 4–5 case; 6–23 'Mr Aplin's Opinion'; 23–24 'The Attorney-Generals Opinion'; 24–25 'The Opinion of Mr Tidd'; 25–26 'The Opinion of Mr Percival'; *26* blank
PAPER: Laid, unmarked; chains vertical 26 mm
TYPOGRAPHY: *Text*: english, old face. *Display*: rules on title are brevier 28 of 1790 Fry and Steele specimen
36 ll., 168 (179) x 102; 93 mm for 20 ll.
NOTES: The question of 'negro servitude' in Nova Scotia came to court when James DeLancey, a slave owning loyalist in Annapolis, sued for recovery of the wages paid in Halifax to one of his runaway slaves. As part of the process DeLancey requested Joseph Aplin, formerly attorney general of Prince Edward Island, to prepare a brief. He also solicited the opinion of English lawyers, printed here in support of Aplin's defence of slavery. The case was inconclusive with DeLancey awarded damages but not recovering Jack the slave before his own death in 1804 (*Dictionary of Canadian Biography* V, s.v. 'DeLancey, James,' by Barry M. Moody; David G. Bell, 'Slavery and the Judges of Loyalist New Brunswick,' *UNB Law Journal* 31 (1982): 9–42).

It was probably Joseph Aplin who initiated publication of the opinions in answer to charges of legal malpractice and sedition which had prompted his hasty departure from Prince Edward Island in 1798 (*Dictionary of Canadian Biography* V, s.v. 'Aplin, Joseph,' by J.M. Bumsted). Certainly Aplin used a copy of the pamphlet to support his request for an allowance from the British government when he addressed a plea to the colonial secretary from Annapolis on 16 Novembr 1802, 'perfectly ruined,' 'indigent,' and incapable of earning his living. He claimed that his ability would be recognized if one of the colonial authorities would 'give yourself the Trouble of running your Eye over the enclosed pamphlet' (GBPRO: CO 226, vol 18, ff 241–2).

Copies were offered 'just published and for sale' at one shilling three pence in the *Royal Gazette* (20 October 1802).
COPIES EXAMINED: QMBM, GBPRO: CO 226, vol 18, ff 243–55
REFERENCES: Gagnon II 1539, MacFarlane

NB15 Spectator

A | FAIR | AND | CANDID REVIEW | Of the Proceedings of the Houſe of *Aſſ*embly | OF THE | PROVINCE OF NEW-BRUNSWICK | IN THEIR LATE SESSION; | ADDRESSED TO THE | LOYAL INHABITANTS | AND | ELECTORS OF THE PROVINCE. | BY | A SPECTATOR. | [thick-thin rule 71 mm] | "BE WISE IN SEASON." | [thin-thick rule 71 mm] | PRINTED FOR THE AUTHOR. | [dotted rule 16 mm] | 1802.
COLLATION: 8° (18.8 x 12.1 cm), *A*[4] B–D[4], [$1 signed], 16 leaves, pp *1–3* 4–32 (pagination flanked by dashes, within [ ])
CONTENTS: *1* title; *2* blank; *3*–32 text
PAPER: Laid, chains horizontal 30 mm; dark with blue fibres
TYPOGRAPHY: *Text*: long primer, old face
53 ll., 175 (186) x 109; 67 mm for 20 ll.
NOTES: 'A Spectator' has been identified by Thomas B. Vincent as Ward Chipman, another of the loyalist founders of New Brunswick. Defeated in the 1795 election, he was indeed a spectator of the third parliament and, although Samuel Denny Street had been his co-counsel in a test case of the legality of slave holding in 1800, he showed little fondness for the 'Creeper Cock' as he called Street (**NB8**).
COPY EXAMINED: NBS

1803

NB16 New Brunswick. Laws (4th Parliament, 1st session: 1803)

[within 6 mm ribbon and stick rules 269 x 143 mm]

ACTS | OF THE | GENERAL ASSEMBLY | OF | HIS MAJESTY'S PROVINCE [open] | OF | NEW-BRUNSWICK. | PASSED IN THE YEAR 1803. | [dot and arrow rule 128 mm] | [royal arms 54 x 109 mm] | [dot and arrow rule 128 mm] | *SAINT JOHN:* | PRINTED BY JOHN RYAN, NO. 9, LONG-WHARF, SOUTH SIDE | MARKET SLIP, PRINTER TO THE KING'S | MOST EXCELLENT MAJESTY. | [leaf ornaments 14 and 14 mm] | 1803.

COLLATION: 2° (34.8 x 21.3 cm), π^2 $2\pi^1$ A–D^2 E^1 [$1 signed], 12 leaves, pp [6] *476* 477–493

CONTENTS: [*1*] title; [*2*] blank; [*3*] session title; [*4*] blank; [*5*] titles of the acts; [*6*] blank; *476*–493 text

PAPER: Laid, unmarked; chains vertical 26 mm

TYPOGRAPHY: *Text*: pica, old face. *Display*: title page with frame of great primer 11 of 1785 Caslon specimen and dot and arrow rule (brevier 28 of Fry and Steele, 1790). Text with long ornamental dashes and rules of ribbon and stick, bead and reel, and foliage (pica 2 and 10 of Caslon, 1785). Royal arms cut signed Lee

58 ll., 246 (264) x 115 (142); 84 mm for 20 ll.

NOTES: Copies of the Acts and Journal (**NB17**) were sent to the Colonial Office on 27 September 1803.

COPIES EXAMINED: NBSM (lacking pp 492–3), GBPRO: CO 188, vol 12, ff 59–70, USMH-L

NB17 New Brunswick. Parliament (4th, 1st session: 1803). House of Assembly

[within 6 mm ribbon and stick rules 302 x 143 mm] JOURNAL | OF THE | VOTES AND PROCEEDINGS | OF THE | HOUSE OF ASSEMBLY | OF THE | PROVINCE | OF | NEW-BRUNSWICK: | From TUESDAY the 8th Day of FEBRUARY, to WED- | NESDAY the 16th Day of MARCH, 1803. | [ornamental rule 130 mm] | [royal arms 58 x 71 mm] | [ornamental rule 130 mm] | SAINT JOHN: | PRINTED BY JACOB S. MOTT, PRINCE WILLIAM-STREET, | OPPOSITE THE MARKET-SQUARE. | 1803.

COLLATION: 2° (32.7 x 20.4 cm), π^2 A^2 B–C^2 (C1 + χ1) D–I^2 K^2 [$1 signed], 23 leaves, pp [2] *1–3* 4–12 ²[2] 13–42 [χ1 is folded leaf 30.2 x 40 cm]

CONTENTS: [*1*] title; [*2*] blank; *1* proclamations; *2* blank; *3*–12 text; ²[*1–2*] imports and duties; public accounts; 13–35 text; 35–42 'Report on the State of the Public Roads in New-Brunswick' by Dugald Campbell

PAPER: Laid, mixed lot with most sheets watermark Britannia; countermark 1801 or fleur de lys; a few sheets watermark Strasbourg lily; countermark 1795; chains vertical

TYPOGRAPHY: *Text*: english, modern face; italic with swash tendrils. *Display*: title page with frame of great primer 11 of 1785 Caslon specimen and rows of tulips. Text with long ornamental dashes and head-piece a panel of snowflakes (english 5 of Caslon, 1785). Tail-piece with FINIS in panel surmounted by urn and palm leaves, swag beneath (86 in Fry and Steele catalogue)

54 ll., 258 (268) x 144; 94 mm for 20 ll.

NOTES: The printer Jacob S. Mott, whose sister was married to John Ryan, had taken over the *Saint John Gazette* when Ryan succeeded to the *Royal Gazette* along with the office of king's printer. Mott, in his turn, succeeded to both (**NB29**).

COPIES EXAMINED: NBFL, NBSM, OOA, GBPRO: CO 188, vol 12, ff 71–92 (lacking χ1)

NB18 The News-Carrier's Address

[within architectural frame made up of rules, brackets, and printer's flowers 335 x 153 mm] | [royal arms 30 x 66 mm] | [ornamental dash 54 mm] | THE | NEWS-CARRIER'S ADDRESS | *TO THE CUSTOMERS OF THE* | ROYAL GAZETTE. [open] | [ornamental dash 78 mm] | TO ALL CHRISTIAN-FOLK, of the Church or the Meeting, [with T open] | I CHARLES, THE CARRIER, send *New-Year's* greeting: | ... | What, tho' now, to myself I this monument raise! | Next season, I'll ſing of your bounty and praise. | [3 ll. braced right] That my office is useful, I think, must appear, | To my conduct, my patrons will not prove severe , | And accept my best pray'rs for a happy New-Year. | ST. JOHN, *(New-Brunswick,)* 1*st. January*, 1803.

Verse: 1 leaf (37.1 x 23.4 cm)

CONTENTS: royal arms; 6 ll. heading and dashes; 54 ll. text; 1 l. closing

PAPER: Laid, marked Strasbourg lily; chains vertical 25 mm

TYPOGRAPHY: *Text*: pica, old and transitional faces. *Display*: the frame is a triumphal arch made up of rules and brackets with half-fluted columns, bases and capitals with rows of O and lattice ornaments, and the arch lined with berry ornaments; a row of bead and reel joins the bases (long primer 11, english 6, and pica 2 of Caslon, 1785)

335 x 153 mm

NOTES: Charles's address is a lively example of the carrier's verse with local references and a satirical twist:

> ...
> From the cradle, *great News, bloody News* taught to cry,

And the fiercene*f*s of tempe*f*ts, and fro*f*ts to defy,
I have weekly your keen curio*f*ities fed,
Brought reliefs for the heart, and recruits for the head.
To the Statesman how bountiful are my supplies!
Revolutions, their causes — all guesses and lies.
...
Then with *New-Brunswick* politics always replete,
With *Atticus, Creon, Amicus,* I treat;
...
In private life also, my aid's of great price,
Of bargains and sales I give early advice.
Into most of the Shops, in my round, take a peep,
See whose Goods are freshest and whose are most cheap.
Try the *wigs, bonnets, dresses,* from London imported;
Know who were last married, and who are now courted.
And with News like the last, or the birth of a son,
The Maidens salute me with "*Charles, you run.*"
But, with wings to my feet, if I fly, with a tale
Of a beauty cast off, or of virtue too frail,
'Tis always "*why, Charles, you move like a snail.*"
...
Romances and *bibles, books* of palm'stry and prayer,
And *powders* will serve for the *teeth, face,* and *hair.*
For lechers lewd *poems,* select *hymns* for Saints,
Plumes, pearl-pins, pomatums, perfumes, plafters, paints,
...

COPY EXAMINED: NBSM

NB19 Odell, Jonathan, 1737–1818

[within 5 mm frame of snowflake rules 348 x 258 mm] | On Seeing the ADDRESS to the Ship AMERICA in which | Governor CARLETON and his FAMILY embark for England. | ...

Verse: 1° (41.5 x 33 cm)

CONTENTS: 2 ll. heading; dash; 74 ll. verse in 2 cols

PAPER: Laid, watermark Britannia; countermark fleur de lys; chains horizontal 25 mm

TYPOGRAPHY: *Text*: english, transitional face. *Display*: frame is english 5 of 1785 Caslon specimen; long ornamental dash used in imprints from the Ryan shop

348 x 258 mm

NOTES: Thomas Carleton, first governor of the province, sailed for England on leave early in October of 1803. Although he never returned to New Brunswick he held the office of lieutenant governor, granted in 1786, until his death in 1817. Appointed provincial secretary along with Carleton in 1784, Jonathan Odell said his farewell in verse:

O may that Power, whose awful sway
Contending elements obey,
With Western Breezes Sweep the Sea,
To clear a smiling path for thee!
...
Attended as he goes, from home,
With happy Omens, back to share,
For us a gracious Monarch's care,
Leaving that Monarch's Realm in Peace,
With wealth and Glory's rich increase,
Triumphant o'er his foes! - and then,
I hope, with tuneful voice, again
To lure sweet Echo from her Cave,
And *welcome Carleton,* while a brave
And Loyal People loudly Sing
"Welcome CARLETON! and GOD Save the KING!"

Odell may have sent a copy to Carleton for in response to a letter from Edward Winslow the lieutenant governor began 'Every word of the information conveyed in your letter of the 7th respecting certain transactions in New Brunswick was new to me, for Odell's letter was nothing more than an introduction to an effusion of his muse, which was enclosed' (*Winslow Papers, A.D. 1776–1826,* ed. by W.O. Raymond. Saint John: New Brunswick Historical Society, 1901, 528). Odell's muse was well known to his loyalist contemporaries particularly for songs and satires published during the Revolutionary War in America.

COPIES EXAMINED: NBSM, OTUTF

1804

NB20 Church of England

[within thick-thin rules 194 x 100 mm] A | FORM | OF | PRAYER, [open] | TO BE USED | In all CHURCHES and CHAPELS, throughout the Province of | *New-Brunswick,* upon FRIDAY the 7th of SEPTEMBER, | 1804, being the day appointed by Proclamation for a | General FAST and HUMILIATION before ALMIGHTY | GOD, to be observed in the mo*f*t Devout and Solemn | Manner, by sending up our Prayers and Supplications | to the DIVINE MAJESTY: | For obtaining Pardon of our SINS, and for averting tho*f*e | heavy Judgments which our manifold Provocations | have mo*f*t ju*f*tly de*f*erved; and imploring his Ble*ff*ing | and A*ffif*tance on the Arms of His MAJESTY by Sea and | Land, and for re*f*toring and perpetuating Peace, Safety, | and

reſtoring and perpetuating Peace, Safety, | and Prosperity to Himself, and to His Kingdom. | [rule 95 mm] | *By the PRESIDENT's Special Command.* | [thick-thin rule 95 mm] | ST. JOHN: | Printed by *JOHN RYAN*, Printer to the King's Moſt Excellent MAJESTY. | [ornamental rule 12 mm] | 1804.
COLLATION: 4° (23.5 x 14 cm), 1^4 2^1, 5 leaves, pp *1–2* 3–10 (3 in [ ])
CONTENTS: *1* title; 2 blank; 3–10 text
PAPER: Wove, unmarked
TYPOGRAPHY: *Text*: pica, transitional face. *Display*: title with dot and arrow rule flanked by leaf ornaments (brevier 28 and 21 of Fry and Steele, 1790). Text with row of ribbon and stick (great primer 11 of Caslon, 1785)
43 ll., 177 (190) x 97; 94 mm for 20 ll.
BINDING: Stitched
NOTES: The president was Gabriel Ludlow, a New York loyalist, who was the first mayor of Saint John and senior member of the Council. After Carleton's departure from the province in 1803 Ludlow served as administrator, commander-in-chief, and president of the Council until his death in 1808.
COPY EXAMINED: NBSM

1805

NB21 New Brunswick. Court of Vice-Admiralty
[dot and arrow rule 148 mm] | THE QUESTION | RESPECTING THE RIGHT OF THE | United States of America, | To the ISLANDS in | Passamaquoddy-Bay, | By virtue of the TREATY of 1783, | CONSIDERED | In the Caſe of the Sloop *Falmouth*, | In the Court of VICE-ADMIRALTY, for | The PROVINCE of | NEW-BRUNSWICK, [open] | In the Year 1805. | [dot and arrow rule 148 mm] | PRINTED BY J. RYAN, PRINTER TO HIS MAJESTY.
COLLATION: 2° (32.2 x 20.2 cm), A^2 B–H^2 [$1 signed], 16 leaves, pp *1–2* 3–31 *32*
CONTENTS: *1* title; 2 blank; 3–31 text; *32* blank
PAPER: Laid, watermark Britannia; countermark H SALMON | 1803; chains vertical 26 mm
TYPOGRAPHY: *Text*: pica, old face. *Display*: dot and arrow rule (brevier 28 of Fry and Steele, 1790) and tail-piece of rosebuds (double pica 3 of Caslon, 1785)
71 ll., 295 (315) x 151; 83 mm for 20 ll.
NOTES: Ever zealous George Leonard sent a copy of this pamphlet to Lord Castlereagh, the colonial secretary, early in 1806 offering his version of the incident: 'Much of the evidence and observations on the trial have been withheld from publication in the pamphlet from delicacy to those officers until a further investigation, if Your Lordship should think any further neceſsary' (CO 188: vol 13, f 173ᵛ). As superintendent of trade and fisheries Leonard had seized the *Falmouth*, an American ship engaged in the plaster trade, in disputed waters between Maine and New Brunswick. It was a rash action noted with disfavour in both London and Washington. At the time Leonard was reprimanded; a recent assessment terms it 'comic opera' (*Dictionary of Canadian Biography* VI, s.v. 'Leonard, George,' by Ann Gorman Condon).
COPIES EXAMINED: OOA, GBPRO (2 copies): CO 188, vol 13, ff 175–90; CO 217, vol 83, ff 29–44

NB22 New Brunswick. Laws (1st Parliament, 1st session: 1786 to 4th Parliament, 2nd session: 1805)
THE | ACTS | OF THE | GENERAL ASSEMBLY, [open] | OF | HIS MAJESTY's PROVINCE | OF | NEW-BRUNSWICK, [open] | From the TWENTY-SIXTH to the FORTY-FIFTH Year | Of the REIGN of | KING GEORGE the THIRD. | [rule 106 mm] | With a COPIOUS INDEX. | [rule 106 mm] | [royal arms 21 x 30 mm] | [thick-thin rule 105 mm] | ST. JOHN: | PRINTED BY JOHN RYAN, PRINTER TO THE KING'S MOST | EXCELLENT MAJESTY, AT HIS OFFICE, NO. 9, LONG- | WHARF, SOUTH SIDE MARKET SLIP. | [rule 18 mm] | M DCCC V.
COLLATION: 4° (23.7 x 14.7 cm), π^2 1^4 2–3^2, A–I^4 K–T^4 V–$2I^4$ 2K–$2T^4$ 2V–$2X^4$ $2Y^3$, $^2A^4$ B–E^4 χ^1 [$1 signed, ^{2}B–E with period], 218 leaves, pp [4] *i* ii–xv *xvi*, *1* 2–374 ^{2}[42] (pp 3–136 with period)
CONTENTS: [*1*] title; [*2*] blank; [*3*] administration of the province; [*4*] blank; *i*–xv table of the acts; xv erratum (1 l.); *xvi* blank; *1*–374 text; ^{2}[*1–40*] index; ^{2}[*40*] erratum (3 ll.); ^{2}[*41*] sittings of the Supreme Court; ^{2}[*42*] blank
PAPER: Wove, marked 1801 twice in corners of sheet
TYPOGRAPHY: *Text*: pica, old face. *Display*: text with head-piece of flowers framing leaves (nonpareil 2 of 1785 Caslon specimen and long primer 40 of Fry and Steele 1790); rows of dot and arrow, bead and reel, and snowflakes (brevier 28 of 1790 Fry and Steele, pica 2 and english 5 of 1785 Caslon) with long ornamental dash and 15 mm leaf ornament dividing sessions
40 ll., 169 (179) x 86 (108); 84 mm for 20 ll.
BINDING: Half calf and bluish gray paper. Laid endpapers (NBSM: 3 copies, one rebacked; one with endpapers marked 1803/2); OTMCL copy rebacked with endpapers marked 1803/2

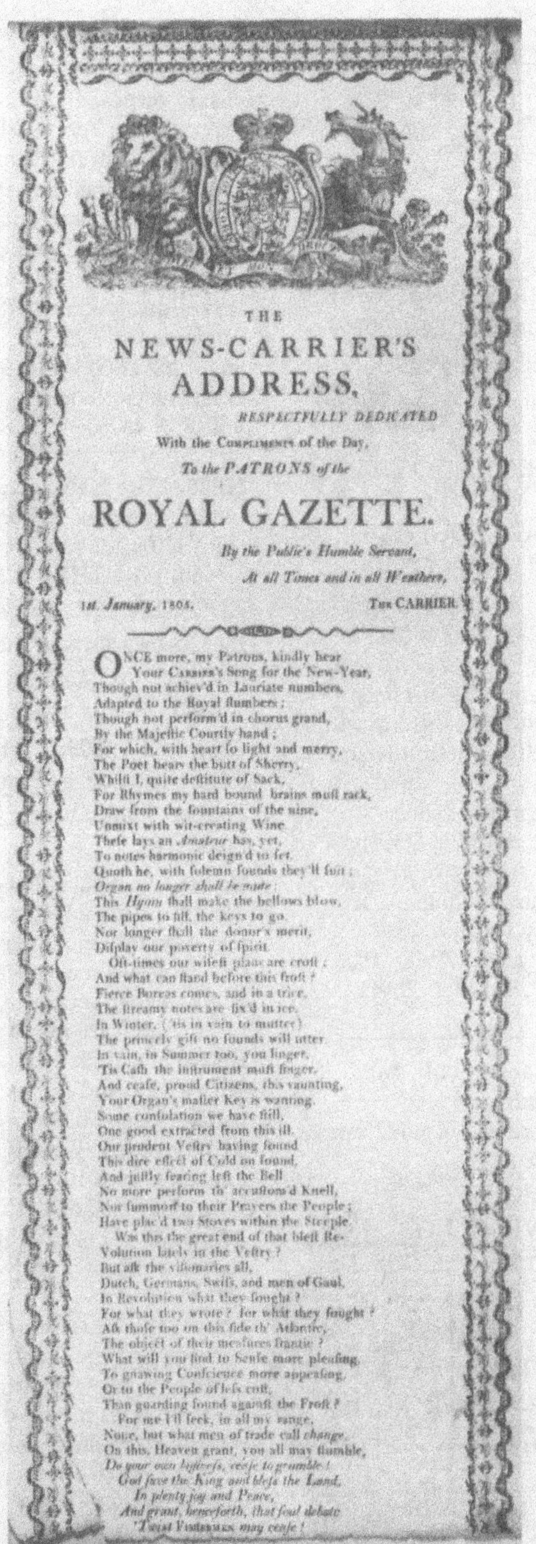

THE

NEWS-CARRIER'S ADDRESS,

RESPECTFULLY DEDICATED

With the Compliments of the Day,

To the PATRONS of the

ROYAL GAZETTE.

By the Public's Humble Servant,

At all Times and in all Weathers,

1st. *January*, 1805. The CARRIER.

ONCE more, my Patrons, kindly hear
Your Carrier's Song for the New-Year,
Though not achiev'd in Lauriate numbers,
Adapted to the Royal ſlumbers;
Though not perform'd in chorus grand,
By the Majeſtic Courtly band;
For which, with heart ſo light and merry,
The Poet bears the butt of Sherry,
Whilſt I, quite deſtitute of Sack,
For Rhymes my hard bound brains muſt rack,
Draw from the fountains of the nine,
Unmixt with wit-creating Wine
Theſe lays an *Amateur* has, yet,
To notes harmonic deign'd to ſet.
Quoth he, with ſolemn ſounds they'll ſuit;
Organ no longer ſhall be mute:
This *Hymn* ſhall make the bellows blow,
The pipes to fill, the keys to go.
Nor longer ſhall the donor's merit,
Diſplay our poverty of ſpirit.
Oft-times our wiſeſt plans are croſt;
And what can ſtand before this froſt?
Fierce Boreas comes, and in a trice,
The ſtreamy notes are fix'd in ice.
In Winter, ('tis in vain to mutter)
The princely gift no ſounds will utter.
In vain, in Summer too, you linger,
'Tis Caſh the inſtrument muſt finger.
And ceaſe, proud Citizens, this vaunting,
Your Organ's maſter Key is wanting.
Some conſolation we have ſtill,
One good extracted from this ill.
Our prudent Veſtry having found
This dire effect of Cold on ſound,
And juſtly fearing leſt the Bell
No more perform th' accuſtom'd Knell,
Nor ſummon'd to their Prayers the People;
Have plac'd two Stoves within the Steeple.
Was this the great end of that bleſt Re-
Volution lately in the Veſtry?
But aſk the viſionaries all,
Dutch, Germans, Swiſs, and men of Gaul,
In Revolution what they ſought?
For what they wrote? for what they fought?
Aſk thoſe too on this ſide th' Atlantic,
The object of their meaſures frantic?
What will you find to Senſe more pleaſing,
To gnawing Conſcience more appeaſing,
Or to the People of leſs coſt,
Than guarding ſound againſt the Froſt?
For me I'll ſeek, in all my range,
None, but what men of trade call *change*.
On this, Heaven grant, you all may ſtumble,
Do your own buſineſs, ceaſe to grumble!
God ſave the King and bleſs the Land,
In plenty joy and Peace,
And grant, henceforth, that foul debate
'Twixt Vestrymen may ceaſe!

NB25 Courtesy New Brunswick Museum, Saint John

NOTES: Planning for this edition of the Acts began as early as 1801 when the Assembly voted £200 for revising and printing two hundred copies 'of all the acts' (*Journal*, 3:5, 1801, p 644).
COPIES EXAMINED: NBSM (3 copies), OTMCL
REFERENCES: Bishop, TPL 787

NB23 New Brunswick. Laws (4th Parliament, 2nd session: 1805)
ACTS | OF THE | GENERAL ASSEMBLY, [open] | OF | HIS MAJESTY'S PROVINCE | OF | NEW-BRUNSWICK, [open] | PASSED IN THE YEAR 1805. | [double rule 107 mm] | [royal arms 21 x 30 mm] | [double rule 107 mm] | ST. JOHN: | PRINTED BY JOHN RYAN, PRINTER TO THE KING'S MOST | EXCELLENT MAJESTY, AT HIS OFFICE, NO. 9 LONG- | WHARF, SOUTH SIDE MARKET SLIP. | [rule 19 mm] | M DCCC V.
COLLATION: 4° (24.5 x 15.5 cm), *2S*^{4} 2T^4 2V–2X^4 2Y^3 [$1 signed], 23 leaves, pp *330–331* 332-374 (332 in ( ))
CONTENTS: *329* title; *330–331* blank; 332–374 text
ISSUE of pp 332–374 of Acts, 1786–1805 (**NB22**) with variant state of gathering 2S printed with title and blanks
PAPER: Wove, marked 1801 in corner of sheet
TYPOGRAPHY: *Text*: pica, transitional face. *Display*: a row of foliage ornament
40 ll., 169 (179) x 86 (108); 84 mm for 20 ll.
NOTES: The Colonial Office copy was not transmitted by Gabriel Ludlow until 17 May 1806.
COPIES EXAMINED: GBPRO: CO 188, vol 13, ff 20–42, USMH-L

NB24 New Brunswick. Parliament (4th, 2nd session: 1805). House of Assembly
[within 6 mm ribbon and stick rules 274 x 142 mm] JOURNAL | OF THE | VOTES AND PROCEEDINGS | OF THE | HOUSE OF ASSEMBLY | OF THE | PROVINCE | OF | NEW-BRUNSWICK: | From TUESDAY the 29th Day of JANUARY, to TUES- | DAY the 5th Day of MARCH, 1805. | [ornamental rule 129 mm] | [royal arms 58 x 71 mm] | [ornamental rule 129 mm] | SAINT JOHN: | PRINTED BY JACOB S. MOTT, AT THE SIGN OF THE BIBLE AND | CROWN, PRINCE WILLIAM-STREET. | 1805.
COLLATION: 2° (32.4 x 20.2 cm), π^1 *A*^{2} B^2 (B1 + χ1) C–H^2 [$1 signed], 18 leaves, pp *43–45* 46–50 [2] 51–76 [χ1 is folded leaf 30.2 x 40 cm]
CONTENTS: *43* title; *44* blank; *45*–50 text; [1–2] imports and duties; public accounts; 51–76 text
PAPER: Laid, watermark Britannia | A B [script]; countermark A BLACKWELL | & | G JONES | 1803; chains vertical 27 mm
TYPOGRAPHY: *Text*: english, modern face. *Display*: title page with frame of great primer 11 of 1785 Caslon specimen and row of tulips. Text with long ornamental dashes and head-piece a panel of snowflakes (english 5 of Caslon, 1785). Tail-piece with FINIS in panel surmounted by urn and palm leaves, swag beneath (86 in Fry and Steele catalogue)
56 ll., 257 (279) x 144; 94 mm for 20 ll.
COPIES EXAMINED: NBFL, NBSM, OOA, GBPRO: CO 188, vol 13, ff 43–60

NB25 The News-Carrier's Address
[within frame of ribbon and stick, foliage, and vine rules 420 x 140 mm cropped at foot] [royal arms 52 x 106 mm] | THE | NEWS-CARRIER'S [open] | ADDRESS, | *RESPECTFULLY DEDICATED* | With the COMPLIMENTS of the Day, | *To the PATRONS of the* | ROYAL GAZETTE. | *By the Public's Humble Servant,* | *At all Times and in all Weathers,* | [to left] 1*st. January*, 1805. [to right] THE CARRIER. | [ornamental dash 75 mm] | ONCE more, my Patrons, kindly hear | Your CARRIER'S Song for the New-Year, | ...
Verse: 1 leaf (42 x 20.3 cm cropped at foot)
CONTENTS: royal arms; 10 ll. heading; dash; 58 ll. text (possibly incomplete)
PAPER: Wove, marked 180[?]
TYPOGRAPHY: *Text*: pica, old face. *Display*: the sides of the frame are made up of three rows of flowers, ribbon and stick then alternating berry and foliage with a vine and leaves closest to the text; the head is five rules with snowflake in the middle flanked on both sides by vines and leaves (great primer 11, english 6, pica 10, and small pica 26; english 5 and long primer 16 of Caslon, 1785; the leaves are long primer 40 of Fry and Steele 1790 specimen). Foot has been cropped. Royal arms cut signed Lee
420 x 140 mm
NOTES: This year's carrier was more skilled at composing type than verse:

Whilſt I, quite deſtitute of Sack,
For Rhymes my hard bound brains muſt rack,
Draw from the fountains of the nine,
Unmixt with wit-creating Wine.

COPY EXAMINED: NBSM

1806

NB26 Norris, Robert
A | CANDID DISCUSSION [open] | OF THE | PRINCIPAL TENETS | OF THE | ROMAN FAITH. | [rule 102 mm] | *BY THE REVEREND ROBERT NORRIS,* | MISSIONARY FROM THE INCORPORATED SOCIETY | FOR THE PROPAGATION OF THE GOSPEL | IN FOREIGN PARTS. | [rule 102 mm] | [thick-thin rule 70 mm] | *SAINT JOHN, NEW-BRUNSWICK:* | PRINTED BY JACOB S. MOTT, AT THE SIGN OF THE | BIBLE AND CROWN, FOR THE AUTHOR. | 1806.
COLLATION: 8° (22.7 x 14.5 cm uncut), A^4 B–I^4 K–O^4 [$1 signed], 56 leaves, pp *1–3* 4–114
CONTENTS: *1* title; 2 blank; 3–114 text
PAPER: Laid, *A*–I marked fleur de lys or BC | 180 | G; K–O unmarked; chains vertical 26 mm (NSHP, NSWA)
TYPOGRAPHY: *Text*: english, modern face. *Display*: long ornamental dash
38 ll., 173 (184) x 102; 94 mm for 20 ll.
NOTES: Norris's response to Edmund Burke's *Letter of Instruction to the Catholic Missionaries of Nova-Scotia, and its Dependencies* (**NS29**) was advertised for sale in Halifax and Saint John in 1807, at a price of 3s 6d (*Weekly Chronicle*, 6 February; *Saint John Gazette*, 20 April). Before joining the Church of England Norris had, like Burke, been a Roman Catholic priest. Burke's reply to Norris was published along with two similar works of earlier date in this controversial series (**NS36**).
COPIES EXAMINED: NSHL, NSHP, NSWA
REFERENCES: Akins, Dennis

1807

NB27 New Brunswick. Laws (4th Parliament, 3rd session: 1807)
[within 6 mm ribbon and stick rules 257 x 143 mm] ACTS | OF THE | GENERAL ASSEMBLY [open] | OF | HIS MAJESTY'S PROVINCE | OF | NEW-BRUNSWICK. [open] | PASSED IN THE YEAR 1807. | [flower rule 132 mm] | [royal arms 52 x 106 mm] | [flower rule 132 mm] | *SAINT JOHN:* | PRINTED BY JOHN RYAN, PRINCE WILLIAM STREET, | PRINTER TO THE KING'S MOST | EXCELLENT MAJESTY. | [ornamental dash 34 mm] | 1807.
COLLATION: 2° (31.1 x 19.5 cm), π^2 $2\pi^1$ A–F^2 G^1 [$1 signed, B as B.], 16 leaves, pp *[6]* *3* 4–28
CONTENTS: [*1*] title; [*2*] blank; [*3*] session title; [*4*] blank; [*5*] titles of acts; [*6*] blank; *3*–28 text
PAPER: Laid, mixed lot with watermark Britannia unframed; countermark RV BROOKE | 1801; watermark W & B O; countermark 1800; some sheets unmarked; chains vertical, varied
TYPOGRAPHY: *Text*: pica, old face. *Display*: title page with frame of great primer 11 of Caslon specimen and flower rule (nonpareil 8 of 1790 Fry and Steele specimen). Text with head-piece of vine ornament framed by bracket flowers (small pica 26 and 7 of Caslon, 1785), long ornamental dashes, foliage rules (pica 10 and long primer 16 of Caslon, 1785); and dot and arrow (brevier 28 of 1790 Fry and Steele); tail-piece of rosebuds (double pica 3 of Caslon, 1785). Royal arms cut signed Lee
57 ll., 241 (256) x 113 (140); 84 mm for 20 ll.
NOTES: The printing account for two hundred copies, eight sheets, was £36 with £2 for folding and stitching (NBFA: RS24/S19/R51).
COPIES EXAMINED: OOA, USMH-L

NB28 New Brunswick. Parliament (4th, 3rd session: 1807). House of Assembly
[within 6 mm ribbon and stick rules 275 x 142 mm] JOURNAL | OF THE | VOTES AND PROCEEDINGS | OF THE | HOUSE OF ASSEMBLY | OF THE | PROVINCE | OF | NEW-BRUNSWICK: | From TUESDAY the 27th Day of JANUARY, to THURS- | DAY the 5th Day of MARCH, 1807. | [ornamental rule 129 mm] | [royal arms 58 x 71 mm] | [ornamental rule 129 mm] | SAINT JOHN: | PRINTED BY JACOB S. MOTT, AT THE SIGN OF THE BIBLE AND | CROWN , PRINCE WILLIAM-STREET. | 1807.
COLLATION: 2° (33.5 x 20.5 cm uncut), π^1 A^2 B^2 $\chi 1$ C–I^2 [$1 signed], 19 leaves, pp *77–79* 80–86 [2] 87–113 *114* [χ1 is folded leaf 33 x 40 mm]
CONTENTS: *77* title; *78* blank; *79*–86 text; [*1–2*] imports and duties; public accounts; 87–113 text; *114* blank
PAPER: Laid, watermark Britannia | G J [script]; countermark G JONES | 1805; chains vertical 28 mm
TYPOGRAPHY: *Text*: english, modern face; italic with swash tendrils. *Display*: title page with great primer 11 of 1785 Caslon specimen and row of tulips. Text with long ornamental dashes and head-piece a panel of snowflakes (english 5 of Caslon, 1785). Tail-piece with FINIS in panel surmounted by urn and palm leaves, swag beneath (86 in Fry and Steele catalogue)
54 ll., 258 (273) x 145; 94 mm for 20 ll.

NOTES: Jacob Mott's account for two hundred copies was £29 13s 6d for printing, £2 for folding and stitching, and £4 13s 9d for the treasurer's accounts (NBFA: RS24/S19/R5.2).
COPIES EXAMINED: NBFL, NBSM (2 copies), OOA, OTMCL

1808

NB29 New Brunswick. Laws (4th Parliament, 4th session: 1808)
[within 6 mm ribbon and stick rules 256 x 143 mm] ACTS | OF THE | GENERAL ASSEMBLY [open] | OF | HIS MAJESTY'S PROVINCE | OF | NEW-BRUNSWICK. [open] | PASSED IN THE YEAR 1808. | [flower rule 130 mm] | [royal arms 58 x 70 mm] | [flower rule 130 mm] | SAINT JOHN: | PRINTED BY JACOB S. MOTT, PRINTER TO THE KING'S MOST | EXCELLENT MAJESTY, AT THE SIGN OF THE BIBLE AND | CROWN, PRINCE WILLIAM-STREET. - 1808.
COLLATION: 2° (30 x 18.7 cm), π^2 $2\pi^1$ A–F^2 G^1 [$1 signed], 14 leaves, pp *1–2* [4] 3 4–27 *28*
CONTENTS: *1* title; 2 blank; [*1*] session title; [2] blank; [3] titles of acts; [4] blank; 3–27 text; *28* blank
PAPER: Laid, watermark Britannia; countermark 1806; chains vertical 28 mm
TYPOGRAPHY: *Text*: english, modern face. *Display*: title page with frame of great primer 11 of 1785 Caslon specimen and flower rule (nonpareil 8 of 1790 Fry and Steele). Text with same flower and foliage rules (long primer 16 of Caslon, 1785) and long ornamental dashes
53 ll., 255 (273) x 121 (145); 94 mm for 20 ll.
NOTES: Jacob Mott, trained as a printer by his father in New York, was appointed king's printer in March of 1808 (*Dictionary of Canadian Biography* V, s.v. 'Mott, Jacob S.,' by Jo-Ann Carr Fellows).
COPY EXAMINED: USMH-L

NB30 New Brunswick. Parliament (4th, 4th session: 1808). House of Assembly
[within 6 mm ribbon and stick rules 276 x 142 mm] JOURNAL | OF THE | VOTES AND PROCEEDINGS | OF THE | HOUSE OF ASSEMBLY | OF THE | PROVINCE | OF | NEW-BRUNSWICK: | From TUESDAY the 5th, to SATURDAY the 30th of | JULY, 1808. | [ornamental rule 129 mm] | [royal arms 58 x 71 mm] | [ornamental rule 122 mm] | SAINT JOHN: | PRINTED BY JACOB S. MOTT, PRINTER TO THE KING'S MOST | EXCELLENT MAJESTY, AT THE SIGN OF THE BIBLE AND | CROWN, PRINCE WILLIAM-STREET. - 1808.
COLLATION: 2° (30.2 x 18 cm), π^1 *A*^{2} B^2 χ1 C–F^2 [$1 signed], 14 leaves, pp *115–117* 118–124 [2] 125–139 *140* [χ1 is folded leaf 3.2 x 40 cm]
CONTENTS: *115* title; *116* blank; *117*–124 text; [*1–2*] imports and duties; public accounts; 125–139 text; *140* blank
PAPER: Laid, watermark Britannia; countermark GR in crowned laurel wreath; chains vertical 25 mm
TYPOGRAPHY: *Text*: english, modern face. *Display*: title page with frame of great primer 11 of 1785 Caslon specimen and row of tulips. Text with long ornamental dash and head-piece a panel of snowflakes (english 5 of Caslon, 1785). Tail-piece with FINIS in panel surmounted by urn and palm leaves, swag beneath (86 in Fry and Steele catalogue)
56 ll., 262 (277) x 147; 94 mm for 20 ll.
NOTES: Two hundred copies were authorized by the House of Assembly (p 132).
COPIES EXAMINED: NBFL, OOA

NB31 The News-Carrier's Address
[within frame of fret, bead, and guilloche rules 343 x 122 mm] [royal arms 52 x 106 mm] | THE | NEWS-CARRIER'S [open] | ADDRESS | TO THE | CUSTOMERS | OF THE | ROYAL GAZETTE. [open] | [ornamental dash 81 mm] | ONCE more my kind PATRONS the season's return'd, [with O open] | So famous for bringing good cheer, | And GEORGE, as is usual, with venders of News, | Again wishes a Happy *NEW-YEAR*. | The comforts last Season your bounty procured, | Are uppermost still in my mind, | And I trust, (if too sanguine I hope you'll excuse,) | This Year the same bounty I'll find: | ... | SAINT JOHN, *New-Brunswick*, January 1st, 1808.
Verse: 1 leaf (39.6 x 15 cm)
CONTENTS: royal arms; 7 ll. heading; ornamental dash; 32 ll. text; 1 l. closing
PAPER: Laid, marked Britannia; chains horizontal 24 mm
TYPOGRAPHY: *Text*: pica, transitional face. *Display*: frame of alternate fret and bead ornaments with guilloche at the foot (pica 5, 2, and 1 of Caslon, 1785). Royal arms cut signed Lee
343 x 122 mm
NOTES: George the news-carrier has been identified as George Lugrin, a native of New Brunswick, who was an apprentice and eventual successor to Jacob Mott (*Dictionary of Canadian Biography* VI, s.v. 'Lugrin, George Kilman,' by C.M. Wallace).
COPY EXAMINED: NBSM

1809

NB32 Address of the Carrier
[within vine and foliage rules 352 x 118 mm]
ADDRESS [open] | *OF THE CARRIER OF THE* | TIMES; OR, TRUE BRITON, [open] | TO HIS GENEROUS PATRONS, | *WISHING THEM A HAPPY NEW-YEAR.* | [ornamental dash 72 mm] | YE PATRONS all and *Patronesses,* | Who feel for CARRIERS distresses, | May Heaven its choicest blessings send you, | ... | *Saint John, New-Brunswick, January* 1, 1809.
Verse: 1 leaf (38.3 x 15.3 cm)
CONTENTS: 5 ll. heading; dash; 38 ll. text; 1 l. closing
PAPER: Laid, watermark arms of England; countermark M[?] & C° | 1807; chains horizontal 24 mm
TYPOGRAPHY: *Text*: pica, transitional face. *Display*: rules are small pica 26 and long primer 15 of 1785 Caslon specimen; swash A, M, N, Y in second italic line of heading
352 x 118 mm
NOTES: *The Times; or, True Briton* was a weekly paper founded in 1808 by William Durant who had served his apprenticeship with John Ryan. He became a freeman of the city in 1801 (J. Russell Harper, *Historical Directory of New Brunswick Newspapers and Periodicals*. Fredericton: University of New Brunswick, 1961, 95–6).
COPY EXAMINED: NBSM

NB33 Andrews, Samuel, 1737–1818
SERMON, [open] | PREACHED IN TRINITY CHURCH, | KINGSTON, JULY 16th, 1809. | [rule 89 mm] | *By the Reverend* SAMUEL ANDREWS, *A.M. Rector of Saint* | *Andrews Church, in the Parifh of Saint Andrews.* | [rule 89 mm] | SAINT JOHN: PRINTED BY JACOB S. MOTT, | PRINTER TO THE KING'S MOST EXCEL- | LENT MAJESTY, AT THE SIGN OF THE | BIBLE AND CROWN, PRINCE WIL- | LIAM STREET, 1809.
COLLATION: 8° (19.1 x 12.5 cm), 1^8, 8 leaves, pp *1–5* 6–16 (pagination in ( ))
CONTENTS: *1* title; *2* blank; *3* dedication: [foliage rule 190 mm] | *MR. ANDREW's SERMON,* | ON THE REWARD OF PIETY. | *In Memory of the Reverend Mr.* JAMES SCOVIL, *late* | *Rector of Trinity Church, Kingston, New-Brunswick,* | *the following Discourse was composed, and delivered in* | *said Church, July 16th,* 1809; *and is now publifhed at the* | *requeft, and respectfully inscribed to the family of Mourn-* | *ers by their Friend and Servant* | *THE AUTHOR.* | [foliage rule 190 mm]; *4* blank; *5*–16 sermon, text: Revelation, 14th chap, 13th verse
PAPER: Wove, possibly marked WHATMAN; partly laminated
TYPOGRAPHY: *Text*: pica, transitional face. *Display*: rule is long primer 16 of 1785 Caslon specimen
37 ll., 154 (165) x 92; 84 mm for 20 ll.
COPY EXAMINED: OOA (with pp 3–4 bound in following 16)
REFERENCES: Casey 922, MacFarlane

1810

NB34 New Brunswick. Laws (5th Parliament, 1st session: 1810)
[within 6 mm ribbon and stick rules 275 x 142 mm]
ACTS | OF THE | GENERAL ASSEMBLY [open] | OF | HIS MAJESTY's PROVINCE | OF | NEW-BRUNSWICK. | PASSED IN THE YEAR 1810. | [ornamental rule 130 mm] | [royal arms 59 x 70 mm] | [ornamental rule 130 mm] | SAINT JOHN: | PRINTED BY JACOB S. MOTT, PRINTER TO THE KING'S MOST EX- | CELLENT MAJESTY, AT THE SIGN OF THE BIBLE AND | CROWN, PRINCE WILLIAM-STREET. | 1810.
COLLATION: 2° (31.4 x 19.5 cm), π^2 $2\pi^1$ A^2 B–I^2 K–T^2 [$1 signed], 41 leaves, pp *1–4* [2] *5* 6–80
CONTENTS: *1* title; *2* blank; *3* session title; *4* blank; [1–2] titles of acts; *5*–80 text
PAPER: Laid, π, *A* watermark Britannia unframed; countermark CH | 1806; 2π, B–T watermark Britannia; countermark F | 1807; chains vertical 26 mm
TYPOGRAPHY: *Text*: english, modern face. *Display*: title page with frame of great primer 11 of 1785 Caslon specimen and row of tulips. Text with foliage and flower rules (long primer 16 of Caslon, 1785; nonpareil 2 of 1790 Fry and Steele specimen) and tail-piece of snowflakes (english 5 of Caslon, 1785)
54 ll., 253 (272) x 122 (141); 94 mm for 20 ll.
BINDING: Half sheep and spot marbled paper in grayish blue and yellowish gray. Upper board with trapezoidal black leather label lettered gilt HOUSE OF | ASSEMBLY | NEW | BRUNSWICK | . Laid endpapers marked arms of England (NBSM)
NOTES: Since the Assembly did not meet in 1811 the 'Few Copies of the Acts of the General Assembly' which Mott was offering for sale on 8 May 1811

were probably copies of this edition (*Royal Gazette*).
COPIES EXAMINED: NBSM, USMH-L

NB35 New Brunswick. Parliament (5th, 1st session: 1810). House of Assembly
[within 6 mm ribbon and stick rules 278 x 143 mm] JOURNAL | OF THE | VOTES AND PROCEEDINGS | OF THE | HOUSE OF ASSEMBLY | OF THE | PROVINCE | OF | NEW-BRUNSWICK: | From SATURDAY the 27th day of JANUARY, to WED- | NESDAY the 14th day of MARCH, 1810. | [ornamental rule 130 mm] | [royal arms 58 x 71 mm] | [ornamental rule 130 mm] | SAINT JOHN: | PRINTED BY JACOB S. MOTT, PRINTER TO THE KING'S MOST EX- | CELLENT MAJESTY, AT THE SIGN OF THE BIBLE AND | CROWN, PRINCE WILLIAM STREET. | 1810.
COLLATION: 2° (30.2 x 18 cm), *A–B*^{2} C–G^2 χ1 H–I^2 K–Q^2 R^1 [$1 signed], 34 leaves, pp *1–5* 6–28 [2] 29–66 [χ1 is folded leaf 30.2 x 40 cm]
CONTENTS: *1* title; 2 blank; *3–4* proclamations; *5*–28 text; [*1–2*] imports and duties; public accounts; 29–66 text
PAPER: Laid, *A*, C–M, χ watermark arms of England; countermark 1806 [in double circle] (*A*, C–I) or GR | 1805 (K–M, χ); *B*, N–R watermark Britannia; countermark NH | 1807 (*B*) or S WISE & PATCH (N–R); chains vertical, varied
TYPOGRAPHY: *Text*: english, modern face. *Display*: title page with frame of great primer 11 of 1785 Caslon specimen and row of tulips. Text with flower rule and tail-piece of snowflakes (nonpareil 8 of 1790 Fry and Steele and english 5 of Caslon, 1785) as well as the tulips reversed
52 ll., 252 (267) x 144; 94 mm for 20 ll.
BINDING: Half sheep edged double blind and spot marbled paper in grayish blue, yellowish gray, grayish red, and black. Spine with black lettering piece JOURNALS 1810 vertically. Upper board with trapezoidal black leather label edged gilt, lettered HOUSE OF | ASSEMBLY | NEW | BRUNSWICK | . Endpapers laid, watermark arms of England; countermark H & C | 1807 (OTMCL)
COPIES EXAMINED: NBFL, NBS, OOA, OTMCL

1811

NB36 An Almanack for the Year of Our Lord, 1812
[within rule frame 156 x 88 mm] AN | ALMANACK | FOR | The Year of our Lord, 1812, | BEING BISSEXTILE OR LEAP YEAR; | Calculated for the Meridian of | Saint John, in New-Brunswick; | Being in Latitude 45° 20′ North, Longitude 66° 3′ West; | *BUT WILL SERVE FOR ANY PART OF THE PROVINCE.* | [ornamental dash 37 mm] | *CONTAINING* | [8 ll. to left of double rule] The UNIVERSAL CALENDAR, | The FEASTS and FASTS of the CHURCH, with other RE- | MARKABLE DAYS, | The ECLIPSES of the LUMI- | NARIES, | The RISING and SETTING of | the SUN and MOON, | [8 ll. to right] The MOON'S PLACE, | The EQUATION of TIME, | The TIME of HIGH WATER, | List of PROVINCIAL OFFICERS, | OFFICERS of the ARMY under | Major-General BALFOUR, | OFFICERS of the MILITIA, | SITTINGS of COURTS, &c. &. | *With a variety of other Matter useful and entertaining.* | [thick-thin rule 85 mm] | *By BERNARD KIERNAN, T.M.* | [thin-thick rule 85 mm] | SAINT JOHN: | PRINTED AND SOLD BY JACOB S. MOTT, KING'S PRINTER, AT HIS | OFFICE, AT THE SIGN OF THE BIBLE AND CROWN, | PRINCE WILLIAM STREET.
COLLATION: 8° (19.7 x 12.5 cm uncut), *A–B*^{4} C–E^4 [$1 signed], 20 leaves, pp [*40*]
CONTENTS: [*1*] title; [*2*] eclipses, zodiac, planets, aspects, vulgar notes; [*3–14*] calendar with poem opening '"WITH care this happy Province may produce "All that Life asks, for Pleasure, or for Use,' running at head of pages to [*19*]; [*15–16*] signals; [*16*] holidays; firewards; [*17–18*] Friendly Fire Club, firemen; [*18*] branch pilots; [*18–19*] roads; [*19*] anecdote: 'An Honest Hibernian'; [*20–22*] civil list; King's College, Public Grammar School; [*23*] established church; [*23–27*] Saint John and county officers; [*27–28*] courts; [*28–29*] army; [*30–35*] militia; [*35–37*] army in Nova Scotia; [*38*] ships; [*39–40*] interest tables; [*40*] amusements
PAPER: Laid, watermark Britannia; countermark ALLEE | 1809; chains vertical 24 mm
TYPOGRAPHY: *Text*: long primer, old face. *Display*: pages in rule frame; ornamental dashes and almanac signs
157 x 90 mm
BINDING: Stitched (NBSM)

NOTES: Jacob Mott announced in August that 'An Almanack for the Year 1812 will be published at the Royal Gazette Office on the 15th of November next' (*Royal Gazette*, 26 August 1811). He advertised that it was just published in the issue of 9 December. This appears to be the first almanac published in New Brunswick since 1791 when Christopher Sower and John Ryan, both of whom had already published local almanacs, joined forces on *The British American Almanack* for 1792. Before this revival of the almanac tradition in New Brunswick Mott had been offering 'Halifax Almanacks' for sale at his office each January.
COPIES EXAMINED: NBS (lacking pp [*39–40*]), NBSM (3 copies, one lacking pp [*1-2*] [*39–40*], another lacking pp [*1–2*] [*35–40*]), OOA

NB37 Saint John [Charter]
THE [open] | *CHARTER* | OF THE [open] | CITY OF SAINT JOHN, | IN THE [open] | *PROVINCE OF NEW-BRUNSWICK.* | [dot and arrow rule 142 mm] | [arms of Saint John with motto, diam 54 mm] | [dot and arrow rule 142 mm] | *SAINT JOHN:* | REPRINTED BY WILLIAM DURANT, & Co. PRINCE WILLIAM STREET. | [ornamental dash 34 mm] | 1811.
COLLATION: 2° (31 x 19 cm), π^1 A^2 B–G^2 H^1 [$1 signed], 16 leaves, pp *1–3* 4–32
CONTENTS: *1* title; 2 blank; *3*–32 text signed Thomas Carleton; 32 statement signed Ward Chipman, 30 April 1785; 26 Geo III, c 46, An Act for Confirming unto the City of Saint John its Rights and Privileges
PAPER: Laid, watermark Britannia; countermark 1810; chains vertical 26 mm
TYPOGRAPHY: *Text*: pica, old face; *CHARTER* with swash tendril *A*. *Display*: title page rules are dot and arrow (brevier 28 of Fry and Steele, 1790). Text with head-piece of bracket flowers and foliage with dot and arrow (small pica 7 and long primer 16 of Caslon, 1785). Long ornamental dashes and royal arms factotum (30 x 32 mm)
59 ll., 247 (264) x 122 (143); 84 mm for 20 ll.
NOTES: Saint John was the first incorporated city in Canada (30 April 1785), with a charter modelled on the document drawn up for New York before the American Revolution. The original text was printed in 1785 by William Lewis and John Ryan (Tremaine 467) and reprinted in this edition.
COPIES EXAMINED: NBSM (2 copies)

1812

NB38 An Almanack for the Year of Our Lord, 1813
[within rules 157 x 88 mm] AN | ALMANACK | FOR | The Year of our LORD, 1813, | BEING THE FIRST AFTER BISSEXTILE OR LEAP YEAR; | Calculated for the Meridian of | Saint John, in New-Brunswick; | Being in Latitude 45° 20′ North, Longitude 66° 3′ West; | BUT WILL SERVE FOR ANY PART OF THE PROVINCE. | [ornamental dash 30 mm] | *CONTAINING* | [8 ll. to left of double rule] The UNIVERSAL CALENDAR, | The FEASTS and FASTS of the | CHURCH, with other RE- | MARKABLE DAYS. | The ECLIPSES of the LUMINA- | RIES, | The RISING and SETTING of | the SUN and MOON, | [8 ll. to right] The MOON'S Place, | The EQUATION of TIME, | The TIME of HIGH WATER. | List of PROVINCIAL OFFICERS, | OFFICERS of the ARMY under | Major-General SMYTH. | OFFICERS of the MILITIA, | SITTINGS of COURTS, &c, &c. | *With a variety of other Matter useful and entertaining.* | [thick-thin rule 87 mm] | BY BERNARD KIERNAN, *T.M.* | [thin-thick rule 87 mm] | SAINT JOHN: | PRINTED AND SOLD BY JACOB S. MOTT, KING'S PRINTER, AT HIS | OFFICE, AT THE SIGN OF THE BIBLE AND CROWN, | PRINCE WILLIAM STREET.
COLLATION: 8° (18.4 x 11.5 cm), *A–B*^{4} C–D^4 E^1 [$1 signed], 17 leaves, pp [*34*]
CONTENTS: [*1*] title; [*2*] eclipses, zodiac, planets, aspects; [*3*] vulgar notes, ember days, feasts, holidays; branch pilots; anecdote; [*4–15*] calendar with seasonal verses opening '"As lightnings play beneath the sable cloud' for August and '"Now whitened vapours to the earth descend' for December; [*16–17*] firewards, Friendly Fire Club, firemen; [*17–18*] roads; [*18–20*] civil list; [*20–21*] Church of England; [*21*] King's College, Public Grammar School; [*21–22*] courts; [*22–25*] county officers; [*26–27*] Saint John officers; [*27–28*] army; [*29*] militia; [*29–31*] army in Nova Scotia; [*31–32*] ships; [*33*] interest tables; [*34*] table of value of sterling at New Brunswick; amusements
PAPER: Laid, watermark post horn in crowned shield; countermark G PIKE | 1810; chains vertical 25 mm
TYPOGRAPHY: *Text*: long primer, modern face. *Display*: pages in rule frame; medium and long ornamental dashes; almanac signs

45 ll., 157 (160) x 88; 67 mm for 20 ll.
BINDING: Rebacked half leather and gloster paper in pale pink, yellow, bluish green, and black. Interleaved as a diary (NBS)
COPIES EXAMINED: NBS, OOA (lacking pp [*33–34*])

NB39 New Brunswick. Administrator (1812–1813: Smyth)
[royal arms 30 x 41 mm] | BY HIS HONOR | GEORGE STRACEY SMYTH, Esquire, | PRESIDENT of His MAJESTY'S Council | and Commander in Chief ... | ... | A PROCLAMATION. | WHEREAS the Government of the United States | of America, by an Act of Congress on the 18th | day of JUNE last, has declared WAR against the United | Kingdom of Great-Britain and Ireland ... | ... | ... I have therefore | thought proper ... | ... to order and direct all His MAJESTY'S | Subjects, under my Government, to abstain from mo- | lesting the Inhabitants living on the shores, and on those | parts of the Territories of the United States, contiguous | to this Province ... | ... | *Given under my Hand and Seal at Fredericton, the* | *tenth day of July, in the Year of our Lord One* | *Thousand Eight Hundred and Twelve ...*
Proclamation: 1 leaf (27.6 x 14.3 cm)
CONTENTS: royal arms; 8 ll. heading; 30 ll. text; 6 ll. closing signed Jon. Odell
PAPER: Wove (laid down)
TYPOGRAPHY: *Text*: english, modern face
257 x 108 mm
NOTES: Although Britain and America were at war the inhabitants of New Brunswick and Nova Scotia were directed to keep the peace with their neighbours as long as possible. The British had for some years encouraged Americans living near Canada to trade in violation of the American embargo.

Recently appointed to New Brunswick, Smyth sent his proclamation to Lord Bathurst, the new colonial secretary, at the end of August, explaining that since the Americans 'were desirous of maintaining an amicable intercourse with us' he had issued an order 'exactly similar' to that of Lieutenant Governor Sherbrooke in Halifax (**NS87**) (GBPRO: CO 188, vol 18, ff 70–71).
COPY EXAMINED: GBPRO: CO 188, vol 18, f 72

NB40 New Brunswick. Executive Council
[royal arms 30 x 41 mm] | PROVINCE OF NEW-BRUNSWICK. | *At a Council holden in the City of Saint John* | *on the* 10*th day of July* 1812 ... | ... | HIS HONOR the PRESIDENT communicated to the | Council for their consideration the copy of a con- | ference and agreement ... | ... | ... for | the purpose of securing the neutrality of those Indians | during the present WAR ...
Report: 1 leaf (30.3 x 14.2 cm)
CONTENTS: royal arms; 5 ll. heading; 18 ll. text; 2 ll. signature, Jon. Odell
PAPER: Wove (laid down)
TYPOGRAPHY: *Text*: english, modern face
245 x 108 mm
NOTES: Since only the St Croix River separated Charlotte County from the United States, Robert Pagan and other local magistrates met native leaders at St Andrews on 6 July seeking assurances of their neutrality in case war reached as far as that peaceful border. Similar agreements were made with natives living near the Saint John and Miramichi Rivers. George Stracey Smyth submitted details to Bathurst along with the proclamation he issued the same day (**NB39**).
COPY EXAMINED: GBPRO: CO 188, vol 18, f 73

NB41 New Brunswick. Laws (5th Parliament, 2nd session: 1812)
[within 6 mm ribbon and stick rules 257 x 143 mm] ACTS | OF THE | GENERAL ASSEMBLY | OF | HIS MAJESTY's PROVINCE | OF | *NEW-BRUNSWICK;* [open] | PASSED IN THE YEAR 1812. | [thick-thin rule 130 mm] | [royal arms 61 x 72 mm] | [thick-thin rule 131 mm] | SAINT JOHN: | PRINTED BY JACOB S. MOTT, PRINTER TO THE KING'S MOST | EXCELLENT MAJESTY, AT THE SIGN OF THE BIBLE AND | CROWN, PRINCE WILLIAM-STREET. | 1812.
COLLATION: 2° (34 x 21 cm), π^2 $2\pi^1$ A–I^2 K^2 [$1 signed], 22 leaves, pp [*6*] *3* 4–39 *40*
CONTENTS: [*1*] title; [*2*] blank; [*3*] session title; [*4*] blank; [*5–6*] titles of acts; *3*–39 text; 39 note (3 ll.) marked with pointing hand; *40* blank
PAPER: Laid, watermark Britannia; countermark F | 1810; chains vertical 26 mm
TYPOGRAPHY: *Text*: english, modern face. *Display*: title page with frame of great primer 11 of 1785 Caslon specimen. Text with long rules of flowers (nonpareil 8 of 1790 Fry and Steele specimen)
55 ll., 256 (278) x 117 (142); 94 mm for 20 ll.
COPIES EXAMINED: NBSM (lacking pp 39–*40*), USMH-L

NB42 New Brunswick. Parliament (5th, 2nd session: 1812). House of Assembly
[within 6 mm ribbon and stick rules 276 x 143 mm] JOURNALS | OF THE | HOUSE OF ASSEMBLY | OF THE | PROVINCE | OF | *NEW-BRUNSWICK:* [open] | From TUESDAY the 4th day of FEBRUARY, to SATUR- | DAY, the 7th day of MARCH, 1812. | [thick-thin rule 130 mm] | [royal arms 61 x 72 mm] | [thin-thick rule 129 mm] | SAINT JOHN: | PRINTED BY JACOB S. MOTT, PRINTER TO THE KING'S MOST | EXCELLENT MAJESTY, AT THE SIGN OF THE BIBLE AND | CROWN, PRINCE WILLIAM STREET – 1812.
COLLATION: 2° (30.2 x 18 cm), *A*[1] *B*[2] C–D[2] χ1 E–I[2] K–O[2] P[1] [$1 signed], 29 leaves, pp *1–3* 4–14 [2] 15–56 [χ1 is folded leaf 30.2 x 40 cm]
CONTENTS: *1* title; 2 blank; *3*–14 text; [*1*–2] imports and duties; public accounts; 15–56 text
PAPER: Laid, *A*–P watermark Vryheyt; countermark 1811; χ watermark posthorn in crowned shield | GP [script]; countermark G PIKE | 1810; chains vertical 27 mm
TYPOGRAPHY: *Text*: english, modern face. *Display*: title page with frame of great primer 11 of 1785 Caslon specimen. Text with long rules of flowers (nonpareil 8 of 1790 Fry and Steele specimen)
56 ll., 264 (278) x 147; 94 mm for 20 ll.
BINDING: Half sheep edged blind and gloster marbled paper. Upper board with trapezoidal black leather label lettered gilt HOUSE OF | ASSEMBLY | NEW | BRUNSWICK | . Spine divided by gilt rules, possibly with a lettering piece. Endpapers laid, watermark arms of England; countermark P COLLINS | 1810 (OOA); NBSM copy rebacked
COPIES EXAMINED: NBFL, NBS, NBSM, OOA (2 copies)

1813

NB43 Church of England
A | FORM | OF | *PRAYER*, [open] | TO BE USED | In all Churches, Chapels, and Places of | PUBLIC WORSHIP, according to the usage of | the CHURCH of ENGLAND, throughout His | Majesty's Province of NEW-BRUNSWICK, on | FRIDAY, the NINETEENTH Day of MARCH, | 1813: being the Day appointed by Proclama- | tion for a GENERAL FAST and HUMILIATION | before ALMIGHTY GOD; to be observed in the | most devout and solemn manner, by sending | up our PRAYERS and SUPPLICATIONS to the | DIVINE MAJESTY: | For obtaining Pardon of our Sins, and for averting those heavy Judg- | ments which our manifold Provocations have most justly deserved; | imploring His Blessing and Assistance on His MAJESTY'S Arms by | Sea and Land, and for restoring and perpetuating Peace, Safety | and Prosperity to Himself, and to His Kingdom. | [rule 92 mm] | *By Command of His Honor the President.* | [rule 91 mm] | SAINT JOHN: PRINTED BY JACOB S. MOTT, PRINTER TO THE KING'S | MOST EXCELLENT MAJESTY, AT THE SIGN OF THE BIBLE AND | CROWN, PRINCE WILLIAM-STREET – 1813.
COLLATION: 4° (21 X 14 cm), *1*[4] 2[2], 6 leaves, pp *1–2* 3–12
CONTENTS: *1* title; 2–11 Morning Prayer; 12 Communion Service
PAPER: Wove, marked J WHATMAN | 1810 in corner of sheet
TYPOGRAPHY: *Text*: english, modern face with long primer for p 12. *Display*: medium and long ornamental dashes
33 ll., 154 (161) x 93; 94 mm for 20 ll.
BINDING: Disbound, stab holes
NOTES: A few days before this Fast Day New Brunswick's 104th regiment completed its famous snowshoe march travelling from Fredericton to Quebec, 350 miles, in twenty-four days during the coldest winter in years. A force numbering about six hundred was welcomed at Quebec on the fifteenth of March by Sir George Prevost who ordered them to continue the march to Upper Canada. There they took part in battles at Niagara and Lundy's Lane (W. Austin Squires, 'The March of the 104TH,' *The Atlantic Advocate* 51, no 6 (February 1961): 33–8).
Copies of the *Form of Prayer* were advertised for sale at the offices of the *New-Brunswick Courier* (18 March) and the *Royal Gazette* (16 March) where the notice was printed at the foot of a broadside extra reporting on the progress of the war in Russia.
COPY EXAMINED: USMWA

NB44 New Brunswick. Laws (5th Parliament, 3rd session: 1813)
[within 6 mm ribbon and stick rules 266 x 143 mm] ACTS | OF THE | GENERAL ASSEMBLY | OF | HIS MAJESTY's PROVINCE | OF | *NEW-BRUNSWICK;* [open] | PASSED IN THE YEAR 1813. | [thick-thin rule 130 mm] | [royal arms 60 x 72 mm] | [thick-thin rule 130 mm] | SAINT JOHN: | PRINTED BY JACOB S. MOTT, PRINTER TO

THE KING'S MOST | EXCELLENT MAJESTY, AT THE SIGN OF THE BIBLE AND | CROWN, PRINCE WILLIAM STREET - 1813.
COLLATION: 2° (31.7 x 19.8 cm), π^1 $2\pi^2$ A^2 B–G^2 H^1 [$1 signed], 18 leaves, pp *1–2* [4] *3* 4–29 *30* 31–32
CONTENTS: *1* title; 2 blank; [1] session title; [2] blank; [3] titles of acts; [4] blank; *3*–29 text; *30* blank; 31–32 text of act with note at foot of p 32 explaining that enactment and ratification were delayed, dated 31 July 1813
PAPER: Laid, watermark Britannia; countermark M [script] | 1812 except π marked F | 1810 in USMH-L copy; chains vertical 25 mm
TYPOGRAPHY: *Text*: english, modern face. *Display*: title page with frame of great primer 11 of 1785 Caslon specimen. Text with long foliage and flower rules (long primer 16 of Caslon, 1785; nonpareil 8 of 1790 Fry and Steele specimen)
56 ll., 255 (272) x 117 (141); 93 mm for 20 ll.
BINDING: Half sheep edged gilt and stormont paper. Upper board with trapezoidal black leather label edged gilt and lettered HOUSE | OF | ASSEMBLY | NEW BRUNSW.[K] | . Endpapers laid, watermark Britannia; countermark T W & R BOTFIELD (NBS). QMM with sheep edged double blind, label lost, and endpapers replaced
NOTES: Mott's account for printing nine sheets, two hundred copies, was £36 with £3 for folding and stitching (NBFA: RS24/S23/R10.10). The 1814 Journal records payment to the administrators of his estate of £69 16s 3d for these Acts and the Journal (**NB45**) as well as other printing completed before his death early that year (*Journal*, 5:4, 1814, p 47).
COPIES EXAMINED: NBS, QMM (both lacking pp 31–2), USMH-L

NB45 New Brunswick. Parliament (5th, 3rd session: 1813). House of Assembly
[within 6 mm ribbon and stick rules 276 x 143 mm] JOURNALS | OF THE | HOUSE OF ASSEMBLY | OF THE | PROVINCE | OF | *NEW-BRUNSWICK:* [open] | From TUESDAY the 12th day of JANUARY, to WEDNES- | DAY, the 3d day of MARCH, 1813. | [thick-thin rule 130 mm] | [royal arms 61 x 72 mm] | [thin-thick rule 130 mm] | SAINT JOHN: | PRINTED BY JACOB S. MOTT, PRINTER TO THE KING'S MOST | EXCELLENT MAJESTY, AT THE SIGN OF THE BIBLE AND | CROWN, PRINCE WILLIAM STREET - 1813.
COLLATION: 2° (30.9 x 20 cm), π^1 A^2 B–D^2 (D1 + χ1) E–I^2 K^2 [$1 signed], 22 leaves, pp *1–3* 4–16 [2] 17–42 [χ1 is folded leaf 30.9 x 40 cm]
CONTENTS: *1* title; 2 blank; 3–16 text; [1–2] imports and duties; public accounts; 17–42 text
PAPER: Laid, π, *A*–G watermark Vryheyt | 1811; H–K watermark Britannia; countermark F | 1810; χ watermark Britannia; countermark J M [script] | 1812 (NBFL, OOA); bound NBFL copy same except π as H–K; chains vertical 27 mm
TYPOGRAPHY: *Text*: english, modern face. *Display*: title page with frame of great primer 11 of 1785 Caslon specimen. Text with long rules of section marks and flowers (nonpareil 8 of 1790 Fry and Steele specimen)
56 ll., 266 (278) x 146; 94 mm for 20 ll.
BINDING: Half sheep and greenish gray spot marbled paper. Upper board with trapezoidal black leather label lettered gilt HOUSE | OF | ASSEMBLY | NEW BRUNSW.[K] | and spine with black lettering piece, vertically JOURNALS 1813 | . Laid endpapers, watermark Britannia; countermark T W & R BOTFIELD (NBFL). OOA copy same with sheep edged gilt
NOTES: Two hundred copies, ten and a half sheets, were printed at a rate of £32 16s 3d with £5 for the accounts, and £3 for folding and stitching (NBFA: RS24/S23/R10.10).
COPIES EXAMINED: NBFL (2 copies), NBS, OOA (2 copies)

NB46 Nova Scotia and New Brunswick Baptist Association
MINUTES | *OF THE* | NOVA-SCOTIA *AND* NEW-BRUNSWICK | *Baptist Association,* | HELD AT THE | *BAPTIST MEETING-HOUSE* | IN | SHEFFIELD, | *June* 21 & 22, 1813; | TOGETHER WITH THEIR | *Circular Letter.* | [ornamental dash 38 mm] | SAINT JOHN: | *Printed by William Durant, & Co.* | 1813.
COLLATION: 8° (15 x 11.5 cm), 1^8, 8 leaves, pp *1–3* 4–16
CONTENTS: *1* title; 2 blank; 3–10 text with 8 ll. note marked pointing hand at end; 11–16 Circular Letter
PAPER: Laid, unmarked; chains vertical 23 mm
TYPOGRAPHY: *Text*: pica, transitional face. *Display*: text with foliage rule at head and tail-piece made up of seven rows of lattice ornament tapering from seven to one (long primer 15 and 11 of Caslon, 1785) and long ornamental dashes
27 ll., 113 (120) x 75; 83 mm for 20 ll.
NOTES: There was a vote at the meeting that five hundred copies of the Minutes be printed under the superintendence of the treasurer, Nathan Garrison (p 7).
William Durant's first paper, *The Times; or, True Briton* had ceased in 1811. Soon afterwards he

founded *The City Gazette and General Advertiser* which continued for more than thirty years.
COPY EXAMINED: NSWA

NB47 Saint John. Town Major
NOTICE | IS hereby given, that all Persons | having any business to transact with the Commandant, are | directed to attend at the Town Major's Office, at Portland | Point ... | ... | ALL Masters of Vessels of any | description are hereby cautioned that under no pretence | whatever are they to presume to Sail from this Harbour | without having previously brought to the above Office a | Return ... | ... | Masters of all Vessels arriving in the Port are without loss | of time to report themselves ... | ... | THE Post at Partridge Island has | received Orders from the Commandant, to stop all Vessels | going out, who cannot produce a Passport signed by him. | By Command. | H. COOPER, | Acting Town Major. | *Saint John, 24th February*, 1813. | [double rule 53 mm] | *J.S. Mott, King's Printer.*
Public notice: 1 leaf (29.1 x 22.5 cm)
CONTENTS: 1 l. heading; 19 ll. text; 4 ll. signature and date; 2 ll. imprint
PAPER: Laid, unmarked; chains vertical 25 mm
TYPOGRAPHY: *Text*: transitional and modern face romans
248 x 138 mm
NOTES: The Return demanded of vessels leaving Saint John included 'the Vessel's and Master's Name and Cargo, whither she is bound, together with the numbers and names of such passengers as may be embarked in her.' A manuscript note on the verso, 'Two Quires for the Town Major, 25th February 1813,' suggests that about one hundred copies of the notice were printed.
COPY EXAMINED: NBFA: RS/23/C8/Printed Documents 1786–1813

1814

NB48 Church of England
A | FORM | OF | *PRAYER,* [open] | TO BE USED | In all Churches, Chapels, and Places of PUBLIC WOR- | SHIP, according to the usage of the CHURCH of | ENGLAND, throughout His MAJESTY'S Province of | NEW-BRUNSWICK, on FRIDAY, the FIFTEENTH | Day of APRIL, 1814; being the Day appointed by | Proclamation for a GENERAL FAST and HUMILI- | ATION before ALMIGHTY GOD; to be observed in | the most devout and solemn manner, by sending up | our PRAYERS and SUPPLICATIONS to the DIVINE | MAJESTY: | For obtaining Pardon of our Sins, and for averting those heavy Judgments | which our manifold Provocations have most justly deserved; imploring a | continuance of His Blessing and Assistance on His Majesty's Arms by | Sea and Land, and on those of His Majesty's Allies; and for restoring and | perpetuating Peace, Safety and Prosperity, to Himself, and to His King- | dom. | [rule 104 mm] | *By Command of His Honor the President.* | [rule 104 mm] | NEW-BRUNSWICK: | PRINTED BY HENRY CHUBB, & Co. AT THE ROYAL GAZETTE OFFICE. | 1814.
COLLATION: 8° (22.2 x 14.2 cm uncut), A^4 B^4 [B1 signed], 8 leaves, pp *1–3* 4–15 *16*
CONTENTS: *1* title; 2 blank; *3*–15 text; *16* blank
PAPER: Wove, unmarked
TYPOGRAPHY: *Text*: english, transitional face with modern face two-line pica on title and two-line great primer drop letters
33 ll., 150 (167) x 102; 93 mm for 20 ll.
BINDING: Stitched
NOTES: Jacob Mott, king's printer since 1808, died on 7 January 1814. Although Ann Mott took over her husband's shop with their son Gabriel the appointment of king's printer went instead to George Lugrin, one of Mott's former apprentices. Dropping 'Royal' from the title Ann Mott continued her newspaper: 'To the Public. The Subscriber begs leave to inform the Public, that she has now the sole conduct and management of this Paper, aided only by the exertions of her Son. – Under these circumstances she ventures to throw herself on their protection, with a grateful sense of their past kindness ... Ann Mott.' (*Gazette*, 11 January 1815). In April of 1815 '& Son' disappeared from the imprint after Gabriel Mott joined his uncle John Ryan in Newfoundland. At the same time Ann Mott advertised for an apprentice to the printing trade (*Gazette*, 20 April 1815). Later that year she discontinued the newspaper and returned to New York. Gabriel also moved to the United States where he was 'Editor of the Blakley Sun, at Blakely, Alabama Territory' in 1819 (marriage notice, *Halifax Journal*, 4 October).

Henry Chubb, another of Mott's former apprentices, had begun publication of his own paper *The New-Brunswick Courier* at Mott's office on 2 May 1811. It is likely that this pamphlet was printed by Chubb at Ann Mott's shop before the designation 'Royal' was transferred to George Lugrin (**NB51**).
COPY EXAMINED: NBSM

NB49 Knowlan, James, 1779–1845

A | REVIEW | OF | EDMUND J. REIS's | SHORT ACCOUNT | OF | *MICHAEL M'COMB, &c.* | AND ALSO, | A | SHORT REFUTATION OF SOME OF THE ERRORS | OF THE | BAPTISTS. | [double rule 93 mm] | BY JAMES KNOWLAN. | [double rule 93 mm] | *To the law and to the testimony: if they speak not according to this* | *word,* it is *because* there is *no light in them* – Isaiah 8, 20. | *If there come any unto you, and bring not this doctrine, receive him* | *not into* your *house, neither bid him God speed. For he that bid-* | *deth him God speed, is partaker of his evil deeds* – 2 John, 10, 11. | [ornamental dash 46 mm] | SAINT JOHN: | PRINTED BY HENRY CHUBB, AND CO. AT THE SIGN OF THE BIBLE AND | CROWN, PRINCE WILLIAM STREET. | 1814.

COLLATION: 8° (21.1 x 13 cm), A^8 B^8 [B1 signed], 16 leaves, pp *1–3* 4–29 *30–32*

CONTENTS: *1* title; *2* blank; *3*–29 text; 29 errata (2 ll.); *30–32* blank

PAPER: Wove, unmarked

TYPOGRAPHY: *Text*: long primer, modern face 47 ll., 159 (171) x 94; 67 mm for 20 ll.

NOTES: Although much documentation of the tangled Knowlan-Reis dispute has survived, essential pieces are lacking, particularly issues of Chubb's newspaper for 1814 and the Saint John edition of Reis's *Short Account* of Michael McComb (Appendix) which prompted Knowlan to write this pamphlet. An American edition of Reis's work published at Newburyport in 1815 is located at USMWA. The case itself was sensational enough to attract attention. McComb, a private in the 104th regiment, was captured several weeks after the murder of Kitty Trafton, convicted, and executed on 'newly erected gallows' in Saint John. The local newspaper reported that McComb was attended on the scaffold by Mr Reis, a Baptist missionary (*City Gazette*, 18 April 1814). In the same issue Mr Reis's account of that 'unhappy youth' was announced for publication 'in order to gratify the mind of the Public.'

Since Henry Chubb published Reis's sixteen page pamphlet in early May and Knowlan's reply, at twice the length, his paper *The New-Brunswick Courier* should be a prime source of information on the dispute but there are no microfilmed issues for 1814 before 21 May, then a gap to 13 August. In both those issues, however, the page of local news is dominated by the Knowlan–Reis controversy with statements by a moderator in the dispute, reports of a public meeting, and letters of accusation and support (*New Brunswick Courier*, 1811–23. Canadian Library Association, Newspaper Microfilming Project, reel 1).

In his reply to Reis, Knowlan, a Methodist, claimed that Reis's publication 'contains several falsehoods respecting myself and my friends, but I am the principal object of the writers malignity' (p 2). Characterizing his adversary's work as 'pernicious' and 'entirely discordant with its title' he described it as 'a libel upon individuals or upon religion' rather than an account of the unfortunate McComb. Knowlan's own work passes quickly from the unseemly struggle over a young prisoner to doctrinal matters: 'the defence of Repentance and Faith, those blessed and comfortable doctrines, and to the refutation of some of the most popular errors among the Baptists' (p 4).

COPIES EXAMINED: NBSM, NSHP

REFERENCE: Akins

NB50 Loyal British Hero

A NEW SONG, | On PEACE, and CONQUERED BONAPARTE, | &c. &c. &c. | *Composed by a Loyal British Hero.* | [swelled rule 21 mm] | HAIL ye British Loyal Heroes, now rejoice every Heart, | We have conquer'd the Tyrant, whose names' Bonaparte<.> | So far has he gone, (but he cannot go further), | He's a scourge been to Nations, with blood-shed and Murder. | ... | Of strife and all dissention, Lord, thou dissolve the bands, | And knit the knot of peace and love throughout our lands, | That we may enjoy thy favor and everlasting peace, | And stop the blustering noise of KNOWLAN and REIS. | *29th* AUGUST, 1814.

Verse: 1 leaf (28 x 14.7 cm)

CONTENTS: 4 ll. heading; rule; 44 ll. of verse in 4 line stanzas; 1 l. date

PAPER: Wove, unmarked

TYPOGRAPHY: *Text*: long primer, modern face 226 x 101 mm

NOTES: Celebrating in capital letters his heroes George Prevost, John Bull, the King, and Lord Wellington, the local loyal British hero reported on the War:

> ...
> The Enemy which we're engaged with, now at this present hour,
> Those villainous Americans, who sported with our power;
> Now their Ports are all blockaded, they can't receive a single Cargo,
> Tho' we shewed them British play, Sirs, and took off their Embargo.
> ...

Napoleon's defeat had freed 15,000 men, many of them veterans of Wellington's force, to serve in Canada under Prevost. In early September he led them in the unheroic Battle of Plattsburgh. At the same time, closer to home, Sir John Sherbrooke took the fort at Castine and brought all of eastern Maine, from the Penobscot river to the New Brunswick border, under British control:

...
I hope this is a warning for the Yankee race,
That no Yankee in Canada will ever shew his face,
For Canadians will fight, they are paid by the King,
And so are the Indians to make the woods ring.
...

The song's closing line refers to the dispute between the clergymen James Knowlan and Edmund Reis (**NB49**).

COPY EXAMINED: NBSM: Otty Family Papers, Box 4, F3-1

NB51 New Brunswick. Laws (5th Parliament, 4th session: 1814)

[within thick-thin rules 260 x 131 mm] ACTS | OF THE | GENERAL ASSEMBLY | OF | HIS MAJESTY'S PROVINCE | OF | NEW-BRUNSWICK; [open] | PASSED IN THE YEAR 1814. | [dot and arrow rule 124 mm] | [royal arms 51 x 113 mm] | [dot and arrow 124 mm] | SAINT JOHN: | PRINTED BY GEORGE K. LUGRIN, PRINTER TO THE | KING'S MOST EXCELLENT MAJESTY: | 1814.

COLLATION: 2° (30.2 x 18.5 cm), π^2 $2\pi^1$ A^2 B–G^2 [$1 signed], 17 leaves, pp *1–4* [2] *5* 6–32

CONTENTS: *1* title; *2* blank; *3* session title; *4* blank; [1] titles of acts; [2] blank; *5*–32 text

PAPER: Laid, watermark Britannia; countermark crown | GR | 1810; RICKFORD MILL | 1811; and [?] initials unreadable; chains vertical 27 mm

TYPOGRAPHY: *Text*: pica, modern face. *Display*: title page with dot and arrow rule as brevier 28 of 1790 Fry and Steele specimen. Royal arms cut signed Lee 57 ll., 245 (262) x 117 (149); 82 mm for 20 ll.

NOTES: George Kilman Lugrin, still in his early twenties and a freeman of the city since 1813, was newly appointed as king's printer succeeding his former master Jacob Mott. On his appointment 'at the Seat of Government' he announced his intention to begin publication of 'The New-Brunswick Royal Gazette' at Fredericton as soon as a press and types arrived from England (**NB55**). Until then Lugrin explained that a page of each issue of the *City Gazette* would be appropriated for the *Royal Gazette* (*City Gazette*, 18 April 1814). It was in that newspaper, the second published by William Durant (**NB32**), that 'A Few Copies' of these Acts were offered for sale on 16 May 1814.

COPY EXAMINED: USMH-L

NB52 New Brunswick. Parliament (5th, 4th session: 1814). House of Assembly

[within thick-thin rules 271 x 141 mm] JOURNAL | OF THE | HOUSE OF ASSEMBLY | OF THE | PROVINCE | OF | *NEW-BRUNSWICK*: [open] | From TUESDAY the 11th day of JANUARY, to MONDAY the 7th | day of MARCH, 1814. | [thick-thin rule 131 mm] | [royal arms 61 x 72 mm] | [thin-thick rule 131 mm] | SAINT JOHN: | PRINTED BY HENRY CHUBB, AND CO. AT THE SIGN OF THE BIBLE AND CROWN, | PRINCE WILLIAM STREET. | 1814.

COLLATION: 2° (32.3 x 20 cm), π^1 A^2 B–C^2 χ1 D–I^2 K–Q^2 [$1 signed], 36 leaves, pp *1–3* 4–14 [2] 15–65 *66* [χ1 is folded leaf 32.3 x 40 cm]

CONTENTS: *1* title; 2 blank; 3–14 text; [*1–2*] imports and duties; public accounts; 15-65 text; *66* blank

PAPER: Laid, π, *A*–I K–Q watermark Britannia; countermark I M [script] | 1812; χ watermark arms of England; countermark S WISE & PATCH | 1808 (NBFL). OOA copy same except Q watermark Britannia; countermark J STEVENS

TYPOGRAPHY: *Text*: english, modern face. *Display*: text with long rules of section marks and flowers (nonpareil 8 of 1790 Fry and Steele specimen) 54 ll., 256 (273) x 147; 94 mm for 20 ll.

BINDING: Half black roan edged gilt and stormont paper. Upper board with trapezoidal black leather label edged gilt and lettered HOUSE | OF | ASSEMBLY | N. BRUNSW.^{K} | . Spine divided and lettered vertically JOURNALS 1814 | . Endpapers laid, watermark Britannia; countermark 1812 (OOA)

NOTES: Typography as well as the familiar Bible and Crown imprint show that the volume was printed at Ann Mott's shop. In the Acts of the fifth session of this parliament which met in 1816 there is a record of payment to her: £95 19s 8d 'for printing Journals, Manifests, &c' (*Acts*, 5:5, 1816, p 57).

COPIES EXAMINED: NBFL, NBS, OOA (2 copies)

NB53 Nova Scotia and New Brunswick Baptist Association

MINUTES | OF THE | NOVA-SCOTIA AND NEW-BRUNSWICK | ASSOCIATION, | HELD AT THE | BAPTIST MEETING HOUSE, | IN |

CHESTER, [open] | JUNE 27th, and 28th, | 1814. | [ornamental dash 47 mm] | SAINT JOHN: | PRINTED BY HENRY CHUBB, AND CO. | 1814.
COLLATION: 8° (20.3 x 12.7 cm) 1^4 2^1, 5 leaves, pp *1–2* 3–10
CONTENTS: *1* title; 2–5 text; 5–10 Circular Letter
PAPER: Wove, unmarked
TYPOGRAPHY: *Text*: long primer and english, modern faces. *Display*: thickened modern face on title; long ornamental dash in text48, 34 ll., 162 (171) x 95; 67, 94 mm for 20. ll
NOTES: According to the nineteenth resolution Edmund J. Reis was to superintend the printing of five hundred copies of the Minutes (p 5).
COPY EXAMINED: NSWA

1815

NB54 Nova Scotia and New Brunswick Baptist Association
MINUTES | OF THE | NOVA-SCOTIA AND NEW-BRUNSWICK | ASSOCIATION, | HELD AT THE | BAPTIST MEETING HOUSE, | IN | *CORNWALLIS*, [open] | JUNE 26th, and 27th, | 1815. | [ornamental dash 29 mm] | SAINT JOHN: | PRINTED BY HENRY CHUBB. | 1815.
COLLATION: 8° (20.1 x 12.5 cm), 1^4 2^2, 6 leaves, pp *1–3* 4–12
CONTENTS: *1* title; 2 blank; *3*–5 text; 6–11 Circular Letter; 11–12 Corresponding Letter
PAPER: Wove, unmarked
TYPOGRAPHY: *Text*: bourgeois, old face, and pica, modern face. *Display*:thickened modern face on title, open italic with swash A, N; swelled and ornamental rules in text
38 ll., 159 (168) x 110; 84 mm for 20 ll.
NOTES: Once again 'brother Edmund J. Reis' was named to superintend the printing of the Minutes in an edition increased this year to six hundred copies (p 5).
COPY EXAMINED: NSWA

1816

NB55 Mountain, George Jehoshaphat, 1789–1863
A | SERMON, | PREACHED IN THE PARISH CHURCH | OF | *FREDERICTON*, | On the 14th January, 1816; | UPON OCCASION OF A COLLECTION MADE IN AID OF THE | WATERLOO SUBSCRIPTIONS. | [thick-thin rule 55 mm] | BY THE REV. GEO. J. MOUNTAIN, A.B. | Rector of Fredericton. | [thin-thick rule 55 mm] | (Published by Desire.) | [*The Profits of the Sale, (if any) to be applied to the above-men-* | *tioned purpose.*] | [thick-thin rule 21 mm] | FREDERICTON: | PRINTED BY GEO. K. LUGRIN, KING'S PRINTER.
COLLATION: 8° (19 x 11.9 cm), 1^8, 8 leaves, pp *1–5* 6–15 *16*
CONTENTS: *1* title; 2 blank; *3* advertisement; *4* blank; *5*–15 sermon, text: JUDGES VII. 34, 35 (corrected in ms to JUDGES VIII); *16* blank
PAPER: Laid, watermark Strasbourg lily; countermark J LARKING | 1814 ; chains vertical 24 mm
TYPOGRAPHY: *Text*: english, transitional face. *Display*: beaded open roman as english two lines ornamented of Fry and Steele in Stower
32 ll., 150 (162) x 90; 92 mm for 20 ll.
NOTES: Son of the first bishop of the Church of England in Quebec, George Mountain had returned to England to study at Trinity College, Cambridge. He was ordained by his father early in 1814 and came to Fredericton later that year. In 1817 he went back to Quebec where he eventually succeeded his father as bishop (**NB62**).

This January sermon is among the earliest imprints of Fredericton's first permanent press established there by George Lugrin in 1815. Although Thomas Carleton had selected Fredericton as the capital of New Brunswick in 1785, the province's first printers, William Lewis and John Ryan, had already set up shop in Saint John (Parr Town) in 1783 and remained there even after the government moved from Saint John to Fredericton in 1788. Christopher Sower, the king's printer from 1785 to 1799, also worked at Saint John and at Brookville his nearby farm except for 1792 when he was paid extra 'for bringing up his printing press and types and staying at Fredericton to print the Journal of the House' (Tremaine 790). His Acts and Journals for 1796 (*ibid* 1005, 1006) and the Acts for 1797 and 1798 (*ibid* 1058, 1096) have a Fredericton imprint on the title page but may have been printed at Saint John.

The capital appears to have remained without a press until 1806 when Michael Ryan, son of John Ryan the king's printer at Saint John, began to publish the short-lived *Fredericton Telegraph* in the summer of that year. Early in 1807 he moved on to Newfoundland where his father established the first press. Together they founded *The Royal Gazette and Newfoundland Advertiser* in August.

A

SERMON,

PREACHED IN THE PARISH CHURCH

OF

FREDERICTON,

On the 14th January, 1816;

UPON OCCASION OF A COLLECTION MADE IN AID OF THE

WATERLOO SUBSCRIPTIONS.

BY THE REV. GEO. J. MOUNTAIN, A. B.
Rector of Fredericton.

(Published by Desire.)

[*The Profits of the Sale, (if any) to be applied to the above-mentioned purpose.*]

FREDERICTON:

PRINTED BY GEO. K. LUGRIN, KING'S PRINTER.

NB55 Courtesy Metropolitan Toronto Reference Library

In 1814 when George Lugrin succeeded Jacob Mott he was appointed His Majesty's printer at Fredericton. Finally, after more than thirty years as capital, Fredericton had a printer and a press furnished with Lugrin's new English types (**NB51**).
COPY EXAMINED: OTMCL
REFERENCES: MacFarlane, TPL 1101

NB56 New Brunswick. Laws (5th Parliament, 5th session: 1816)
[within 6 mm Greek key rules 278 x 154 mm] ACTS | OF THE | *GENERAL ASSEMBLY* | OF | *HIS MAJESTY's PROVINCE* | OF | *NEW-BRUNSWICK.* | PASSED IN THE YEAR 1816. | [wavy rule 142 mm] | [royal arms 73 x 86 mm] | [wavy rule 142 mm] | FREDERICTON: | PRINTED BY GEORGE K. LUGRIN, PRINTER TO THE KING'S | MOST EXCELLENT MAJESTY: | 1816.
COLLATION: 2° (33.4 x 20.5 cm), π^2 $2\pi^1$ A^2 B–I^2 K–Q^2 [$1 signed], 35 leaves, pp *1–4* [2] *5* 6–67 *68*
CONTENTS: *1* title; 2 blank; *3* session title; *4* blank; [*1*] titles of acts; [2] blank; *5*–67 text; *68* blank
PAPER: Laid, watermark Britannia, *A*–E countermark JL | 1814; F–H, K, L countermark <G> A [script] | 1815; π, I, M countermark C ANSELL | 1813; N–Q countermark 3 | 1814; chains vertical 27 mm
TYPOGRAPHY: *Text*: english, modern face. *Display*: title with wavy rule (brevier 29 of Fry and Steele in Stower); text with beaded open roman as english two lines ornamented of Fry and Steele in Stower; fat faces
57 ll., 265 (282) x 117 (151); 94 mm for 20 ll.
BINDING: Rebacked, blue spot marbled boards, the upper with mark of lost trapezoidal label edged gilt. Endpapers replaced (QMM)
NOTES: George Lugrin was offering 'A Few Copies' of the Acts and Journals for sale on 2 July 1816 (*Royal Gazette*). His account for 250 copies, each seventeen and a half sheets, was £105 with £3 for folding and stitching (NBFA: RS24/S19/R51).
COPIES EXAMINED: NBSM, QMM, USMH-L

NB57 New Brunswick. Parliament (5th, 5th session: 1816). House of Assembly
[within 6 mm ribbon and rosette rules 278 x 156 mm] JOURNAL | OF THE | *HOUSE OF ASSEMBLY* | OF THE | PROVINCE | OF | *NEW-BRUNSWICK:* | FROM THURSDAY THE 11th DAY OF JANUARY, TO SATURDAY THE 16th DAY OF MARCH, 1816. | [zigzag rule 140 mm] | [royal arms 57 x 70 mm] | [zigzag rule 140 mm] | FREDERICTON: | PRINTED BY GEORGE K. LUGRIN, KING'S PRINTER. | 1816.
COLLATION: 2° (31.4 x 20 cm), π^1 A^2 B–I^2 K^2 χ1 2χ1 L–T^2 V–Z^2, $2A^1$ [$1 (–C) signed], 52 leaves, pp *1–3* 4–42 [*4*] 43–99 *100* (misprinting 46 as 40) [χ1, 2χ1 folded leaves 31.4 x 40 cm]
CONTENTS: *1* title; 2 blank; *3*–42 text; [*1–4*] imports and duties; public accounts; 43–99 text; *100* blank
PAPER: Laid, all but χ, 2χ watermark Britannia; countermark JL | 1811; χ, 2χ arms of England; countermark G & A [script] | 1812; chains vertical 25 mm
TYPOGRAPHY: *Text*: english, modern face. *Display*: title page with frame of double pica 7 of 1790 Fry and Steele specimen and rule of brevier 30 of Fry and Steele in Stower; second line of italic on title with swash K, N
56 ll., 262 (284) x 152; 94 mm for 20 ll.
BINDING: Half sheep and shell marbled paper. Upper board with light brown trapezoidal leather label edged gilt and lettered HOUSE | OF | ASSEMBLY | N. BRUNSW.[K] | and spine divided and lettered vertically JOURNAL 1816 | . Front endpaper laid, watermark Britannia; countermark HARRIS | 1810; back endpaper wove (OOA)
NOTES: Two hundred copies were printed at a charge of £100 for the twenty-five sheets, with £15 for the treasurer's report, and £3 for folding and stitching (NBFA: RS24/S19/R51).
COPIES EXAMINED: NBFL, NBS, OOA (2 copies)

NB58 Nova Scotia and New Brunswick Baptist Association
MINUTES | OF THE | NOVA-SCOTIA AND NEW-BRUNSWICK | ASSOCIATION, | HELD AT THE | BAPTIST MEETING HOUSE, | IN | NICTAU, N.S. | JUNE 26th, 27th and 28th, | 1816. | [thick-thin rule 32 mm] | SAINT JOHN: | PRINTED BY WILLIAM DURANT. | 1816.
COLLATION: 12° (20.2 x 12.5 cm), 1^6, 6 leaves, pp *1–3* 4–11 *12*
CONTENTS: *1* title; 2 blank; 3–6 text; 7–10 Circular Letter; 10–11 Corresponding Letter; *12* blank
PAPER: Wove, unmarked
TYPOGRAPHY: *Text*: long primer, modern face
48 ll., 161 (168) x 109; 67 mm for 20 ll.
NOTES: With their twenty-third resolution the members 'Voted, that brother JOSHUA LANE of *St. John* superintend the Printing of the Minutes, and that 600 copies be printed' (p 6).
COPIES EXAMINED: NSWA, QMMRB
REFERENCE: Lande S115

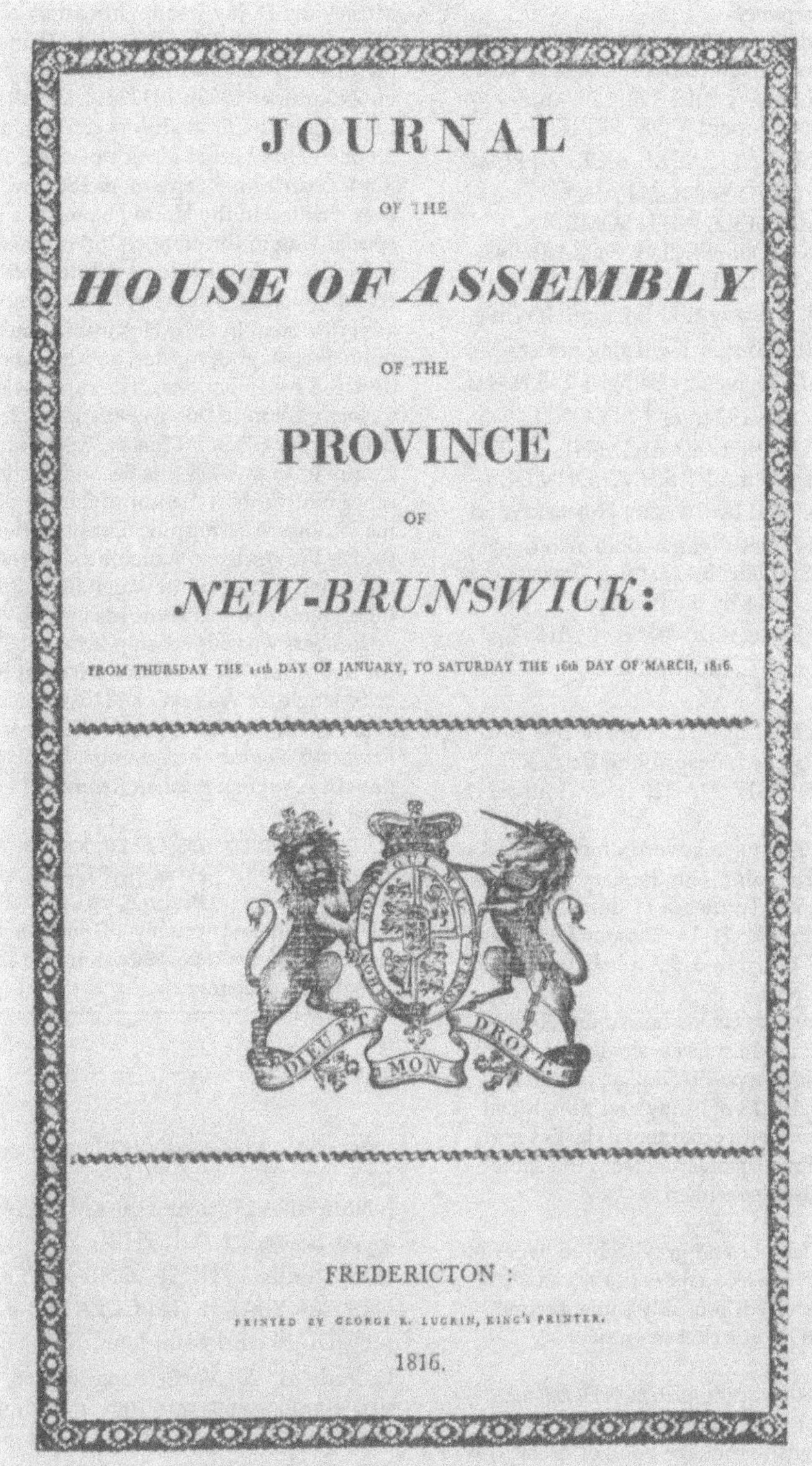

JOURNAL

OF THE

HOUSE OF ASSEMBLY

OF THE

PROVINCE

OF

NEW-BRUNSWICK:

FROM THURSDAY THE 11th DAY OF JANUARY, TO SATURDAY THE 16th DAY OF MARCH, 1816.

FREDERICTON:

PRINTED BY GEORGE K. LUGRIN, KING'S PRINTER.

1816.

NB57 Courtesy Legislative Library, Fredericton

NB59 Union Harmony

[within frame made up of short sections of reeded bead and scallop ornament composed base to base, the whole enclosing wavy rules 122 x 207 mm] UNION HARMONY: [open] | OR | BRITISH AMERICA'S SACRED VOCAL MUSICK. | FROM THE MOST APPROVED ENGLISH AND AMERICAN COMPOSERS, WITH SOME ORIGINAL MUSICK ON SPECIAL OCCASIONS. | TO WHICH IS PREFIXED A CONCISE INTRODUCTION. | [wavy rule 192 mm] | While I live, will I praise the Lord: | I will sing praises unto my God, while I have any being. | 146 PSALM, 2d VERSE. | [wavy rule 192 mm] | SECOND EDITION, MUCH IMPROVED AND ENLARGED. | [ornamental dash 70 mm] | *SAINT JOHN (New-Brunswick:)* | Published by STEPHEN HUMBERT, and sold at his Store, Market Wharf. - Sold also by MARTIN G. BLACK, *Halifax:* BENJAMIN & GEORGE DEWOLF, *Windsor:* | and by the principal Booksellers in the BRITISH PROVINCES. | 1816. | [dotted rule 22 mm] | C. NORRIS & CO. PRINTERS.

COLLATION: Broad 8° (12.8 x 22.2 cm), A^4 B–I^4 K–U^4 W–$2I^4$ 2K–$2Q^4$ [$1 signed, misprinting B2 as R2], 160 leaves, pp *1–5* 6–'317' *318–320* (misprinting 211 as 111, 317 as 217)

CONTENTS: *1* title; 2 blank; *3* advertisement signed Stephen Humbert at Saint John, January 1816; *4* 'A Dictionary of Musical Terms'; *5*–11 'Introduction to the Grounds of Musick'; 11–14 'Lessons for Tuning the Voice'; *15*–317 text; *318–319* Alphabetical Index; *319–320* Metrical Index

PAPER: Laid, unmarked; chains horizontal 26 mm

TYPOGRAPHY: *Text*: modern faces, small pica, pica, and english. Music is typeset. *Display*: title page with frame of english 13 of Binny and Ronaldson 1812 specimen. Text with ornamental dashes and long primer two line ornamented from the same Binny and Ronaldson specimen

118 (120) x 198

BINDING: Quarter leather and grayish blue paper on wooden boards. Wove endpapers (NBSM); OONL copy rebacked, repaired, probably same; second copy at NBSM with linen jacket sewn over scabboard

NOTES: Since an 1801 edition of *Union Harmony*, well documented but not located, is considered Canada's first English-language book of music this second edition has been studied with particular interest by historians of Canadian music (*Encyclopedia of Music in Canada*, s.v. 'Union Harmony: or British America's Sacred Vocal Musick' by D. Jay Rahn, with an illustration of the title page, p 944; John Beckwith, 'Tunebooks and Hymnals in Canada, 1801–1939,' *American Music* 6, no 2 (Summer 1988): 193–234). Despite its Saint John origin the first edition, offered for sale by Stephen Humbert at a price of one dollar in the *Royal Gazette* on 8 September 1801, would have been printed in the United States at a shop specializing in the compositon of music type. C. Norris & Co, named as printers of the second edition, worked at Exeter, New Hampshire. In his advertisement in 1816 Humbert, a merchant, politician, singing master, and Methodist leader declared his intentions: 'The rapid sale of the former edition of this work, and the increasing demand for Church Musick, has induced the Compiler to publish this Second Edition, with no other motive than the improvement of psalmody in the various Worshipping Congregations in the British Provinces; to which he sincerely hopes it may contribute, and in which he will not only be highly gratified but compensated' (p 3).

Humbert was advertising it for sale 'Published by the Subscriber' at his store, priced at 50s per dozen or 5s single, in August of 1816. Copies were also available in Halifax through the autumn (*New-Brunswick Courier*, 7 September 1816 with notice dated 14 August; *Acadian Recorder*, 14 September 1816 *et seq*.).

COPIES EXAMINED: NBSM (2 copies, one lacking pp 215–320); OONL (lacking pp 317–20); NSHP fragment lacking title page, prelims, pp 197–200, 209–18, 297–320 is most probably 1816 rather than 1801 since it includes types shown in the 1812 Binny and Ronaldson specimen.

1817

NB60 An Almanack for the Year of Our Lord, 1818

[within rules 157 x 90 mm] AN | ALMANACK, [open, beaded] | FOR THE | Year of our Lord, | 1818; | BEING THE SECOND AFTER BISSEXTILE OR LEAP YEAR. | CALCULATED FOR THE MERIDIAN OF | Saint John, N.B. | Being in Latitude 45° 20' North, Longitude 66° 3' West; | *BUT WILL SERVE FOR ANY PART OF THE PROVINCE.* | [ornamental dash 34 mm] | CONTAINING | [6 ll. to left of rule] The *Universal Calendar,* | *Feasts* and *Fasts* of the | *Church, &c.* | *Eclipses* of the *Luminaries,* | *Rising* and *Setting* of the | *Sun* and *Moon,* | [6 ll. to right] The *Moon's*

AN

ALMANACK,

FOR THE

Year of our Lord,

1818;

BEING THE SECOND AFTER BISSEXTILE OR LEAP YEAR.

CALCULATED FOR THE MERIDIAN OF

Saint John, N. B.

Being in Latitude 45° 20' North, Longitude 66° 3' West;

IT WILL SERVE FOR ANY PART OF THE PROVINCE.

CONTAINING

The *Universal Calendar*,
Feasts and *Fasts* of the *Church*, &c.
Eclipses of the *Luminaries*,
Rising and *Setting* of the *Sun* and *Moon*,
The *Moon's* Place,
Equation of *Time*,
Time of *High Water*,
List of *Provincial Officers*,
Sitting of *Courts*,
&c. &c. &c.

By BERNARD KIERNAN, *T. M. & L. S.*

SAINT JOHN:

PRINTED AND SOLD BY HENRY CHUBB, AT THE SIGN OF THE CROWN AND MITRE, PRINCE WILLIAM STREET.

NB60 Courtesy National Archives, Ottawa

Place, | *Equation* of *Time,* | Time of *High Water,* | List of *Provincial Officers,* | *Sitting* of *Courts,* | *&c. &c. &c.* | [thick-thin rule 89 mm] | BY BERNARD KIERNAN, *T.M. & L.S.* | [thin-thick rule 89 mm] | SAINT JOHN: | PRINTED AND SOLD BY HENRY CHUBB, AT THE SIGN OF THE CROWN AND | MITRE, PRINCE WILLIAM STREET.
COLLATION: 12° (17.7 x 10.4 cm), A^6 B–C^6 [$1 signed], 18 leaves, pp [36]
CONTENTS: [*1*] title; [*2*] blank; [*3*] eclipses, zodiac, planets; [*4*] aspects, vulgar notes, ember days, feasts, holidays; [*5–16*] calendar with notes about names of the months; [*17–19*] civil list; [*19*] customs, revenue; [*20*] College of New Brunswick, Public Grammar School, clergy of established church, Kirk of Scotland; [*21–24*] county officers; [*25*] courts; [*25–26*] army; [*27–28*] Saint John officers; [*28–30*] firewards, Friendly Fire Club, firemen; [*30–31*] roads; [*31–33*] puzzles, riddles, charades; [*33*] time table; [*34*] harbour signals; the Falls; [*35–36*] freemasons; [*36*] ships
PAPER: Wove, unmarked
TYPOGRAPHY: *Text*: long primer, modern face, with old faces. *Display*: beaded open roman as english two lines ornamented of Fry and Steele in Stower; pages in rule frame; ornamental dashes including leaf ornaments (14 mm), often used in pairs by John Ryan; almanac signs
45 ll., 155 (161) x 91; 67 mm for 20 ll.
NOTES: With this almanac, probably his first, Henry Chubb began a series of almanacs which continued almost uninterrupted until the 1850s. During the years after Jacob Mott's last Saint John almanac in 1813 (**NB38**) New Brunswickers had been offered Halifax editions by local printers and booksellers. In January of 1817 Chubb himself had advertised 1817 Halifax and Boston almanacs for sale (*New-Brunswick Courier*, 18 January 1817). In October he again offered Nova Scotia almanacs for the coming year (18 October) then announced 'In the Press and speedily will be published, An Almanack for the Year of our Lord, 1818; Calculated for the Meridian of Saint John, (New Brunswick)' (25 October). It was 'Just Published' and for sale by early December (6 December). A convenient excerpt from the *City Gazette* was inserted as an indirect form of advertisement in the same issue of Chubb's paper: 'We understand that a large quantity of Almanacks for the year 1818 have lately been clandestinely imported into the Province from the United States.' Warning that American almanacs were contraband and purchasers 'liable to a prosecution' the article continues 'Nor can there be any justifiable pretext for smugglers bringing such articles into this City, as the Printers here have, at a great expence and with a laudable industry, published an Almanack for next year, equal, if not superior to any extant in the United States' (*New-Brunswick Courier*, 6 December 1817).
COPIES EXAMINED: NBS, NBSM (lacking pp [*1–2*]), OOA

NB61 Burns, George, 1790?–1876
A VIEW | OF THE | PRINCIPLES AND FORMS | OF THE | CHURCH OF SCOTLAND, AS BY LAW ESTABLISHED. | ADDRESSED TO THE PRESBYTERIAN CONGREGATION OF SAINT JOHN, NEW- | BRUNSWICK. | [ornamental dash 27 mm] | BY GEORGE BURNS, D.D. | *Minister of Saint Andrews Church, in the City of Saint John.* | [ornamental dash 27 mm] | "Neglect not the gift that is in thee, which was given thee by prophecy, | with the laying on of the hands of the Presbytery." 1 Tim. iv. 14. | [thick-thin rule 55 mm] | SAINT JOHN: | PRINTED BY HENRY CHUBB, PRINCE WILLIAM-STREET. | 1817.
COLLATION: 8° (21.7 x 12.7 cm), A^4 B–D^4 [$1 signed], 16 leaves, pp *1–3* 4–32 (pagination in ( ))
CONTENTS: *1* title; 2 advertisement signed GB at Saint John, 13 Decmeber 1817; *3*–32 text; 32 erratum (1 l.)
PAPER: Laid, unmarked
TYPOGRAPHY: *Text*: long primer, modern face
47 ll., 162 (172) x 100; 67 mm for 20 ll.
NOTES: Chosen in 1816 as minister of the new Presbyterian church in Saint John, the first in the province, George Burns arrived from Aberdeen the following year. He explained the need for this work in his advertisement: 'In organizing our Infant Church by the appointment of Office-Bearers, I thought it might be useful to some of my hearers who had left Scotland at an early period of life, and to others who had been trained in the principles of Presbyterian Government in different quarters of the world, to explain the Constitution of the Church of Scotland, with a particular reference to the design and duties of the Eldership.' Although Burns claimed 'I deprecate all controversy on the subject' he and the new congregation were soon involved in old disputes with the Church of England about establishment of the Church of Scotland in New Brunswick (**NB72**). Henry Chubb's first notice that the work was 'just published' is dated 7 January (*New-Brunswick Courier*, 10 January 1818).
COPIES EXAMINED: NBSM, USMBAt
REFERENCE: MacFarlane

NB62 Mountain, George Jehoshaphat, 1789–1863
A | VALEDICTORY | *SERMON,* | PREACHED | IN | CHRIST CHURCH, | FREDERICTON, | ON THE 29TH JUNE, | 1817. | [thick-thin rule 42 mm] | BY THE REVEREND | GEORGE J. MOUNTAIN. | [thin-thick rule 42 mm] | *"Hold fast the faithful word as you have been taught."* | *"Am I therefore your enemy because I tell you* the truth? | [thick-thin rules 11, 11 mm] | FREDERICTON, | PRINTED BY GEO. K. LUGRIN, | KING'S PRINTER.

COLLATION: 8° (22.2 x 14 cm), 1^8, 8 leaves, pp *1–5* 6–15 *16*
CONTENTS: *1* title; *2* blank; *3* dedication: 'To the Parishioners of Fredericton and especially to the members of the vestry' signed Geo. J. Mountain at Quebec, 1 September 1817; *4* blank; *5*–15 sermon, text: Thessalonians. IV. 1, 2; 15 note headed *.* (7 ll.); *16* blank
PAPER: Wove, unmarked
TYPOGRAPHY: *Text*: english, transitional modern face. *Display*: beaded open roman as english two lines ornamented of Fry and Steele in Stower
36 ll., 166 (175) x 92; 94 mm for 20 ll.
BINDING: Stitched (NBFL)
NOTES: After three years in Fredericton George Mountain and his wife Mary Hume Mountain, whose name is inscribed on the title of the OTMCL copy, returned home to Quebec (**NB55**).
COPIES EXAMINED: NBFL, OOA (lacking pp *1–2*, 15–*16*), OTMCL
REFERENCES: Casey 1035, MacFarlane, TPL 1124

NB63 New Brunswick
[Agricultural Export Prohibition Act] 57 Geo III, 1817, c. 1
Published by Authority. | [ornamental dash 74 mm] | AN ACT | To prohibit the exportation of Corn, Meal, Flour and Potatoes, out of the | Province for a limited time. | Passed the 17th February, 1817. | ... | [wavy rule 65 mm] | Printed by GEO. K. LUGRIN, King's Printer.
Act: 1/2° (32.4 x 20 cm)
CONTENTS: 1 l. heading; dash; 4 ll. title and date; 32 ll. text; rule; 1 l. imprint
PAPER: Laid, marked Britannia; chains vertical 25 mm
TYPOGRAPHY: *Text*: english, modern face
277 x 172 mm
NOTES: 'Owing to the failure of the late crops' a prohibition on the export of foodstuffs was ordered for four months.
COPY EXAMINED: NBFA: 'Misc Records'

NB64 New Brunswick. Laws (4th Parliament, 3rd session: 1807 to 6th Parliament, 1st session: 1817)
THE | ACTS | OF THE | GENERAL ASSEMBLY | OF | HIS MAJESTY'S PROVINCE | OF | *NEW-BRUNSWICK,* | FROM THE | FORTY-SEVENTH to the FIFTY-SEVENTH | Year of the REIGN of | KING GEORGE THE THIRD. | [double rule 103 mm] | WITH A COPIOUS INDEX. | [double rule 104 mm] | [royal arms 20 x 30 mm] | [double rule 104 mm] | FREDERICTON: | PRINTED BY GEORGE K. LUGRIN, PRINTER TO THE KING'S MOST | EXCELLENT MAJESTY. | [dotted rule 15 mm] | MDCCCXVII.

COLLATION: 4° (23 x 14.2 cm), π^4 (π1 + χ1) A^4 B–I^4 K–U^4 X–$2B^4$ 2C–$2I^8$ 2K–$2N^8$ (2N5 + χ1) 2O–$2Q^4$ $2R^2$ [\$1, \$^{8}1, 2, 3 signed], 208 leaves, pp [4] *i* ii–ix *x*, *1* 2–365 *366* χ366 χ367 ^{2}[34]
CONTENTS: [*1*] title; [*2*] blank; [*3*] administration of the province 1805–1817; [*4*] blank; *i*–ix table of acts; *x* blank; *1*–365 text; *366* blank; χ366 text headed '(Omitted in its place.) Page 366'; χ367 blank; ^{2}[*1–32*] index; ^{2}[*33*] table of acts; ^{2}[*34*] errata (3, 14 ll.)
PAPER: Wove, unmarked except X–2B laid, marked post horn in crowned shield; chains horizontal 26 mm
TYPOGRAPHY: *Text*: english, moderate modern face. *Display*: beaded open roman as english two lines ornamented of Fry and Steele in Stower; modern face italic drop letters; wavy rule as brevier 29 of same Fry and Steele
36 ll., 172 (180) x 86 (107); 94 mm for 20 ll.
BINDING: Calf, boards edged in blind with rope roll, turnovers with dotted and hatched rolls. Spine divided into six panels by double blind rule, in second a black lettering piece edged gilt with leaf and lozenge roll, lettered NEW | BRUNSWICK | LAWS | (NBSM). Half calf edged in blind with bead and ball roll and grayish blue wove paper. Spine as full calf copy with gilt lozenge roll on lettering piece. Endpapers and binder's leaf wove, marked JM | 1816 (NBFL, 2 copies at NBSM); NBS copy same except calf edged gilt with chain roll and lettering piece red, edged gilt with bellflower and daisy; OTMCL copy half calf without finish except triple blind on spine and gilt chain on black lettering piece
COPIES EXAMINED: NBFL, NBS, NBSM (3 copies), OTMCL

NB65 New Brunswick. Laws (6th Parliament, 1st session: 1817)
[within 6 mm Greek key rules 278 x 154 mm] ACTS | OF THE | *GENERAL ASSEMBLY* | OF | HIS MAJESTY'S PROVINCE | OF | *NEW-BRUNSWICK.* | PASSED IN THE YEAR 1817. | [wavy rule 143 mm] | [royal arms 70 x 88 mm] | [wavy rule 143 mm] | FREDERICTON: | PRINTED BY GEORGE K. LUGRIN, PRINTER TO THE KING'S | MOST EXCELLENT MAJESTY. | 1817.
COLLATION: 2° (31.1 x 19.5 cm), π^2 (π1 + 1) $2\pi^2$ A^2 B–E^2 [$1 signed], 15 leaves, pp *1–2* [2] *3–4* ²[4] *5* 6–23 *24*
CONTENTS: *1* title; 2 blank; [1] session title; [2] blank; 3 titles of acts; *4* blank; ²[*1–3*] 'An Act for the Encouragement of the Trade of this Province in Plaster of Paris, otherwise called Gypsum' passed 11 March 1816; ²[4] proclamation dated 31 January 1817; *5*–23 text; *24* blank
PAPER: Laid, *A*, C watermark Vryheyt; countermark J BUDGEN | 1815; B, 1 wove, unmarked; D, E, π, 2π watermark Britannia; countermark RADWAY | 1814; second copy with *A*, 1 BUDGEN, rest RADWAY; chains vertical 26 mm
TYPOGRAPHY: *Text*: modern face. *Display*: title with wavy rule brevier 30 of Fry and Steele in Stower; beaded open roman as english two lines ornamented of same Fry and Steele
57 ll., 265 (282) x 114 (146); 94 mm for 20 ll.
NOTES: George Lugrin's account for printing 250 copies of the Acts, each seven and one-half sheets, was £45; folding and stitching was £3 (NBFA: RS24/S26/R6.22). On 27 May he was offering a 'Few Copies for sale at the Royal Gazette office (*New Brunswick Royal Gazette*, 27 May 1817).
COPIES EXAMINED: OOA (2 copies)

NB66 New Brunswick. Parliament (6th, 1st session: 1817). House of Assembly
[within 6 mm ribbon and rosette rules 281 x 158 mm] JOURNAL | OF THE | *HOUSE OF ASSEMBLY* | OF THE | PROVINCE | OF | *NEW-BRUNSWICK:* | FROM TUESDAY THE 4TH DAY OF FEBRUARY, TO SATURDAY THE 22D DAY OF MARCH, 1817. | [zigzag rule 142 mm] | [royal arms 57 x 70 mm] | [zigzag rule 142 mm] | FREDERICTON: | PRINTED BY GEORGE K. LUGRIN, KING'S PRINTER. | 1817.
COLLATION: 2° (34 x 21 cm), π^1 A^2 B–F^2 χ1 G–I^2 K–T^2 V^1 [$1 signed], 41 leaves, pp *1–3* 4–18 χ18–26 [2] 27–78 *79* [χ1 is folded leaf 34 x 40 cm]
CONTENTS: *1* title; 2 blank; 3–26 text; [*1*–2] imports and duties; public accounts; 27–78 text; *79* blank
PAPER: Laid, watermark Britannia; *A*, E–L, S countermark JELLYMAN | 1813; B–D, M–T countermark AM^c^G | 1813; *V* countermark E SMITH | 1816; χ countermark fleur de lys | MOLINEUX & JOHNSTON | 1813; chains vertical 27 mm
TYPOGRAPHY: *Text*: english, modern face. *Display*: title page with frame of double pica 7 of 1790 Fry and Steele specimen and rule of brevier 30 of Fry and Steele in Stower; beaded open roman as english two lines ornamented of same Fry and Steele
56 ll., 263 (282) x 149; 94 mm for 20 ll.
NOTES: The usual edition of two hundred copies was printed with charges for twenty-one sheets of £80 for printing, £10 for the treasurer's report, and £3 for folding and stitching (NBFA: RS24/S26/P6.22).
COPIES EXAMINED: NBFL (lacking title), NBSM, OOA

NB67 Saint John
[within 6 mm ribbon and stick rules 278 x 143 mm] LAWS | AND | ORDINANCES, | ORDAINED AND ESTABLISHED | BY THE | *MAYOR, ALDERMEN, AND COMMONALTY,* | OF THE | CITY | OF | *SAINT JOHN* [open] | IN COMMON COUNCIL CONVENED. | Published the *first* day of *March*, 1817, in the first year of the Mayoralty of | JOHN ROBINSON, Esquire. | [dot and arrow rule 131 mm] | [arms of Saint John 31 x 36 mm] | [thick-thin rule 131 mm] | SAINT JOHN, *(New-Brunswick,)* | PRINTED BY WILLIAM DURANT, AT THE SIGN OF THE CROWN AND MITRE, PRINCE WILLIAM-STREET. | 1817.
COLLATION: 2° (30.6 x 19.2 cm), π^2 $2\pi^2$ πA–C^2, A^2 B–E^2 F^1 G–I^2 J^1 [$1 signed], 28 leaves, pp *i–v* vi–xx, *1* 2–36
CONTENTS: *i* title; *ii* blank; *iii–iv* index; *v*–xx laws confirmed 1 April 1796; *1*–36 'subsequent laws'
PAPER: Laid, watermark Britannia; countermark JJ[?] except π, 2π, F countermark G & A [script] | 1813; chains vertical 24 mm
TYPOGRAPHY: *Text*: pica, old face. *Display*: title page with frame of great primer 11 of 1785 Caslon specimen and dot and arrow rule (brevier 28 of Fry and Steele, 1790); modern faces on title; italic with swash A, M, N, Y (except *N* in *ALDERMEN*); text with long ornamental dashes and rows of flowers (nonpareil 8 of 1790 Fry and Steele)
58 ll., 243 (260) x 112 (137); 84 mm for 20 ll.
COPY EXAMINED: NBSM

1818

NB68 An Almanack for the Year of Our Lord, 1819

[within rules 149 x 92 mm] AN | ALMANACK, | FOR THE | Year of our Lord, | 1819; | BEING THE THIRD AFTER BISSEXTILE OR LEAP YEAR. | *CALCULATED FOR THE MEREDIAN OF* | SAINT JOHN, N.B. | BEING IN LATITUDE 45° 20′ N. LONGITUDE 66° 03′ W. | BUT WILL SERVE FOR ANY PART OF THE PROVINCE. | [ornamental dash 55 mm] | CONTAINING: | [8 ll. to left of rule] *Signals* made on the approach of | Vessels; also, all the Merchants | *Private Signals.* | *UNIVERSAL KALENDAR*, con- | taining the *Feasts* and *Fasts* of the | *Church; Equation of Time; Ris-* | *ing* and *Setting* of the *Sun* and | *Moon;* the *Moon's Place; Time* of *High Water, &c.* | [8 ll. to right] *Eclipses* of the *Luminaries.* | *Vulgar Notes.* | *Staff* of the *Army.* | List of *Provincial Officers.* | *Sittings* of *Courts.* | *Masonic Lodges.* | *Roads* through the Province. | Valuable *Receipts, &c. &c.* | [rule 90 mm] | BY *COPERNICUS.* | [rule 90 mm] | SAINT JOHN: | PRINTED AND SOLD BY WILLIAM REYNOLDS AND COMPANY, CORNER OF | PRINCE WILLIAM AND CHURCH STREETS.
Stent MEREDIAN Merchants
COLLATION: 12° (19.4 x 11.5 cm), *1–2*^{6} 3^4 *4–5*^{2}, 20 leaves, pp [*40*]
CONTENTS: [*1*] title; [*2*] blank; [*3*] astronomical; [*4*] royal family, sovereigns of Europe; [*5*] harbour signals; the Falls; [*6–17*] calendar; [*18–19*] civil list; [*19–20*] courts, legal; [*20*] customs, revenue; [*21*] education, ecclesiastical; [*22–24*] local officers; [*25–26*] Saint John officers; [*26–27*] fire officers; [*28*] merchants' signals; [*29–30*] army; [*31*] navy; [*32–33*] roads; [*33*] local officers; [*34*] courts; holidays; [*35*] freemasons; [*36–40*] domestic and agricultural hints including Lady Derby's soap, 'Rules for plucking geese'
PAPER: Laid, unmarked
TYPOGRAPHY: *Text*: modern faces. *Display*: zigzag rule brevier 30 of Fry and Steele in Stower; pages in rule frame; almanac signs
149 x 92 mm
BINDING: Stitched
NOTES: Williams Reynolds, a Saint John bookseller, began a new weekly in the spring of 1818, *The Star; and New Brunswick Literary, Political and Commercial Intelligencer.*
COPY EXAMINED: NBS

NB69 An Almanack for the Year of Our Lord, 1819

[within rules 154 x 85 mm] AN | ALMANACK, [open, beaded] | FOR THE | Year of our Lord, | 1819; | BEING THE THIRD AFTER BISSEXTILE OR LEAP YEAR. | CALCULATED FOR THE MERIDIAN OF | Saint John, N.B. | Being in Latitude 45° 20′ North, Longitude 66° 3′ West; | *But will serve for any part of the Province.* | [ornamental dash 36 mm] | CONTAINING | [7 ll. to left of double rule] The *Universal Calendar,* | *Feasts* and *Fasts* of the | *Church, &c.* | *Eclipses* of the *Lumina-* | *ries,* | *Rising* and *Setting* of the | *Sun* and *Moon,* | [6 ll. to right] The *Moon's* Place, | *Equation* of *Time,* | Time of *High Water,* | List of *Provincial Officers,* | *Sitting* of *Courts,* | *&c. &c. &c.* | [double rule 86 mm] | BY BERNARD KIERNAN, *T.M. & L.S.* | [double rule 86 mm] | *SAINT JOHN:* | PRINTED AND SOLD BY HENRY CHUBB, AT THE SIGN OF THE CROWN | AND MITRE, PRINCE WILLIAM STREET.
COLLATION: 12° (19 x 13 cm uncut), *A*^{4} B^4 C^8 D^6 [$1 signed], 22 leaves, pp [*44*]
CONTENTS: [*1*] title; [*2*] eclipses, zodiac, planets, aspects; [*3*] vulgar notes, ember days, feasts, holidays; the Falls; [*4–15*] calendar with verses opening '"April returns – thoſe early ſonnets bring' for April and '"Bleſt be the cult'ters of New-Brunſwick's ſoil' for October; [*16–18*] civil list; [*18*] customs, revenue; [*19–20*] College of New Brunswick, Public Grammar School, National School, clergy of established church, Kirk of Scotland; [*20–23*] county officers; [*23*] courts; [*24–25*] army; [*25*] hints; [*26–27*] Saint John officers; [*28–29*] firewards, Friendly Fire Club, firemen; [*29–30*] roads; [*31–32*] harbour signals; [*32*] hint; [*33*] ships; [*33–34*] freemasons; [*34*] royal family; [*35–36*] answers to 1818 puzzles, new puzzles, selections; 'A Fable to the Ladies' and 2 ll. note inviting contributions; [*37–44*] advice on crops and livestock
PAPER: Laid, unmarked; chains horizontal 27 mm
TYPOGRAPHY: *Text*: long primer, bourgeois, and brevier, modern and old faces. *Display*: beaded open roman as english two lines ornamented of Fry and Steele in Stower; pages in rule frame; long ornamental dashes; almanac signs
46 ll., 156 (158) x 86
NOTES: Chubb's almanac was promised for 'next week' on 17 October 1818 (*New-Brunswick Courier*).
COPIES EXAMINED: NBS (lacking pp [*31–44*]), NBSM (one copy lacking pp [*1–2*] [*43–44*], the other lacking pp [*33–36*] [*43–44*]), OOA

NB70 Burns, George, 1790?–1876
LETTER | ADDRESSED TO THE | *REV. JAMES MILNE, A.M.* | IN CONSEQUENCE OF HIS | REMARKS [open] | ON | DR. BURNS'S VIEW | OF THE | PRINCIPLES AND FORMS | OF THE | CHURCH OF SCOTLAND, | AS BY LAW ESTABLISHED. | [ornamental dash 34 mm] | BY THE | AUTHOR OF THAT WORK. | [ornamental dash 34 mm] | "After the way which they call heresy, so worship I the God of my | fathers." – Acts xxiv. 14. | "The bane and antidote are both before you." | Audi alteram partem. | [thick-thin rule 53 mm] | SAINT JOHN: | PRINTED BY HENRY CHUBB, PRINCE WILLIAM-STREET. | 1818.
COLLATION: 8° (21.5 x 13 cm), A^4 B–H^4 [$1 signed], 32 leaves, pp *1–3* 4–64 (pagination in ( ))
CONTENTS: *1* title; 2 blank; *3*–64 text
PAPER: Laid, unmarked; chains vertical 26 mm
TYPOGRAPHY: *Text*: pica, transitional face with *f*
38 ll., 159 (170) x 101; 83 mm for 20 ll.
NOTES: Written promptly in response to the Rev Milne's *Remarks* (**NB72**) on his first work (**NB61**), Burns's *Letter* was advertised by Henry Chubb as 'Just Published in 64 pages, Octavo' for sale at the Courier office on 7 April 1818 (issue of 11 April). George Lugrin was offering copies for sale in Fredericton on 5 May (*Royal Gazette*). Both pamphlets, Milne's attack and Burns's counterattack, were printed by the same printer in the same shop with the same ornamental dash, an outline swelled rule with lozenges midway, setting off the statement of authorship on both title pages.
COPIES EXAMINED: NBSM, USMBAt
REFERENCE: MacFarlane

NB71 Hay-Drummond, George William Auriol, 1761–1807
SELECT PORTIONS | OF THE | *NEW VERSION OF PSALMS,* | FOR EVERY SUNDAY | THROUGHOUT THE YEAR; | WITH | THE PRINCIPAL FESTIVALS AND FASTS; | FOR THE USE OF | *PARISH CHURCHES.* | THE WORDS | SELECTED | *BY THE REV. GEORGE HAY DRUMMOND;* | WITH | A SELECTION OF HYMNS, | FOR PARTICULAR OCCASIONS. | TO WHICH IS ADDED, | SUCH PARTS OF THE CHURCH SERVICE | AS IS USUALLY CHAUNTED. | [thick-thin rule 25 mm] | *Re-printed* from the TWENTY-THIRD, *London Edition,* | BY WILLIAM DURANT, | *Saint John, New Brunswick.* | 1818.
COLLATION: 12° (17.3 x 10.2 cm), A^6 B–I^6 K–M^6 N^2 [$1 signed], 74 leaves, pp *[4]* *1* 2–144
CONTENTS: [*1*] title; [2] blank; [*3–4*] preface; *1* 'Advertisement to the Twenty-Third Edition' dated October 1817; 2–115 text; 116–120 appendix; 121–135 hymns; *136*–140 'Instructions for Chaunting the Hymns'; *141*-144 index
PAPER: Laid, marked fleur de lys; chains horizontal 26 mm
TYPOGRAPHY: *Text*: long primer, modern face. *Display*: ornamental dashes
38 ll., 129 (163) x 71; 67 mm for 20 ll.
BINDING: Although stab holes confirm that the work was issued stitched, probably in the blue wrapper promised by the publisher, two copies are half very deep red leather with spine ruled gilt and light brown spanish marbled paper. Wove endpapers (OTMCL, QMMRB)
NOTES: Durant advertised this as an edition of Tate and Brady's version of the psalms, 'being the selections now in use at St. John and Fredericton.' It was 'in the press' on 30 September 1818. He promised a work 'neatly Printed on a good Type and Paper ... stitched in blue, and delivered to Subscribers at two shillings and six-pence each' (*Royal Gazette*, 6 October 1818). The notice was carried at Halifax, in Anthony Holland's *Acadian Recorder* where subscriptions were being taken (24 October 1818). Merchants in both Saint John and Halifax were also accepting subscriptions. The following year copies were offered 'for Cash, on delivery' at the same price in Fredericton (*New Brunswick Royal Gazette*, 16 March 1819).
COPIES EXAMINED: NSHD, OTMCL, QMMRB
REFERENCES: Lande S678, MacFarlane, MTL7014

NB72 Milne, James, d. 1823
REMARKS | ON | DR. BURNS'S VIEW | OF THE | PRINCIPLES AND FORMS | OF THE | PRESBYTERIAN KIRK, AS BY LAW ESTABLISHED | IN | SCOTLAND. | [ornamental dash 34 mm] | BY THE | REV. JAMES MILNE, A.M. | FREDERICTON, NEW-BRUNSWICK. | [ornamental dash 34 mm] | *Art thou a master of Israel, and knowest not these things?* – St. John, 3, 10. | *If the blind lead the blind, both shall fall into the ditch* – St. Mat. 15, 10. | *Thus saith the Lord, stand ye in the ways, and see, and ask for the old* | *paths, where is the good way, and walk therein, and ye shall find rest* | *for your souls.* – Jeremiah 6, 16. | [thick-thin rule 54 mm] | SAINT JOHN: | PRINTED BY WILLIAM DURANT, PRINCE WILLIAM-STREET. | 1818.
COLLATION: 8° (21.8 x 13 cm), A^4 B–E^4 [$1 signed], 20 leaves, pp *1–3* 4–40 (pagination in ( ))

CONTENTS: *1* title; 2 letter of dedication addressed to His Excellency Major-General Smyth, lieutenant governor, signed James Milne; *3–40* text; errata slip (58 x 130 mm) inserted facing dedication (8 ll.)
PAPER: Unmarked; *A*–D wove; E laid, chains vertical 26 mm (NBSM); *A*–E laid (USMBAt)
TYPOGRAPHY: *Text*: pica, transitional face with *f*; letter (p 2) in italic
38 ll., 153 (164) x 94 mm; 84 mm for 20 ll.
NOTES: James Milne, Church of England rector at Fredericton, described George Burns's *View* (**NB61**) as 'an attack on our National Church, which, although weak in itself, is yet by the boldness of its manner calculated to make on the minds of the unlearned and unstable impressions unfavorable to her.' He continued 'I have no wish to feed the flame of Religious controversy so inconsiderately kindled. My sole object is to warn the Members of the Church of the arts of seduction which are practised against us' (p 2).

Henry Chubb, Burns's printer, offered Milne's *Remarks* 'This Day is Published (And May be had at this office)' in a notice dated 25 March 1818 (*New-Brunswick Courier*, 11 April). George Lugrin had copies for sale in Fredericton within a week (*New Brunswick Royal Gazette*, 31 March 1818).
COPIES EXAMINED: NBSM, USMBAt
REFERENCE: MacFarlane

NB73 New Brunswick. Laws (6th Parliament, 2nd session: 1818)
ACTS | OF THE | *GENERAL ASSEMBLY* | OF | HIS MAJESTY'S PROVINCE | OF | *New-Brunswick*: | PASSED IN THE YEAR | 1818. | [thick-thin rule 105 mm] | [royal arms 20 x 30 mm] | [thin-thick rule 105 mm] | FREDERICTON: | PRINTED BY GEORGE K. LUGRIN, | *Printer to the King's Most Excellent Majesty.* | [swelled rule 9 mm] | MDCCCXVIII.
COLLATION: 4° (26.5 x 19.5 cm), π^3 A^4 B–H^4 I^2 [$1 signed], 37 leaves, pp [6] *1* 2–67 *68*
CONTENTS: [*1*] title; [*2*] blank; [*3*] session title; [*4*] blank; [*5–6*] titles of acts; *1*–67 text; *68* blank
PAPER: Wove, marked at edge of sheet RC & SON | 1816
TYPOGRAPHY: *Text*: english, modern face. *Display*: beaded open roman as english two lines ornamented of Fry and Steele in Stower
37 ll., 167 (181) x 86 (107); 94 mm for 20 ll.
NOTES: This edition of the annual laws marks a break with the eighteenth century style established by Christopher Sower and imitated by John Ryan and Jacob Mott. Their laws were folios with grand title pages framed in Caslon ornaments. George Lugrin maintained the format in a simpler style with thick-thin rules for 1814 (**NB51**) and a neo-classical frame for 1816 and 1817 (**NB56, 65**). For the collected acts, 1807 to 1817, he dispensed with the frame, selected a small royal arms cut, and printed the date in roman numerals (**NB64**). These innovations together with the adoption of quarto format established a new image for New Brunswick's laws.

Lugrin's account for 1818 does not specify how many copies he printed. The number of sheets, 111 1/2, suggests that several accounts were combined in the total of £63, with the usual £3 for folding and stitching (NBFA: RS24/S27/R7.15).
COPIES EXAMINED: NBSM, OOA

NB74 New Brunswick. Parliament (6th, 2nd session: 1818). House of Assembly
[within 6 mm ribbon and rosette rules 280 x 158 mm] JOURNAL | OF THE | *HOUSE OF ASSEMBLY* | OF THE | PROVINCE | OF | *NEW-BRUNSWICK*, | FROM TUESDAY THE TWENTIETH DAY OF JANUARY, TO WEDNESDAY THE ELEVENTH DAY OF | MARCH, 1818. | [zigzag rule 144 mm] | [royal arms 74 x 90 mm] | [zigzag rule 144 mm] | FREDERICTON: | PRINTED BY GEORGE K. LUGRIN, PRINTER TO THE KING'S MOST | EXCELLENT MAJESTY. | 1818.
COLLATION: 2° (31.8 x 19.5 cm), π^2 A^2 B–C^2 χ1 D–I^2 K–U^2 X–Y^2 Z^1 [$1 signed], 48 leaves, pp [4] *1* 2–12 ²[2]13–89 *90* [χ1 is folded leaf 32 x 40 cm]
CONTENTS: [*1*] title; [*2*] blank; [*3*] proclamations; [*4*] blank; *1*–12 text; ²[*1–2*] import duties; public accounts; 13–89 text; *90* blank
PAPER: Laid, watermark Britannia; some sheets without countermark; *A*–I countermark R COLLINS | 1817; N, O countermark SNELGROVE | 1816; P–Y countermark W[space]M | 1816 (NBFL, NBSM); OOA copy same except N countermark GR | 1815; χ in OOA copy and π in NBSM countermark W[space]M | 1816; chains vertical 25 mm
TYPOGRAPHY: *Text*: english, modern face. *Display*: title page with frame of double pica 7 of 1790 Fry and Steele specimen and rule of brevier 30 of Fry and Steele in Stower; open beaded roman as english two lines ornamented of same Fry and Steele
58 ll., 270 (284) x 150; 94 mm for 20 ll.
NOTES: Although the number of copies is not specified in Lugrin's account of £98 for twenty-four and a half sheets, with £10 for the accounts and £3 for folding and stitching, comparison with previous

years indicates that the customary edition of two hundred copies was printed (NBFA: RS24/S27/R7.15).
COPIES EXAMINED: NBFL (lacking pp 89–*90*), NBSM lacking ^{2}[2], OOA

NB75 Nova Scotia and New Brunswick Baptist Association

MINUTES | OF THE | *NOVA-SCOTIA* AND *NEW-BRUNSWICK* | BAPTIST ASSOCIATION, | HELD AT | NEWPORT, N.S. | JUNE 24th and 25th, | 1818. | [thick-thin rule 27 mm] | SAINT JOHN: | PRINTED BY WILLIAM DURANT. | 1818.

COLLATION: 8° (25 x 12.7 cm), *1*^{4}, 4 leaves, pp *1–2* 3–8 (pagination in ( ))
CONTENTS: *1* title; 2–5 text with 5 ll. note at foot; 6–7 Circular Letter; 8 Corresponding Letter with 5 ll. note at foot
PAPER: Laid, unmarked; chains vertical 25 mm
TYPOGRAPHY: long primer, modern face. *Display*: swash A, N, V in italic on title. Text with thick-thin rules and leaf ornament
51 ll., 171 (180) x 92; 67 mm for 20 ll.
NOTES: An edition of six hundred copies was ordered with Brother Griffin delegated to superintend the work (p 4). According to the report there were 1367 members in the two provinces.
COPY EXAMINED: NSWA

NB76 Order of Procession

[3 mm rule 153 mm] | *FREDERICTON, 27th NOVEMBER*, 1818. | [thick-thin rule 53 mm] | ORDER OF PROCESSION | FOR THE | *FUNERAL* | OF THE LATE | HONOURABLE AND REVEREND | *Jonathan Odell*, | Member of His Majesty's Council. | ... | The Funeral to take place To-morrow precisely at one o'clock, from the late | Mansion of the Deceased. | [3 mm rule 153 mm]

Notice: 1/2° (32x 20 cm)
CONTENTS: mourning rule; 1 l. place and date; rule; 7 ll. heading; ornamental dash; 26 ll. text and rules; rule; 2 ll. closing; mourning rule
PAPER: Laid, one copy marked Britannia, the other 1817 | H; chains vertical 26 mm
TYPOGRAPHY: *Text*: english, transitional face. *Display*: coffin cut 20 x 10 mm
NOTES: A leading citizen of Fredericton from its founding, the loyalist Jonathan Odell had served as provincial secretary from 1784 to 1812. He is remembered now primarily as a satirist of the American Revolution and a poet of early New Brunswick (**NB19**) (*Dictionary of Canadian Biography* v, s.v. 'Odell, Jonathan,' by Alfred G. Bailey).
COPIES EXAMINED: NBSM: Odell Papers F22–4, 4a (2 copies)

1819

NB77 An Almanack for the Year of Our Lord, 1820

[within rules 156 x 87 mm] AN | ALMANACK, [open, beaded] | FOR THE | Year of our Lord, | 1820; | BEING BISSEXTILE OR LEAP YEAR. | CALCULATED FOR THE MERIDIAN OF | Saint John, N.B. | Being in Latitude 45° 20′ North, Longitude 66° 3′ West; | *But will serve for any part of the Province.* | [ornamental dash 28 mm] | CONTAINING | [6 ll. to left of row of section marks] The *Universal Calendar,* | *Feasts* and *Fasts* of the | *Church, &c.* | *Eclipses* of the *Luminaries,* | *Rising* and *Setting* of the | *Sun* and *Moon.* | [6 ll. to right] The *Moon's Place,* | *Equation* of *Time,* | *Time* of *High Water,* | *List* of *Provincial Officers,* | *Sitting* of *Courts,* | *&c. &c. &c.* | [thick-thin rule 86 mm] | BY BERNARD KIERNAN, *T.M. & L.S.* | [thin-thick rule 86 mm] | SAINT JOHN: | PRINTED AND SOLD BY HENRY CHUBB, AT THE SIGN OF THE | CROWN AND MITRE, PRINCE WILLIAM STREET.

COLLATION: 12° (17.3 x 10.8 cm), *A*^{6} B^6 C^6 [B1 signed], 18 leaves, pp [*36*]
CONTENTS: [*1*] title; [*2*] eclipses, zodiac; [*3*] planets, aspects, vulgar notes, cycles, ember days, feasts, holidays; [*4–15*] calendar with poem: 'First to the Gods thy humble homage pay'; [*16–18*] civil list; [*18*] customs, revenue; [*19–20*] College of New Brunswick, Public Grammar School, Madras School, clergy of established church, Kirk of Scotland; [*20–23*] county officers; [*23–24*] courts; [*24–25*] army; [*25*] cure for gout (leeks); [*26–27*] Saint John officers; [*28–29*] firewards, Friendly Fire Company, firemen; [*29–30*] roads; [*31*] harbour signals; [*32*] ships; [*32–33*] freemasons; [*33–35*] recipes and remedies, domestic and veterinary; [*36*] table of interest
PAPER: Wove, unmarked
TYPOGRAPHY: *Text*: long primer, bourgeois, and brevier, both old and modern faces. *Display*: beaded open roman as two lines ornamented of Fry and Steele in Stower; pages in rule frame; ornamental dashes and almanac signs
155 x 87 mm

COPIES EXAMINED: NBS, NBSM (lacking pp [*35–36*]), OOA (lacking pp [*33–36*])

NB78 Burns, George, 1790?–1876

ACTIVE GOODNESS | RECOMMENDED AND ENFORCED. | [swelled rule 20 mm] | A | SERMON | DELIVERED AT SAINT JOHN, | ON JANUARY 1ST. 1819. | WHEN A COLLECTION WAS MADE FOR THE BENEFIT | OF THE POOR. | BY | GEORGE BURNS, D.D. | CLERGYMAN OF THE ESTABLISHED CHURCH OF SCOTLAND, AND MINISTER | OF THE PRESBYTERIAN CHURCH OF SAINT ANDREW, | IN THE CITY OF SAINT JOHN, | *NEW BRUNSWICK.* | [ornamental dash 16 mm] | SAINT JOHN: | PRINTED AT THE STAR OFFICE, BY W. REYNOLDS, AND CO. | CORNER OF PRINCE WILLIAM AND CHURCH STREETS. | 1819.

COLLATION: 8° (20.3 x 12 cm), *1–3*[4], 12 leaves, pp [4] *1* 2–20

CONTENTS: [1] title; [2] blank; [3] dedication: TO THE | MEMBERS OF SESSION | AND | CONGREGATION IN GENERAL, | OF THE | SCOTCH CHURCH, ST. JOHN; | ... | BY | *THE AUTHOR;* [4] advertisement; *1*–20 sermon, text: ECCLES. CHAP.IX. VER. 10

PAPER: Wove, unmarked except *3* marked 1816 in NBSM copy

TYPOGRAPHY: *Text*: pica, modern face. *Display*: drop letter two-line great primer fat roman; notched french rule

35 ll., 146 (161) x 93; 84 mm for 20 ll.

NOTES: In his advertisement Burns explained that this discourse was first delivered 'to a country congregation in the parish Church of Lochwinnock in the west of Scotland' and 'has been THRICE asked for publication in different parts of the world' (p [4]).

Copies were available at George Eaton's store in Halifax on 23 February (*Free Press*).

COPIES EXAMINED: NBSM, USMBAt

NB79 Freemasons. Solomon's Lodge, No XXII (Fredericton)

BY-LAWS | OF | SOLOMON'S LODGE, | *No. XXII.* | HELD AT | FREDERICTON, N.B. | ON THE | *First Tuesday after every Full Moon,* | *throughout every Year.* | [thick-thin rule 70 mm] | FREDERICTON: | PRINTED BY GEO. K. LUGRIN, | *Printer to the King's Most Excellent Majesty.* | [french rule 9 mm] | 1819.

COLLATION: 8° (17.7 x 10.7 cm uncut), *1*[4] 2[2], 6 leaves, pp *1–3* 4–11 *12*

CONTENTS: *1* title; 2 blank; *3*–11 text; *12* blank

PAPER: Laid, unmarked; chains vertical 28 mm

TYPOGRAPHY: *Text*: long primer, modern face. *Display*: row of flowers, brevier 16 of 1790 Fry and Steele specimen

35 ll., 123 (131) x 71; 72 mm for 20 ll.

BINDING: Stitched

COPY EXAMINED: NBSM

NB80 Milne, James, d. 1823

A | FRIENDLY ADDRESS | TO THE | CONGREGATION | OF | *CHRIST'S CHURCH,* | FREDERICTON. | [thick-thin rule 53 mm] | BY THE | *REV. JAMES MILNE, A.M.* | [thick-thin rule 53 mm] | FREDERICTON: | Printed by GEO. K. LUGRIN, Printer to the KING'S Most Excellent Majesty.

COLLATION: 8° (17.2 x 10.5 cm), *1–2*[4], 8 leaves, pp *1–3* 4–<14> *15–16* (pagination in [ ]; 7–8, 11–14 cropped)

CONTENTS: *1* title; 2 blank; *3*–<14> sermon, text: 2d Peter, 3d.I., dated at Fredericton, 15 February 1819; *15–16* blank

PAPER: Laid, 2 marked, probably Strasbourg lily; chains vertical 25 mm

TYPOGRAPHY: *Text*: long primer, modern face

40 ll., 144 (157) x 96; 72 mm for 20 ll.

NOTES: The sermon was for sale at the office of the *New Brunswick Royal Gazette* (27 April 1819).

COPY EXAMINED: USMBAt

NB81 New Brunswick. Laws (6th Parliament, 3rd session: 1819)

ACTS | OF THE | *GENERAL ASSEMBLY* | OF | HIS MAJESTY'S PROVINCE | OF | *New-Brunswick,* | PASSED IN THE YEAR | 1819. | [thick-thin rule 114 mm] | [royal arms 20 x 30 mm] | [thin-thick rule 114 mm] | FREDERICTON: | PRINTED BY GEORGE K. LUGRIN, | *Printer to the King's Most Excellent Majesty.* | [swelled rule 9 mm] | MDCCCXIX.

COLLATION: 4° (22.9 x 14 cm), π[1] 2π[2] *A*[4] B–F[4] G[2] [$1 signed], 29 leaves, pp [6] *1* 2–52

CONTENTS: [1] title; [2] blank; [3] session title; [4] blank; [*5–6*] titles of the acts; *1*–52 text

PAPER: π, *A*–G laid, marked probably post horn in crowned shield; chains horizontal 26 mm; 2π wove, unmarked

TYPOGRAPHY: *Text*: english, modern face. *Display*: thickened modern faces; beaded open roman as english two lines ornamented of Fry and Steele in Stower

38 ll., 178 (190) x 94 (115); 94 mm for 20 ll.
COPY EXAMINED: NBSM

NB82 New Brunswick. Parliament (6th, 3rd session: 1819). House of Assembly
[within 6 mm ribbon and rosette rules 267 x 155 mm] JOURNAL | OF THE | *HOUSE OF ASSEMBLY* | OF THE | PROVINCE | OF | *NEW-BRUNSWICK,* | FROM TUESDAY THE 2D DAY OF FEBRUARY, TO WEDNESDAY THE 24TH DAY OF MARCH, 1819. | [wavy rule 142 mm] | [royal arms 56 x 70 mm] | [wavy rule 142 mm] | FREDERICTON: | PRINTED BY GEO. K. LUGRIN, KING'S PRINTER. | [swelled rule 19 mm] | 1819.
COLLATION: 2° (34 x 21 cm), π^2 A^2 B^2 χ1 2χ1 3χ1 C–I^2 K–U^2 W–X^2 [$1 signed], 51 leaves, pp [4] 91–98 ²[6] 99–178 (page numbers with square bracket on gutter side except (91)) [χ1, 3χ1 folded leaves 34 x 42 cm, 2χ1 is 30.5 x 22.5 cm]
CONTENTS: [1] title; [2] blank; [3] proclamations; [4] blank; 91–98 text; ²[*1–6*] imports and duties; public accounts; 99–178 text
PAPER: *A–G* laid, unmarked; chains vertical 30 mm; H–O watermark Britannia; countermark M CORBETT | 1816[?] ; P–Z, π watermark Britannia; countermark 1815; chains vertical 26 mm; χ, 2χ, 3χ wove, unmarked
TYPOGRAPHY: *Text*: english, modern face. *Display*: title page with frame of double pica 7 of 1790 Fry and Steele specimen and rule of brevier 29 of Fry and Steele in Stower
54 ll., 255 (268) x 149; 94 mm for 20 ll.
COPIES EXAMINED: NBFL, NBSM, OOA

NB83 Nova Scotia and New Brunswick Baptist Association
MINUTES | OF THE | *NOVA-SCOTIA AND NEW-BRUNSWICK* | BAPTIST ASSOCIATION, | HELD AT | *SAINT JOHN*, N.B. [italic open] | JUNE 23d and 24th, | 1819. | [thick-thin rule 32 mm] | SAINT JOHN: | PRINTED BY HENRY CHUBB, AT THE SIGN OF THE CROWN AND MITRE, PRINCE | WILLIAM-STREET.
COLLATION: 8° (20.2 x 12.7 cm), *1*⁴, 4 leaves, pp *1–2* 3–8 (pagination in ( ))
CONTENTS: *1* title; 2–5 text with 4 ll. note at foot; 6–8 Circular Letter; 8 Corresponding Letter
PAPER: Laid, unmarked; chains vertical 27 mm
TYPOGRAPHY: *Text*: long primer, modern face. *Display*: swash A, N in italic on title (except *N* in *AND*); long ornamental dash in text
52 ll., 172 (178) x 100; 67 mm for 20 ll.
NOTES: The members appointed John M. Wilmot to superintend the printing of six hundred copies (p 4). Membership had risen to 1570 in twenty-six congregations.
COPY EXAMINED: NSWA

1820

NB84 An Almanack for the Year of Our Lord, 1821
[within rules 155 x 87 mm] An | ALMANACK, [open, beaded] | FOR THE | Year of our Lord, | 1821; | BEING THE FIRST AFTER BISSEXTILE OR LEAP YEAR. | CALCULCATED FOR THE MERIDIAN OF | Saint John, N.B. | Being in Latitude 45° 20′ North, Longitude 66° 3′ West; | *But will serve for any part of the Province.* | [ornamental dash 28 mm] | CONTAINING | [6 ll. to left of row of section marks] The *Universal Calendar,* | *Feasts* and *Fasts* of the | *Church, &c.* | *Eclipses* of the *Luminaries* | *Rising* and *Setting* of the | *Sun* and *Moon,* | [6 ll. to right] The *Moon's Place,* | *Equation* of *Time,* | *Time* of *High Water,* | *List* of *Provincial Officers,* | *Sitting* of *Courts,* | *&c. &c. &c.* | [thick-thin rule 84 mm] | BY BERNARD KIERNAN, *T.M. & L.S.* | [thin-thick rule 84 mm] | SAINT JOHN: | PRINTED AND SOLD BY HENRY CHUBB, AT THE SIGN OF THE | CROWN AND MITRE, PRINCE WILLIAM STREET.
COLLATION: 12° (17.4 x 10.9 cm), *A*⁶ B–C⁶ [$1 signed, C printed C.], 18 leaves, pp [*36*]
CONTENTS: [*1*] title; [*2*] eclipses, zodiac, planets, aspects, vulgar notes, cycles; [*3*] ember days, feasts, holidays, note on the 'Apparent Rising and Setting of the Sun and Moon'; the Falls; [*4*] harbour signals; [*5–16*] calendar with seasonal verses opening '"Once more the new-born year, all gaily drest' for January, '"To hail the morn a thousand warbler's wake!' for July, and '"Her painted carpet Flora lays aside' for September; [*17–19*] civil list; [*19*] customs, revenue; [*20–21*] College of New Brunswick, Public Grammar School, Madras Schools, S.P.C.K., New Brunswick Auxiliary Bible Society; [*22*] Bank of New Brunswick; New Brunswick Central Society for Promoting the Rural Economy of the Poor, Fredericton Emigrant Society; [*23*] vaccine establishment, officials; [*23–24*] clergy of established churches of England and Scotland; [*24–27*] county officers; [*27–28*] courts; [*28–29*] army; [*30–32*] Saint John officers; [*32–34*] firewards, Friendly Fire Company, Union Fire Club ('This club

is composed exclusively of young men'), firemen; [34] national societies; [34–35] roads; [36] post days, recipes, 'eratta' (2 ll.)
PAPER: Wove, unmarked
TYPOGRAPHY: *Text*: long primer and other faces, old and transitional. *Display*: beaded open roman as english two lines ornamented of Fry and Steele in Stower; pages in rule frame; ornamental dashes and almanac signs
44 ll., 156 (158) x 87 mm
NOTES: George Lugrin offered 'Almanacks for 1821' at his office on 5 December without specifying title or publisher but this almanac is probably the one he was selling. It was the only New Brunswick almanac for that year and Chubb was both a former colleague and his brother-in-law (*Royal Gazette*, 5 December 1820).
COPIES EXAMINED: NBS, OOA (lacking pp [*15–16, 21–22, 35–36*])

NB85 Burns, George, 1790?–1876
LECTURES | AND | SERMONS, | DELIVERED IN THE | SCOTS CHURCH OF SAINT JOHN, | ON SEVERAL ORDINARY OCCASIONS. | [thick-thin rule 11 mm] | DEDICATED (BY PERMISSION) TO HIS EXCELLENCY | THE RIGHT HONOURABLE | *The Earl of Dalhousie.* | [thin-thick rule 11 mm] | BY | GEORGE BURNS, D.D. | CLERGYMAN OF THE NATIONAL ESTABLISHED CHURCH OF SCOTLAND, | FORMERLY OF THE UNIVERSITY OF EDINBURGH, AND NOW | MINISTER OF ST. ANDREW'S, IN THE CITY OF ST. JOHN, | PROVINCE OF NEW BRUNSWICK, | BRITISH NORTH AMERICA. | [thick-thin rule 15 mm] | SAINT JOHN, NEW BRUNSWICK. | PRINTED BY WILLIAM REYNOLDS AND CO. AT THE STAR OFFICE, | CORNER OF PRINCE WILLIAM AND CHURCH STREETS. | [rule 8 mm] | 1820.
IMPRINT: [rule 48 mm] | William Reynolds, and Co. Printers.
COLLATION: 8° (23 x 14.5 cm uncut), π^2 A–I^8 K–V^8 X–2A^8 [$1–4 (–V4) signed, misprinting T2 as 2T], 202 leaves, pp [4] *I* II–XIV *15–17* 18–400
CONTENTS: [*1*] title; [*2*] blank; [*3–4*] dedication: 'To His Excellency the Right Honourable Lieutenant General George, Earl of Dalhousie signed George Burns, at Saint John, New Brunswick, 1 June 1820; *I*–III contents; *IV* blank; *V*–XIV preface; *15* half title: LECTURES.; *16* blank; *17*–149 text; *150* blank; *151* half title SERMONS.; *152* blank; *153*–400 text; 400 imprint
PAPER: Wove, unmarked
TYPOGRAPHY: *Text*: pica, modern face
26 ll., 140 (153) x 84; 108 mm for 20 ll.
BINDING: Quarter light grayish yellowish brown paper and grayish blue paper boards. Spine with printed label [thick-thin rule 30 mm] | LECTURES | AND | SERMONS | BY THE | REV. G. BURNS, D.D. | [swelled rule 15 mm] | 1<2>s 6*d* BOARDS. | [thin-thick rule 30 mm] (NSHD). Rebacked and repaired light grayish yellowish brown paper boards. Edges paste ornamented with swirl pattern (OTMCL)
NOTES: Well before publication Burns's volume was announced to potential subscribers in Nova Scotia and New Brunswick: 'There will be at least *eighteen* Discourses in all, embracing a variety of practical subjects. The Volume will be 8 vo, consisting of from 3 to 400 pages – paper of a very superior quality – and will sell in boards for *two dollars*. As only a very limited number of copies will be thrown off, those who are desirous of being put in possession of the work are requested to leave their name ...' (*Acadian Recorder*, 11 December 1819). In Saint John the notice specified a price of two dollars to subscribers and two dollars and a half to others (*New-Brunswick Courier*, 18 December) while a similar notice in Fredericton quoted 10s and 12s 6d (*Royal Gazette*, 21 December). Copies were available to subscribers in Halifax on the first of July (*Acadian Recorder*, 15 July 1820).

Burns, the first and only Presbyterian clergyman in the province at that time, dedicated his work to George Ramsay, Earl of Dalhousie, who was the Scottish Presbyterian lieutenant governor of Nova Scotia, citing 'The enlightened attachment to the Church of Scotland, which has ever distinguished your Noble House' and 'the dignified and important political relation in which you now stand to that Province of His Majesty's Dominions in which my lot is cast' (p [*3*]). In the preface he assured readers that promises made in the prospectus were fulfilled although he had altered the arrangement of the text: 'One circumstance more requires explanation. In the first advertisement of these discourses it was stated that there would be EIGHTEEN in all, whereas there appears to be in reality only FIFTEEN ... while the full complement of pages is given, there are, instead of eighteen discourses as originally promised, or fifteen as apparently realized, virtually and truly TWENTY-TWO discourses in all' (pp xiii–xiv).
COPIES EXAMINED: NBS, NBSM, NSHD, NSWA, OTMCL (2 copies)
REFERENCES: MacFarlane, TPL 1191

NB86 Burns, George, 1790?–1876
A | SERMON | PREACHED AT | *SAINT JOHN,* [open] | BEFORE THE SAINT JOHN'S AND UNION LODGES OF | FREE AND ACCEPTED ANCIENT MASONS. | ON THE ANNIVERSARY OF | *ST. JOHN THE EVANGELIST,* | 1819; | WHEN A COLLECTION WAS MADE FOR THE POOR | OF THE PARISH IN GENERAL. | [ornamental dash 27 mm] | BY GEORGE BURNS, D.D. | CLERGYMAN OF THE NATIONAL ESTABLISHED CHURCH OF SCOTLAND, | AND MINISTER OF ST. ANDREW'S IN THE CITY OF | SAINT JOHN, NEW-BRUNSWICK. | [ornamental dash 27 mm] | [The profits arising from the sale of this Discourse are to be applied | to the charitable purposes for which the Collection was made.] | [thick-thin rule 27 mm] | SAINT JOHN: | PRINTED BY HENRY CHUBB, PRINCE WILLIAM-STREET. | 1820.
COLLATION: 8° (19.5 x 13 cm), *1*[8], 8 leaves, pp *1–3* 4–15 *16* (pagination in ( ))
CONTENTS: *1* title; 2 dedication: 'To the Masters, Wardens, and Brethren of the St. John's, and Union Lodges' by the Author; *3*–15 sermon, text: 2 Peter I. 5, 7; *16* blank
PAPER: Wove, unmarked
TYPOGRAPHY: *Text*: pica, old face; script for dedication. *Display*: modern faces on title; long ornamental dashes in text
38 ll., 157 (169) x 96; 82 mm for 20 ll.
COPY EXAMINED: NBS

NB87 Lockwood, Anthony, 1775–1855
REPORT | ON THE | *PROJECTED CANAL* | ACROSS THE ISTMUS | THAT DIVIDES | NOVA-SCOTIA AND NEW-BRUNSWICK, | EXPLORED AND LEVELLED IN THE AUTUMN OF | 1819, | BY ORDER OF | HIS EXCELLENCY MAJOR-GENERAL *GEORGE STRACEY SMYTH,* | LIEUTENANT-GOVERNOR OF THE PROVINCE | OF NEW-BRUNSWICK. | [double rule 102 mm] | FREDERICTON: | PRINTED BY GEORGE K. LUGRIN, PRINTER TO THE KING'S MOST | EXCELLENT MAJESTY. | 1820.
COLLATION: (25.5 x 16 cm uncut), *1–2*[6], 12 leaves, pp *1–9* 10–24
CONTENTS: *1* title; 2 blank; *3* letter dated 27 December 1819, to Lieutenant Governor Smyth presenting report, signed A Lockwood, surveyor-general; *4* blank; *5* note about printing the report; sheet of reference; *6* blank; *7* extract from the Journal of the House of Assembly, 3 March 1819; *8* blank; *9*–22 text signed A. LOCKWOOD 'Employed to explore the Istmus'; 23–24 tides
PAPER: Wove, unmarked
TYPOGRAPHY: *Text*: pica, modern face; script for letter
36 ll., 168 (178) x 83 (108); 84 mm for 20 ll.
BINDING: Stitched (USMBAt, USMWA)
NOTES: A canal across the Chignecto Isthmus joining the Bay of Fundy and Baie Verte in the Northumberland Strait had been proposed as early as the seventeenth century. Anthony Lockwood's survey was completed soon after his appointment by Lord Bathurst as surveyor general of New Brunswick in April of 1819.

Preliminaries of the report include details of the printing: 'The House of Assembly of New-Brunswick having expressed a desire, to have Printed a few Copies, for their immediate use, of the Report on the practicability of Cutting a Canal across the Istmus; His Excellency General Smyth in complying with this request, has directed a sheet of reference to be attached. The plan to which the letters refer, cannot be engraved in this Country' (p 5).
COPIES EXAMINED: NSHP, OOA (lacking pp 23–24), USMBAt, USMWA
REFERENCES: Bishop, Casey 1090

NB88 Madras School
Annual Report | OF THE STATE OF THE | MADRAS SCHOOL, | IN | *NEW-BRUNSWICK,* | FOR THE YEAR | 1820. | [thick-thin rule 27 mm] | SAINT JOHN: | PRINTED BY WILLIAM DURANT.
COLLATION: 8° (20.2 x 12.8 cm), *1–2*[4], 8 leaves, pp *1–3* 4–14 *15–16* (pagination in ( ))
CONTENTS: *1* title; 2 blank; 3–13 text; 13–14 rules and regulations, 1 to 6, dated at Saint John, 6 July 1820; *15–16* blank
PAPER: Wove, marked [?] I | 1818
TYPOGRAPHY: *Text*: pica, modern face. *Display*: swash N in italic on title; thickened and shadowed romans, ornamental dashes
37 ll., 152 (162) x 95; 84 mm for 20 ll.
NOTES: Lieutenant Governor Smyth had encouraged the establishment of Madras schools conducted on a monitorial system of instruction. He sent his own son to the first one in Saint John and in 1819 he granted a charter allowing the trustees to establish more schools. According to this report there were eight Madras schools in the province a year later with a total daily attendance of 454 boys and 225 girls (*Dictionary of Canadian Biography* VI, s.v.

'Smyth, George Stracey,' by D.M. Young).
COPY EXAMINED: OOA
REFERENCES: Bishop, Casey 1081

NB89 New Brunswick. Laws (7th Parliament, 1st session: 1820)
ACTS | OF THE | *GENERAL ASSEMBLY* | OF | HIS MAJESTY'S PROVINCE | OF | *New-Brunswick,* | PASSED IN THE YEAR | 1820. | [double rule 104 mm] | [royal arms 21 x 31 mm] | [double rule 104 mm] | FREDERICTON: | PRINTED BY GEORGE K. LUGRIN, | *Printer to the King's Most Excellent Majesty.* | [swelled rule 9 mm] | MDCCCXX.
COLLATION: 4° (24.3 x 15 cm), π^2 $2\pi^1$ A^4 B–I^4 K–L^4 [$1 signed], 47 leaves, pp [*6*] *1* 2–88
CONTENTS: [*1*] title; [*2*] blank; [*3*] session title; [*4*] blank; [*5–6*] titles of acts; *1*–88 text
PAPER: Wove, unmarked
TYPOGRAPHY: *Text*: english, transitional face. *Display*: thickened modern faces on title; beaded open roman as english two lines ornamented of Fry and Steele in Stower
38 ll., 177 (188) x 83 (104); 93 mm for 20 ll.
COPIES EXAMINED: NBSM (2 copies), OOA (lacking pp [*1–2*])

NB90 New Brunswick. Parliament (7th, 1st session: 1820). House of Assembly
[within 6 mm ribbon and rosette rules 256 x 145 mm] JOURNAL | OF THE | *HOUSE OF ASSEMBLY* | OF THE | PROVINCE | OF | *NEW-BRUNSWICK,* | FROM THURSDAY THE 3D DAY OF FEBRUARY, TO WEDNESDAY THE 29TH DAY OF MARCH, 1820. | [wavy rule 130 mm] | [royal arms 57 x 70 mm] | [wavy rule 130 mm] | FREDERICTON: | PRINTED BY GEO. K. LUGRIN, KING'S PRINTER. | [swelled rule 19 mm] | 1820.
COLLATION: 2° (30.2 x 18.5 cm), π^2 A^2 B–C^2 χ1 2χ1 D–I^2 K–U^2 W–$2A^2$ [$1 signed], 54 leaves, pp [*4*] 179–190 [2][*4*] 191–274 (pagination with square bracket on gutter side except (179)) [χ1, 2χ1 folded leaves 30.2 x 40 cm]
CONTENTS: [*1*] title; [*2*] blank; [*3–4*] proclamations; 179–190 text; [2][*1*] public accounts; [2][*2*] blank; [2][*3–4*] imports and duties; 191–274 text
PAPER: *A–O* laid, unmarked; P–2A, π watermark Britannia; countermark M | 1818; χ, 2χ wove, unmarked (NBFL); OOA copy same except *A*–T laid, unmarked; chains vertical 28 mm
TYPOGRAPHY: *Text*: english, modern face. *Display*: title page with frame of double pica 7 of 1790 Fry and Steele specimen and rule of brevier 30 of Fry and Steele in Stower
55 ll., 259 (269) x 150; 94 mm for 20 ll.
COPIES EXAMINED: NBFL, OOA

NB91 New Brunswick Central Society for Promoting the Rural Economy of the Province
[text begins p [2]] AT a meeting held in Fredericton, on the 4th day of March 1820 --- | WILLIAM BOTSFORD, Esquire, in the Chair; | The promoting the Agricultural interests of the Province being taken into con- | sideration, it was proposed as highly expedient, in order to promote so desirable | an object, to establish a Society ... | ... | The New-Brunswick Central Socie- | ty, for promoting the Rural Eco- | nomy of the Province:
COLLATION: 2° (22.5 x 20 cm), 1^2, 2 leaves, pp [*4*]
CONTENTS: [*1*] circular letter headed Province Hall, Fredericton, inviting 'with the request of His Excellency the President and others' the recipient to become a member and to 'render such other aid as you may think fit'; [*2–3*] founding meeting, rules and regulations, officers; [*4*] blank
PAPER: Laid, watermark Britannia; countermark IA | 1815; chains vertical 26 mm
TYPOGRAPHY: *Text*: english, modern face; script for circular letter
269 x 151 mm
NOTES: A similar society had been founded in Halifax late in 1819.
COPIES EXAMINED: NSHP: RG 8, vol 2, 68; NBFA: 'Misc. Records' (lacking pp [*1–2*])

NB92 Nova Scotia and New Brunswick Baptist Association
MINUTES | OF THE | *NOVA-SCOTIA AND NEW-BRUNSWICK* | BAPTIST ASSOCIATION, [shadowed] | HELD AT | SACKVILLE, N.B. | JUNE, 21*st*, 22*d*, 23*d*, | 1820. | [thick-thin rule 42 mm] | *SAINT JOHN:* | PRINTED BY HENRY CHUBB, PRINCE WILLIAM-STREET. *Stet* JUNE,
COLLATION: 8° (20.2 x 12.2 cm), 1^4 2^2, 6 leaves, pp *1*–2 3–12 (pagination in ( ))
CONTENTS: *1* title; 2–5 text; 6–10 Circular Letter; 11–12 Corresponding Letter
PAPER: Wove, unmarked
TYPOGRAPHY: *Text*: long primer and pica, modern faces. *Display*: swash A, N, V in first line of italic on title (except *N* in *AND*); ornamental dash in text
51, 40 ll., 157 (175) x 96; 67, 84 mm for 20 ll.
NOTES: The size of edition was increased to seven hundred copies with Elder Richard Scott requested to superintend the printing (p 5). Membership now totalled 1786.
COPY EXAMINED: NSWA

NB93 Priestley, James
A | SERMON | OCCASIONED BY THE LAMENTED DEMISE OF HIS LATE MAJESTY, | GEORGE III. [shadowed] | DELIVERED IN THE METHODIST CHAPEL ON THE | 14TH APRIL, 1820, | *By J. PRIESTLEY.* | [outline swelled rule 35 mm] | PUBLISHED IN COMPLIANCE WITH THE REQUESTS OF MANY WHO HEARD IT. | [thick-thin rule 32 mm] | *SAINT JOHN:* | PRINTED BY HENRY CHUBB, PRINCE WILLIAM-STREET. | 1820.
COLLATION: 8° (19 x 11 cm), *A*⁴ B–C⁴ [$1 signed], 12 leaves, pp *1–5* 6–24 (pagination in ( ))
CONTENTS: *1* title; 2 blank; *3–4* advertisement signed J. Priestley at Saint John, 1 May 1820; *5*–24 sermon, text: 2 Kings, xxiii, 25
PAPER: Wove, *A*, B mark unreadable
TYPOGRAPHY: *Text*: pica, transitional face, with long primer to finish, midway p 22 to p 24
37 ll., 158 (169) x 96; 82 mm for 20 ll.
NOTES: James Priestley's advertisement is traditionally modest explaining that his sermon was written in less than two days 'when the writer was bowed down by sickness' (p 3).
COPY EXAMINED: NBFL
REFERENCE: MacFarlane

NB94 Saint John
[running title] [between double rules 131 mm] LAWS AND ORDINANCES OF THE CITY OF SAINT JOHN. | [text headed] LAWS AND ORDINANCES [shadowed] | ORDAINED AND ESTABLISHED THE 21ST JANUARY, 1820.
COLLATION: 2° (27.9 x 18 cm), *1–2*², 4 leaves, pp [*8*]
CONTENTS: [*1–7*] text of 4 laws; [*8*] blank
PAPER: Laid, 2 marked Britannia; chains vertical 26 mm
TYPOGRAPHY: *Text*: pica, old face. *Display*: modern faces; dot and arrow rule (brevier 28 of Fry and Steele, 1790)
59 ll., 248 (266) x 110 (130); 84 mm for 20 ll.
COPY EXAMINED: NBSM

NB95 St George's Society (Saint John)
RULES | FOR THE | SAINT GEORGES' [shadowed] | SOCIETY | IN | ST. JOHN, N.B. [shadowed] | [thick-thin rule 42 mm] | SAINT JOHN: | PRINTED BY HENRY CHUBB, PRINCE WILLIAM-STREET. | 1820. *Stet* GEORGES'
COLLATION: (19.7 x 12.7 cm), *1*⁶, 6 leaves, pp *1–3* 4–12 (pagination in ( ))
CONTENTS: *1* title; 2 blank; *3*–11 text; 12 'Members Names – April 1820' (62)
PAPER: Wove, marked probably with initials (I) and year (18)
TYPOGRAPHY: *Text*: pica, old face
33 ll., 137 (148) x 90; 82 mm for 20 ll.
NOTES: The printers Henry Chubb and William Reynolds were members of this society which was open to 'any Man of good character and reputation, being a native of England or Engliſh deſcent' (p 4). Each member was to be furnished with a copy of the rules 'for which he ſhall pay the ſum of one ſhilling' (p 11).
COPY EXAMINED: OOA
REFERENCE: Casey 1089

Newfoundland

1807

Nfld1 Benevolent Irish Society (St John's)
A REPORT [open] | OF THE | MEMBERS NAMES | BELONGING TO THE | Benevolent Iriſh Society, | WITH THE NAMES OF | DONORS AND THEIR DONATIONS, | STATEMENT of the TREASURERS Account with the SOCIETY, | STATEMENTS of the TREASURERS to the COMMITTEE | of CHARITY'S Account, | The NAMES of the OBJECTS relieved, and what they have received | From the 3d of MARCH, 1806, to the 12th OCTOBER, 1807. | ALSO, | SHEWING the GROSS AMOUNT of TICKETS Sold for a | PLAY performed in 1806, for the Benefit of the | above INSTITUTION, and how the Net | proceeds thereof has been applied. | [thick-thin rule 19 mm] | *St. John's, Newfoundland*: | Printed by *John Ryan & Son,* | Printers to the KING'S MOST | EXCELLENT MAJESTY. | 1807.

COLLATION: 8° (22.9 x 14.6 cm uncut), *1*–3[4], 12 leaves, pp *1–2* 3–24 (3 with period)
CONTENTS: *1* title; 2 blank; 3–5 members; 6–9 donors; 9 Committees of Charity 1806, 1807; 10–24 treasurer's account; 24 meeting October 1807
PAPER: Laid, unmarked; chains vertical 28 mm
TYPOGRAPHY: *Text*: long primer, modern face with old face pica. *Display*: double pica, both open modern and old face; long ornamental dash
52 ll.; 179 (188) x 114; 67 mm for 20 ll.
BINDING: Stitched in wrapper of faded grayish yellowish brown laid paper
NOTES: John Ryan, a loyalist who served as apprentice to John Howe in Rhode Island, had already published the first newspaper in Saint John, New Brunswick before he came to Newfoundland (**NB1**). With public support and having consented to official censorship he was permitted to establish a press in the summer of 1807. *The Royal Gazette and Newfoundland Advertiser* began publication in August.
This report and the Society's rules (**Nfld2**) may be the earliest Newfoundland imprints.
COPY EXAMINED: NFSM
REFERENCE: O'Dea 292

Nfld2 Benevolent Irish Society (St John's)
RULES [open] | AND | CONSTITUTION | OF THE | BENEVOLENT | *IRISH SOCIETY*. [open] | FEBRUARY 17th, 1806. | [thick-thin rule 18 mm] | *St. John's, Newfoundland*: | Printed by *John Ryan & Son,* | Printers to the KING'S MOST | EXCELLENT MAJESTY. | 1807.

COLLATION: 8° (22.5 x 14.2 cm), *1*–2[4], 8 leaves, pp *1–2* 3–16 (pagination in ( ))
CONTENTS: *1* title; 2 blank; 3–4 meetings 5 February, 8 February 1806; 4–12 rules and constitution; 12–15 meeting of 17 February with list of members and officers signed Winckworth Tonge, president; 15–16 approval by magistrates at General Quarter Sessions of the Peace, held April 1806, signed Lionel Chancey, clerk of the peace.
PAPER: Laid, unmarked; chains vertical 26 mm
TYPOGRAPHY: *Text*: pica, old face. *Display*: double pica, both old face and open modern roman and italic
35 ll., 162 (175) x 95 (110); 94 mm for 20 ll.
BINDING: Stitched in wrapper of faded grayish yellowish brown laid paper
NOTES: Founded by a group of Irish gentlemen meeting at the London Tavern on 5 February 1806, this non-denominational charitable society continued into the twentieth century (James M. Kent,

A REPORT

OF THE

MEMBERS NAMES

BELONGING TO THE

Benevolent Irifh Society

WITH THE NAMES OF

DONORS AND THEIR DONATIONS,

STATEMENT of the TREASURERS Account with the SOCIETY,

STATEMENTS of the TREASURERS to the COMMITTEE of CHARITY'S Account,

The NAMES of the OBJECTS relieved, and what they have received From the 3d of MARCH, 1806, to the 12th OCTOBER, 1807.

ALSO,

SHEWING the GROSS AMOUNT of TICKETS Sold for a PLAY performed in 1806, for the Benefit of the above INSTITUTION, and how the Net proceeds thereof has been applied.

St. John's, Newfoundland:
Printed by John Ryan & Son,
Printers to the KING'S MOST
EXCELLENT MAJESTY.
1807.

Nfld1 Courtesy Queen Elizabeth II Library, Memorial University of Newfoundland, St John's

'The Benevolent Irish Society,' *Newfoundland Quarterly* I, no 4 (March 1902): 13–16).
COPY EXAMINED: NFSM
REFERENCE: O'Dea 293

1808

Nfld3 Benevolent Irish Society (St John's)
[text headed] 1 | [thick-thin rule 107 mm] | APPENDIX [open] | TO THE FOREGOING | REPORT, | From the 12th *OCTOBER*, to the 17th *FEBRUARY*, 1808. | [thin-thick rule 108 mm]
COLLATION: 8° (22.9 x 14.6 cm uncut), 1^4, 4 leaves, pp 1–8
CONTENTS: 1 members; 1–3 donors; 4–8 accounts; 8 donations; officers for 1808
PAPER: Laid, marked 180[?]; chains vertical 28 mm
TYPOGRAPHY: *Text*: long primer, modern face. *Display*: three long and two short ornamental dashes
52 ll., 179 (188) x 114; 67 mm for 20 ll.
BINDING: Stitched in wrapper with *Report* (**Nfld1**)
COPY EXAMINED: NFSM
REFERENCE: O'Dea 292n

Nfld4 Society for Improving the Condition of the Poor (St John's)
AN | ACCOUNT [open] | OF THE | RISE, PROGRESS and ESTABLISHMENT | OF THE | SOCIETY | For IMPROVING the CONDITION of the | *POOR* [open] | OF | ST. JOHN'S, NEWFOUNDLAND. | [thick-thin rule 20 mm] | *St. John's, Newfoundland*: | Printed by J. RYAN & SON, | Printers to the King's | Moſt Excellent | Majeſty. | 1808.
COLLATION: 8° (19.2 x 12.2 cm), *1*–2^4, 8 leaves, pp *1–2* 3–14 *15–16*
CONTENTS: *1* title; *2* blank; 3–13 text; 13–14 receipts and disbursements 1805 to 1807; *15–16* blank
PAPER: Laid, marked post horn in crowned shield; chains vertical 28 mm
TYPOGRAPHY: *Text*: long primer, modern face
38 ll., 143 (153) x 71; 72 mm for 20 ll.
BINDING: Stitched in wrapper of light bluish gray laid paper
NOTES: Part of the account recalls the efforts of James Gambier who proposed the institution of Sunday Schools during his first visit as governor in 1802. When denominational resistance delayed the schools he directed the missionary of the established church and the magistrates to form a committee to continue his initiative. In the winter of 1803 they opened a School for Female Children to teach reading, spinning, knitting, and 'plain work.' The next step was to combine the Charitable Fund which had been supported by the previous governors Waldegrave and Pole, the Widow's Fund, and the Charity Schools into this new society. With donations and annual subscriptions of one guinea for members, five for directors, the society founded a School of Industry for children aged four to fourteen. The course of study planned for boys included twine spinning, netmaking and mending, reading, and writing. This school opened on 20 October 1804, three months after the arrival of Gambier's successor Erastus Gower.
COPY EXAMINED: USMWA

1810

Nfld5 Newfoundland. Governor (1810–1813: Duckworth)
[to left of heading a circle of type oranaments enclosing text: *Seal*. diam 38 mm] By SIR JOHN THOMAS DUCKWORTH, K.B. | Admiral of the Blue, Governor and Commander in Chief, in and over the | Island of NEWFOUNDLAND, and its dependencies. | WHEREAS it has been found requisite that certain alterations should | take place in the Table of Fees, heretofore established for the several Courts of this Island, and | the following appearing to me to be just and reasonable — I do hereby approve thereof, and such Fees are in | future to be received accordingly, and none other. | GIVEN under my Hand and Seal at FORT TOWNSHEND, ST. JOHN'S, Newfoundland, this First | day of *October*, One thousand Eight hundred and Ten. | J.T. DUCKWORTH. | ...
Proclamation: 1 leaf (47.5 x 38.4 cm)
CONTENTS: 12 ll. heading; rule; table of fees in 2 cols
PAPER: Laid, watermark post horn in crowned shield | 1809; countermark T EDMONDS | 1809; chains horizontal 26 mm
TYPOGRAPHY: *Text*: old and modern faces, pica, double pica, two-line english. *Display*: 19 mm drop initial, probably wooden type
421 x 328 mm
NOTES: Appointed on 26 March Duckworth arrived in St John's on 9 July 1810. Later that same month he sailed in his flagship, the 50-gun *Antelope*, for a tour of settlements in Newfoundland and Labrador. On his return to St John's early in September he worked on social and administrative

improvements for the island population, then numbering 30,000 with 7000 in the capital. In mid-October he returned, as had all the governors before him, to England until the next summer.
COPY EXAMINED: NFSPR
REFERENCE: O'Dea 305

Nfld6 Violet, Edmund
REMARKS | UPON THE LIFE AND MANNERS | OF | THE REV. | JOHN JONES, | FORMERLY PASTOR | OF THE INDEPENDENT CHURCH, | ST. *JOHN'S*, | NEWFOUNDLAND. | [swelled rule 15 mm] | *BY EDMUND VIOLET.* | [swelled rule 15 mm] | With eloquence innate his soul was arm'd, | Tho' harsh the precept, yet the preacher charm'd, | He bore his great commission in his look, | But sweetly temper'd awe, and soften'd all he spoke. | DRYDEN. | [thick-thin 15 mm] | *NEWFOUNDLAND.* | ST. JOHN'S: | PRINTED BY MICHAEL RYAN, | *AT HIS OFFICE*, | In the Lane opposite *Parker Knight & Bulley's.* | [swelled rule 11 mm] | 1810.
COLLATION: 8° (22.3 x 12.2 cm), *1*–2^8 3^2, 18 leaves, pp *1–2* 3–36
CONTENTS: *1* title; *2* blank; 3–4 preface; *5* blank; 6 contents; 7–35 text; 36 errata (3 ll.)
PAPER: Wove, unmarked
TYPOGRAPHY: *Text*: long primer, modern face. *Display*: swelled rule in text
41 ll., 137 (144) x 83; 67 mm for 20 ll.
NOTES: Induced by the 'singular and insulated situation of this Church' Violet prepared his memoir of the first Congregational pastor in Newfoundland for his own improvement and as 'a treat' for his friends. Only when 'it attained its present size' did he consider publishing it (p 3). Drawing useful lessons for his readers on the rewards of piety he described Jones's conversion in 1770 from 'irreligious practices' and even 'wickedness' as a soldier, his founding of a dissenting society, his ordination and ministry, and the school he maintained for poor children. Despite early hostility from the Church of England and the government, a dissenting congregation was well established in St John's by the time of Jones's death in 1800.

Chapter III includes comment on Newfoundland:

> This Island is of considerable extent, and seems to have been designed by Providence for a Fishery. It is locally fit for this end, and can scarcely be appropriated to any other without herculean labour and pains. The coasts swarm with fish, and the country abounds with wood. To the Agriculturist Newfoundland promises nothing. The soil is bad and superficial ... The Country is of an irregular surface, and so covered with wood, and intersected by morasses and large ponds, as to defy the courage of him that would explore it. The Aborigines have never been civilized, but remain in their original state of barbarism and independence. The settlers are absorbed in the Fishery. It is the exclusive trade of the island, and is therefore the object of universal pursuit. The interests of individuals ultimately terminate in the aggregate interests of the fishery ... It is governed by a British Admiral, who takes the title of His Excellency, assumes the station usually for three years, and comes and returns periodically' (pp 17–19).

Violet, one of Jones's successors, was himself pastor of the Congregational Church in St John's from 1807 to 1810 (D.W. Prowse, *A History of Newfoundland*, 2d ed. London: Eyre and Spottiswoode, 1896, 630).
COPY EXAMINED: USICRL
REFERENCE: O'Dea 308

1811

Nfld7 Newfoundland. Governor (1810–1813: Duckworth)
CONDITIONS | For Leaſing by Public Auction, certain Lots of Ground, heretofore Fiſhing Ships' Rooms in the | Town of ST. JOHN'S, by order of SIR JOHN THOMAS DUCKWORTH, K.B. Governor of | Newfoundland, in purſuance of the Statute 51st of GEORGE the 3d. Chapter 45th, entituled | an Act for taking away the Public uſe of certain Ships' Rooms in the Town of ST. JOHN's, in | the Iſland of Newfoundland; and for inſtituting Surrogate Courts on the Coaſt of Labrador, | and in certain Iſlands adjacent thereto. (31st May, 1811.) | ...
Public notice: 1 leaf (41 x 31 cm)
CONTENTS: 7 ll. heading; 38 ll. text of 13 conditions
PAPER: Laid, marked Britannia; countermark J ANSELL | 1810; chains horizontal 26 mm
TYPOGRAPHY: *Text*: double pica old face. *Display*: two-line double pica Caslon for heading
370 x 274 mm
NOTES: Reserved originally for West-Country fishing vessels during the migratory season, the water-front lots or ship's rooms in St John's harbour were being used instead by merchants and other inhabitants for wharves, storage, and boat building. In the session of Britain's Parliament after Duckworth's first visit to Newfoundland legislation

passed allowing these lands to be converted to private property. Following a survey the governor offered lots at auction with renewable leases of thirty years on condition that buildings of timber, stone, or brick be erected. Since the revenue was likely to exceed £1000 (or even £1600 by Duckworth's private estimate) citizens organized to petition that the money be used for local improvement (**Nfld8, Nfld10**).

The MacBraire copy is signed to lower left: St Johns | 24 Oct 1811 | J.T. Duckworth | and to right: Mac braire | . The copy now in the Public Record Office was sent to the Earl of Liverpool by Duckworth from 'Antelope at Sea' on 1 November 1811. He enclosed a sample of the printed indenture which would be completed in manuscript as part of the transaction. Signatures of the witnesses were prefaced: 'Sealed and Delivered, at St. John's aforesaid, (where no Stamped Paper is Used), in the Presence of Us.'

COPIES EXAMINED: NFSA: James MacBraire Collection, P3/B/22 file 25; GBPRO: CO194, vol 51, f10

Nfld8 At a General Meeting (St John's)

At a General Meeting of the Merchants and principal [script] | Inhabitants of the Town of Saint John's, in the Island [script] | of Newfoundland, held at Merchants'-Hall, on Thurs- [script] | day the 7th November, 1811. [script] | Mr. BOUCHER being called to the Chair, briefly stated the object of the meeting – which was for the purpose of | petitioning the PRINCE REGENT for the appropriation of Monies arising from the Sale of the Ships' Rooms. | ... | Alex. Boucher, Chairman. [script]

Report: 1 leaf (32.2 x 20 cm)

CONTENTS: 4 ll. heading; 54 ll. text; 1 l. signature

PAPER: Wove, marked KG | 1804

TYPOGRAPHY: *Text*: long primer, modern face

229 x 162 mm

NOTES: Mr Boucher, foreman of the grand jury, announced this meeting in the *Royal Gazette* on 31 October and 7 November. Both the report and petition were printed in the issue of 28 November sparking an exchange of correspondence in subsequent issues. William Carson included both texts in the first of his reform pamphlets, *A Letter to the Members of Parliament of the United Kingdom of Great Britain and Ireland*, published in Greenock, Scotland the following year. The *Royal Gazette* carried a notice of publication advising readers that copies could 'be had of Dr. Carson' (21 May 1812).

COPY EXAMINED: GBPRO: CO 194, vol 51, f 61

Nfld9 Newfoundland. Governor (1810–1813: Duckworth)

[royal arms 62 x 119 mm] | By His EXCELLENCY | SIR JOHN THOMAS DUCKWORTH, | ... | WHEREAS the great want of SPECIE in this ISLAND is | continuing to increase ... | ... | IT is hereby earnestly recommended, that in future it be tendered and accepted at | the same rate which it bears at Home ... | ... | GIVEN at FORT TOWNSHEND, ST. JOHN'S, Newfoundland, *September* the | Fourteenth, One thousand Eight hundred and Eleven. | J.T. DUCKWORTH, Governor. | ... | NOTICE. | MAJOR-GENERAL FRANCIS MOORE, Commanding the | Forces in this Island, having the authority of His MAJESTY'S Government to pass the | Bank of England DOLLAR in payment of the Troops ... | ... | [thick-thin rule 40 mm] | ST. JOHN'S: Printed by J. RYAN.

Proclamation: 1° (42 x 30.2 cm)

CONTENTS: royal arms; 5 ll. heading; 8 ll. text; 5 ll. closing; rule; 1 l. heading; 12 ll. text; 2 ll. closing including 2 ll. imprint

paper: Laid, marked Britannia; countermark RADWAY | 1808; chains horizontal 26 mm

TYPOGRAPHY: *Text*: double pica, transitional modern face. *Display*: two-line double pica for heading, 15 mm drop letter

372 x 243 mm

NOTES: This copy, included with a long report on the paymaster, was sent from 'Antelope, at Sea' on 29 October 1811. The text had been published in the *Royal Gazette* along with seven other proclamations on subjects as diverse as the creation of a public hospital, illegal use of buoys by merchants, sanctions against the concealment of deserters, and vandalism of the gallows (24 October).

COPY EXAMINED: GBPRO: CO 194, vol 50, f 339

Nfld10 Petition of Inhabitants of St John's

May it please Your Royal Highneſs, [script] | WE His MAJESTY'S most dutiful and loyal subjects, Inhabitants of the Town of St. John's, | in the Island of Newfoundland, humbly beg leave to approach Your ROYAL HIGHNESS ... | ... | ... the Town of Saint John's contains ten | thousand Inhabitants, and that upwards of five hundred sail of Vessels from Great-Britain and other Countries en- | tered the Harbour during the preceding season – That the Island has been governed by Laws of an ancient date, cal- | culated at the time they were enacted to promote the welfare of the

Fishery ... | ... | ... we are without a Police, without a Public estab- | lishment for the education of our Youth, without a Market-place, and without any legal provision for the Poor. | ... | *ST. JOHN'S (Newfoundland), November 7th*, 1811. | (Signed by the Merchants and principal Householders). [script]
Petition: 1 leaf (32.2 x 20 cm)
CONTENTS: 1 l. heading; 43 ll. text; 4 ll. closing
PAPER: Wove, marked KG | 1804
TYPOGRAPHY: *Text*: long primer, modern face
208 x 162 mm
NOTES: Since St John's was, with one exception, built of wood with narrow streets unpaved and unlighted, the inhabitants were requesting that money from the sale of ship's rooms be used to improve the town. They also proposed a Police Board of seven members including Alexander Boucher, William Carson, and James MacBraire to govern St John's.

When Governor Duckworth received a letter from Newfoundland enclosing the report (**Nfld8**) and this petition at Wear House, his country seat near Exeter, on 28 December he sent both on to Lord Liverpool, the colonial secretary, with his opinion of a Board of Police so formed: 'it will not be poſsible to give any countenance whatever to this particular part of the Petition without rendering the Merchants of Newfoundland the Masters of the Fishermen; and overturning at once the whole policy which has been hitherto observed with a view of discouraging the idea of a neceſsity for the colonization of the Island' (CO194, vol 51, ff 57–8).

The Petition of the inhabitants was not granted.
COPY EXAMINED: GBPRO: CO 194, vol 51, f 62

1812

Nfld11 Newfoundland. Governor (1810–1813: Duckworth)
[royal arms 62 x 119 mm] | By His Excellency | Sir JOHN THOMAS DUCKWORTH, K.B. | ... | I do hereby declare that the said Wharf has been erected at the Government expence, to be appropriated exclusively to the | Fishing Ships fitted out from Great Britain ... | Nevertheless, as it is to be expected that those ships will not resort hither until the return of Peace, it is the gracious inten- | tion of HIS ROYAL HIGHNESS the PRINCE REGENT, that the said Wharf shall, in the mean time, be free to the general Use ... | ... | GIVEN at FORT TOWNSHEND, Saint John's, Newfoundland, this 12th Day of October, 1812. | J.T. DUCKWORTH. | [ornamental dash 78 mm] | RULES. | ...
Public notice: 1° (52 x 46 cm)
CONTENTS: royal arms; 2 ll. heading; 12 ll. text; 4 ll. signature; dash; 1 l. heading; 14 ll. text of 8 rules
PAPER: Laid, watermark Strasbourg bend and lily | B & W [script]; countermark BUDGEN & WILMOTT | 1808; chains horizontal 28 mm
TYPOGRAPHY: *Text*: double and two-line pica, transitional face. *Display*: two-line double pica and 15 mm transitional face
510 x 377 mm
NOTES: Two new wharves costing £1000 for this one at the western end of the harbour, and £500 for the other at the foot of Church Hill (**Nfld12**), may have been built as part of the governor's plan to strengthen the town's defenses in case of American attack.

This was Duckworth's last visit to Newfoundland. He left for England at the end of October and resigned soon after his arrival home on 2 December.
COPY EXAMINED: GBPRO: CO 194, vol 52, f 141

Nfld12 Newfoundland. Governor (1810–1813: Duckworth)
[royal arms 62 x 119 mm] | WHEREAS it is the intention of His MA- | JESTY'S Government, that the Wharf recently built in SAINT JOHN'S Harbour by | my direction, should be used for the general accommodation of the Town ... | ... | ... the GOVERNOR'S Wharf, is and will | continue FREE to all persons willing to make use of the same, provided that a due | adherence be observed to the following | RULES. | ... | (Signed) J.T. DUCKWORTH, | *Governor*.
Public notice: 1° (49.3 x 37.3 cm)
CONTENTS: royal arms; 8 ll. preamble; 1 l. heading; 16 ll. text of 8 rules; 2 ll. signature
PAPER: Laid, watermark Strasbourg bend and lily | B & W [script]; countermark BUDGEN & WILMOTT | 1808; chains horizontal 28 mm
TYPOGRAPHY: *Text*: two-line pica, transitional. *Display*: 12 and 15 mm transitional face
473 x 312 mm
NOTES: Rules included a daily charge of 2s 6d for landing goods, with passengers and their baggage free. No wheeled carriages were allowed on the wharf and heavy goods were prohibited from the wooden part of the structure.
COPY EXAMINED: GBPRO: CO 194, vol 52, f 140

1818

Nfld13 Cubit, George, 1791–1850
JESUS CHRIST THE SUPREME GOVERNOR | AND ONLY FOUNDATION | OF THE CHRISTIAN CHURCH. | [thin-thick rule 43 mm] | A | SERMON | ON | MATTHEW XVI. – 13–19. | PREACHED AT THE | METHODIST CHAPEL, [open] | SAINT JOHN's, NEWFOUNDLAND: | [thick-thin rule 22 mm] | BY GEORGE CUBIT, | METHODIST MISSIONARY. | [double rule 83 mm] | Thus saith the Lord, stand ye in the ways, and see, and inquire for | the old paths, where is the good way, and walk therein, and ye shall | find rest to your souls. | JEREMIAH. | [double rule 83 mm] | SAINT JOHN's: | PRINTED FOR THE AUTHOR, BY JOHN RYAN, PRINTER | TO THE KING'S MOST EXCELLENT MAJESTY, | AND SOLD AT HIS OFFICE, | KING'S PLACE. | [thick-thin rule 15 mm] | 1818. | *Price Three Shillings.*
COLLATION: 8° (21.2 x 13.2 cm), *A*[4] B–G[4] [$1 signed], 28 leaves, pp *i–iii* iv–vi, *1* 2–50 (iv–vi with period)
CONTENTS: *i* title; *ii* blank; *iii*–vi preface; *1*–50 sermon: text Matthew XVI.13–19
PAPER: Wove, unmarked
TYPOGRAPHY: *Text*: english, modern face
27 ll., 152 (166) x 82 mm; 114 mm for 20 ll.
NOTES: A Methodist noted for the eloquence of his preaching Mr Cubit was in Newfoundland from 1816 to 1818 (*Dictionary of Canadian Biography* VII, s.v. 'Cubit (Cubick) George' by Calvin D. Evans). This sermon was available for sale from the author, at Mr James Bayly's Auction Mart, and at the printer's office (*Royal Gazette*, 31 March 1818).
COPY EXAMINED: OTCC

Nfld14 Cubit, George, 1791–1850
OBSERVATIONS [open] | ON THE | NATURE, EVIDENCES, AND AUTHORITY | OF THE | CHRISTIAN RELIGION; | BEING THE SUBSTANCE OF | TWO SERMONS | Preached at the WESLEYAN CHAPEL, St. John's Newfoundland, | August 2d and 9th, 1818. | [thick-thin rule 22 mm] | BY | GEORGE CUBIT, [open] | METHODIST MISSIONARY. | [double rule 82 mm] | SOCIAL order can only rest in the basis of these relations – TRUTH | – JUSTICE; these are its immutable laws. Far from us be | the dangerous maxim, that it is sometimes useful to mislead, | to deceive, and enslave mankind, to insure their happiness. – | Cruel experience has at all times proved, that with impunity | the sacred laws can never be infringed. LA PLACE. | [double rule 82 mm] | SAINT JOHN's: | PRINTED FOR THE AUTHOR, BY JOHN RYAN, PRINTER | TO THE KING'S MOST EXCELLENT MAJESTY, | AND SOLD AT HIS OFFICE, | KING'S PLACE. | [thick-thin rule 14 mm] | 1818. | PRICE – 3s.*9d.*
COLLATION: 8° (21.2 x 13.2 cm), *A–B*[4] C–I[4] K–L[4] *M*[2] [$1 signed], 46 leaves, pp *i–v* vi–viii, *1* 2–81 *82–84* (vi–viii with period)
CONTENTS: *i* title; *ii* blank; *iii* dedication: TO THE | REVEREND JOHN BELL, | CHAIRMAN OF THE NEWFOUNDLAND | METHODIST MISSIONARY DISTRICT, | ... signed THE AUTHOR at St. John's, 31 August 1818; *iv* blank; *v*–viii preface; 1–81 sermon: text HEBREWS, 2 – 1, 2, 3, 4; *82–84* blank
PAPER: Wove, unmarked
TYPOGRAPHY: *Text*: english, modern face
27 ll., 154 (168) x 82; 115 mm for 20 ll.
BINDING: Half calf and gloster paper. Spine divided into six compartments by double gilt rule, the second with a red lettering piece lettered towards the head SERMONS | . Wove endpapers and binder's leaf. Remnants of a blue paper wrapper and stab holes suggest that the work was first issued in pamphlet form.
NOTES: When Cubit returned to England for reasons of health in December 1818 he was succeeded in St John's by John Bell, named here in his dedication. Bell was the senior of six Methodist missionaries who had come to Newfoundland in 1816.
COPIES EXAMINED: OTCC, GBL

Nfld15 Sabine, James

A | SERMON, | IN | COMMEMORATION | OF THE | BENEVOLENCE [open] | OF THE | CITIZENS OF BOSTON, | Who, on occasion of the dreadful FIRES of the 7th and 21st | of NOVEMBER, 1817, in ST. JOHN'S, NEWFOUNDLAND, sent | down GRATUITOUS SUPPLIES for the RELIEF of the SUFFERERS | during the inclement season of Winter. | Preached in the CONGREGATIONAL CHURCH, ST. JOHN'S, on | LORD'S-DAY, February 22, 1818. | – WITH AN APPENDIX. – | [thick-thin rule 22 mm] | BY REV. JAMES SABINE. | [double rule 82 mm] | SAINT JOHN'S: | PRINTED FOR THE AUTHOR, BY JOHN RYAN, PRINTER | TO THE KING'S MOST EXCELLENT MAJESTY, AND | SOLD BY BURTON AND BRIGGS, LONDON, | AND BY S. ARMSTRONG, BOSTON. | [thick-thin rule 14 mm] | 1818.

COLLATION: 8° (22.3 x 13.7 cm), *A*[4] B–F[4] [$1(–E) signed], 24 leaves, pp *1–5* 6–31, *i* ii–xvi *xvii* (roman pagination with period)

CONTENTS: *1* title; *2* blank; *3* preface signed J.S., Pastoral House, 23 February 1818; *4* blank; *5*–31 sermon, text: Job XLII.–11, 12; *i*–xvi appendix, parts first and second; *xvii* blank

PAPER: Wove, unmarked

TYPOGRAPHY: *Text*: english, modern face with long primer pp *i*–xvi. *Display*: short and medium ornamental dashes

34 ll., 147 (161) x 83; 113 mm for 20 ll.

BINDING: Rebound retaining wrapper of grayish blue wove paper printed [thick-thin rule 83 mm] | A | SERMON | IN | COMMEMORATION | OF THE | BENEVOLENCE [open] | OF THE | CITIZENS OF BOSTON; | WITH AN APPENDIX. | [swelled rule 15 mm] | BY | THE REV. JAMES SABINE. | [thick-thin rule 14 mm] | 1818. | [thin-thick rule 83 mm] (QMBM)

NOTES: The two fires destroyed most of the waterfront, left a quarter of the population without habitation, and consumed much of the winter stores. In December a group of Bostonians chartered a brig to send flour, rice, meal, and bread to Francis Pickmore, governor and president of the Society for the Improvement of the Poor of St John's. Mr Sabine, pastor of the Congregational Church from 1816 to 1818, preached this sermon of thanks two days before the death of Pickmore, the first governor to stay the winter. According to one biographer he was 'literally worked to death by his effort to alleviate the worst sufferings' (*Dictionary of Canadian Biography* V, s.v. 'Pickmore, Francis' by Frederic F. Thompson).

The Houghton copy is inscribed on the title 'Mr Thomas Jackson from the Author' and on the verso: 'I was one of the many Citizens of this Town who met to devise some plan of relief [sic] for the Sufferers at St Johns – we collected much [word illegible] and in return each of the Committee were presented with Mr Sabine's Sermon' [Signed] Thos Jackson (USMH-H).

COPIES EXAMINED: NSHP, OTMCL, QMBM, USMBAt, USMH-H, USMWA

REFERENCES: Akins, Gagnon II 1898, O'Dea 339, TPL 4843

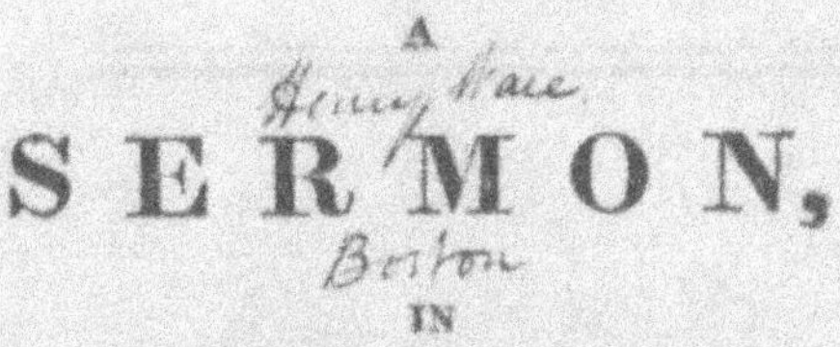

A

SERMON,

IN

COMMEMORATION

OF THE

BENEVOLENCE

OF THE

CITIZENS OF BOSTON,

Who, on occasion of the dreadful FIRES of the 7th and 21st of NOVEMBER, 1817, in ST. JOHN'S, NEWFOUNDLAND, sent down GRATUITOUS SUPPLIES for the RELIEF of the SUFFERERS during the inclement season of Winter.

Preached in the CONGREGATIONAL CHURCH, ST. JOHN'S, ON LORD'S-DAY, February 22, 1818.

—WITH AN APPENDIX.—

BY REV. JAMES SABINE.

SAINT JOHN'S:

PRINTED FOR THE AUTHOR, BY JOHN RYAN, PRINTER TO THE KING'S MOST EXCELLENT MAJESTY, AND SOLD BY BURTON AND BRIGGS, LONDON, AND BY S. T. ARMSTRONG, BOSTON.

1818.

Nfld15 Courtesy Metropolitan Toronto Reference Library

Nova Scotia

1800

NS1 An Almanack for the Year of Our Lord, 1801

[within thick-thin rules 144 x 84 mm] AN | ALMANACK [open] | FOR THE | Year of our Lord, 1801; | Being the Fifth after BISSEXTILE, or LEAP YEAR, | CALCULATED FOR THE MERIDIAN OF | HALIFAX IN NOVA-SCOTIA, | BUT WILL SERVE FOR ANY PART OF THE PROVINCE. | GONTAINING | [7 ll. to left of rule 22 mm] THE ECLIPSES | RISING and SETTING of the | SUN and MOON | TIME of HIGH WATER | FEASTS and FASTS of the | CHURCH | LIST OF PROVINCIAL OFFI | CERS | [8 ll. to right] SITTINGS of the COURTS | OFFICERS of the NAVY on | this STATION | OFFICERS of the ARMY, un- | der his Royal Highneſs the | DUKE of KENT | OFFICERS of the NAVY- | YARD and HOSPITAL. | WITH EVERY MATTER USEFUL OR NECESSARY. | [rule 75 mm] | By THEOPHRASTUS. | [rule 76 mm] | HALIFAX, | Printed and Sold by JOHN HOWE, at his Printing-Office | in George Street, near the Parade. *Stet* GONTAINING

STATE: NAVY | YARD

COLLATION: 12° (19.2 x 11.8 cm), *A*[4] B–C[6] [$1, 3 signed; $3 signed 2], 16 leaves, pp [*32*]

CONTENTS: [*1*] title; [*2*] signals; vulgar notes; [*3*] eclipses; man of signs; [*4*] ephemeris; firewards; [*5–16*] calendar with seasonal verses; [*17–22*] civil list; courts; [*23*] navy yard; [*23–24*] freemasons; [*25*] clergy of established church, Presbyterian ministers; holidays; [*26*] ships; [*27–30*] army, militia; fire engine company; [*31–32*] roads and distances with houses of entertainment; Parrsborough packet; buoys

PAPER: Unmarked, *A* wove; B, C laid; chains horizontal 27 mm

TYPOGRAPHY: *Text*: minion, old face. *Display*: pages within thick-thin rules; man of signs cut (46 x 44 mm) is 1804 in Reilly; almanac signs 143 (145) x 80 mm

BINDING: Stitched (NSHD)

NOTES: John Howe, a native of Boston and an active loyalist printer, had been working in Halifax since 1780. In Howe's first almanac published for 1790 Theophrastus had introduced himself as a novice calculator.

COPIES EXAMINED: NSHD, NSHL, NSHP (lacking pp [*17–20, 25–30*]), OOA

REFERENCE: Tremaine 1158

NS2 Astronomical Calculations for the Year 1801

[within frame of ornamental dashes 138 x 85 mm] ASTRONOMICAL | CALCULATIONS, [open] | FOR THE YEAR | 1801. | Being the Fifth after Leap Year, | CONTAINING, | [10 ll. to left of rule 29 mm] The riſing, ſetting, places, and | Eclipſes of the Sun and Moon, | The Southing, Phaſes, Age & | Latitude of the Moon, Long- | itude of her aſcending Node, | &c. | The geocentric Places and Aſ- | pects of the Planets (inclu- | ding the Georgian diſcovered | [9 ll. to right] by HERSCHELL) with the | riſing, ſetting and ſouthing of | the moſt conſpicuous Planets | and fixed Stars, | The paſſage of Alioth over the | Meridian, | The Equation of Time, | Sun's declination, and Time of | High Water, &c. | ALSO, | The increaſe, decreaſe, and length of Days, with the | Feſtivals, &c. | Calculated for the Latitude and

Der

Neu-Schottländische

CALENDER.

Auf das Jahr, nach der heilbringenden Geburt

unsers HErrn JEsu Christi,

1801.

Welches ein Gemein Jahr von 365 Tagen ist.

Darinnen, nebst richtiger Festrechnung, die Sonn- und Monds-Finsternisse, des Monds Gestalt und Viertel, Monds-Auf- und Niedergang Monds-Zeichen, Aspecten der Planeten und Witterung, Sonnen Auf- und Untergang, das hohe Wasser zu Halifax, Courten und andere zu einem Calender gehörige Sachen, zu finden sind.

Imgleichen verschiedene nützliche und lehrreiche Erzählungen, &c.

Mit sonderbarem Fleiß nach dem Horizont und Nordhöhe zu Halifax, und andern Theilen der Provinz Neu-Schottland, berechnet.

Zum Dreyzehntenmahl herausgegeben.

HALIFAX,

Gedruckt und zu haben bey Anthon Henrich, in der Sackville-Strasse.

NS3 Courtesy J.J. Stewart Collection, Special Collections Department, Dalhousie University Library, Halifax

Meridian of | HALIFAX IN NOVA-SCOTIA. | [rule 79 mm] | BY ABRAHAM SHOEMAKER, OF NEW-YORK. | [thick-thin rule 79 mm] | HALIFAX, | Printed and Sold by ANTHONY HENRY, at his Printing | Office, in Sackville Street, Corner of Grafton-Street.

COLLATION: 12° (19.4 x 12 cm), 1^4 2^1 $3–5^6$, 23 leaves, pp [46]

CONTENTS: [1] title; [2] 'Notes to the Reader' explaining calculations; common notes; [3] astronomical, eclipses; [4] tides; [5] man of signs; 'Female Attachment and Heroism'; [6–26] calendar with astronomical calculations and miscellany: agricultural observation and hints; 'The Wonderful Ape of Marseilles'; 'A Curious Sermon'; and 'Verses upon Gaming'; [27–29] calendar with astronomical calculations and civil list; [30–32] civil list; levee days; [33–34] courts; [34] holidays; [34–37] army; [37–38] ships; [38] sheriffs; firewards, fire engine company; [39] miscellany: 'Old Parr's Maxims of Health'; 'A Bill of Fare'; 'Extraordinary Character'; [40–41] currency; [42] signals; [43] 'Erratas' (35 ll.); [44] Parrsborough packet; advertisement by William Cobbett about *Porcupine's Gazette*; [45–46] roads and distances with houses of entertainment; [46] buoys

PAPER: Laid, unmarked; chains horizontal 27 mm

TYPOGRAPHY: *Text*: long primer, old face. *Display*: pages framed by ornamental dashes of rimmed oval flanked by tapered arrows; man of signs cut (28 x 23 mm) not in Reilly but similar to 1802 and 1803 except right leg extended beyond globe; rows of penwork oval and bead and reel (long primer 2 of 1790 Fry and Steele specimen); almanac signs 140 x 82 mm

NOTES: Although Marie Tremaine noted an advertisement for this almanac in Henry's *Royal Gazette* she did not locate a copy. It is one of Henry's last imprints since he died on 1 December 1800, after forty years as a printer in Halifax, the last twelve of them as the king's printer. Mrs Henry carried on the shop and newspaper until the end of that month then announced that Gay and Merlin would be taking over the business (**NS11**).

COPIES EXAMINED: NSHD, NSHL

REFERENCE: Tremaine 1159 (not located)

NS3 Der Neu-Schottländische Calender, 1801

[within thick-thin rules 193 x 148 mm] *Der | Neu-Schottländische* | CALENDER. | *Auf das Jahr, nach der heilbringenden Geburt | unsers HErrn JEsu Christi,* | **1801.** | *Welches ein Gemein Jahr von* 365 *Tagen ist.* | *Darinnen, nebst richtiger Festrechnung, die Sonn- und Monds-Finsterniffe, | des Monds Gestalt und Viertel, Monds-Auf- und Niedergang Monds-Zeicheu, | Afpecten der Planeten und Witterung, Sonnen Auf- und Untergang, | das hohe Waffer zu <H>alifax, Courten und andere zu einem | Calender gehörige Sachen, zu finden find. | Imgleichen verfchiedene nützliche und lehrreiche Erzählungen, &c. | Mit fonderbarem Fliefz nach dem Horizont und Nordhöhe zu Halifax, und andern Theilen der | Provinz Neu-chottland, berechnet.* | [thick-thin rule 138 mm] | *Zum Dreyzehntenmahl herausgegeben.* | [thin-thick rule 138 mm] | *HALIFAX,* | *Gedruckt und zu haben bey Anthon Henrich, in der Sackville-Straffe. Stent Zeicheu Neu-chottland*

COLLATION: 4° (20.5 x 16.8 cm), 1^3 $2–4^4$ 5^1, 16 leaves, pp [32] incomplete

CONTENTS: [1] title; [2–3] astronomical, holidays; [3–5] sovereigns in Europe; [6–29] calendar on verso with calendar information, court sittings, anecdotes, and stories on recto; [30–32] miscellany continued from calendar

PAPER: Laid, unmarked; chains vertical, 26 to 30 mm

TYPOGRAPHY: *Text*: small pica, black letter. *Display*: pages within thick-thin rules; man of signs cut (63 x 47 mm) with bellflower frame not in Reilly but somewhat similar to 1809 Binny and Ronaldson cut except figure opened and without garment; ornaments in text are penwork lozenge, bead (as english 14 of 1790 Fry and Steele), and foliage (long primer 15 of 1785 Caslon specimen); almanac signs 187 x 149 mm

BINDING: Stitched

NOTES: Anthony Henry or Anthon Henrich had published his first German almanac in Halifax for the year 1788 (Tremaine 503). The series ended with this edition.

COPY EXAMINED: NSHD

1801

NS4 An Almanack for the Year of Our Lord, 1802

[within thick-thin rules 142 x 80 mm] AN | ALMANACK, | FOR THE | *YEAR of our LORD*, 1802; | Being the *Sixth* after BISSEXTILE, or LEAP-YEAR; | CALCULATED FOR THE MERIDIAN OF | *HALIFAX, in NOVA-SCOTIA*; | BUT WILL SERVE FOR ANY PART OF THE PROVINCE. | CONTAINING, | [7 ll. to left of rule 18 mm] The

Eclip*f*es, | Ri*f*ing and Setting of the Sun and | Moon, | Time of High-Water, | Fea*f*ts and Fa*f*ts of the Church, | Li*f*t of Provincial Officers, | Sittings of the Courts, | [7 ll. to right] Officers of the Navy on this | Station, | Officers of the Army, under his | Royal Highne*f*s, the Duke of | Kent. | Officers of the Navy-Yard and | Ho*f*pital. | *ALSO*, | A GREAT VARIETY OF | *Inftructive, Entertaining, and Ufeful* | *Matter, &c. &c.* | [rule 73 mm] | BY THEOPHRASTUS. | [rule 74 mm] | *HALIFAX:* | Printed and Sold by A. GAY, at his Printing-Office, SACK- | VILLE-STREET, near the HALIFAX GRAMMAR-SCHOOL.

COLLATION: 12° (16.2 x 10 cm), *1*[12] 2[6], 18 leaves, pp [*36*]

CONTENTS: [*1*] title; [*2*] table of planets; agricultural; [*3*] man of signs; eclipses, vulgar notes; [*4*] hints: fattening calves, 'receipt' for salve; [*5–16*] calendar with verses; [*17–21*] civil list; [*21*] holidays; [*22*] levee days; civil list; firewards; [*23*] fire engine company; [*23–24*] courts; [*24–25*] account of 'three finger'd Jack'; recipes; [*26–28*] army; [*28–33*] prose pieces; domestic and agricultural hints; 'To Know the Age of a Horse' with five woodcuts; [*34*] free-masons; [*35–36*] roads and distances with houses of entertainment; [*36*] buoys; Parrsborough packet

PAPER: Laid, 2 marked 1796; chains vertical 26 mm

TYPOGRAPHY: *Text*: old faces. *Display*: pages within thick-thin rules; man of signs cut (28 x 23 mm) as **NS2**; almanac signs

142 x 80 mm

ILLUSTRATION: Five woodcuts of horses' teeth at ages two and a half to six years (maximum 24 x 28 mm) on p [*30*]

BINDING: Stitched

NOTES: Archibald Gay printed this almanac at Anthony Henry's old office using types and ornaments familiar to readers of Henry's imprints.

COPY EXAMINED: NSHD

NS5 An Almanack for the Year of Our Lord, 1802

[within thick-thin rules 153 x 90 mm] AN | ALMANACK | FOR THE | Year of our Lord, 1802; | Being the Sixth after BISSEXTILE, or LEAP YEAR, | *Calculated for the Meridian of* | HALIFAX IN NOVA-SCOTIA, | BUT WILL SERVE FOR ANY PART OF THE PROVINCE. | CONTAINING | [8 ll. to left of rule 24 mm] THE ECLIPSES | RISING and SETTING of the | SUN and MOON | TIME of HIGH WATER | FEASTS and FASTS of the | CHURCH | LIST of PROVINCIAL OFFI- | CERS | [8 ll. to right] SITTINGS of the COURTS | OFFICERS of the NAVY on | this STATION | OFFICERS of the ARMY under | His Royal Highne*f*s the | DUKE of KENT | OFFICERS of His Maje*f*ty's NA- | VY-YARD and HOSPITAL. | WITH EVERY OTHER MATTER USEFUL OR NECESSARY. | [rule 84 mm] | BY THEOPHRASTUS- | [rule 84 mm] | HALIFAX: | Printed and Sold by JOHN HOWE, at his Printing-Office, in | George-Street, near the Parade.

COLLATION: 12° (16.5 x 10.5 cm), *1–2*[6] 3[4], 16 leaves, pp [32]

CONTENTS: [*1*] title; [2] signals; vulgar notes; [3] eclipses; man of signs; [*4*] planets; fire engine company; [*5–16*] calendar with poem 'Machina Orrereana' by Dr Shaw of the British Museum; [*17*] conclusion of poem and anecdotes; [*18–22*] civil list; [22–23] courts; [*24–25*] holidays; navy; [*25–26*] free-masons; [*26–27*] clergy of established church, Presbyterian ministers; [*27*] firewards; [*27–30*] officers and army; [*31–32*] roads and distances with houses of entertainment; [32]Parrsborough packet; buoys

PAPER: Unmarked, *1*, 2 laid; chains horizontal 27 mm; *3* wove (NSHP); OOA copy all wove

TYPOGRAPHY: *Text*: bourgeois, old face. *Display*: pages within thick-thin rules; man of signs cut (46 x 44 mm) is 1804 in Reilly; almanac signs

152 x 90 mm

BINDING: Stitched (NSHD)

COPIES EXAMINED: NSHD, NSHP, OOA

NS6 Inglis, Charles, 1734–1816

A | SERMON | ON | CONFIRMATION: | Preached in St. John's Church, Cornwallis, | ON SUNDAY, SEPTEMBER 13, 1801. | [double rule 129 mm] | BY THE RIGHT REVEREND CHARLES INGLIS, D.D. | BISHOP OF NOVA-SCOTIA. | [double rule 130 mm] | HALIFAX: | Printed by JOHN HOWE, Printer to the KING's Mo*f*t Excellent Maje*f*ty.

COLLATION: 8° (23.5 x 18.5 cm), A[4] B[4] C[2] [$1 signed], 10 leaves, pp *1–5* 6–20 (pagination in [ ])

CONTENTS: *1* title; 2 blank; 3 letter of thanks to the Right Reverend the Bishop of Nova Scotia with a request for a copy to be printed signed at Cornwallis, 14 September, by the rector and church-wardens; *4* dedication to the requestors, Rev Mr Twining and John Burbidge and Benjamin Belcher, E*f*quires, 'by the AUTHOR; who fervently prays, that it may be accompanied with a ble*ff*ing, and promote the edification of his Brethren, and of all who *f*hall favor it with a peru*f*al' signed at Clermont, 28 October 1801; *5*–20 sermon, text: ACTS VIII. xvii

PAPER: Laid, watermark Strasbourg lily; countermark E[?] | 1798; chains horizontal 29 mm
TYPOGRAPHY: *Text*: pica, transitional old face, with notes in bourgeois
36 ll., 173 (184) x 130; 94 mm for 20 ll.
BINDING: Wrapper of spot marbled paper in greenish pale blue, dark pink, light orange yellow, and black with conjugate paste-downs
NOTES: Appointed in 1787 as the first bishop of the Church of England in Nova Scotia, Inglis held the position until his death almost thirty years later. Throughout his term the established church in Nova Scotia and New Brunswick struggled against religious 'enthusiasm' which accompanied the growing influence of New Light, Methodist, and Baptist preachers. Cornwallis, where Inglis delivered this sermon, was a particular problem since William Twining, rector of St John's Church from 1789 to 1805, was himself slipping into Methodist practices. During visits to Cornwallis the bishop preached, administered confirmation, and tried to reconcile Twining with his congregation, particularly churchwardens John Burbidge and Benjamin Belcher (Brian Cuthbertson, *The First Bishop*. Halifax: Waegwoltic Press, 1987).

John Howe was newly appointed king's printer succeeding Anthony Henry in 1801.
COPY EXAMINED: NSHK

NS7 Nova Scotia. Laws (8th Parliament, 2nd session: 1801)
[text begins] At the GENERAL ASSEMBLY of | the Province of NOVA-SCOTIA, begun and | holden at Halifax, on the Ninth Day of June, | 1801
COLLATION: 2° (34.4 x 21.5 cm), U5–A6² [$1 signed, U–X with period], 14 leaves, pp 566–592 *593* (pagination with period except 566, 567, 571, 573)
CONTENTS: 566–592 text; *593* blank
PAPER: Laid, watermark Britannia; countermark JC | 1800; chains vertical 26 mm
TYPOGRAPHY: *Text*: pica, old face
55 ll., 235 (251) x 117 (146); 84 mm for 20 ll.
BINDING: Stitched
NOTES: The spare style of these annual laws printed without caption title, imprint, half title, or title page continues a practice established for the province's laws in the eighteenth century. They are paged in continuation of the 1800 edition of the temporary laws (Tremaine 1192).
COPY EXAMINED: OTMCL

NS8 Nova Scotia. Laws (8th Parliament, 2nd session: 1801)
[text begins] At the GENERAL ASSEMBLY of the Province of | NOVA-SCOTIA, begun and holden at Halifax, | on the Ninth Day of June, 1801
COLLATION: 2° (34 x 20.8 cm), M5–N5² O¹ [$1 signed], 5 leaves, pp 548–556 *557* (pagination with period)
CONTENTS: 548–556 text; *557* blank
PAPER: Laid, watermark Britannia; countermark JC | 1800; chains vertical 26 mm
TYPOGRAPHY: *Text*: pica, old face
56 ll., 247 (265) x 117 (147); 84 mm for 20 ll.
BINDING: Stitched
COPY EXAMINED: OTMCL

NS9 Nova Scotia. Legislature. Joint Committee on the Indians
[text begins] *HALIFAX, 23d January*, 1801. | SIR, | IN performance of the duty aſſigned to us by the two Houſes of the General Aſſembly; | of which we form a joint Committee, and with the approbation of His Excellency | the Lieutenant-Governor, we take leave to ſubmit to your conſideration the following | Queries, intended to procure information neceſſary for us to form ſome plan for the ſet- | tlement of the Indians, to be laid before the Legiſlature at its next meeting.
COLLATION: 2° (33.4 x 20.1 cm), *1*², 2 leaves, pp [4]
CONTENTS: [1–2] text (to be completed in ms); [*3–4*] blank
PAPER: Laid, watermark Britannia; countermark HAS [script] | 1798; chains vertical 26 mm
TYPOGRAPHY: *Text*: pica, old face. *Display*: two-line great primer drop letter
253 x 150 mm
NOTES: The list of queries being sent to community leaders in different parts of the province asked for information about the number of natives; the identity and character of heads of families and influential leaders; whether any of them had settled or taken up trades; whether any local people knew native languages; which priests the natives saw and how often; what lands would be suitable for their settlement and whether these lands would furnish staves, hoops, shingles, and clapboard; local costs of potatoes, clearing land, and building huts with log, stone, and mud chimneys; prospects for the fishery; the availability of wool, flax, and wheels; whether natives would place their children in families 'to learn our domestic arts'; and whether natives could be induced to fish if they were given

At the GENERAL ASSEMBLY of the Province of NOVA-SCOTIA, begun and holden at Halifax, on the Ninth Day of June, 1801; in the Forty-first Year of the Reign of our Sovereign Lord GEORGE the Third, by the Grace of God, of the United Kingdom of Great-Britain and Ireland King, Defender of the Faith, &c. &c. being the Second Session of the Eighth GENERAL ASSEMBLY, convened in the said Province.

CAP. I.

An Act to revive and continue an Act made in the thirty-sixth year of His Majesty's Reign, entitled an Act to encourage the Killing of Wolves, Bears, Loup Cerviers, and Wild Cats.

WHEREAS an Act made in the thirty sixth year of his present Majesty's Reign, to encourage the killing of Wolves, Bears, Loup Cerviers, and Wild Cats, was found to be of great public utility: And whereas great damage still continues to be done to the Farmers in different parts of this Province, by Wolves, Bears, Loup Cerviers, and Wild Cats, killing and destroying their Sheep and other Cattle. For remedy whereof, Preamble;

I. *Be it enacted by the Lieutenant Governor, Council and Assembly,* That the before recited Act, and every clause, matter, and thing therein contained, be revived, and that the same shall continue and be in force for and during the term of three years, from and after the publication hereof and no longer, Act continued to 31st July 1804.

CAP. II.

An Act, to continue an Act, made and passed in the Thirty-fourth Year of His present Majesty's Reign, entitled, An Act to provide for the support of the Grammar School in Halifax, and for other public purposes therein contained.

WHEREAS the above recited Act is near expiring, and it is expedient that the same should be continued; Preamble.

I. *Be it Enacted, by the Lieutenant Governor, Council and Assembly,* That the said Act, and every Matter and Thing therein contained, shall be and continue, and the same is hereby continued in force until the Thirty-first day of July, which will be in the Year of Our Lord One Thousand Eight Hundred and Two. Act continued to 31st July 1802.

U 5. CAP.

NS7 Courtesy Metropolitan Toronto Reference Library

shares in the boats as well as clothing and support for their families.
COPY EXAMINED: NSHP: RG1, vol 430, no 481/2

NS10 Nova Scotia. Parliament (8th, 2nd session: 1801). House of Assembly
[half title] [rule 147 mm] | JOURNAL | AND | PROCEEDINGS | OF THE | HOUSE OF ASSEMBLY. [full caps open] | 1801. | [rule 146 mm]
COLLATION: 2° (30.3 x 19.4 cm), A^2 B–I^2 K–T^2 χ^1, [$1 signed], 37 leaves, pp [2] 1–75 *76* (pagination in ( ) except [1])
CONTENTS: [*1*] half title; [2] proclamation; 1–75 text; *76* blank
PAPER: Laid, watermark Britannia; countermark JG | 1800 (NSHL); GBPRO copy with χ same and *A*–T countermark MB | 1797; chains vertical 26 mm
TYPOGRAPHY: *Text*: pica, old face. *Display*: royal arms cut 40 x 88 mm
56 ll., 236 (248) x 146; 84 mm for 20 ll.
NOTES: Certification of the copy sent to the Colonial Office by the speaker is dated 4 February 1802.
COPIES EXAMINED: NSHL, NSHP, GBPRO: CO 217, vol 76, ff 61–99

NS11 St Peter's Church (Halifax)
RESOLVES | OF THE | DELEGATES, [open] | *Appointed by the Congregation* | OF THE | ROMAN CATHOLIC CHURCH, | *IN HALIFAX*; | TO MAKE AMENDMENTS AND ALTERATIONS IN THE BYE LAWS AND | REGULATIONS OF THE TEMPORAL AFFAIRS OF SAID CHURCH, | AT A VESTRY MEETING, | HELD BY ORDER OF THE | *REVEREND Mr. BURKE, P.P* | ON EASTER MONDAY, BEING THE 6th DAY OF APRIL, 1801. | [ornamental rule 40 mm] | *HALIFAX:* | [thin-thick rule 21 mm] | PRINTED, BY GAY AND MERLIN.
COLLATION: 8° (22.1 x 14.2 cm), 1^8 (–*1*8), 7 leaves, pp [2] *1–3* 4–12 (pagination in ( ))
CONTENTS: [*1*] 'To the Roman Catholic Reader'; [2] 'The Extracts from the Rules and Regulations made by the committee of St. Peter's Church, Halifax, on the 17th August, 1800'; *1* title; *2* blank; *3*–12 text I to XXIII signed by the delegates and dated at Halifax, 10 April 1801
PAPER: Laid, unmarked; chains vertical 26 mm
TYPOGRAPHY: *Text*: english, old face. *Display*: title page and p [*1*] with bead and reel rule (long primer 2 of Fry and Steele 1790 specimen)
34 ll., 158 (173; 187) x 97; 93 mm for 20 ll.
BINDING: Stitched in wrapper of coarse paper
NOTES: Under John Jones, the first anglophone Catholic priest in Nova Scotia, members of St Peter's in Halifax had demanded a role in the governance of their parish. In August of 1800 Jones, his health failing, sailed for England leaving the troublesome congregation to Edmund Burke, a Dominican who had been serving in Newfoundland. During that same month a committee of elders approved a set of regulations so stringent that the rites of interment were denied to Mrs Redfern who belonged to the church, and to Thomas Butler. More than two hundred parishioners signed a protest. In response Mr Burke ordered a vestry meeting to select delegates to revise the elders' regulations which required a payment of 10s each year from families and single men and imposed a schedule of charges for funerals: 7s 6d for tolling the bell, 7s 6d for the pall, 7s 6d for opening the grave, and 7s 6d for digging the grave. The delegates meeting in 1801 resolved that never again would any 'ſtranger or native, reſident or ſojourner' professing the Roman Catholic religion be denied interment in the churchyard (p 4). Moreover, expenses such as paying for the pall, opening the ground, and tolling the bell were not in future to be 'extracted' from anyone. Costs would be borne by the church with revenues gathered through an increase in the annual rent of pews from £3 to £4 (*Dictionary of Canadian Biography* v, s.v. 'Burke, Edmund,' by Raymond J. Lahey; 'Jones, James,' by A.A. MacKenzie).
The printers Gay and Merlin had taken over the shop of Anthony Henry, late king's printer.
COPY EXAMINED: QQA: NE, II, 34

1802

NS12 An Almanack for the Year of Our Lord, 1803
[within thick-thin rules 150 x 89 mm] AN | ALMANACK | FOR THE | Year of our Lord, 1803; | BEING THE SEVENTH AFTER BISSEXTILE OR LEAP YEAR. | *Calculated for the Meridian of* | HALIFAX, IN NOVA-SCOTIA, | BUT WILL SERVE FOR ANY PART OF THE PROVINCE. | CONTAINING | [8 ll. to left of rule 24 mm] THE ECLIPSES | RISING and SETTING of the | SUN and MOON | TIME of HIGH WATER | FEASTS and FASTS of the | CHURCH | LIST of PROVINCIAL OFFI- | CERS | [8 ll. to right] SITTINGS of the COURTS | OFFICERS of the

NAVY on | this STATION | OFFICERS of the ARMY under | Lieutenant-General HENRY | BOWYER | OFFICERS of His Maje*f*ty's NA- | VY-YARD and HOSPITAL. | WITH EVERY OTHER MATTER USEFUL OR NECESSARY. | [rule 82 mm] | By THEOPHRASTUS. | [rule 80 mm] | HALIFAX: | Printed and *f*old by JOHN HOWE, at his Printing-Office, in | George-Street, near the Parade.
COLLATION: 12° (17 x 10.4 cm), *A*⁶ B–C⁶ [$1, 3 signed, $3 signed 2], 18 leaves, pp [*36*]
ISSUE as **NS13** *An Almanack for the Year of Our Lord, 1803* (Gay), pp [*2–32*] [*35–38*]
CONTENTS: [*1*] title; [*2–3*] signals; [*3*] eclipses; man of signs; [*4*] holidays, levee days; buoys; [*5*] firewards, fire engine company; clergy of established church; [*6–7*] roads and distances with houses of entertainment; [*7*] Parrsborough packet; [*8*] planets, vulgar notes; [*9–20*] calendar with verses and selections: 'Winter Song' by Robert Bloomfield; 'Ode to Old May-Day'; 'A Hint for a Rich Man'; 'Common Friendship'; 'Verses'; [*21–25*] civil list; [*25-27*] courts; [*27*] hospital; navy yard; [*27–29*] freemasons; [*30*] ships; [*31–32*] army; [*33–34*] observations on hemp; anecdotes: 'The Fountain of Memory and Forgetfulness'; 'A Wonderful Dog'; [*35–36*] sun's declination
PAPER: Wove, unmarked except *A* marked 1801
TYPOGRAPHY: *Text*: long primer and bourgeois, old face. *Display*: pages within thick-thin rules; man of signs cut (46 x 44 mm) is 1804 in Reilly; almanac signs
153 (155) x 89 mm
BINDING: Stitched (NSHD)
NOTES: John Howe advertised that his almanac was 'ready for sale' on 11 November (*Royal Gazette*, 1802).
COPIES EXAMINED: NSHD, NSHL (lacking pp [*1–2*] [*35–36*]

NS13 An Almanack for the Year of Our Lord, 1803

[within thick-thin rules 150 x 89 mm] AN | ALMANACK | FOR THE | Year of our Lord, 1803; | BEING THE SEVENTH AFTER BISSEXTILE OR LEAP YEAR. | *Calculated for the Meridian of* | HALIFAX, IN NOVA-SCOTIA; | BUT WILL SERVE FOR ANY PART OF THE PROVINCE. | CONTAINING | [8 ll. to left of rule 24 mm] THE ECLIPSES | RISING and SETTING of the | SUN and MOON | TIME of HIGH WATER | FEASTS and FASTS of the | CHURCH | LIST of PROVINCIAL OFFI- | CERS | [8 ll. to right] SITTINGS of the COURTS | OFFICERS of the NAVY on | this STATION | OFFICERS of the ARMY under | Lieutenant-General HENRY | BOWYER | OFFICERS of His Maje*f*ty's NA- | VY-YARD and HOSPITAL. | WITH EVERY OTHER MATTER USEFUL OR NECESSARY. | [rule 81 mm] | By THEOPHRASTUS. | [rule 80 mm] | *Halifax*: | Printed and *f*old by A. GAY, at his Printing-Office, SACKVILLE- | STREET, near the HALIFAX GRAMMAR-SCHOOL.
COLLATION: 12° (18.4 x 11.7 cm), *A*⁶ B–C⁶ (C4 + χ1) [$1, 3 signed, $3 signed 2], 19 leaves, pp [*38*]
ISSUE as **NS12** *An Almanack for the Year of Our Lord, 1803* (Howe), pp [*2–36*]
CONTENTS: [*1*] title; [*2–3*] signals; [*3*] eclipses; man of signs; [*4*] holidays, levee days; buoys; [*5*] firewards, fire engine company; clergy of established church; [*6–7*] roads and distances with houses of entertainment; [*7*] Parrsborough packet; [*8*] planets, vulgar notes; [*9–20*] calendar with verses and selections: 'Winter Song' by Robert Bloomfield; 'Ode to Old May-Day'; 'A Hint for a Rich Man'; 'Common Friendship'; 'Verses'; [*21–25*] civil list; [*25-27*] courts; [*27*] navy yard; hospital; [*27–29*] freemasons; [*30*] ships, navy; [*31–32*] army; [*33–34*] anecdotes and hints including 'Fre*f*h and Salt Water'; 'Surpri*f*ing Proof of Healthine*f*s; 'Fact upon Fact'; 'William Tell'; 'A Remarkable Story of Prede*f*tination'; 'To prevent the Biting of Mu*f*ketoes'; 'For the ague. – By Dr. Mead.'; [*35–36*] observations on hemp; anecdotes: 'The Fountains of Memory and Forgetfulness'; 'A Wonderful Dog'; [*37–38*] sun's declination
PAPER: Wove, unmarked
TYPOGRAPHY: *Text*: bourgeois, old face. *Display*: pages within thick-thin rules; man of signs cut (46 x 44 mm) is 1804 in Reilly; almanac signs
148 (153) x 87 mm
BINDING: Stitched (NSHD)
NOTES: Comparison with Howe's almanac for the same year (**NS12**) suggests that much of this text was printed from the same setting of type with slight shifts caused by moving the formes.
COPIES EXAMINED: NSHD (lacking pp [*33–36*], misfolded), NSHP (lacking pp [*37–38*]), OOA, OTMCL
REFERENCE: MTL 6810

NS14 Church of England

[within thick-thin rules 149 x 107 mm] A | FORM | OF | PRAYER | and | THANKSGIVING | TO | ALMIGHTY GOD; [open] | *TO BE USED* | In all Churches and Chapels throughout His Maje*f*ty's

Pro- | vince of *Nova-Scotia*, on *Thurſday* the Eighth Day of *July* | next, being the Day appointed by Proclamation for a | General THANKSGIVING to Almighty God, for putting | an End to the late bloody, extended, and expenſive War | in which we were engaged. | [rule 100 mm] | By deſire of his Excellency, the LIEUTENANT-GOVERNOR. | [rule 100 mm] | HALIFAX: | Printed by JOHN HOWE, Printer to the KING'S Moſt Excellent Majeſty.
COLLATION: 4° (22 x 16.5 cm), A⁴ *B*² [A1, 2 signed], 6 leaves, pp *1–3* 4–12 (pp 5–8, 10–12 with period; 6 printed in gutter; 9 in ( ))
CONTENTS: *1* title; 2 blank; *3*–12 text
PAPER: Laid, unmarked; chains horizontal 26 mm
TYPOGRAPHY: *Text*: pica, old face
25 ll., 130 (147) x 102; 94 mm for 20 ll.
NOTES: Although the *Form of Prayer* is undated, July eighth was the day of thanksgiving designated in 1802 by Council to mark the Peace of Amiens which interrupted the Napoleonic Wars until the following year. A similar proclamation was issued for 27 July in New Brunswick.
COPY EXAMINED: NSHL

NS15 Hand in Hand Fire Company (Halifax)
RULES AND ARTICLES, [full caps open] | TO BE OBSERVED BY | THE HAND IN HAND | FIRE COMPANY, | IN | *THE TOWN OF HALIFAX*, | INSTITUTED | THE 28th DAY of JANUARY, 1789. | REVISED | *AND ORDERED TO BE RE-PRINTED*, | AT | A QUARTERLY MEETING | Held the 5th of Auguſt, 1801. | [row of section marks 35 mm] | HALIFAX: | Printed by JOHN HOWE, Printer to the KING's Moſt Excel- | lent Majeſty.
COLLATION: 12° (18.5 x 11.3 cm), *1*⁶, 6 leaves, pp *1–3* 4–10 *11–12* (page numbers in [ ])
CONTENTS: *1* title; 2 blank; 3–10 text: introduction, rules I to XII; 10 'Present Members, 1802' *11–12* blank
PAPER: Laid, marked Strasbourg lily | GR; chains vertical 28 mm
TYPOGRAPHY: *Text*: pica, old face. *Display*: long swelled rule
31 ll., 149 (162) x 89; 94 mm for 20 ll.
BINDING: Wrapper of dutch marbled paper in dark pink, greenish gray, light orange yellow, and pale yellow. Laid endpapers, free front lacking
NOTES: 'Whereas it is the indiſpenſable duty of every member of a community, more especially in compact towns to guard againſt the fatal effects of Fire' the forty members of this society agreed to assist fellow townsmen in general, but more particularly members of their own company (p 3). They would try to save whatever they could and then 'ſtand as centinel at the door' to guard against looting (pp 7–8). Within one month of admission each man was to furnish himself with bags, one and three-quarters yards long, to carry goods to safety and two sturdy leather buckets of three gallon capacity marked with his name and 'two claſped hands, handſomely painted, to deſignate them as the property of the members of this company' (p 6). Among the members were Michael Wallace, the provincial treasurer, R.J. Uniacke, the attorney general, merchant Andrew Belcher, physician W.J. Allmon, and William Cochran, the president of King's College.
COPY EXAMINED: NSHL

NS16 Nova Scotia. Laws (8th Parliament, 3rd session: 1802)
[text begins] At the GENERAL ASSEMBLY of the | Province of NOVA-SCOTIA, begun and holden | at Halifax, on Thurſday the Twenty-fifth Day of February, 1802
COLLATION: 2° (33.5 x 21 cm), B6–F6² *G6*¹ [$1 signed, D and E with 6. and F as F.6.], 11 leaves, pp 593–613 *614*
CONTENTS: 593–613 text; *614* blank
PAPER: Laid, watermark Britannia; B–C countermark crown | GR | 179[?] ; D–F countermark J LARKING | 1799 ; chains vertical 26 mm
TYPOGRAPHY: *Text*: pica, old face
50 ll., 231 (248) x 118 (147); 95 mm for 20 ll.
BINDING: Stitched
COPY EXAMINED: OTMCL

NS17 Nova Scotia [Laws etc.]
[caption title] [thick-thin rule 100 mm] | PROVINCE OF NOVA-SCOTIA. | REVENUE LAWS | IN FORCE, IN 1802. | [swelled rule 32 mm]
COLLATION: 4° (19.4 x 15 cm), *A*⁴ B–F⁴ [$1 signed], 24 leaves, pp *1* 2–48
CONTENTS: *1*–48 text
PAPER: Laid, watermark Britannia; countermark J LARKING | 1799; chains horizontal 27 mm
TYPOGRAPHY: *Text*: long primer, old face
44 ll., 149 (159) x 98 (122); 68 mm for 20 ll.
BINDING: Wrapper of spot marbled paper in greenish pale blue, dark pink, light orange yellow, and black
COPY EXAMINED: NSHL

NS18 Nova Scotia. Parliament (8th, 3rd session: 1802) House of Assembly
[half title] [lattice and flower rule 145 mm] | JOURNAL | AND | PROCEEDINGS | OF THE | HOUSE OF ASSEMBLY, | 1802. | [lattice and flower rule 145 mm]
COLLATION: 2° (30.3 x 19.4 cm), *A*² B–I² K–Y² Z¹ [$1(–D) signed], 49 leaves, pp *1–3* 4–97 *98* (pagination in ( ) except [4])
CONTENTS: *1* half title; 2 proclamation; *3*–97 text; *98* blank
PAPER: Laid, mixed lot with much watermark Britannia or Vryheyt; countermark 1800; *A*–C watermark propatria; countermark crown | GR [circled] (NSHL, GBPRO); NSHL copy countermark crown | GR | 1795 | H | for V, W, Y; J LARKING | 1799 for X, Z; chains vertical, varied
TYPOGRAPHY: *Text*: pica, old face. *Display*: title with rule as english 12 in Fry and Steele 1790 specimen; two-line pica open roman, royal arms cut 40 x 88 mm
53 ll., 222 (237) x 145; 84 mm for 20 ll.
NOTES: Although the Colonial Office file does not include a letter of transmittal this folio was probably sent by Lieutenant Governor Wentworth on 18 October 1802.
COPIES EXAMINED: NSHL, NSHP, GBPRO: CO 217, vol 77, ff 59–107

NS19 Signal Orders and Instructions
[text headed p 1] SIGNAL ORDERS AND INSTRUCTIONS.
COLLATION: (6.6 x 14 cm), *1–16*² *17*¹, 33 leaves, pp [*8*] 1–42 ²[*8*] 43–50 (pagination in ( ))
CONTENTS: [*1*] blank; [2–3] charts of signals; [*4–8*] blank; 1–49 text with ²[*1–8*] blank, following 42; 50 index
PAPER: Laid, marked, possibly propatria; chains horizontal 26 mm
TYPOGRAPHY: *Text*: pica, old face.
57 (61) x 118
BINDING: Flexible boards in calf, edged blind with bead and leaf wavy roll. Paste-downs of laid paper. Slipcase with same tooling and marbled paper lining
NOTES: Identified by its owner as 'the system of Telegraph as used in the Province of Nova Scotia' the vocabulary of messages includes warnings of adverse weather and other alarms as well as notices of court martial and desertion.

This neatly bound copy is signed 'W Tonge A.D.C.' on the front paste-down and is accompanied by a letter to George Stracey Smyth, senior aide-de-camp and quartermaster general to Edward, Duke of Kent, the commander-in-chief in British North America, signed by Tonge at Spanish Town, 28 February 1802. William Cottnam Tonge, known mainly as an adversary of Sir John Wentworth, had succeeded his father Winckworth Tonge as provincial naval officer (*Dictionary of Canadian Biography* VI, s.v. 'Tonge, William Cottnam,' by Judith Tilloch).
COPY EXAMINED: NSHD

1803

NS20 An Almanack for the Year of Our Lord, 1804
[within thick-thin rules 149 x 87 mm] AN | ALMANACK, [open] | FOR THE | Year of Our LORD, 1804; [script] | BEING BISSEXTILE, OR LEAP-YEAR. | *Calculated for the Meridian of* | HALIFAX, IN NOVA-SCOTIA; | *BUT WILL SERVE FOR ANY PART OF THE PROVINCE.* | CONTAINING, | [9 ll. to left of rules 24 mm] THE ECLIPSES, | RISING AND SETTING OF THE | SUN AND MOON, | SUN'S DECLINATION, | TIME OF HIGH WATER, | FEASTS AND FASTS OF THE | CHURCH, | LIST OF PROVINCIAL OFFI- | CERS. | [9 ll. to right] SITTINGS OF THE COURTS, | OFFICERS OF THE NAVY ON | THIS STATION, | OFFICERS OF THE ARMY UN- | DER LIEUTENANT-GENERAL | HENRY BOWYER. | OFFICERS OF HIS MAJESTY'S | NAVY-YARD AND HOSPI- | TAL. | *With every other Matter Ufeful or Neceffary.* | [rule 80 mm] | BY ABRAHAM SHOEMAKER, OF NEW-YORK. | [rule 80 mm] | *Halifax*: | Printed and Sold by A. GAY, at his Printing-Office, SACKVILLE- | STREET, near the HALIFAX GRAMMAR-SCHOOL.
COLLATION: 12° (19.5 x 11.8 cm), *A*⁶ B⁶ C⁸ [$1 (+B3) signed], 20 leaves, pp [*40*]
CONTENTS: [*1*] within reeded rules [150 x 92 mm] woodcut scene in oval frame on plinth with tablet: VIEW OF HALIFAX; [*2*] blank; [*3*] title; [*4*] table of planets, common notes; [*5*] table of the equation of time, eclipses; [*6*] astronomical characters; high water tables; table of life; [*7*] man of signs; [*7–8*] signals; [8] holidays, levee days; [*9*] firewards, fire engine company; clergy of established church; [*10–11*] roads and distances with houses of entertainment; [*12*] 'To Know the Age of a Horse' with five woodcuts; [*13–24*] calendar with seasonal verses, 4 ll., opening 'From heavy dreary clouds the snow descends' in February and 'Now Pomona

pours her treasure' in October; [25–29] civil list; [29–30] courts; [30] navy yard, hospital; [30–31] freemasons; [32] ships; buoys; [33–35] army lists; [35–40] remedies, anecdotes including 'Sagacity of Rats'; excerpt from the Minutes of the Methodist Episcopal Church for 1803; 'Extreme Cold'; 'French Sympathy'; and 'Puerile Fortitude'
PAPER: Unmarked, *A*, B wove; C laid, chains horizontal 27 mm
TYPOGRAPHY: *Text*: old faces, much bourgeois. *Display*: pages within thick-thin rules; man of signs cut (28 x 23 mm) as **NS2**; almanac signs
147 (149) x 86 mm
ILLUSTRATION: First leaf with woodcut of architectural frame enclosing a scene of Halifax across the harbour with a hunter and dog in the foreground, ships at anchor, and the town with steeples and a flag on Citadel Hill. Five woodcuts of horses' teeth at ages two and a half to six years (maximum 24 x 28 mm) on p [12]
BINDING: Stitched (NSWA)
NOTES: The scene of Halifax is one of three cuts of the town used by Anthony Henry in his eighteenth century *Nova-Scotia Calender* in English and German. The first appeared in the 1777 edition and was a crude imitation of the Paul Revere cut of Boston from the Edes and Gill almanac for 1770. This more conventional and decorative version was published in the 1793 edition and in later years.
COPIES EXAMINED: NSHD (2 copies), NSHP, NSWA (2 copies)

NS21 An Almanack for the Year of Our Lord, 1804

[within thick-thin rules 150 x 90 mm] AN | ALMANACK | FOR THE | Year of our Lord, 1804; | BEING BISSEXTILE OR LEAP YEAR. | *Calculated for the Meridian of* | HALIFAX IN NOVA-SCOTIA | BUT WILL SERVE FOR ANY PART OF THE PROVINCE. | CONTAINING | [9 ll. to left of rule 27 mm] THE ECLIPSES | RISING and SETTING of the | SUN and MOON | TIME of HIGH WATER | FEASTS and FASTS of the | CHURCH | LIST of PROVINCIAL OFFI- | CIERS | SITTINGS of the COURTS | [9 ll. to right] OFFICERS of the NAVY on | this STATION | OFFICERS of the ARMY under | Lieutenant-General HENRY | BOWYER | OFFICERS of His Majeſty's | NAVY-YARD and HOSPI- | TAL. | WITH EVERY OTHER MATTER USEFUL OR NECESSARRY. | [rule 84 mm] | BY THEOPHRASTUS. | [rule 83 mm] | HALIFAX. | Printed and ſold by JOHN HOWE, at his Printing-Office in | George-Street, near the Parade. *Stent* OFFI- | CIERS NECESSARRY
COLLATION: 12° (19.4 x 11.2 cm), A–C⁶ [$1, 3 signed, $3 signed 2; STATE: A3 signed A], 18 leaves, pp [36]
CONTENTS: [1] title; [2–3] signals; [3] eclipses; firewards; [4] man of signs; levee days; buoys; [5] holidays; Parrsborough packet; 'Sugar from the Beet-Root'; [6] planets, vulgar notes; [7–18] calendar with seasonal verses: 'Winter'; 'The Hay Field; a Morning Scene by Miſs Seward' continued to p [19]; [20–23] civil list; [23-25] courts; [25–26] civil list; [26] fire engine company; [27] clergy of established church; navy yard, hospital; [28–30] freemasons; [30] ships, navy; [31–33] army; [33–36] miscellaneous selections including anecdote about animals; 'On Avarice'; 'Cleanliness and Washing'; and 'Observations on the Weather'
PAPER: Wove, unmarked
TYPOGRAPHY: *Text*: long primer, old face. *Display*: pages within thick-thin rules; man of signs cut (46 x 44 mm) is 1804 in Reilly; almanac signs
148 (151) x 89 mm
BINDING: Stitched (NSHD, NSWA)
COPIES EXAMINED: NSHD, NSHP, NSWA, OOA

NS22 Nova Scotia. Laws (8th Parliament, 4th session: 1803)

[text begins] At the GENERAL ASSEMBLY of the | Province of NOVA-SCOTIA, begun and holden | at Halifax, on Wedneſday the Firſt Day of June, | 1803
COLLATION: 2° (32.8 x 21 cm), G6–H6² χH6²–I6² K6² [$1 signed], 10 leaves, pp 614–633
CONTENTS: 614–633 text
PAPER: Laid, H6–K6 watermark Britannia; H6, χH6 countermark JC | 1800; I6, K6 countermark CH | 1797 ; G6 marked CAP | | C HAMERTON | 1801; chains vertical 26 mm
TYPOGRAPHY: *Text*: pica, old face
49 ll., 228 (248) x 118 (147); 95 mm for 20 ll.
BINDING: Stitched
COPY EXAMINED: OTMCL

NS23 Nova Scotia. Laws (8th Parliament, 4th session: 1803)

[text begins] At the GENERAL ASSEMBLY of the | Province of NOVA-SCOTIA, begun and holden | at Halifax, on Wedneſday the Firſt day of June, | 1803
COLLATION: 2° (31.7 x 20 cm), Q5² Q6¹ [Q51 signed 3; printed as Q.5.], 3 leaves, pp 565–569 *570*
CONTENTS: 565–569 text; *570* blank

THE

STATUTES, RULES AND ORDINANCES,

OF THE

UNIVERSITY

OF

KING's COLLEGE

AT

WINDSOR,

IN THE

PROVINCE OF NOVA-SCOTIA.

HALIFAX:

Printed by JOHN HOWE, Printer to the KING's Most Excellent Majesty.

NS26 Courtesy Archives of Ontario, Toronto

PAPER: Laid, watermark Britannia; countermark CH | 1797; chains vertical 27 mm
TYPOGRAPHY: *Text*: pica, old face. *Display*: long swelled rule; two-line great primer drop letter
45 ll., 233 (238) x 116 (145); 94 mm for 20 ll.
BINDING: Stitched
COPY EXAMINED: OTMCL

NS24 Nova Scotia. Parliament (8th, 4th session: 1803). House of Assembly
[half title] [lattice and flower rule 145 mm] | JOURNAL | AND | PROCEEDINGS [open] | OF THE | HOUSE OF ASSEMBLY. | 1803. | [lattice and flower rule 145 mm]
COLLATION: 2° (30.3 x 19.4 cm), *A*² B–I² K–Z² [$1 signed], 50 leaves, pp *1–3* 4–98 *99–100* (pagination in ( ))
CONTENTS: *1* half title; 2 proclamation; *3*–98 text; *99–100* blank
PAPER: Laid, mixed lot with watermark Britannia; countermarks CH | 1797; GATER | 1801; C HAMERTON | 1801; crown | GR | 1791; J LARKING; chains vertical, varied
TYPOGRAPHY: *Text*: pica, old face. *Display*: two-line pica open roman; title rule as english 12 in Fry and Steele 1790 specimen; royal arms cut 40 x 88 mm
55 ll., 232 (243) x 147; 84 mm for 20 ll.
NOTES: The Colonial Office copy was certified on 16 December 1803 by Richard John Uniacke, speaker of the House until 1805.
COPIES EXAMINED: NSHL, NSHP, GBPRO: CO 217, vol 78, ff 144–93

NS25 Shreve, Thomas
A | SERMON, [open] | PREACHED | *At St. Paul's Church, in Halifax,* | BEFORE | *THE PROVINCIAL GRAND LODGE* | OF | *Free and Accepted ANCIENT MASONS,* | JUNE 24*th*, 1803. | *On the celebration of St. John the Baptift,* | BY | THE REVEREND THOMAS SHREVE, A.M. | *RECTOR OF St. GEORGE'S, PARRSBORO',* | AND | *P.G.C. for the Province of Nova Scotia.* | [ornamental dash 45 mm] | *Halifax*: | PRINTED BY A. GAY. *Stet On*
COLLATION: 12° (19.7 x 11.8 cm uncut), A–B⁶ [$1, 2, 3 signed], 12 leaves, pp *1–2* 3–23 *24* (pagination in ( ))
CONTENTS: *1* title; *2* blank; 3 resolution extracted from the Minutes thanking Reverend Brother Shreve and requesting a copy 'for the Prefs' signed John Selby, grand secretary, 24 June 1803; 4 dedication to the R.W. Grand Lodge; 5–20 sermon, text: First Epistle of St Peter, 2d chap. and part of the 17th verse; 21–23 prayer; *24* blank
PAPER: Wove, unmarked
TYPOGRAPHY: *Text*: english, old face. *Display*: two-line double pica open roman; dash is rimmed oval with tapered arrow sides
32 ll., 150 (158) x 90; 93 mm for 20 ll.
BINDING: Stitched in wrapper of bluish gray laid paper
NOTES: Thomas Shreve, a loyalist and former soldier, had been named in 1787 as missionary from the Society for the Propagation of the Gospel after the churchmen in Parrsboro petitioned the Bishop of London for his ordination and appointment. He remained in Parrsboro until 1804 when he moved to Lunenburg (Judith Fingard, *The Anglican Design in Loyalist Nova Scotia, 1783–1816.* London: S.P.C.K., 1972, 47).
COPY EXAMINED: NSHP

NS26 University of King's College (Windsor)
THE | STATUTES, RULES AND ORDINANCES | OF THE | UNIVERSITY [open] | OF | KING'S COLLEGE, | AT | WINDSOR, | IN THE | PROVINCE OF NOVA-SCOTIA. | [swelled rule 44 mm] | HALIFAX: | Printed by JOHN HOWE, Printer to the KING'S Moft Excellent Majefty.
COLLATION: 4° (18.8 x 15 cm), π⁴ *A*⁴ B–F⁴ [$1 signed], 28 leaves, pp [2] *i–iii* iv–v *vi*, *1* 2–48 (roman pagination with period, 5 in ( ))
CONTENTS: [1–2] blank; *i* title; *ii* blank; *iii*–v table of contents; *vi* blank; *1*–4 The Ratification witnessed by the governors 18 July 1803; 5–18 Book I. Of the College. – Of Persons; 19–22 Book II. Of the College. – Of Things; 23–28 Book III. Of the College. – Of Discipline; 29–38 Book IV. – Of the University; 39–40 conclusion (sanctions); 41–48 appendix: oaths, petitions, scheme of lectures, grace, fees
PAPER: Laid, watermark Britannia; countermarks CAP | 1801; C HAMERTON; and JC | 1800; chains horizontal 28 mm
TYPOGRAPHY: *Text*: long primer, old face
45 ll., 147 (156) x 115; 69 mm for 20 ll.
NOTES: Founded by Bishop Charles Inglis as an academy in 1788, King's College was granted a Royal Charter in 1802. At a meeting in September of that year the governors determined that statutes should be drafted by three of their number, Bishop Inglis, Alexander Croke, and Sampson Salter Blowers, using the statutes of Oxford as a model. After a series of meetings the text was approved in July of 1803 and an edition of one hundred copies was authorized (Brian Cuthbertson, *The First Bishop*. Halifax: Waegwoltic Press, 1987, 137–66). Since students as well as teachers at King's were required to subscribe to the Thirty-Nine Articles of the Church of England the majority of Nova

Scotians were excluded from the new college.
COPIES EXAMINED: OTAR, GBL (copy belonging to Sir Joesph Banks)

1804

NS27 An Almanack for the Year of Our Lord, 1805
[within 3 mm ornamental rules, plume head and foot, bellflower sides 194 x 90 mm] AN | ALMANACK, | FOR THE | YEAR OF OUR LORD, 1805; | BEING THE FIRST AFTER BISSEXTILE, OR LEAP-YEAR. | *Calculated for the Latitude and Meridian of* | HALIFAX, IN NOVA-SCOTIA; | *BUT WILL SERVE FOR ANY PART OF THE PROVINCE.* | CONTAINING, | [10 ll. to left of rule 27 mm] THE ECLIPSES, | RISING AND SETTING OF THE | SUN AND MOON, | EQUATION OF TIME, | SUN'S DECLINATION, | TIME OF HIGH WATER, | FEASTS AND FASTS OF THE | CHURCH, | LIST OF PROVINCIAL OFFI- | CERS, | [9 ll. to right] SITTINGS OF THE COURTS, | OFFICERS OF THE NAVY ON | THIS STATION, | OFFICERS OF THE ARMY UN- | DER LIEUTENANT-GENERAL | HENRY BOWYER, | OFFICERS OF HIS MAJESTY'S | NAVY-YARD AND HOSPI- | TAL. | [rule 80 mm] | *With every other Matter Uſeful or Neceſſary.* | [rule 80 mm] | BY ABRAHAM SHOEMAKER, OF NEW-YORK. | [rule 78 mm] | *Halifax,* | Printed and Sold by A. GAY, at his Printing-Office, *Sackville-* | *Street,* near the *Halifax Grammar-School.* [below ornamental rule] A
COLLATION: 12° (19.3 x 12.2 cm), A–D⁶ [$1, 3 (+A1) signed, $3 signed 3], 24 leaves, pp *[48]*
CONTENTS: *[1]* title; *[2]* table of planets, common notes; *[3–4]* man of signs; harbour signals; holidays, levee days; *[5]* clergy of established church; fire-wards, fire engine company; *[6–7]* roads and distances with houses of entertainment; *[8]* astronomical characters; table of high water; *[9–10]* sun's declination; *[11]* eclipses; *[11–12]* remedies: blackberry jelly, hooping-cough, hydrophobia; recipe: copal varnish; *[13–24]* calendar with seasonal verses, 4 ll., opening 'Now gloomy winter ſhews his hoary head' for January and 'Pomona joyous ſpreads her copious ſtores' for October; *[25–26]* 'An Explanation of Several Terms used in the Almanac – for the information of the vulgar'; *[26]* anecdotes: Ulysses' dog; malt spirits; *[27–30]* civil list; *[30–31]* courts; *[31–33]* civil list including corrrected list of firewards; [33] buoys; hint: 'to preserve wheat from the Weaſel'; *[34–36]* army; *[36]* recipe for milk paint; *[37]* ships; 'From a Young Lady to her Friend the day previous to her Marriage'; *[38–39]* army and militia; *[39]* remedy; *[40–44]* farmers calendar; *[45]* to calculate bricks in a wall; cure for cancer; *[46]* tables of interest; hooping-cough, 'From Shenstone'; *[47]* planets; *[47–48]* miscellaneous including 'Ridiculous Cuſtoms and Superſtitions in different nations'; 'Vaccination'; 'Journal of Elizabeth Woodville'; 'Description of Love'; an acrostic 'Love'; and 'Preſerve Plumbs'
PAPER: Laid, unmarked; chains horizontal 28 mm
TYPOGRAPHY: *Text*: brevier, old face. *Display*: pages within frames of plumes, bellflower, and penwork lozenge ornaments (plume is long primer 10 and bellflower is long primer 42 of 1790 Fry and Steele specimen); man of signs cut (28 x 23 mm as **NS2**); almanac signs
149 (151) x 90 mm
BINDING: Stitched (NSHD)
COPIES EXAMINED: NSHD (lacking pp *[11–12]*, *[45–46]*), NSHP

NS28 An Almanack for the Year of Our Lord, 1805
ANOTHER EDITION with title and text reset
[within 3 mm ornamental rules, plume head and foot, ribbon and stick sides 194 x 90 mm] [title as transcribed except no rule below two columns; imprint is | *Halifax:* | ; and no signature letter below ornamental rules]
(21 x 13.5 cm uncut)
TYPOGRAPHY: *Display*: ribbon and stick on title is great primer 6 of 1790 Fry and Steele specimen
BINDING: NSWA copy interleaved, with marbled paper wrapper
COPIES EXAMINED: NSHD, NSHL, NSWA, OOA

NS29 Catholic Church. Diocese of Quebec. Vicar General of Nova Scotia (1801-1817: Burke)
LETTER | OF | *INSTRUCTION* | TO THE | CATHOLIC MISSIONARIES | *OF* | *Nova-Scotia, and its Dependencies.* | [thick-thin rule 58 mm] | BY THE REVEREND MR. BOURKE. | [thin-thick rule 58 mm] | *Halifax:* | PRINTED BY A. GAY: AND SOLD AT THE STORE OF MICHAEL | BENNETT, WATER-STREET. | [row of section marks 18 mm] | 1804.
[MISSIONARIES with wf S]
COLLATION: 12° (21.5 x 13.5 cm uncut), A–E⁶ [$1, 2, 3 (–B3) signed], 30 leaves, pp *1–3* 4–58 *59–60* (pagination in ( ))
CONTENTS: *1* title; 2 blank; 3–48 letter, text: St Paul's Epiſtle to Titus, Ch. 3. v. 1; *49–57* postscript signed E.B. at Halifax, 3 February 1804; 57–58 letter to Sir

Richard Musgrave by order of Marquis Cornwallis, signed E.B. Littlehales, dated at Dublin Castle, 24 March 1801, requesting that Musgrave's dedication to Cornwallis be omitted from that author's history of the rebellions in Ireland; *59–60* blank
PAPER: Laid, marked in the corner of the sheet 1798; chains horizontal 27 mm
TYPOGRAPHY: *Text*: english, old face. *Display*: two-line great primer open roman; text headed with pica rule of penwork chain ornaments; long dash of rimmed oval with tapered arrow sides
32 ll., 148 (161) x 183; 92 mm for 20 ll.
BINDING: Rebound retaining wrapper of bluish greenish gray laid paper (OTMCL)
NOTES: Appointed to Nova Scotia in 1801, Edmund Burke, an Irish priest educated in France, had taught philosophy and mathematics at the Séminaire de Québec and served parishes on the Ile d'Orléans and in Upper Canada. His plan to establish a seminary in Nova Scotia was vigorously opposed by Charles Inglis who had overseen the development of his own school into King's College, recently chartered as a university (**NS26**). In a charge delivered to the clergy of the established church in June of 1803, then revised in August after the renewal of war with France, Bishop Inglis had linked the French Revolution with Catholicism which he declared to be 'encumbered with ʃuperʃtitious ceremonies, and degraded with idolatrous worʃhip of Images, of Saints and of angels' and 'by no means calculated to oppoʃe the torrent of atheiʃm' (**NS30**, p 13). His apocalyptic vision of republicanism implicated Catholics, the Irish, and dissenters. For his part Mr Burke had prepared this letter to Catholic missionaries citing as his text St Paul's Epistle to Titus, chapter 3, verse 1: 'Remind them to be ʃubjet to Princes and Powers, to obey the Magiʃtrates and be prepared for every good work' (p 3). Then, as he explained 'The laʃt ʃheet of this Letter was in the Preʃs, when a charge from a Prelate of the eʃtablished Church accidentally fell into my hands' (p 49). Incensed that Inglis was encouraging discord with his attacks on Catholics and the Irish, and with questions about the loyalty of the Methodists who constituted a great proportion of the inhabitants of the province, Burke added a postscript. He admitted the following year that it had been 'written in a haʃty manner, under a ʃtrong irritation, with ʃome unjuʃtifiable aʃperity of language' (**NS36**, p ²1). In the postscript he mocked the bishop's erudition: 'few Catholics or Non-Conformiʃts are envious of the ʃtock of ʃcience which he poʃʃeʃʃes' (p 49); and his personal inactivity: 'by what extraordinary precaution he has prolonged a life, ʃo neceʃʃary to the peace of the world.' Burke in fact condemned the *Charge* absolutely: 'I don't remember to have ʃeen a more wretched performance: it ʃeems compoʃed of borrowed pieces badly aʃʃorted; written in a languid ʃtyle; replete with dark inʃinuations' (p 56).

Charles Inglis countered with an Appendix to his *Charge* refuting this Postscript to Burke's *Letter*. He also published unfavourable comments addressed to Burke by the lieutenant governor and the attorney general (**NS30**). With the battle joined Robert Stanser, Robert Norris, William Cochran, and Thomas McCulloch lined up in opposition to the formidable Mr Burke (**NS33, NB26**). He answered them all (**NS36, 60, 69**).
COPIES EXAMINED: NSHD, NSHL, OTMCL, QMBM, USMH-H
REFERENCES: Gagnon I 546, TPL 772

NS30 Church of England. Diocese of Nova Scotia. Bishop (1787–1816: Inglis)
A | CHARGE | DELIVERED TO THE CLERGY | *of* | THE DIOCESS OF NOVA-SCOTIA, | AT THE | TRIENNIAL VISITATION | HOLDEN IN | THE MONTHS OF JUNE AND AUGUST, 1803. | [row of double daggers 18 mm] | By the Right Reverend CHARLES INGLIS, D.D. | BISHOP OF NOVA-SCOTIA. | [row of double daggers 18 mm] | [thick-thin rule 88 mm] | The *Second* Edition: To which is ʃubjoined an Appendix, containing | ʃome Papers relative to the Reverend Mr. Bourke's late publication. | [thin-thick rule 89 mm] | [swelled rule 44 mm] | HALIFAX: | Printed by JOHN HOWE, Printer to the King's Moʃt Excellent Majeʃty. | MDCCCIV.
COLLATION: 8° (22.2 x 14.5 cm uncut), *A–B*⁸ C⁸ D⁴ [$1 signed], 28 leaves, pp *I–III* IV–V *VI 7* 8–56 (arabic pagination in ( ))
CONTENTS: *I* title; *II* blank; *III*–V advertisement dated at Clermont, 2 December 1803; *VI* note: [*The first Edition of the Bishop's* Charge, *is strictly followed in the* | *present; which is given merely to gratify many persons who inquired for* | *it, after the few Copies, first printed, had been disposed of*]; 7–43 text; 44–47 Appendix I; 48–56 Appendix II; 56 errata (4 ll.)
PAPER: Wove, marked 1801 at edge of sheet on *B* (NSHL), *A* (NSHP), *B*, C (OTMCL); rest unmarked
TYPOGRAPHY: *Text*: pica, old face, with bourgeois for notes; two-line great primer drop letter
30 ll., 150 (162) x 90; 94 mm for 20 ll.
BINDING: Stitched (NSHL)
NOTES: Although Charles Inglis revised his charge for the August visitation at Annapolis he published the text as he had delivered it first at Halifax in

June, before news of the resumption of England's war with France reached Nova Scotia. He began by celebrating the establishment of King's College at home then warned at length against 'the de*ſ*olating ravages' of republican ideas spreading abroad from France to other Catholic countries (p 44). In Appendix II he responded to Edmund Burke who had 'thought fit to animadvert, in a manner very unbecoming, and with as little regard to Truth, as to decency, on the Bi*ſ*hop of Nova Scotia's Charge' (p 48). The Appendix includes two rebukes sent by allies of Inglis to Mr Burke in answer to his *Letter of Instruction*: first from the lieutenant governor: 'Sir John Wentworth herewith returns it, and with much regret that any *ſ*uch *ſ*hould have been publi*ſ*hed, and more *ſ*o, that it *ſ*hould have been *ſ*ubmitted for his peru*ſ*al' (p 49); and from Richard John Uniacke, the attorney general: 'I have written thus plainly to you, in the hope that you will not think it nece*ſſ*ary to publi*ſ*h any thing further on the *ſ*ubject' (p 52).

Signing himself Charles Nova Scotia, Inglis sent a copy of his *Charge* to Lord Hobart, secretary of state, on 16 February. He enclosed a copy of Burke's *Letter* identifying the author as 'the Popish Priest at Halifax, & Vicar General of the Popish Bishop of Quebec' and his work as 'evidently Democratic' and 'of a dangerous tendency.' Inglis described the situation: 'The Roman Catholics are now labouring to procure a Licence for a Seminary in this town, which they have erected contrary to the sentiments of the Lieut. Governor, & of every other person in authority. Protestants of all denominations in the Province, are greatly alarmed at the progre*ſ*s which this Intolerant Sect has lately made, & dread the consequences of a more extensive diffusion of its principles among the lower Cla*ſ*ses of people, for which this Seminary is calculated.' Of the pamphlet war he wrote 'Mr Bourke had a sight of this *Charge* whilst his *Letter* was in the Pre*ſ*s; & he added a Postscript, replete with abuse & slander again*ſ*t me' (GBPRO: CO 217, vol 79, ff 167–8).

John Howe offered a few copies of the *Charge* 'Just Published and ... to be disposed of by the Printer' on 9 February 1804 (*Royal Gazette*).

COPIES EXAMINED: NSHL, NSHP, OTMCL, GBPRO: CO 217, vol 79, ff 169–96

REFERENCES: Akins, TPL 776

NS31 Gray, Archibald

A | SERMON, | PREACHED ON 10TH AUGUST, 1804: | THE DAY APPOINTED, BY GOVERNMENT, | FOR | A GENERAL FAST, | BY | ARCHIBALD GRAY, | *MINISTER OF THE CHURCH OF SCOTLAND, AND PASTOR OF* | *THE PROTESTANT DISSENTING CONGREGATION,* | HALIFAX, NOVA-SCOTIA. | [row of section marks 15 mm] | HALIFAX: | Printed by JOHN HOWE, and SON, | PRINTERS to the KING'S MOST EXCELLENT MAJESTY. | 1804.

COLLATION: 8° (15.4 x 9.9 cm), *1–2*[8] 3[4], 20 leaves, pp *1–3* 4–38 *39–40* (pagination in ( ))

CONTENTS: *1* title; 2 note by the author; *3*–38 sermon, text: Psalm CXLVII–12; *39–40* blank

PAPER: Laid, marked Britannia; chains vertical 26 mm

TYPOGRAPHY: *Text*: pica, old face 24 ll., 113 (123) x 66; 94 mm for 20 ll.

BINDING: Stitched in wrapper of spot marbled paper in greenish pale blue, dark pink, light orange yellow, and black (NSHD)

NOTES: Archibald Gray continued to preach in Halifax on into the next decade. Shortly after his arrival as lieutenant governor in 1816 the Earl of Dalhousie noted in his journal: '15th December. Sunday. Went to the Scotch Kirk today where a seat had been provided for us by the Elders & Session. Dr. Gray is clergyman of it, a poor preacher rather ...' (p 23). Three years later Dalhousie commented again on Mr Gray: '14th November. Sunday. I have during my stay in Halifax made it a rule of going one Sabbath in each month to the Scotch Presbyterian Church, which is connected with the Established Kirk of Scotland. I went there today. Dr. Gray as usual preached. He is much respected by his congregation, which was more numerous some years ago than now. Dissenters & sectarians are pulling the people all ways, but aim chiefly to seduce from the Established Church. Dr. Gray is naturally corpulent & very lazy – gives himself no trouble, pays none of those visits in family devotion to which Scotch people are accustomed, writes & reads his sermons, an unpardonable offence (p 171) (*The Dalhousie Journals*, vol 1, ed. Marjorie Whitelaw. Ottawa: Oberon, 1978).

With the new imprint of John Howe and Son marking the entry of John Jr into the business, this sermon was offered for sale by booksellers, by merchants, and at the circulating library, until the spring of 1805 (*Weekly Chronicle*, 2 March 1805, *et seq.*).

COPIES EXAMINED: NSHD, NSHP (lacking pp 21–22, *39–40*), NSWA

REFERENCES: Akins, Dennis

NS32 Nova Scotia. Parliament (8th, 5th session: 1804). House of Assembly
[half title] [lattice and flower rule 145 mm] | JOURNAL | AND | PROCEEDINGS | OF THE | HOUSE OF ASSEMBLY, | 1804. | [lattice and flower rule 145 mm]
COLLATION: 2° (30.3 x 19.4 cm), A^2 B–H^2 I^2 K–R^2 [$1 (–C) signed], 34 leaves, pp *1–3* 4–67 *68* (pagination in ( ))
CONTENTS: *1* half title; 2 proclamation; *3*–67 text; *68* blank
PAPER: Laid, watermark Britannia; countermark CH | 1797; chains vertical 26 mm
TYPOGRAPHY: *Text*: pica, old face. *Display*: title with rule as english 12 in Fry and Steele 1790 specimen; royal arms cut 40 x 88 mm
60 ll., 250 (262) x 145; 84 mm for 20 ll.
NOTES: The Assembly adjourned in July; publication of the Journal was probably completed by November.
COPIES EXAMINED: NSHP, GBPRO: CO 217, vol 79, ff 121–54

NS33 Stanser, Robert, 1760–1828
AN | EXAMINATION | OF THE | *Reverend Mr. BURKE's* | LETTER *of* INSTRUCTION, | TO THE | CATHOLIC MISSIONARIES | OF | *Nova-Scotia, and its Dependencies.* | ADDRESSED TO | *CHRISTIANS* | OF EVERY DENOMINATION. | [ornamental dash 45 mm] | *Halifax*: | PRINTED BY A. GAY. | [row of section marks 13 mm] | 1804.
COLLATION: 12° (21.5 x 14 cm uncut), π^1 A–G^6 H^5 [$1, 2, 3 signed], 48 leaves, pp *1–3* 4–95 *96* (pagination in ( ))
CONTENTS: *1* title; 2 advertisement (21 ll.); *3*–95 text signed Robert Stanser, Halifax, 7 March 1804; *96* addendum: 'Omitted in page 12, after line 12' (12 ll. with 3 ll. footnote)
PAPER: Laid, marked in the corner of the sheet 1798; chains horizontal 26 mm
TYPOGRAPHY: *Text*: english, old face. *Display*: two-line pica and two-line great primer open romans; dash is rimmed oval with tapered arrow sides
33 ll., 152 (166) x 85; 93 mm for 20 ll.
NOTES: Appointed in 1791 to St Paul's Church in Halifax by the Society for the Propagation of the Gospel, Stanser remained rector until 1824 although he was consecrated bishop in 1816 and lived in England after 1817. With this reply to Edmund Burke, Robert Stanser joined his bishop in the pamphlet war (**NS30**). Burke responded the following year (**NS36**).
COPIES EXAMINED: NSHD (2 copies, one lacking title), NSHL (lacking title, pp 91–*96*), USMWA (lacking title)

1805

NS34 An Almanack for the Year of Our Lord, 1806
[within thick-thin rules 146 x 88 mm] AN | ALMANACK, | FOR THE | YEAR OF OUR LORD, 1806; | BEING THE SECOND AFTER BISSEXTILE, OR LEAP-YEAR. | *Calculated for the Latitude and Meridian of* | HALIFAX, IN NOVA-SCOTIA; | *BUT WILL SERVE FOR ANY PART OF THE PROVINCE.* | CONTAINING, | [10 ll. to left of rule 28 mm] THE ECLIPSES, | RISING AND SETTING OF THE | SUN AND MOON, | EQUATION OF TIME, | SUN'S DECLINATION, | TIME OF HIGH WATER, | FEASTS AND FASTS OF THE | CHURCH, | LIST OF PROVINCIAL OFFI- | CERS, | [9 ll. to right] SITTINGS OF THE COURTS, | OFFICERS OF THE NAVY ON | THIS STATION, | OFFICERS OF THE ARMY UN- | DER LIEUTENANT-GENERAL | WILLIAM GARDINER, | OFFICERS OF HIS MAJESTY'S | NAVY-YARD AND HOSPI- | TAL. | [rule 82 mm] | *With every other Matter Ufeful or Neceffary.* | [rule 81 mm] | BY ABRAHAM SHOEMAKER, OF NEW-YORK. | [rule 81 mm] | *Halifax*, | Printed and Sold by E. GAY, at her Printing-Office, SACKVILLE | STREET, near the *Halifax Grammar-School.*
COLLATION: 4° (18.4 x 13.6 cm uncut), A^4 B–E^4 [$1 signed], 20 leaves, pp [40]
CONTENTS: [*1*] within reeded rules [150 x 92 mm] woodcut scene in oval frame on plinth with tablet: VIEW OF HALIFAX; [*2*] blank; [*3*] title; [*4*] table of planets, common notes; [*5*] man of signs; [*5–6*] signals; [*6*] clergy of established church; [*7*] astronomical characters; table of high water; [*8*] holidays, levee days; firewards, fire engine company; [*9–10*] roads and distances with houses of entertainment; [*11–12*] sun's declination; [*13–24*] calendar with seasonal verses, 4 ll., opening 'A life of love is endless May' for August and 'Where are the walks that blush'd with flowers?' for October; [*25–28*] civil list; [*28–29*] courts; [*29–30*] civil list; [*31*] navy yard; buoys; hint: cattle and clover; [*31*] 'Scrap'; [*32–35*] army; [*35*] 'Berengeria, Queen of Castile,' 'On seeing a Beautiful Woman in a Passion'; [*36*] ships; [*37*] eclipses; [*37–40*] miscellany including 'Spartan Heroism'; 'A Religious

NS34 Courtesy J.J. Stewart Collection, Special Collections Department, Dalhousie University Library, Halifax

AN

ALMANACK,

FOR THE

YEAR OF OUR LORD, 1806;

BEING THE SECOND AFTER BISSEXTILE, OR LEAP-YEAR.

Calculated for the Latitude and Meridian of

HALIFAX, IN NOVA-SCOTIA;

BUT WILL SERVE FOR ANY PART OF THE PROVINCE.

CONTAINING,

THE ECLIPSES,
RISING AND SETTING OF THE SUN AND MOON,
EQUATION OF TIME,
SUN'S DECLINATION,
TIME OF HIGH WATER,
FEASTS AND FASTS OF THE CHURCH,
LIST OF PROVINCIAL OFFICERS,
SITTINGS OF THE COURTS,
OFFICERS OF THE NAVY ON THIS STATION,
OFFICERS OF THE ARMY UNDER LIEUTENANT-GENERAL WILLIAM GARDINER,
OFFICERS OF HIS MAJESTY'S NAVY-YARD AND HOSPITAL.

With every other Matter Uſeful or Neceſſary.

BY ABRAHAM SHOEMAKER, OF NEW-YORK.

Halifax,

Printed and Sold by E. GAY, at her Printing-Office, SACKVILLE STREET, near the *Halifax Grammar-School.*

NS34 Courtesy J.J. Stewart Collection, Special Collections Department, Dalhousie University Library, Halifax

Hypocrite'; 'On the Summer Complaint of Infants' by Joseph Brevitt; and short selections headed Scrap, Epigram, Anecdote, and Remark
PAPER: Laid, unmarked; chains horizontal 26 mm
TYPOGRAPHY: *Text*: old faces. *Display*: pages within thick-thin rules; man of signs cut (28 x 23 mm) as **NS2;** almanac signs
145 (149) x 88 mm
ILLUSTRATION: Woodcut vignette of Halifax (p [*1*]) first seen in Anthony Henry's *Nova-Scotia Calender* for 1793 and, most recently, in Archibald Gay's *Almanack* for 1804 (**NS20**).
BINDING: Stitched (NSHD)
NOTES: The imprint of this almanac 'Printed and Sold by E. GAY, at her Printing-Office' is exceptional in early Canadian printing, not because women did not print but because their work was traditionally private rather than public. Printing was often a family craft passed from generation to generation and through marriage between printing families. The frequent combination of shop and dwelling with apprentices living in the family brought the printing business, the routine work and the rush jobs, into the domestic sphere. In these circumstances it was inevitable that women who were daughters, sisters, wives, and mothers of printers would learn to print. However they were not eligible for entry to the craft through a regular apprenticeship so their work was seldom recorded in imprints, contracts, or pay books.

Elizabeth Gay is typical of the women printers known to historians. Like Ann Mott in New Brunswick ten years later (**NB47, 51**) she was a widow who took over the shop. Her husband Archibald Gay, who had himself taken over Anthony Henry's shop from Mrs Henry in 1801, died on 30 April 1805 leaving his wife and four young children 'to deplore the loss' (*Weekly Chronicle*, 4 May 1805). Elizabeth Gay assumed charge of the office and published this almanac and a magazine (**NS41**) under her own imprint. Their newspaper, the *Nova-Scotia Gazette* continued until at least 22 July 1806 (issue in NSHP) but in the autumn the 'Printing Press, Types and Materials of Every kind, The Property of the late Archibald Gay' were announced for sale at auction (*Royal Gazette*, 14 October 1806). In July of the following year Charles Stuart Powell, actor and theatre manager, bought Gays' printing office and announced a new paper to be called the *Halifax Telegraph* (*Weekly Chronicle*, 17 July 1807). The first number was published on 20 July at Sackville Street. In November Powell suspended publication 'for want of proper assistance in the office' (*Weekly Chronicle*, 13 November 1807) and, although he proposed to renew it in partnership with James Bagnall the following year, no later issues of the *Halifax Telegraph* are known (*Weekly Chronicle*, 5 August 1808). Printing continued however in 'Sackville Street, near the Halifax Grammar School' with the Henry / Gay equipment when James Bagnall published an almanac there in 1808 (**NS49**). In that same year Bagnall founded the *Novator* which lasted until 18 June 1810, and perhaps longer but not past 27 July when John Howe Jr announced his purchase of Bagnall's materials and his intention to publish the *Halifax Journal* at the Sackville Street office (*Weekly Chronicle*).
COPIES EXAMINED: NSHD (2 copies, one lacking pp [*1–2*], the other pp [*39–40*]), NSHL (lacking pp [*1–2*], [*39–40*]), NSWA, OOA

NS35 An Almanack for the Year of our Lord, 1806

[within 4 mm reeded rules 150 x 90 mm] AN | ALMANACK | FOR THE | Year of our Lord 1806. | BEING THE SECOND AFTER BISSEXTILE OR LEAP YEAR. | *Calculated for the Meridian of* | HALIFAX IN NOVA-SCOTIA: | BUT WILL SERVE FOR ANY PART OF THE PROVINCE. | CONTAINING | [9 ll. to left of rule 30 mm] THE ECLIPSES | RISING and SETTING of | the SUN and MOON | TIME of HIGH WATER | FEASTS and FASTS of | the CHURCH | LIST of PROVINCIAL | OFFICERS | SITTINGS of COURTS | [8 ll. to right] OFFICERS of the NAVY | on this STATION | OFFICERS of the ARMY | under Lieutenant General | WILLIAM GARDINER. | OFFCERS of His Maje*f*ty's | NAVY-YARD and HOS- | PITAL. | WITH EVERY OTHER MATTER USEFUL OR NECESSARY. | [rule 79 mm] | BY THEOPHRASTUS. | [rule 79 mm] | HALIFAX: | Printed and *f*old by *JOHN HOWE*, & *SON*, at their Office | *Bedford Row. Stet* OFFCERS
COLLATION: 12° (18.6 x 12 cm uncut), *1–3*^{6}, 18 leaves, pp [*36*]
CONTENTS: [*1*] title; [*2*] ephemeris, vulgar notes; [*3*] eclipses, planets; [*4*] man of signs; levee days, holidays; [*5–6*] signals; [*6*] Parrsborough packet; firewards; epigram; [*7–18*] calendar with domestic and seasonal verses: 'Wife, Children and Warm Fire Side'; 'To Spring'; and 'Morning'; [*19–23*] civil list; [*23–24*] courts; [*25*] civil list; [*26–27*] freemasons; [*27*] fire engine company; [*28*] clergy of established church; navy yard; [*29–32*] army; [*32*] bail commissioners; [*33*] ships; [*34–35*] roads and

distances with houses of entertainment; buoys; [*36*] blank
PAPER: Unmarked, *1* wove; *2–3* laid, chains horizontal 25 mm
TYPOGRAPHY: *Text*: long primer, old face. *Display*: pages within thick-thin rules; man of signs cut (46 x 44 mm) is 1804 in Reilly; almanac signs
146 x 86 mm
BINDING: Stitched (NSHD)
NOTES: On 5 December the Howes promised the almanac for 'Saturday next' (*Royal Gazette*, 1805).
COPIES EXAMINED: NSHD, NSWA (lacking pp [*33–36*])

NS36 Burke, Edmund, 1753–1820
REMARKS | ON THE | *Rev. Mr.* STANSER's *EXAMINATION* | OF THE | Rev. Mr. BURKE's LETTER OF INSTRUCTION | TO THE | *C.M. of Nova-Scotia;* | Together with | A REPLY | TO THE | *Rev. Mr. COCHRAN's Fifth and Last LETTER* | *to Mr. B.* | PUBLISHED IN THE NOVA-SCOTIA GAZETTE; | *As alſo* | *A Short Review of his former Letters,* | AND THE | *REPLIES WHICH WERE MADE.* | Chohàmar Jehovah, imedou al derachim ou reouve ſhaelou lenithboth hòlam éi zeh derek | ha tòb ou lechou bah ou mitſeou margoha le naphſhechim. – IRMIH. | Thus ſaith the Lord: ſtand on the ways, and ſee, and aſk of the old paths if this be the | right way, and walk in it. – JER. vi. 16. | [ornamental dash 46 mm] | *Halifax*: | PRINTED BY A. GAY. | [cross rule 15 mm] | 1805.
COLLATION: 8° (23 x 14.5 cm uncut), A–I[4] K–U[4] X–2E[4], [2]A–I[4] K–2D[4] 2E[2] [$1, 2 (+[2]A1, –[2]L2, [2]2E2) signed], 230 leaves, pp *1–3* 4–222 *223–224*, [2]*1* 2–150 [2]150–234 postscript; *235–236*
CONTENTS: *1* title; *2* blank; 3–222 text of Remarks; *223–224* blank; [2]*1*–150 text of Review; [2]150–234 postscript; [2]*235* errata: 69 ll. for volume I, 31 ll. for volume II; [2]*236* blank
PAPER: A–O, [2]B–G, [2]K–2E laid, unmarked; chains vertical 28 mm; P–2E, [2]A, [2]H–I wove, unmarked
TYPOGRAPHY: *Text*: A–[2]K english, transitional face; [2]L–[2]2E pica, old face. *Display*: text with head-pieces: row of lattice for Remarks, bead and reel for Review (long primer 10 and 2 of Fry and Steele 1790 specimen); ornamental dash on title is rimmed oval with tapered arrow sides, long swelled rule; open roman in double pica and two-line great primer
38 ll., 179 (190) x 101 / 180 (191) x 99; 94 mm for 20 ll.
BINDING: Remarks and Review possibly issued separately in wrappers since stab holes do not align and OTMCL copy of Remarks rebound retaining wrapper of bluish light greenish gray laid paper. Bound together in sprinkled sheep, spine divided into six compartments by double gold rule, brown lettering piece in second edged rope roll gilt and lettered D.[R] BURKE'S | WORKS | . Wove endpapers and binder's leaf, lacking all but front paste-down (OTMCL)
NOTES: Burke began with Robert Stanser (**NS33**) whose pamphlet 'if ſtripped of theſe adventitious ornaments, and confined to logical reaſoning, would be reduced to half a ſheet' (p 31). He then moved on to the letters published in Archibald Gay's *Nova-Scotia Gazette* under the name Palæologus by William Cochran of King's College. In a postscript (pp [2]150–234) which follows the Review of Cochran's letters without evidence of interruption to the printing, Burke answered, section by section, the 'pretended Discussion' of Robert Norris of Saint John (**NB26**). Recalling Norris's former life as a Catholic priest Burke chided him: 'If the pleaſures of matrimony had not totally effaced from that *ci-devant* Catholic Ecclеſiaſtic's mind, the remembrance of the faith which he formerly profeſſed' (pp [2]150–51). Since Norris's *Candid Discussion* was not published until 1806 Burke must have added to his 1805 manuscript while it was in the press. His postscript begins midway on the verso of leaf [2]T3. The death of his publisher Archibald Gay in April of 1805 and the sale of the shop by Elizabeth Gay the following year may well have delayed publication of Burke's essays.
It was Thomas McCulloch, the Pictou Presbyterian, who answered Burke with *Popery Condemned by Scripture and the Fathers: Being a Refutation of the Principal Popish Doctrines and Assertions Maintained in the Remarks on the Rev. Mr. Stanser's Examination of the Rev. Mr. Burke's Letter of Instruction to the Catholic Missionaries of Nova Scotia, and in the Reply to the Rev. Mr. Cochran's Fifth and Last Letter to Mr. Burke, &c.*
Published in Edinburgh, McCulloch's refutation was advertised for sale in Halifax priced at 6s in boards in the spring of 1808 (*Weekly Chronicle*, 20 May 1808 *et seq.*). Mr Burke responded to McCulloch the following year (**NS60**).
COPIES EXAMINED: NSHD (lacking pp [2]*233–36*), NSHP (Remarks only), OTMCL (2 copies, one Remarks only), OTUTF (Remarks only), QMBM, GBL, USMBAt, USMH-H, USMWA
REFERENCES: Akins, Dennis, Gagnon II 270, TPL 788

NS37 Nova Scotia. Laws (1st Parliament, 1st session: 1758 to 8th Parliament, 5th session: 1804)
THE | STATUTES AT LARGE, | PASSED IN THE SEVERAL | GENERAL ASSEMBLIES | HELD IN | HIS MAJESTY's PROVINCE OF NOVA-SCOTIA: | FROM | The Firſt ASSEMBLY, which met at HALIFAX the ſecond Day of October, | in the thirty-ſecond year of His late Majeſty Geo. II. A.D. 1758. | TO | The forty-fourth year of His preſent Majeſty Geo. III A.D. 1804, incluſive; | WITH | A Complete Index and Abridgement of the whole. | PUBLISHED BY ORDER OF | THE GOVERNOR, COUNCIL, AND HOUSE OF ASSEMBLY, | BY | RICHARD JOHN UNIACKE. | [royal arms 53 x 107 mm] | HALIFAX: | PRINTED by JOHN HOWE and SON, Printers to the KING's Moſt Excellent Majeſty. | 1805.

AN | ABRIDGEMENT | OF THE | STATUTES OF NOVA-SCOTIA: | FROM | The Firſt Seſſion of GENERAL ASSEMBLY, held at Halifax on the Second day of October in | the year of our LORD 1758, and in the 32d year of the Reign of His late Majeſty King | GEORGE II. to the end of the Seſſion of GENERAL ASSEMBLY held at Halifax on the 21ſt day | of June, in the year of our LORD 1804, and in the 44th year of the Reign of His preſent | Majeſty King GEORGE III. | [rule 165 mm] | BY RICHARD JOHN UNIACKE, Eſq. ATTORNEY GENERAL. | [rule 164 mm] | ÆQUUM ET BONUM EST LEX LEGUM. | [cross rule 14 mm] | IGNORANTIA JURIS NON EXCUSAT. | [swelled rule 39 mm] | HALIFAX: | PRINTED by JOHN HOWE and SON, Printers to the King's Moſt Excellent Majeſty.
COLLATION: 4° (28.5 x 22.7 cm), π–4π^2 A^2 B^2 C–I^4 K–U^4 W–2I^4 2K–3E^4 χ3E–3I^4 3K–3L^4 3M^2, ${}^2A^4$ B–I^4 K–M^4, ${}^3A^2$ B–D^2 χ^2 [$1 (–2T) signed; second alphabet signed with a, third with b; 3I signed I.b.], 308 leaves, pp *i–v* vi–x *xi–xii* [4] *1* 2–483 *484*, ^{2}*1–3* 4–95 *96* ^{2}[*20*]
CONTENTS: *i* title; *ii* blank; *iii* dedication to HIS EXCELLENCY | SIR JOHN WENTWORTH ... | signed RICHARD JOHN UNIACKE; *iv*–x 'To the Reader' signed as dedication; *xi–xii* blank; [*1–4*] 'Sessions of General Assembly'; *1*–483 text of Statues; *484* blank; ^{2}*1* title; ^{2}2 blank ^{2}3–95 text of Abridgement; ^{2}*96* ^{2}[*1–15*] General Index to the Abridgement; ^{2}[*16–20*] Index to the Expired Laws
PAPER: Mixed lot, almost entirely wove, much unmarked or marked in corner 1801; some sheets marked 1804; or HS | 1801; or M & E [script] | 180[?]
TYPOGRAPHY: *Text*: pica, transitional face. *Display*: royal arms cut signed Lee; swelled rules
49 ll., 230 (243) x 158 (183); 94 mm for 20 ll.
BINDING: The commonest binding is calf or sheep with boards outlined blind in plain or rope rule. Spine divided by double gilt rule into six compartments, the second with a red lettering piece NOVA-SCOTIA | LAWS. | Endpapers laid or wove (NSHD, NSWA (2 copies)). OOA copy calf with ribbon and lozenge roll in blind on boards and red lettering piece on upper board edged gilt double and lozenge and bead rules, lettered DAVID CRANDLE | . Endpapers laid, watermark Strasbourg lily | GR; countermark DEMY | 1793. OONL copy same except foliage roll blind on boards and gilt on black lettering piece with name PELEG. WISWALL | . Endpapers marked EDMEADS & PINE. OTMCL copy half dark green leather and reddish brown shell marbled paper. Spine divided as full leather copies and lettered in second NOVA SCOTIA | LAWS | and I | in fourth. Lettering piece on upper board edged gilt with fleur de lys roll and lettered W.H.O. HALIBURTON. for William Hersey Otis Haliburton, a member of the House of Assembly from 1806 to 1824 and father of Thomas Chandler Haliburton. This copy has a worked headband and wove endpapers.
NOTES: Richard John Uniacke, the attorney general and speaker of the House of Assembly until 1805, explained his work in a note 'To the Reader':

> I have carefully abridged every Act under its appropriate head, and have added thereto a copious Index, with proper references, in the hope thereby, to make our Laws intelligible to the meaneſt capacity; and I have no doubt the reader will with pleaſure contemplate the exertions of this infant Colony, in every ſtage of its Legiſlation, to eſtablish religion, and ſuppreſs vice and immorality. I am ſenſible that the patience of the public has been nearly exhauſted on the account of the great length of time this work has been in hand; to me, it has been painful and highly diſtreſſing: but when I conſider the great difficulty that attends a printer, who has to execute an extenſive work like this in a new country, where he is obliged to attend to all his other buſineſs and avocations, it has been to me I confeſs a ſufficient excuſe, and I hope the public will receive it in the ſame light. The only merit I can pretend to in completing a work which has required much labour and attention, is that of diligence and fidelity (p x).

The Journals and Laws of the House of Assembly

record various payments for this extensive work: £100 to Alexander Morrison, bookbinder, for binding eighty sets for the public service and 'to pay for ſewing in blue paper covers, the remainder of the ſaid edition, which are to be offered for ſale to the Inhabitants of the Province' for £1 5s (*Journal*, 8:5, 1804, p 45); £400 advance to John Howe in 1802 (Laws, 8:3, 1802, p 597) with a balance of £150 for printing, and £350 to the attorney general for revising the laws (*Journal*, 8:6, 1805–1806, p 68).

In October of 1806 Alexander Morrison was offering 'Laws of the Province' for sale (*Royal Gazette*, 21 October). A calf-bound copy at NSHD with a lettering piece (probably later) on the upper board, edged floral gilt and lettered JOHN CREIGHTON | , has an engraved blue paper label on the front paste-down showing a native couple flanking an oval lettered GEORGE EATON. | Bookſeller and Stationer | HALIFAX. | NOVA-SCOTIA | [beneath the oval] Bookbinding of all kinds executed with | Neatneſs & Dispatch. [49 x 71 mm]. The endpapers of this volume are laid, watermark fleur de lys | 1802; countermark EDMEADS & PINE. George Eaton, Alexander Morrison's former apprentice, took over Morrison's stock and on 18 April 1811, 'commenced Business on his own account, in the store lately occupied' by Mr Morrison (*Weekly Chronicle*, 26 April; *Halifax Journal*, 29 April).
COPIES EXAMINED: NSHD (2 copies), NSHP, NSWA (2 copies), OOA (2 copies), OONL, OTMCL, GBL, USMH-L
REFERENCES: Bishop, TPL 778

1806

NS38 An Almanack for the Year of Our Lord, 1807

[within thick-thin rules 151 x 86 mm] AN | ALMANACK | FOR THE | Year of our Lord, 1807. | BEING THE THIRD YEAR AFTER BISSEXTILE OR LEAP YEAR. | *Calculated for the Meridian of* | HALIFAX IN NOVA-SCOTIA: | BUT WILL SERVE FOR ANY PART OF THE PROVINCE; | CONTAINING | [8 ll. to left of rule 24 mm] THE ECLIPSES | RISING and SETTING of | the SUN and MOON | TIME of HIGH WATER | FEASTS and FASTS of the | CHURCH | LIST of PROVINCIAL OF- | FICERS | [8 ll. to right] SITTINGS of COURTS | OFFICERS of the NAVY on | this STATION | OFFICERS of the ARMY un- | der Major-General HUNTER | OFFICERS of His Majeſty's | NAVY-YARD and HOS | PITAL. | WITH EVERY OTHER MATTER USEFUL OR NECESSARY. | [thick-thin rule 79 mm] | BY THEOPHRASTUS. | [thin-thick rule 79 mm] | HALIFAX: | Printed and ſold by *JOHN HOWE & SON*, at their Office, | *Bedford Row*.
COLLATION: 12° (19.5 x 11.5 cm), *A–B*[6] C[6] [C1 signed], 18 leaves, pp [36]
CONTENTS: [*1*] title; [*2*] ephemeris, vulgar notes; [*3*] eclipses, planets; Parrsborough packet; [*4*] man of signs; levee days, holidays; [*5–6*] signals; [*6*] firewards; verse: 'A Reflection'; remedy; [*7–18*] calendar with verses: 'Lines Addressed to a Little Redbreast'; 'Approach of Summer'; 'Cheerfulness' by Dr Akinside; [*19–23*] civil list; [*23–24*] courts; [*24–25*] civil list; [*26–27*] freemasons; [*27*] fire engine company; [*28*] clergy of established church; navy yard; [*29–32*] army; [*32*] civil list; [*33–34*] ships; [*34–35*] roads and distances with houses of entertainment; [*36*] buoys; advice: 'Duties to Self' and 'Duties to Society' (described as 'An Antidote to the Contagion of French principles and manners'); anecdote: 'The Physiognomy' by Burke
PAPER: Wove, unmarked
TYPOGRAPHY: *Text*: long primer, old face. *Display*: pages within thick-thin rules; man of signs cut (46 x 44 mm) is 1804 in Reilly; almanac signs
150 (153) x 86 mm
BINDING: Stitched (NSHD); OOA copy in spot marbled wrapper, interleaved and used in the Military Secretary's Office to record sailings
NOTES: Copies were announced for sale 'on Friday next' (31 October) at the Howe office (*Weekly Chronicle*, 24 October 1806); *Royal Gazette*, 28 October).
COPIES EXAMINED: NSHD (2 copies, one lacking pp [*33–36*], the other [*35–36*]), NSHL, NSHP (2 copies), NSWA (lacking pp [*32–36*]), OOA (2 copies)

NS39 Nova Scotia. Laws (8th Parliament, 6th session: 1805–1806)

[text begins] At the GENERAL ASSEMBLY of the Province of | Nova-Scotia, begun and holden at Halifax, on the | Twentieth day of February, Anno Domini, 1800, and | continued by ſeveral Prorogations to Thurſday the | Twenty-Eighth day of November, 1805
COLLATION: 2° (29.4 x 21 cm), Nb–Sb[2] [$1 signed], 12 leaves, pp 484–507
CONTENTS: 484–507 text
PAPER: Wove, Sb marked 1801
TYPOGRAPHY: *Text*: pica, old face

48 ll., 220 (238) x 157 (181); 94 mm for 20 ll.
NOTES: The annual laws are signed and paged in continuation of the *Statutes at Large* (**NS37**).
COPY EXAMINED: USMH-L

NS40 Nova Scotia. Parliament (8th, 6th session: 1805–1806). House of Assembly
[half title] [lattice and flower rule 144 mm] | JOURNAL | AND | PROCEEDINGS | OF | THE HOUSE OF ASSEMBLY, | 1805. | [lattice and flower rule 144 mm]
COLLATION: 2° (30.5 x 19.4 cm), *A*² B–I² K–U² [$1 signed, with C wf, misprinting N as L], 40 leaves, pp *1–3* 4–79 *80* (pagination in ( ))
CONTENTS: *1* half title; *2* proclamation; *3*–79 text; *80* blank
PAPER: Laid, mixed lot with watermark Britannia; countermarks IVY MILL | 1801; BIXON | 1802; J & M | 1803; RADWAY | 180[?]; crown | GR | 1805; watermark Vryheyt; countermark BUDGEN | 1802; chains vertical, varied
TYPOGRAPHY: *Text*: pica, old face. *Display*: rule as english 12 in Fry and Steele 1790 specimen
55 ll., 246 (260) x 145; 94 mm for 20 ll.
COPIES EXAMINED: NSHL, NSHP, GBPRO: CO 217, vol 80, ff 190–229

NS41 The Nova-Scotia and New-Brunswick Magazine
[wrapper title] THE | NOVA-SCOTIA [open] | AND | NEW-BRUNSWICK | *MAGAZINE;* | OR, | *The HISTORICAL, LITERARY, THEO- | LOGICAL, and MISCELLANEOUS* | *REPOSITORY.* | Vol. I. FEBRUARY 1st, 1806. No. 1. | *Conditions:* – | [26 ll. text] | [swelled rule 43 mm] | PRINTED BY E. GAY.
COLLATION: 8° (23 x 14.5 cm), A–B⁴ C² [$1, 2 signed], 10 leaves, pp *1* 2–20
CONTENTS: *1*–20 text headed [ornamental rule 89 mm] | COMPEND | OF | UNIVERSAL HISTORY. [open] | [swelled rule 35 mm]
PAPER: Laid, marked fleur de lys; chains vertical 25 mm
TYPOGRAPHY: *Text*: pica, modern face. *Display*: head-piece of penwork chain ornaments
40 ll., 162 (173) x 91; 84 mm for 20 ll.
BINDING: Wrapper of bluish greenish gray wove paper, the upper printed as transcribed, the lower with 'Contents' (8 ll.) and 'To the Public' (24 ll.)
NOTES: Introducing himself 'To the Public' the editor assured them of his loyalty and explained his motives: 'Solicitous for the spread of useful knowledge the editor has, for some time, employed his moments of reflection, in concerting the plan of a new periodical work, the first number of which, as a specimen, he now offers to the public ... His ultimate aim is to elucidate and defend the great doctrines and duties of revealed religion.' And, given the religious discord in Nova Scotia, he was espousing tolerance: 'His religious sentiments will be found conformable to the confession and catechisms of the church of Scotland, the doctrinal articles of the church of England, and the creeds of the other reformed churches' (lower wrapper). On a more practical note the editor explained that a scarcity of paper had obliged him to begin his journal on a smaller scale than he had intended.
COPY EXAMINED: NSHD

1807

NS42 An Almanack for the Year of Our Lord, 1808
[within thick-thin rules 151 x 88 mm] AN | ALMANACK | FOR THE | Year of our Lord, 1808. | BEING BISSEXTILE OR LEAP YEAR: | *Calculated for the Meridian of* | HALIFAX IN NOVA-SCOTIA: | BUT WILL SERVE FOR ANY PART OF THE PROVINCE; | CONTAINING | [8 ll. to left of rule 24 mm] THE ECLIPSES | RISING and SITTING of | the SUN and MOON | TIME of HIGH WATER | FEASTS and FASTS of the | CHURCH | LIST of PROVINCIAL OF- | FICERS | [8 ll. to right] SITTINGS of COURTS | OFFICERS of the NAVY on | this STATION | OFFICERS of the ARMY un- | der Major-General HUNTER | OFFICERS of His Maje*f*ty's | NAVY-YARD and HOS- | PITAL. | WITH EVERY OTHER MATTER USEFUL OR NECESSARY. | [thick-thin rule 79 mm] | BY THEOPHRASTUS. | [thin-thick rule 79 mm] | HALIFAX: | Printed and *f*old by *JOHN HOWE & SON*, at their Office, | *Bedford Row. Stet* RISING and SITTING
COLLATION: 12° (20 x 12.4 cm uncut), *A*⁶ B–C⁶ [$1, 3 signed, $3 signed 2], 18 leaves, pp [*36*]
CONTENTS: [*1*] title; [*2*] ephemeris, vulgar notes; [*3*] eclipses, planets; [*4*] man of signs; Parrsborough packet; [*5–6*] signals; [*6*] levee days, holidays; [*7–18*] calendar with verses including extracts from Cowper's 'Winter Evening'; 'On the Grasshopper'; [*19–23*] civil list; [*23–24*] courts; [*25*] civil list; [*26–27*] freemasons; [*27*] firewards; [*28*] clergy of established church; navy yard; [*29–32*] army;

[32–33] ships; [34–35] roads and distances with houses of entertainment; [36] civil list; fire engine company; buoys
PAPER: Wove, unmarked
TYPOGRAPHY: *Text*: long primer, old face. *Display*: pages within thick-thin rules, man of signs cut (64 x 55 mm) is 1816 in Reilly; almanac signs
151 (154) x 86 mm
BINDING: OOA copy with lower wrapper of spot marbled paper, interleaved and used in the Military Secretary's Office to record sailings
NOTES: The man of signs cut revived this year had been used by Anthony Henry and John Howe in *The Nova-Scotia Calender* for 1783, a joint publication. Howe continued to use it for his almanacs through the 1790s.
COPIES EXAMINED: NSHD (2 copies), NSHL, NSHP (2 copies), NSWA, OOA

NS43 Church of England
[within thick-thin rules 150 x 108 mm] A | FORM | OF | PRAYER, | TO BE USED | In all Churches, Chapels and Places of | PUBLIC WORSHIP, according to the u*ſ*age of the CHURCH | of ENGLAND, throughout his Maje*ſ*ty's Province of NOVA- | SCOTIA, on FRIDAY, the Twelfth Day of JUNE, 1807: | being the Day appointed by Proclamation for a GENERAL | FAST and HUMILIATION before ALMIGHTY GOD; to be | ob*ſ*erved in the mo*ſ*t devout and *ſ*olemn manner, by *ſ*end- | ing up our PRAYERS and SUPPLICATIONS to the DIVINE | MAJESTY; | For obtaining the pardon of our Sins, and for averting tho*ſ*e heavy Judg- | ments which our manifold provocations have mo*ſ*t ju*ſ*tly de*ſ*erved; and | imploring His Ble*ſſ*ing on the Arms of His Maje*ſ*ty by Sea and Land, | and for re*ſ*toring and perpetuating peace, *ſ*afety and pro*ſ*perity to Him- | *ſ*elf, and to His Kingdom. | [rule 100 mm] | By Command of His Excellency the Lieutenant-Governor. | [thin-thick rule 101 mm] | HALIFAX: | Printed by JOHN HOWE and SON, Printers to the KING'S Mo*ſ*t Excellent | Maje*ſ*ty. 1807.
COLLATION: 4° (19 x 12.6 cm cropped), 1^4 2^1, 5 leaves, pp *1–3* 4–10
CONTENTS: *1* title; *2* blank; *3*–10 text
PAPER: Laid, watermark circles with cross | 1803; countermark P MIR^E; chains horizontal 26 mm
TYPOGRAPHY: *Text*: pica, old face
28 ll., 137 (151) x 109; 92 mm for 20 ll.
NOTES: In response to desertions from Royal Navy ships the British government claimed the right to search American vessels for British sailors. During 1807 this policy and the impressment of American seamen brought the two nations close to war. On 22 June, shortly after the Fast Day, HMS *Leopard* opened fire on USS *Chesapeake* then dispatched a boarding party which seized four members of the crew. One of them, Jenkin Ratford, a deserter from HMS *Halifax*, was tried by court martial that summer (**NS47**).
COPY EXAMINED: NSHP

NS44 Nova Scotia. Laws (9th Parliament, 1st session: 1806–1807)
[text begins] At the GENERAL ASSEMBLY of the Province of | Nova-Scotia, begun and holden at Halifax, on the | Eighteenth day of November, 1806
COLLATION: 2° (29.4 x 21 cm), Tb^2 Vb–Yb^2 Zb^1 [$1 signed], 11 leaves, pp 508–529
CONTENTS: 508–529 text
PAPER: Wove, unmarked
TYPOGRAPHY: *Text*: pica, old face
49 ll., 217 (231) x 155 (180); 94 mm for 20 ll.
COPY EXAMINED: USMH-L

NS45 Nova Scotia. Lieutenant Governor (1792–1808: Wentworth)
SECRETARY'S OFFICE, | HALIFAX, 12th OCTOBER, 1807. | SIR, | HIS Excellency the Lieutenant-Governor has ordered me to de*ſ*ire, that you will, | immediately, a*ſſ*emble the Magi*ſ*trates of your County, or Di*ſ*trict, and that you | do agree, with them, on the mo*ſ*t effectual *ſ*teps to be taken to carry into the fulle*ſ*t | effect an Act pa*ſſ*ed in the 38th year of His pre*ſ*ent Maje*ſ*ty's reign, entitled, *An Act* | *re*ſ*pecting Aliens coming into this Province, or re*ſ*iding therein.* | ...
Order: 1 leaf (32.2 x 20 cm)
CONTENTS: 2 ll. heading; 1 l. salutation; 25 ll. text; 4 ll. signature
PAPER: Wove, unmarked
TYPOGRAPHY: *Text*: pica, old face. *Display*: two-line great primer drop letter
221 x 146 mm
NOTES: Under threat of war between the British and the Americans, government leaders in New Brunswick and Nova Scotia called up the militia and took measures to secure their territory. By this order masters of vessels and keepers of public houses and taverns could suffer a penalty of £100 for failure to give notice of 'Foreigners' in the province.
COPY EXAMINED: NSHP: RG1, vol 225, no 14

THE

TRIAL

OF

JOHN WILSON, *alias* JENKIN RATFORD,

FOR

MUTINY, DESERTION, AND CONTEMPT:

TO WHICH ARE SUBJOINED,

A FEW CURSORY REMARKS.

HALIFAX:
PRINTED BY JOHN HOWE AND SON.

NS47 Courtesy Metropolitan Toronto Reference Library

NS46 Nova Scotia. Parliament (9th, 1st session: 1806–1807). House of Assembly
[half title] [lattice and flower rule 150 mm] | JOURNAL | AND | PROCEEDINGS | OF | THE HOUSE OF ASSEMBLY, | 1806. | [lattice and flower rule 150 mm]
COLLATION: 2° (28.7 x 20.6 cm), *A*² B–I² K–T² V–2C² [$1 signed], 54 leaves, pp *1–4* 5–107 *108* (pagination in [ ])
CONTENTS: *1* half title; *2–3* proclamations; 4–107 text; *108* blank
PAPER: Laid, marked circles; chains vertical 26 mm
TYPOGRAPHY: *Text*: pica, old face. *Display*: title with rule as english 12 in Fry and Steele 1790 specimen; royal arms cut 40 x 88 mm
51 ll., 226 (238) x 151; 94 mm for 20 ll.
NOTES: The copy transmitted to the Colonial Office was certified by the speaker on 26 May 1807.
COPIES EXAMINED: NSHL, NSHP, GBPRO: CO 217, vol 81, ff 93–148

NS47 Wilson, John, defendant
THE | TRIAL | OF | JOHN WILSON, *ALIAS* JENKIN RATFORD, | FOR | MUTINY, DESERTION, AND CONTEMPT: | TO WHICH ARE SUBJOINED, | A FEW CURSORY REMARKS. | [thick-thin rule 29 mm] | HALIFAX: | PRINTED BY JOHN HOWE AND SON.
COLLATION: 8° (23.2 x 19.5 cm uncut), *A*⁸ B⁸ [B1 signed], 16 leaves, pp *1–3* 4–23, *i* ii–ix
CONTENTS: *1* title; 2 blank; *3*–23 trial; 23 execution; *i*–ix 'Remarks' dated at Halifax, 5 September 1807
PAPER: Laid, unmarked; chains vertical 29 mm
TYPOGRAPHY: *Text*: old face, pica with long primer for 'Remarks'
32 ll., 150 (162) x 92; 94 mm for 20 ll.
NOTES: Curiously the real name and the alias of the British seaman tried and executed at Halifax were reversed on the title page of this report. Jenkin Ratford, as he was known to the Royal Navy and at his trial, was a native of London serving on HMS *Halifax*. In March of 1807 he deserted with several companions and entered the American service as John Wilson on the frigate *Chesapeake*. Captured when the *Chesapeake* was taken by HMS *Leopard* on 22 June, Ratford was tried by court martial abord HMS *Belleisle* in Halifax harbour on 26 August. He was found guilty and sentenced 'to suffer death by being hung at the yard-arm' of His Majesty's sloop *Halifax* (p 22).

The day before his execution the *Weekly Chronicle* announced that Messrs Howe & Son would be publishing the proceedings 'in a few days' (28 August 1807). The unsigned 'Remarks,' probably John Howe's, are a review of the increasing tension between Britain and the United States, a mood exacerbated by the *Leopard–Chesapeake* incident. According to the writer 'The above ſtatement of facts is given, not to irritate or widen the breach between two nations, who ought to be in amity with each other. — Who, ſhould a conteſt enſue, might materially mar their mutual proſperity, without deriving any benefit from that conteſt' (p ix). Later when the breach between those two nations became war the *Chesapeake* was captured again, off Boston, on 1 June 1813, by HMS *Shannon* and towed into Halifax harbour.
COPIES EXAMINED: OTMCL, USMH-H
REFERENCE: TPL 816

1808

NS48 An Almanack for the Year of Our Lord, 1809
[within thick-thin rules 150 x 86 mm] AN | ALMANACK | FOR THE | Year of our Lord, 1809. | BEING THE FIRST YEAR AFTER BISSEXTILE OR LEAP YEAR: | *Calculated for the Meridian of* | HALIFAX IN NOVA-SCOTIA: | But will ſerve for any part of the Province; | CONTAINING [9 ll. to left of rule 26 mm] THE ECLIPSES | RISING and SITTING of | the SUN and MOON | TIME of HIGH WATER | FEASTS and FASTS of the | CHURCH | LIST of PROVINCIAL OF- | FICERS | SITTINGS of COURTS | [8 ll. to right] OFFICERS of the NAVY on | this STATION | OFFICERS of the ARMY | under Lieutenant-General | Sir GEORGE PREVOST, Bart. | OFFICERS of His Majeſty's | NAVY-YARD and HOS- | PITAL. | WITH EVERY OTHER MATTER USEFUL OR NECESSARY. | [thick-thin rule 79 mm] | BY THEOPHRASTUS. | [thin-thick rule 79 mm] | HALIFAX: | Printed and ſold by *JOHN HOWE & SON*, at their Office, | Barrington Street, near the Parade. *Stet* RISING and SITTING
COLLATION: 8° (22 x 13.2 cm), *A–B*⁸ C² [C1 signed], 18 leaves, pp [*36*]
CONTENTS: [*1*] title; [*2–3*] signals; [*3*] levee days, holidays; [*4–5*] roads and distances with houses of entertainment; [*6*] firewards, fire engine company; buoys; [*7*] eclipses, planets, vulgar notes; [*8*] man of signs; Parrsborough packet; [*9–20*] calendar; [*21–25*] civil list; [*25–26*] courts; [*27*] civil list; [*28–29*] freemasons; [*29*] civil list; [*30*] clergy of established

church; navy yard; [31–35] army; [36] ships; Marine Humane Society
PAPER: Laid, unmarked; chains vertical 27 mm
TYPOGRAPHY: *Text*: bourgeois, old face. *Display*: pages within thick-thin rules; man of signs cut (64 x 55 mm) is 1816 in Reilly; almanac signs
151 (156) x 87 mm
BINDING: Stitched (NSHD)
NOTES: A somewhat later date of publication this year is suggested by the Howes' *Royal Gazette* advertisement on 13 December and Archibald Cunningham's note 'Rec'd 22 Dec.r 1808' in the NSWA copy.
COPIES EXAMINED: NSHD (2 copies), NSWA, OOA

NS49 An Almanack for the Year of Our Lord, 1809

AN | ALMANACK, [open] FOR THE YEAR OF OUR LORD | 1809. [open] | *BEING THE FIRST AFTER BESEXTILE OR LEAP YEAR.* | CALCULATED FOR THE MERIDIAN OF | HALIFAX, *N.S.* [roman open] | *But will ferve for any part of the Province.* | CONTAINING | [7 ll. to left of thick-thin rule 18 mm] The Eclipfes | Rifing and fitting of the Sun | and Moon, | Time of high Water, | Feafts and Fafts of the Church, | Lift of Provincial Officers, | Sittings of Courts, | [7 ll. to right] Officers of the Navy on this | Station, | Officers of the Army, under | command of Lt. General | Sir GEORGE PREVOST, Bart. | Officers of His Majefty's Na- | vy Yard and Hofpital, &c. | *With other useful matter.* | [thick-thin rule 25 mm] | *BY A NATIVE.* | [thin-thick rule 27 mm] | *Halifax*: | Printed and fold by JAMES BAGNALL, at his Office in Sack- | ville Street, near the Halifax Grammar School. *Stent* BESEXTILE Rifing and fitting
COLLATION: 8° (15.7 x 10.6 cm), *1–4*^{4} 5^1, 17 leaves, pp [34]
CONTENTS: [1] title; [2–3] signals; [3] levee days, holidays; [3–5] roads and distances with houses of entertainment; [5] firewards, fire engine company; [6] clergy of established church; sheriffs; buoys; [7] eclipses; Parrsborough packet; miscellaneous: 'On Crowded Rooms'; [8] man of signs; planets, vulgar notes; [9–18] calendar with seasonal verses, September to December printed in 2 cols; [19–23] civil list; [23–24] courts; [24–25] civil list; [25–26] freemasons; [27–29] army, [30–31] ships; [32–34] army; [34] 'husbandry'; Maritime Humane Society
PAPER: Laid, 3 with part of mark SON; chains vertical 25 mm
TYPOGRAPHY: *Text*: brevier and bourgeois, old face. *Display*: man of signs cut (63 x 47 mm) with bellflower frame as NS3; almanac signs
133 x 76 mm
BINDING: Stitched (NSHD)
NOTES: James Bagnall, a native of Nova Scotia raised in Prince Edward Island, learned printing in Virginia as an apprentice to his brother-in-law William Alexander Rind. In 1804 Bagnall established a press in Charlottetown which had been without a printer since Rind's departure in 1798. Since the small and scattered population of the Island still offered little support Bagnall left the press in the charge of his brother and nephew in 1808 and moved to Halifax where he worked for two years in the old Henry / Gay shop before returning home (NS34). He advertised this almanac in the *Novator* on 10 April 1809.
COPIES EXAMINED: NSHD (lacking pp [33–34]), NSHP

NS50 Burke, Edmund, 1753–1820

A | TREATISE | ON | THE FIRST PRINCIPLES OF CHRISTIANITY, | IN WHICH ALL DIFFICULTIES STATED BY ANCIENT | AND MODERN SCEPTICS, ARE DISPASSION- | ATELY DISCUSSED. | [swelled rule 32 mm] | HALIFAX: | PRINTED BY JOHN HOWE and SON. | 1808.
COLLATION: 8° (23.3 x 14.8 cm uncut), π^2 A–I^4 K–T^4 χV^4 U–2I^4 2K^4 2L^2 [$1 (+A1) signed], 148 leaves, pp *i–iii* iv, *1* 2–292
CONTENTS: *i* title; *ii* blank; *iii*–iv dedication: To the Honorable HENRY AUGUSTUS DILLON, Colonel of the 101ft, or Duke of York's Irifh Regiment, &c. &c. &c. signed '*E. B.* V.G. QUE.' at Halifax, 8 November 1808; *1*–292 text headed [thick-thin rule 92 mm] | LAUS CHRISTO DEO NOSTRO EJUS QUE MATRI SEMPER | VIRGINI. E.B. | and signed on p 292 as dedication.
PAPER: π laid, marked 180[?]; A–X laid, unmarked; Y–2H wove, unmarked; 2I laid, marked M^S & C | 180[?]; 2K, 2L laid, marked fleur de lys (NSHP); OTMCL as NSHP except π laid, marked M^S & C; S laid, marked 1803; 2C laid, unmarked; OTUTF as NSHP except 2B, 2C, 2K laid, unmarked and 2E, 2H wove, marked M^S & C | 1807
TYPOGRAPHY: *Text*: pica, old face. *Display*: two-line great primer drop letter
36 ll., 169 (183) x 92; 94 mm for 20 ll.
NOTES: Perhaps a lull in the pamphlet war allowed Burke to prepare a work in which 'his ftrictures are confined to Anti-Chriftian Works' (p *iii*) rather than to his Protestant contemporaries in Nova Scotia.

COPIES EXAMINED: NSHP, OTMCL, OTUTF, QMBM, GBL, USMWA
REFERENCES: Akins, Gagnon II 271, TPL 821

NS51 Nova Scotia. [Billeting Act] 48 Geo III, 1808, c. 2
EXTRACTS from Provincial Acts relative to the marching of | His Maje*f*ty's Troops through Nova-Scotia: | [swelled rule 64 mm] | ...
Notice: 1 leaf (22.7 x 18.7 cm)
CONTENTS: 2 ll. heading; rule; 13 ll. text
PAPER: Laid, marked Britannia; chains vertical 26 mm
TYPOGRAPHY: *Text*: great primer, old face
158 x 147 mm
NOTES: An 'Abstract of Payments made for Rations to the Embodied Militia on the March to and from Halifax' in 1807 and 1808 has been recorded in manuscript on the verso of printed extracts from 'An Act to provide for the Accommodation and Billeting of His Majesty's Troops or of the Militia when on the march from one part of the province to another.' The total payment for meals, carts, and other supplies was £1040 5s 7½d.
COPY EXAMINED: NSHP: RG1, vol 440, no 1

NS52 Nova Scotia. Adjutant General of Militia
RULES AND REGULATIONS, | FOR THE | MILITIA FORCES | OF | NOVA-SCOTIA. | ALSO, | An Ab*f*tract of the Militia Laws; | And a Circular Letter to the In*f*pecting Field Officers of | DISTRICTS. | [thick-thin rule 14 mm] | HALIFAX: | PRINTED BY JOHN HOWE AND SON. | 1808.
COLLATION: 8° (15.5 x 11 cm), A^6 B–I^8 K^8 L^2 χ^1 [$1 signed], 80 leaves, pp *i–ii* iii–iv [4] *5* 6–156 [2] [χ^1 is a folded leaf (30.5 x 37 cm)]
CONTENTS: *i* title; *ii* blank; iii–iv introduction signed J. Beckwith Adjt. Genl. of Militia at Halifax, 9 July 1808; [1–3] index; [4] blank; *5*–152 text; 153–156 Circular letter to Field Officers from deputy adjutant general's office; [*1*] abstract of Militia laws; [2] table for return of arms
PAPER: Laid, watermark circles with cross | 1803; countermark G B[or R]INO; chains vertical 25 mm
TYPOGRAPHY: *Text*: long primer, old face
32 ll., 110 (120) x 63 (78); 69 mm for 20 ll.
ISSUED WITH
Nova Scotia [Militia Act] 48 Geo III, 1808, c. 1; [Billeting Act] 48 Geo III, 1808, c. 2
[caption title] *An* ABRIDGEMENT *of the Act, paffed in | 48th year of His prefent Majefty's reign, | for the better regulation of the* MILITIA *| of Nova-Scotia; and alfo of an Act, | paffed the fame year, for Quartering | and Billeting His Majefty's Troops, or | the Militia, on a March.*
COLLATION: 8° (14.5 x 9.5 cm), A^8 B^8 C^2 [$1 signed], 18 leaves, pp *1* 2–35 *36*
CONTENTS: *1*–35 text; *36* blank
PAPER: Laid, watermark circles with cross | 1803; countermark G B[or R]INO; chains vertical 25 mm
TYPOGRAPHY: *Text*: pica, old face. *Display*: two-line great primer
23 ll., 109 (117) x 63 (76); 95 mm for 20 ll.
BINDING: Leather pocket binding with boards outlined double blind and upper fore-edge extended all round to fit under a flap on the upper board. Wrapper of bluish gray paper retained under the leather (NSHD). Another copy in bluish gray wrapper with laid endpapers (NSHD). NSHP copy quarter sheep and shell marbled paper.
NOTES: Although the separately paged abridgement of the two militia acts is not indicated on the title page as a component of the *Rules and Regulations* volume it is cited in the index following 'Return of arms, accoutrements, &c.'

The printing account of John Howe and Son for 1808 includes 'one thou*f*and books of In*f*truction for the Militia' (Nova Scotia. Parliament (9th, 3rd session; 1808) House of Assembly. *Journal*, p 46).
COPIES EXAMINED: NSHD (2 copies), NSHL, NSHP
REFERENCES: Akins, Bishop

NS53 Nova Scotia. Court of Vice-Admiralty
THE | RIGHTS AND POWERS | OF | CAPTORS AND PRIZE AGENTS, | OVER | CAPTURES AND PROCEEDS, | BEFORE FINAL SENTENCE, CONSIDERED: | BEING THE SUBSTANCE OF A JUDGMENT PRONOUNCED | IN THE COURT OF VICE-ADMIRALTY AT HALIFAX, | UPON THE RETURN TO A MONITION IN | THE CASE OF THE HERKIMER, | ON THE 26th JANUARY, 1808. | [thick-thin rule 94 mm] | PUBLISHED AT THE REQUEST OF MANY OF THE GENTLEMEN | CONCERNED IN PRIZE CAUSES. | [thin-thick rules 94 mm] | HALIFAX: | PRINTED BY HOWE AND SON. | 1808.
COLLATION: 8° (18.9 x 12.4 cm cropped), A^4 B–E^4 F^2 [$1 signed], 22 leaves, pp <1–6> 7–41 *42–44*
CONTENTS: <1> title; <2> blank; <3>–41 text headed THE SUBSTANCE OF A JUDGMENT, | &c. &c. |; *42–44* blank
PAPER: Wove, *A* marked 1805; B–*F* unmarked
TYPOGRAPHY: *Text*: pica, old face, probably Caslon
35 ll., 165 (175) x 94; 94 mm for 20 ll.
NOTES: The case began when the *Herkimer*, loaded with copper in 'pigs,' Jesuit's bark (*cinchona*), and

cocoa, was taken on a voyage from Lima to New York by the *Leander* in February of 1806. The Court of Vice-Admiralty at Halifax condemned the captured ship as a prize to the privateers. Both the *Herkimer* and the cargo were then sold at auction in Halifax on 29 September for £41,671 19s 4d to Andrew Belcher, a local merchant. The owners of the *Herkimer* appealed the judgment but did not follow through before the time limit expired on 16 January 1808. The second case which came to court ten days later involved payment by Belcher of the hammer price for the ship and cargo, much of it captured or lost at sea in the interim. Belcher was ordered to pay the full amount with interest. The decision of Alexander Croke, judge of the Court of Vice-Admiralty from 1801 to 1815, was 'Just Published And for Sale' in March (*Royal Gazette*, 15 March 1808).
COPY EXAMINED: NSHP

NS54 Nova Scotia. Laws (9th Parliament, 2nd session: 1807–1808)
[text begins] At the GENERAL ASSEMBLY of the Province of | Nova-Scotia, begun and holden at Halifax, on Tueſday | the Eighteenth day of November, Anno Domini, | 1806 and continued by ſeveral Prorogations to Thurſ- | day the third day of December, 1807
COLLATION: 2° (29.4 x 21 cm), Aaa–Iii² Kkk¹ [$1 signed], 19 leaves, pp 530–567
CONTENTS: 530–567 text
PAPER: Wove, unmarked
TYPOGRAPHY: *Text*: pica, old face
47 ll., 223 (238) x 150 (177); 94 mm for 20 ll.
COPY EXAMINED: USMH-L

NS55
Nova Scotia. Laws (9th Parliament, 3rd session: 1808)
[text begins] At the GENERAL ASSEMBLY of the Province of | Nova-Scotia, begun and holden at Halifax, on | Tueſday the Eighteenth day of November, Anno | Domini, 1806, and continued by ſeveral Proroga- | tions to Thurſday the Nineteenth day of May, | 1808
COLLATION: 2° (29.4 x 21 cm), *A*² B² Mmm–Ppp² χ^1 [$1 signed], 13 leaves, pp 568–593
CONTENTS: 568–593 text
PAPER: Laid, unmarked; chains horizontal 28 mm; greenish
TYPOGRAPHY: *Text*: pica, old face
47 ll., 220 (234) x 150 (175); 94 mm for 20 ll.
NOTES: The House of Assembly voted a payment of £150 to John Howe and Son for printing 'on account of the extra Seſſion of the General Aſſembly, in May laſt' (*Journal*, 9:3, 1808, p 46).
COPY EXAMINED: USMH-L

NS56 Nova Scotia. Lieutenant Governor (1792–1808: Wentworth)
SECRETARY'S OFFICE, | HALIFAX, 20th FEBRUARY, 1808. | SIR, | I HAVE it in command from his Excellency the Lieutenant Governor, to acquaint | you, that in the event of the Negociation now pending between his Majeſty and | the Government of the *United States of America*, not terminating amicably; it may be | apprehended that attempts will be made, to distreſs this and the neighbouring Province | of *New-Brunſwick*, not only by land, but alſo by deſultory attacks upon the Settlements | on our Sea Coaſt. | In this mode of warfare, the enemy will naturally look for ſupplies of Proviſions in | the ſettlements they approach, from the Cattle, and other Live Stock that may be | found within their reach. | ...
Circular letter: 1/2° (32 x 20 cm)
CONTENTS: 3 ll. heading; 28 ll. text;
PAPER: Laid, marked [?] & M | 1803; chains vertical 27 mm
TYPOGRAPHY: *Text*: pica, old face
177 x 147 mm
NOTES: Still anticipating an outbreak of hostilities the lieutenant governor directed local leaders to organize a census of livestock including horses, cattle, sheep, and pigs, with a record of owners, the location of their settlements, and a route for removing the animals to safety. By this time the British policy of replacing civil governors by military men more able to take command in case of war had brought John Wentworth's long term to an end. Sir George Prevost, appointed lieutenant governor on 15 January 1808, arrived in Halifax on 7 April and assumed his duties later that month.
COPY EXAMINED: GBPRO: CO 217, vol 82, f 121

NS57 Nova Scotia. Parliament (9th, 2nd session: 1807–1808). House of Assembly
[half title] [lattice and flower rule 145 mm] | JOURNAL | AND | PROCEEDINGS | OF THE | HOUSE OF ASSEMBLY, | 1807. | [lattice and flower rule 145 mm]
COLLATION: 2° (28.7 x 20.6 cm), *A*² B–I² K–2C² 2D¹ [$1 signed], 57 leaves, pp *1–3* 4–114 (pagination in [ ])
CONTENTS: *1* half title; 2 proclamation; *3*–114 text
PAPER: Laid, most sheets watermark circles with cross | 1803; countermark P MIR^{B}; chains vertical 26 mm

TYPOGRAPHY: *Text*: pica, old face. *Display*: title with rule as english 12 in Fry and Steele 1790 specimen; royal arms cut 40 x 88 mm
49 ll., 223 (235) x 145; 94 mm for 20 ll.
COPIES EXAMINED: NSHL, NSHP

NS58 Nova Scotia. Parliament (9th, 3rd session: 1808). House of Assembly
[half title] [thick-thin rule 145 mm] | JOURNAL | AND | PROCEEDINGS | OF THE | HOUSE OF ASSEMBLY, 1808. | [thin-thick rule 145 mm]
COLLATION: 2° (28.7 x 20.6 cm), A^2 B–I^2 K^2 [$1 signed], 20 leaves, pp *1–3* 4–40 (pagination in [ ])
CONTENTS: *1* half title; *2* proclamation; *3*–40 text
PAPER: Laid, watermark circles with cross | 1803; countermark P MIR[E]; chains vertical 26 mm
TYPOGRAPHY: *Text*: pica, old face. *Display*: royal arms cut 40 x 88 mm
52 ll., 248 (254) x 141; 94 mm for 20 ll.
NOTES: This 'extra' session was the first summoned by George Prevost, the new lieutenant governor of the province.
COPY EXAMINED: NSHP

1809

NS59 An Almanack for the Year of Our Lord, 1810
[within thick-thin rules 150 x 84 mm] AN | ALMANACK | FOR THE | Year of Our Lord, 1810, | BEING THE SECOND AFTER BISSEXTILE OR LEAP YEAR: | *Calculated for the Meridian of* | HALIFAX IN NOVA-SCOTIA: | BUT WILL SERVE FOR ANY PART OF THE PROVINCE; | *CONTAINING:* | [9 ll. to left of rule 27 mm] THE ECLIPSES | RISING and SITTING of | the SUN and MOON | TIME of HIGH WATER | FEASTS and FASTS of the | CHURCH | LIST of PROVINCIAL OF- | FICERS | SITTINGS of COURTS | [8 ll. to right] OFFICERS of the NAVY on | this STATION | OFFICERS of the ARMY | under Lieutenant-General Sir | GEORGE PREVOST. Bart. | OFFICERS of His Maje*ſ*ty's | NAVY-YARD and HOS- | PITAL. | WITH EVERY OTHER MATTER USEFUL OR NECESSARY. | [thick-thin rule 76 mm] | BY THEOPHRASTUS. | [thick-thin rule 76 mm] | HALIFAX: | Printed and *ſ*old by *JOHN HOWE & SON*, at their office, | Barrington Street, near the Parade. *Stet* RISING and SITTING
COLLATION: 8° (21.5 x 13.8 cm uncut), A^8 B^8 C^2 [$1 signed], 18 leaves, pp *[36]*
CONTENTS: [*1*] title; [*2–3*] signals; [*3*] levee days, holidays; [*4–5*] roads and distances with houses of entertainment; [*6*] firewards, fire engine company; buoys; [*7*] eclipses, planets, vulgar notes; Marine Humane Society; [*8*] man of signs; Parrsborough packet; [*9–20*] calendar; [*21–25*] civil list; [*25–26*] courts; [*27*] civil list; [*28–29*] freemasons; [*29*] sheriffs; [*30*] clergy of established church; [*31–35*] army; [*35–36*] ships
PAPER: Laid, unmarked; chains vertical 27 mm
TYPOGRAPHY: *Text*: bourgeois, old face. *Display*: pages within thick-thin rules; man of signs cut (64 x 55 mm) is 1816 in Reilly; almanac signs
152 (154) x 87 mm
BINDING: Stitched (NSHD); OOA copy with lower wrapper of spot marbled paper, interleaved and used in the Military Secretary's Office to record sailings; NSWA copy interleaved, with wrapper
NOTES: The *Royal Gazette* and the *Weekly Chronicle* both carried an announcement of this almanac (5, 8 December 1809)
COPIES EXAMINED: NSHD, NSHL, NSHP, NSWA, OOA

NS60 Burke, Edmund, 1753–1820
REMARKS | *ON A PAMPHLET* | ENTITLED | POPERY CONDEMNED | BY | *Scripture and the Fathers.* | [rule 95 mm] | *Eftai gar kairos óte tēs ugiainousēs didafkalias ouk anexontai. Alla kata tas* | *epithumias tas idias, éautois episōreufoúfi didafkalous knēthomenoi tên akouên,"* | 2nd. Tim. iv. 3. | For there will he a time when they will not endure *ſ*ound doctrine, but | according to their *ſ*en*ſ*ual de*ſ*ires will heap to themselves teachers with | itching ears. | [rule 95 mm] | HALIFAX: | PRINTED BY HOWE AND SON, | 1809. *Stet* he
COLLATION: 8° (22.5 x 14 cm uncut), π^2 A^4 B–I^4 K–T^4 V^4 U^4 W–$2I^4$ 2K–$2T^4$ 2V–$3A^4$ $3B^2$ [$1 signed, missigning 2X as X], 204 leaves, pp [4] *1* 2–403 *404*
CONTENTS: [*1*] title; [*2*] blank; [3] introduction; [*4*] blank; *1*–403 text signed *E.B.* V.G.Q.; *404* 'Errata Correcta' (24 ll.)
PAPER: Wove, mixed lot of unmarked and marked at edge of sheet 1808 or IR & C° | 1804
TYPOGRAPHY: *Text*: pica, old face
38 ll., 178 (189) x 95; 93 mm for 20 ll.
NOTES: Characterizing *Popery Condemned* as 'a Pamphlet of uncommon bulk' (p *1*) Burke wrote almost twenty pages more than McCulloch's 386 to prove his opponent's work 'a thick veil of artifice, concealing an unbounded fund of ignorance' (p 3). McCulloch replied at even greater length with

Popery Again Condemned published in Edinburgh in 1810. Burke's response appeared the same year in a postscript to another work (**NS69**).
COPIES EXAMINED: NSHD, OTMCL, OTUTF, QMBM, GBL, USMBAt, USMWA
REFERENCES: Dennis, Gagnon II 272, TPL 847

NS61 Nova Scotia. Laws (9th Parliament, 4th session: 1808–1809)
[text begins] At the GENERAL ASSEMBLY of the Province of | Nova-Scotia, begun and holden at Halifax, on | Tueſday the Eighteenth day of November, Anno | Domini 1806, and continued by ſeveral Proroga- | tions to Thurſday the Twenty-fourth day of No- | vember, 1808
COLLATION: 2° (29.4 x 21 cm), Qqq–Sss² [$1 signed], 6 leaves, pp 594–604 *605*
CONTENTS: 594–604 text; *605* blank
PAPER: Unmarked, Qqq, Rrr laid, chains horizontal 28 mm, greenish; Sss wove
TYPOGRAPHY: *Text*: pica, old face
47 ll., 220 (232) x 150 (175); 94 mm for 20 ll.
COPY EXAMINED: USMH-L

NS62 Nova Scotia. Laws (9th Parliament, 5th session: 1809)
[text begins] At the GENERAL ASSEMBLY of the Province of | Nova-Scotia, begun and holden at Halifax, on | Tueſday the Eighteenth day of November, Anno | Domini 1806, and continued by ſeveral Proroga- | tions to Wedneſday the Seventh day of June, | 1809
COLLATION: 2° (29.4 x 21 cm), Ttt² Vvv² Uuu² [$1 signed], 6 leaves, pp 605–615 *616*
CONTENTS: 605–615 text; *616* blank
PAPER: Wove, unmarked
TYPOGRAPHY: *Text*: pica, old face
47 ll., 215 (233) x 148 (169); 94 mm for 20 ll.
COPY EXAMINED: USMH-L

NS63
Nova Scotia. Laws (9th Parliament, 6th session: 1809)
[text begins] At the GENERAL ASSEMBLY of the Province of | Nova-Scotia, begun and holden at Halifax, on | Tueſday the Eighteenth day of November, Anno | Domini 1806, and continued by ſeveral Proroga- | tions to Thurſday the Ninth day of November, | 1809
COLLATION: 2° (29.4 x 21 cm), Vvv² Uuu² Www–Zzz² [$1 signed], 12 leaves, pp 617–640
CONTENTS: 617–640 text
PAPER: Laid, Yyy marked in corner, probably 1805; chains vertical 30 mm
TYPOGRAPHY: *Text*: pica, old face
47 ll., 218 (230) x 145 (170); 94 mm for 20 ll.
BINDING: Rebound
COPY EXAMINED: USMH-L

NS64 Nova Scotia. Lieutenant Governor (1808–1811: Prevost)
[royal arms 40 x 90 mm] | PROCLAMATIONS. | [swelled rule 62 mm] | *PROCLAMATION.* [open] | BY HIS EXCELLENCY | SIR GEORGE PREVOST, Bart. | *Lieutenant Governor and Commander in Chief,* | *in and over His Majesty's Province of Nova-* | *Scotia and its Dependencies, &c. &c. &c.* | AND I DO ORDER ... | ... | that no Trade or Intercourſe, whatſoever, | ſhall be carried on between this Province, | and the United States of America, ſave and | except ſuch Trade and Intercourſe as is al- | lowed, and permitted, in and by the ſaid two | Acts of Parliament, and His Majeſty's Order | in Council, herein before mentioned. | ... | GIVEN under my Hand and Seal at Arms | at Halifax, this 27 day of April 1809, | in the 49th Year of His Majesty's | Reign. | GEORGE PREVOST. | ... | *God Save the King!*
Proclamation: 1 leaf (31.7 x 20.2 cm)
CONTENTS: royal arms; 1 l. heading; rule; text in three cols: 6 ll. heading; 60 ll. proclamation; 8 ll. closing; rule; 6 ll. heading; 55 ll. order in council dated 26 October 1808; 1 l. closing; rule; 6 ll. heading; 42 ll. proclamation; 8 ll. closing
PAPER: Laid, unmarked; chains vertical 26 mm
TYPOGRAPHY: *Text*: small pica, old face. *Display*: modern face open italic with swash A, M, N
301 x 87 mm
NOTES: In the aftermath of the *Leopard* and *Chesapeake* affair (**NS43**) the American government passed a series of laws forbidding trade with Britain. To counter this threat to Atlantic shipping Lieutenant Governor Prevost actively encouraged Americans to violate Jefferson's embargo by trading illegally at ports in Nova Scotia. The imperial order in council of 26 October 1808, published in his proclamation, designated Halifax and Shelburne, as well as Saint John, New Brunswick, as free ports. Prevost's involvement in trade policy is apparent in the dispatch to Lord Castlereagh enclosing this proclamation: 'so soon as I arrived I caused Proclamations conformable to the King's Order in Council to be iſsued, a printed copy of which I have the honor to inclose for Your

Lordships consideration – and in order to give the whole as much publicity as poſsible, copies have been forwarded to His Majesty's Minister, and Consuls in the United States' (GBPRO: CO 217, vol 85, ff 151–2). He issued the proclamation within two weeks of his arrival back in Halifax from a successful expedition against Martinique.
COPY EXAMINED: GBPRO: CO 217, vol 85, f 153

NS65 Nova Scotia. Parliament (9th, 4th session: 1808–1809). House of Assembly
[half title] [thick-thin rule 145 mm] | JOURNAL | AND | PROCEEDINGS | OF THE | HOUSE OF ASSEMBLY, | 1808. | [thin-thick rule 145 mm]
COLLATION: 2° (28.7 x 20.6 cm), A^2 B–I^2 K–T^2 V–2B $2C^2$ [$1 signed, missigning V2 as T], 54 leaves, pp *1–3* 4–102 *103–108* (4 in [ ])
CONTENTS: *1* half title; 2 proclamation; *3–108* text
PAPER: Laid, many sheets watermark circles with cross | 1803; countermark P MIR^E; chains vertical 26 mm
TYPOGRAPHY: *Text*: pica, old face. *Display*: royal arms cut 40 x 88 mm
47 ll., 221 (232) x 143; 93 mm for 20 ll.
COPIES EXAMINED: NSHL, NSHP

NS66 Nova Scotia. Parliament (9th, 5th session: 1809). House of Assembly
[half title] [thick-thin rule 143 mm] | JOURNAL | AND | PROCEEDINGS | OF | THE HOUSE OF ASSEMBLY, | 1809. | [thin-thick rule 143 mm]
COLLATION: 2° (28.7 x 20.6 cm), A^2 B–C^2 [$1 signed], 6 leaves, pp *1–3* 4–12
CONTENTS: *1* half title; 2 proclamation; 3–12 text
PAPER: Laid, watermark circles with cross | 1803; countermark P MIR^E; chains vertical 26 mm
TYPOGRAPHY: *Text*: pica, old face. *Display*: royal arms cut 40 x 88 mm
48 ll., 235 (247) x 143; 93 mm for 20 ll.
COPIES EXAMINED: NSHL, NSHP

NS67 Nova Scotia. Parliament (9th, 6th session: 1809). House of Assembly
[half title] [thick-thin rule 143 mm] | JOURNAL | AND | PROCEEDINGS | OF | THE HOUSE OF ASSEMBLY, | 1809. | [thin-thick rule 143 mm]
COLLATION: 2° (28.7 x 20.6 cm), A^2 B–I^2 K–T^2 χ^2 [$1 signed], 40 leaves, pp *1–3* 4–79 *80*
CONTENTS: *1* half title; 2 proclamation; 3–79 text; *80* blank
PAPER: Laid, watermark circles with cross | 1808; countermark P MIR^E; chains vertical 26 mm
TYPOGRAPHY: *Text*: pica, old face. *Display*: royal arms cut 40 x 88 mm
48 ll., 230 (242) x 142; 94 mm for 20 ll.
COPIES EXAMINED: NSHL, NSHP

1810

NS68 An Almanack for the Year of Our Lord, 1811
[within thick-thin rules 150 x 86 mm] AN | ALMANACK | FOR | *The Year of our Lord*, 1811, | BEING THE THIRD AFTER BISSEXTILE OR LEAP YEAR. | Calculated for the Meridian of | *Halifax, in Nova-Scotia;* | BUT WILL SERVE FOR ANY PART OF THE PROVINCE; | CONTAINING: | [9 ll. to left of rule 24 mm] THE ECLIPSES | RISING and SITTING of the | SUN and MOON | TIME of HIGH WATER | FEASTS AND FASTS OF THE | CHURCH | LIST of PROVINCIAL OFFI- | CERS. | SITTINGS of COURTS | [9 ll. to right] OFFICERS of the NAVY on | this STATION | OFFICERS of the ARMY, un- | der Lieutenant-General Sir | GEORGE PREVOST, Bart. | OFFICERS of the PROVINCI- | AL MILITIA | OFFICERS of His Majeſty's NA- | VY-YARD and HOSPITAL, | *With every other matter uſeful or neceſſary.* | [thick-thin rule 78 mm] | *By THEOPHRASTUS.* | [thin-thick rule 78 mm] | *Halifax*: | Printed and ſold by JOHN HOWE & SON, at their Office, Bar- | rington Street, near the Parade. *Stet* RISING and SITTING
COLLATION: 8° (21.5 x 13.5 cm uncut), *1–2*^{8} 3^1, 17 leaves, pp [34]
CONTENTS: [1] title; [2] signals; [3] levee days, holidays; firewards, fire engine company; [4] man of signs; eclipses; [*5–16*] calendar with verses including 'Rural Life'; an extract from Virgil; and 'Winter – An Ode'; [*17–21*] civil list; [*21–22*] courts; [*22–23*] civil list; [*24–25*] freemasons; [*25*] navy yard; Marine Humane Society; [*26*] clergy of established church; King's College; [*27–30*] army; [*30*] militia; [*31–32*] ships; [32] Parrsborough packet; buoys; planets, signs; [*33–34*] roads and distances with houses of entertainment
PAPER: Laid, unmarked; chains vertical 27 mm
TYPOGRAPHY: *Text*: bourgeois, old face. *Display*: pages within thick-thin rules; man of signs cut (63 x 47 mm) with bellflower frame as **NS3**; long dash of rimmed oval with tapered arrow sides; almanac signs
150 x 86 mm

BINDING: Stitched (NSHD); both OOA copies interleaved, one stitched in coarse grayish yellowish brown wrapper, the other, from the Military Secretary's Office, with upper wrapper of spot marbled paper. NSWA copy interleaved, retaining lower marbled wrapper
NOTES: Since John Howe Jr bought Bagnall's shop in 1810 it is not surprising to find here Anthony Henry's eighteenth century man of signs cut which Bagnall had used in his almanac the year before (NS49). The new Howe paper, John Jr's *Halifax Journal*, offered this almanac first on 26 November 1810 with repeats through December, then or into the spring with a last notice in September of 1811.
COPIES EXAMINED: NSHD (2 copies), NSHP (lacking pp [33–34]), NSWA, OOA (2 copies), QMMRB
REFERENCE: Lande S34

NS69 Burke, Edmund, 1753–1820
CONTINUATION | OF | THE FIRST PRINCIPLES | OF | CHRISTIANITY. | [swelled rule 36 mm] | HALIFAX: | PRINTED BY JOHN HOWE & SON. | 1810.
COLLATION: 8° (23 x 14.7 cm uncut), π^2 A–I[4] K–T[4] V–2I[4] 2K–2T[4] 2V–3H[4] 3I[2] [$1 (+A1) signed], 228 leaves, pp [4] *1* 2–449 *450–452*
CONTENTS: [*1–2*] blank; [3] title; [4] blank; *1*–400 text signed E.B. *V.G.Q.*; *401*–449 postscript; *450–451* contents; *452* errata (18 ll.)
PAPER: Wove, unmarked
TYPOGRAPHY: *Text*: pica, old face
38 ll., 178 (187) x 95; 94 mm for 20 ll.
BINDING: Wrapper of bluish greenish gray wove paper with light grayish yellowish brown paper spine. Wove endpapers (QMMRB); NBSAM copy unopened, binder's leaf at front
NOTES: Burke took an ironic tone in his postscript which was a reply to Thomas McCulloch's *Popery Again Condemned* published that same year in Edinburgh: 'Our Edinburgh Caſtigator, whoſe ſpirit of divination has opportunely diſcovered an inexhauſtible repertory of amuſing tales, and whoſse induſtry in tranſcribing is indefatigable; has once more condeſcended to gratify the curioſity of his readers with a new collection judiciouſly ſelected, and aſſorted' (p *401*).
A curious couplet signed 'Psalmanazer' was printed at end of a conventional advertisement for *Popery Again Condemned*, 444 pages bound in boards and priced at six shillings:

In hoc est hoax, cum quiz et joksez
Et smokem, roastem, toastem folksez;'
(*Weekly Chronicle*, 30 November 1810)

COPIES EXAMINED: NBSAM, NSHP, OTMCL, OTUTF, QMBM, QMMRB, GBL
REFERENCES: Dennis, Gagnon II 273, Lande S534, TPL 821

NS70 Fairbanks, Charles Rufus, 1790–1841 and Cochran, Andrew William, 1793–1849
REPORT | OF | *THE TRIAL* [open] | OF | EDWARD JORDAN, | AND | *MARGARET JORDAN HIS WIFE*, | FOR | PIRACY & MURDER, [open] | *AT HALIFAX ON THE* 15th *DAY OF NOVEMBER*, 1809, | TOGETHER WITH EDWARD JORDAN'S | DYING CONFESSION: | *TO WHICH IS ADDED* | THE TRIAL OF JOHN KELLY, | *FOR* | *PIRACY AND MURDER*, | ON THE 8th DAY OF DECEMBER, 1809. | *Tompilev* | *From Official Documents and Notes of the Trials.* | [thick-thin rule 48 mm] | BY C.R. FAIRBANKS & A.W. COCHRAN, | *STUDENTS at LAW*. | [thick-thin rule 48 mm] | HALIFAX, *Nova-Scotia*: | PRINTED BY JAMES BAGNALL, AT THE NOVATOR | OFFICE, SACKVILLE STREET. | [double dotted rule 14 mm] | 1810. *Stet Tompilev*
COLLATION: 4° (19.8 x 12.8 cm), *A*[4] (*A*1 + χ1) B–I[2] K–N[2] *O*[2], 31 leaves, pp *I–II* [2] *III* IV *5* 6–59 *60*
CONTENTS: *I* title; *II* blank; [*1*] dedication: 'To His Excellency Lieutenant-General Sir George Prevost' signed 'The Publishers' at Halifax, 5 March 1810; [*2*] blank; *III*–IV introduction; *5*–33 Jordan trial; 34–36 Jordan's confession; *37*–59 Kelly trial; *60* appendix
RT: TRIAL OF EDWARD AND MARGARET JORDAN. | | misprinted MAGARET pp 11, 24, 32; lacking period pp 7, 11, 16, 17, 20, 26, 27, 30, 33, 34; TRIAL OF JOHN KELLY. | | printed as THE ... p 44; lacking period pp 48, 54
PAPER: Laid, unmarked except *A* with mark unreadable and dedication leaf marked 18[?]; chains horizontal 27 mm
TYPOGRAPHY: *Text*: brevier, old face with double pica and script; printing Gaſpè. *Display*: short dash with penwork chain and long dash of rimmed oval with tapered arrow sides. Tail-piece with FINIS in panel surmounted by urn and palm leaves, swag beneath (86 in Fry and Steele catalogue)
44, 47 ll., 160 (170) x 93; 70 mm for 20 ll.
NOTES: The crimes of piracy and murder were committed aboard the *Three Sisters* by Edward Jordan who had built the schooner then lost it to the Tremains of Halifax, his creditors. Sailing as a passenger with his wife Margaret and their four young children, a nine-year old boy and his three sisters, Jordan seized the vessel on 13 September, killing two seamen and intimidating the mate John

Kelly. The captain escaped and gave notice of Jordan's crime. When the *Three Sisters* was captured both the Jordans and Kelly were returned to Halifax for trial. Margaret Jordan was found not guilty; Edward was condemned and hanged on 23 November; John Kelly was sentenced to death but recommended for pardon.

James Bagnall gave notice early in the new year that the Jordan trial was 'In the Press' (*Novator*, 22 January 1810). He announced it as 'just published' on 5 March (*ibid*); the same date appears on a dedication to the lieutenant general printed on a separate leaf and inserted between the title page and introduction. Bagnall sent copies for sale to New Brunswick (*Royal Gazette*, 2 April 1810) and Newfoundland (*Royal Gazette*, 14 June 1810).
COPY EXAMINED: NSHP
REFERENCE: Akins

NS71 Nova Scotia and New Brunswick Baptist Association
MINUTES, | *OF THE* | BAPTIST, NOVA-SCOTIA AND | NEW-BRUNSWICK, ASSOCIATION, | *HELD AT* | *Sackville in the Tounty of Weftmoreland,* | JUNE 25 & 26, | 1810; | TOGETHER WITH THEIR | CIRCULAR AND CORRESPONDING LETTERS. | [swelled rule 37 mm] | *HALIFAX*: | PRINTED BY JOHN HOWE & SON, | 1810. *Stent* NEW-BRUNSWICK, ASSOCIATION *Tounty*
COLLATION: 8° (16 x 11 cm), 1^8, 8 leaves, pp *1–3* 4–13 *14–16*
CONTENTS: *1* title; 2 blank; 3–7 text; 8–11 Circular Letter; 12–13 Corresponding Letter; *14–16* blank
PAPER: Laid, watermark postilion; countermark whale | ADRIAAN ROGGE (Churchill 81; Gravell and Miller, *Foreign*: 594, 595, 597); chains vertical 27 mm
TYPOGRAPHY: *Text*: english, old face; script for signatures. *Display*: tail-piece with FINIS banner on lance with laurel wreath and olive branch (84 in Fry and Steele catalogue)
28 ll., 131 (140) x 92; 92 mm for 20 ll.
NOTES: The Association voted to have six hundred copies printed. There were 924 members in fourteen congregations.
COPIES EXAMINED: NSWA, QMMRB
REFERENCE: Lande S114

1811

NS72 An Almanack for the Year of Our Lord, 1812
[within thick-thin rules 151 x 86 mm] AN | ALMANACK | FOR | *The Year of our Lord*, 1812, | BEING BISSEXTILE OR LEAP YEAR. | Calculated for the Meridian of | *Halifax, in Nova-Scotia;* | BUT WILL SERVE FOR ANY PART OF THE PROVINCE: | CONTAINING: | [8 ll. to left of rule 24 mm] THE ECLIPSES | RISING and SITTING of the | SUN and MOON | TIME of HIGH WATER | FEASTS AND FASTS OF THE | CHURCH | LIST of PROVINCIAL OFFI- | CERS. | [7 ll. to right] SITTINGS of COURTS | OFFICERS of the NAVY on | this STATION | OFFICERS of the ARMY, un- | der Major-General HUNTER | OFFICERS of His Majefty's NA- | VY-YARD and HOSPITAL, | *With every other matter ufeful or neceffary.* | [thick-thin rule 79 mm] | *By THEOPHRASTUS.* | [thin-thick rule 79 mm] | *Halifax*: | Printed and fold by JOHN HOWE & SON, at their Office, Bar- | rington Street, near the Parade. *Stet* RISING and SITTING
COLLATION: 8° (21.8 x 13.7 cm uncut), A^8 B^8 C^1 [B1 signed], 17 leaves, pp [34]
CONTENTS: [*1*] title; [*2*] signals; [*3*] levee days, holidays; firewards, fire engine company; [*4*] man of signs; eclipses; [*5–16*] calendar with verses including 'A Winter Song'; 'The Peasant's Comfort'; and an extract from Thomson's 'Hymn to the Seasons'; [*17–21*] civil list; [*21–22*] courts; [*22–23*] civil list; [*24–25*] freemasons; [*25*] navy yard; Marine Humane Society; [*26*] clergy of established church; King's College; [*27–31*] army; [*31–32*] ships; [*32*] buoys, planets, signs, vulgar notes; [*33*] Parrsborough packet; [*33–34*] roads and distances with houses of entertainment
PAPER: Laid, unmarked; chains vertical 27 mm
TYPOGRAPHY: *Text*: bourgeois, old face. *Display*: pages within thick-thin rules; man of signs cut (63 x 47 mm) with bellflower frame as **NS3**; almanac signs
151 (153) x 86 mm
BINDING: Stitched (NSHD); NSWA copy interleaved, with wrapper of spot marbled paper
NOTES: This edition was advertised in the usual format, folded and stitched, or interleaved for use as a journal or diary, a refinement available in marbled paper copies of Anthony Henry's *Nova-Scotia Calender* more than thirty years earlier (Tremaine 302; *Royal Gazette*, 20 November 1811; *Halifax Journal*, 18 November, 16 December).
COPIES EXAMINED: NSHD, NSHL, NSHP (lacking pp [33–34]), NSWA, OOA (lacking pp [1–2])

NS73 Monro, James, d. 1819

A | TREATISE | ON | BAPTISM: | WHEREIN IS BRIEFLY SHEWN WHEN BAPTISM WAS IN- | TRODUCED INTO THE CHURCH. | II; JOHN'S BAPTISM BRIEFLY CONSIDERED. | III. THE BAPTISM OF SUFFERINGS. | IV. THE BAPTISM OF THE HOLY GHOST. | V. CONSIDERED AT LARGE CHRISTIAN BAPTISM, OR | THAT APPOINTED BY OUR LORD, AND WHICH WE | FIND RECORDED BY THE EVANGELIST, MATTHEW, | CHAP. 28. 16. TO THE END. | [double rule 95 mm] | BY JAMES MONRO, | MINISTER OF THE GOSPEL DORCHESTER, NOVA-SCOTIA. | [double rule 95 mm] | Acts 2.38.39. Then Peter ſaid unto them Repent, and be Baptiſed every | one of you for the Remiſſion of Sins, and ye ſhall receive the gift of the | Holy Ghoſt: for the promiſe is to you, and to your Children and to all | that are afar off: even as many as the Lord our God ſhall call. | [swelled rule 47 mm] | HALIFAX: | PRINTED BY HOWE & SON. | 1811.

COLLATION: 8° (23 x 14.5 cm uncut), A^4 B–I^4 K–T^4 V–$2C^4$ 2D–$2I^2$ 2K–$2T^2$ $2V^2$ $2W^4$ [$1 signed], 146 leaves, pp *1–5* 6–212, [2]*1–3* 4–78 *79–80*

CONTENTS: *1* title; 2 blank; *3–4* preface dated at Dorchester, 19 July 1811; *5*–208 text; 209–212 Postscript; [2]*1* half title APPENDIX: | IN WHICH THERE IS A CANDID ENQUIRY OR | EXAMINATION OF DIVERS TEXTS, WHICH | THOSE THAT ARE OPPOSED TO IN- | FANT BAPTISM AND SPRINKLING, | THINK MAKE FOR THEM. |; [2]2 blank; [2]3–78 text; *79–80* blank

PAPER: Wove, unmarked

TYPOGRAPHY: *Text*: pica, old face

38 ll., 174 (186) x 96; 94 mm for 20 ll.

BINDING: Wrapper made up of several layers of coarse brownish paper pasted and sewn over blue; wove endpapers, free lacking at front (NBSM); NSHD copy retaining upper wrapper of bluish gray paper pasted over stiff yellowish white paper

NOTES: An obituary notice for Mr Monro published in 1819 by John Howe identified him as 'in the 80th year of his age' and a 'Minister of the National Church of Scotland' who had 'distinguished himself for diligence and fidelity as a Preacher of the Gospel, in his native country and in this Province' for fifty years. Mr Howe, Monro's printer, added: 'Some years ago he published in this town, a valuable treatise on Baptism, which is less known than it ought to be' (*Halifax Journal*, 31 May 1819). Monro's death at Antigonish was also noted in the *Chronicle* (28 May) and *Free Press* (1 June).

COPIES EXAMINED: NBSAM, NSHD (lacking pp [2]11–*80*), NSWA, QMBM, QMMRB

REFERENCES: Dennis, Gagnon I 2417

NS74 Nova Scotia. [School Act] 51 Geo III, 1811, c. 8

SCHOOL ACT. | The following ACT, paſſed in the laſt Seſſion of the General Aſſembly, is Publiſhed by Authority. | An ACT for Encouraging the Eſtabliſhment of Schools throughout the Province. | ... | NOVA-SCOTIA ROYAL GAZETTE OFFICE, APRIL, 1811.

Act: 1° (30.8 x 42.4 cm)

CONTENTS: 3 ll. heading; 2 cols of text with imprint

PAPER: Laid, unmarked; chains vertical 26 mm

TYPOGRAPHY: *Text*: pica, old face. *Display*: old face canon for heading

285 x 304 mm

NOTES: By this act communities of thirty families or households were permitted to organize schools and receive grants from the provincial government. A grammar school act (c. 9) passed the same year.

COPY EXAMINED: NSHP: MG1, vol 106, no 37

NS75 Nova Scotia. Court of Vice-Admiralty

The | *SUBSTANCE OF A DECISION,* | IN | The Court of Vice-Admiralty at Halifax, | UPON A PETITION FROM THE DEPUTY TO | *The Treaſurer of Greenwich Hoſpital,* | AGAINST | *The Prize Agents of the Bermuda,* | FOR CERTAIN UNCLAIMED SHARES OF PRIZE-MONEY DUE TO | THE HOSPITAL, | Delivered on the 8th May, 1811. | [thick-thin rule 92 mm] | *Published at the suggestion of some of the Gentlemen of the Profession.* | [thin-thick rule 92 mm] | HALIFAX: | PRINTED BY HOWE AND SON. | 1811.

COLLATION: 8° (19.9 x 12.8 cm), A^4 B–C^4 D^2 [$1 signed], 14 leaves, pp *1–3* 4–28

CONTENTS: *1* title; 2 blank; 3–27 text; 27–28 Act: 1 Geo III, 1760, c.8, § 1, 2, 7, 8

PAPER: Wove, unmarked

TYPOGRAPHY: *Text*: english, old face

34 ll., 158 (166) x 95; 94 mm for 20 ll.

NOTES: Unclaimed prize money from the capture by the *Bermuda* of the ships *Venus* and *Charles* amounted to £45 2d, the share due to Owen Cotten for his work as captain's clerk on the *Bermuda*. However Cotten had since been declared an absent or absconding debtor opening the way for a petition by Greenwich Hospital which was entitled by the prize act to all unclaimed shares. The Court of Vice-Admiralty decided in favour of the hospital and ordered the prize agents of the *Bermuda* to pay out Cotten's share.

The printed decision was advertised for sale at the shop of William Minns, John Howe's brother-in-law, for a price of 1s 6d early in July (*Journal*, 8 July; *Royal Gazette*, 17 July).
COPY EXAMINED: NSHP
REFERENCE: Akins

NS76 Nova Scotia. Laws (9th Parliament, 7th session: 1811)
[text begins] At the GENERAL ASSEMBLY of the Province of | Nova-Scotia, begun and holden at Halifax, on | Tuefday the Eighteenth day of November, Anno | Domini, 1806, and continued by feveral Prorogati- | ons to Thurfday the Fourteenth Day of February, | 1811
COLLATION: 2° (29.4 x 21 cm), A3–I3² K3¹ [$1 signed], 19 leaves, pp 641–678
CONTENTS: 641–678 text
PAPER: Laid, A3 marked 1809, D3–G3 marked [?] C | 1804; chains horizontal 30 mm
TYPOGRAPHY: *Text*: pica, old face
46 ll., 215 (230) x 150 (174); 94 mm for 20 ll.
COPY EXAMINED: USMH-L

NS77 Nova Scotia. Parliament (9th, 7th session: 1811). House of Assembly
[half title] [thick-thin-thin rule 136 mm] | JOURNAL | AND | PROCEEDINGS | OF THE | HOUSE OF ASSEMBLY, | 1811. | [thin-thin-thick rule 136 mm]
COLLATION: 2° (28.7 x 20.6 cm), *A–B*² C–I² K–U² W–2C² 2D¹ [$1 (-F) signed], 55 leaves, pp *1–3* 4–110
CONTENTS: *1* half title; 2 proclamation; 3–110 text
PAPER: Laid, *A*–N, S watermark circles with cross | 1803; countermark P MIR^E; rest unmarked; chains vertical 26 mm
TYPOGRAPHY: *Text*: pica, old face. *Display*: royal arms cut 40 x 88 mm
47 ll., 225 (238) x 145; 94 mm for 20 ll.
COPIES EXAMINED: NSHL, NSHP

NS78 Nova Scotia and New Brunswick Baptist Association
MINUTES, | *OF THE* | NOVA-SCOTIA AND NEW-BRUNSWICK | BAPTIST ASSOCIATION, | *HELD AT THE* | *Meeting-House* | *IN* | ONSLOW, | *JUNE 24th* & *25th*, | 1811; | TOGETHER WITH THEIR CIRCULAR AND CORRESPONDING LETTERS. | [swelled rule 37 mm] | *HALIFAX:* | PRINTED BY JOHN HOWE & SON, | 1811.
COLLATION: 8° (19.1 x 12.5 cm), *1*⁸, 8 leaves, pp *1–3* 4–14 *15–16*
CONTENTS: *1* title; 2 blank; 3–8 text; 9–12 Circular Letter; 13–14 Corresponding Letter; *15–16* blank
PAPER: Laid, watermark post horn in crowned shield | [J H]ONIG; countermark J HO[NIG]; chains vertical 27 mm
TYPOGRAPHY: *Text*: pica, old face. *Display*: row of section marks; tail-piece (p 14) with FINIS in panel surmounted by urn and palm leaves, swag beneath (86 in Fry and Steele catalogue)
28 ll., 131 (141) x 87; 95 mm for 20 ll.
NOTES: The twentieth resolution 'Appointed Brother Burton to fuperintend printing of the Minutes: feven hundred Copies to be printed' (p 7). Membership now exceeded twelve hundred an increase of three hundred in a year.
COPY EXAMINED: NSWA

1812

NS79 An Almanack for the Year of Our Lord, 1813
[within thick-thin rules 152 x 86 mm] AN | ALMANACK | FOR | *The Year of our Lord*, 1813, | BEING THE FIRST AFTER BISSEXTILE OR LEAP YEAR. | Calculated for the Meridian of | *Halifax, in Nova-Scotia*, | BUT WILL SERVE FOR ANY PART OF THE PROVINCE. | CONTAINING: | [8 ll. to left of rule 22 mm] THE ECLIPSES | RISING and SITTING of the | SUN and MOON | TIME of HIGH WATER | FEASTS and FASTS of the | CHURCH | LIST of PROVINCIAL OFFI- | CERS | [8 ll. to right] SITTINGS of COURTS | OFFICERS of the NAVY on | this STATION | OFFICERS of the ARMY, un- | der Lieutenant-General Sir | JOHN COAPE SHERBROOKE, K.B., | OFFICERS of His Majefty's NA- | VY-YARD and HOSPITAL. | *With every other matter ufeful or neceffary.* | [thick-thin rule 78 mm] | *By THEOPHRASTUS.* | [thin-thick rule 78 mm] | *Halifax*: | Printed and fold by JOHN HOWE & SON, at their Office, Bar- | rington-Street, near the Parade. *Stet* RISING and SITTING
COLLATION: 8° (21.7 x 13 cm uncut), *1*–2⁸ 3¹, 17 leaves, pp [34]
CONTENTS: [1] title; [2] signals; [3–4] roads and distances with houses of entertainment;

Parrsborough packet; [5] levee days, holidays; firewards, fire engine company; [6] man of signs; eclipses, chronological notes; [7–18] calendar with verses including 'Lines addressed to a young Lady on New Year's Day, 1813'; 'Sonnet'; and 'On an Hour Glass'; [19–23] civil list; [23–24] courts; [24–25] civil list; [26–27] freemasons; [27] navy yard; Marine Humane Society; [28] clergy of established church; King's College; [29–33] army; [33–34] ships
PAPER: Laid, unmarked; chains vertical 27 mm
TYPOGRAPHY: *Text*: bourgeois, old face. *Display*: pages within thick-thin rules with corner ornaments; man of signs cut (63 x 47 mm) with bellflower frame as **NS3**; long dash of rimmed oval with tapered arrow sides; almanac signs
149 x 85 mm
BINDING: Stitched (NSHD); NSHD, NSWA, and one OOA copy in wrappers of spot marbled paper with interleaving
NOTES: The almanac was announced for sale on 23 December (*Royal Gazette*).
COPIES EXAMINED: NSHD (2 copies), NSHL (lacking pp [33–34]), NSHP (2 copies), NSWA, OOA (2 copies)

NS80 Bermuda. Court of Vice-Admiralty
THE CASE | OF | THE LEGAL TENDER, | ARGUED BEFORE, AND DECIDED BY, THE JUDGE OF | THE VICE-ADMIRALY COURT AT BERMUDA, | 1812, | FOR A BREACH OF THE REVENUE LAWS. | [row of section marks 14 mm] | HALIFAX: | PRINTED BY HOWE AND SON.
Stet ADMIRALY
COLLATION: 8° (19 x 12 cm), *1*⁴ 2¹, 5 leaves, pp *1–3* 4–10
CONTENTS: *1* title; 2 blank; 3–10 text
PAPER: Laid, marked JOHN [?]; chains vertical 24 mm
TYPOGRAPHY: *Text*: pica, old face, Caslon
29 ll., 136 (144) x 82; 94 mm for 20 ll.
COPY EXAMINED: NSHP

NS81 British North America. Commander of British Forces (1811–1815: Prevost)
(CIRCULAR.) | HALIFAX, 10th JULY, 1812. | SIR, | HIS Excellency the Commander in Chief, having given ſufficient time to | put the General Order of the 1ſt Inſt. into force, is now pleaſed to expreſs his in- | tention, to call out, and Embody, in the diſtrict of each Battalion, one Company, | conſiſting of the fifth of the firſt Claſs, (agreeably to the detail herewith ſent) to be | Stationed at [space] for the purpoſe of being drilled and | diſciplined. | ...
COLLATION: 2° (32.2 x 20.2 cm), *1*², 2 leaves, pp [4]
CONTENTS: [*1–2*] text (to be completed in ms); [*3–4*] blank
PAPER: Laid, watermark Britannia; countermark TAVERHAM | 1809; chains vertical 28 mm
TYPOGRAPHY: *Text*: english, transitional old face
214 x 150 mm
NOTES: Appointed in 1811 as governor-in-chief of British North America and commander of the British forces serving there Prevost faced the United States, which had declared war on Britain on 18 June 1812, with fewer than 6000 regular troops. He called out the militia in July to guard coastal areas from attack (**NS85**).
COPY EXAMINED: NSHP: RG1, vol 440, no 20

NS82 Church of England
[within thick-thin rules 159 x 110 mm] | A | FORM | OF | PRAYER, | TO BE USED | In all Churches, Chapels, and Places of | PUBLIC WORSHIP, according to the uſage of the CHURCH | of ENGLAND, throughout His Majeſty's Province of NOVA- | SCOTIA, on WEDNESDAY, the NINETEENTH Day of FEBRU- | ARY, 1812: being the Day appointed by Proclamation | for a GENERAL FAST and HUMILIATION before ALMIGH- | TY GOD; to be obſerved in the moſt devout and ſolemn | manner, by ſending up our PRAYERS and SUPPLICATIONS | to the DIVINE MAJESTY: | For obtaining Pardon of our Sins, and for averting thoſe heavy Judg- | ments which our manifold Provocations have moſt juſtly deſerved; | imploring his Bleſſing and Aſſiſtance on His Majeſty's Arms by Sea | and Land, and for reſtoring and perpetuating Peace, Safety and | Proſperity, to Himſelf, and to His Kingdom. | [rule 100 mm] | By Command of His Excellency the Lieutenant Governor. | [thin-thick rule 102 mm] | HALIFAX: | Printed by JOHN HOWE and SON, Printers to the KING'S Moſt | Excellent MAJESTY. 1812.
COLLATION: 4° (18.7 x 13.3 cm cropped), *A*⁴ B⁴ [B1 signed], 8 leaves, pp *1–3* 4–16
CONTENTS: *1* title; 2 blank; 3–16 text
PAPER: Laid, *A* watermark circles with cross | 1803; countermark B JUMERE | ; B unmarked; chains horizontal 26 mm
TYPOGRAPHY: *Text*: english, old face
33 ll., 153 (166) x 102; 94 mm for 20 ll.
COPY EXAMINED: NSHP

NS83 Directions for Avoiding the Sambro Ledges

Directions, | [swelled rule 68 mm] | For avoiding the Ledges lying to the Ea*f*tward and We*f*tward of Sambrô-I*f*land, whereon | is now erected a Light-Hou*f*e; for entering the Harbour of Halifax. in Nova-Scotia, | Sambrô-I*f*land is in 44. 32. North Latitude, and 63. 10. We*f*t Longitude from London. | ...

Notice: 1/2° (23 x 19.5 cm)

CONTENTS: 1 l. heading; rule; 35 ll. text

PAPER: Laid, marked CURTEIS & SONS | 1794; chains vertical 28 mm

TYPOGRAPHY: *Text*: pica, old face

216 x 154 mm

NOTES: As early as 1752 the government of Nova Scotia had tried to raise money to build a light-house on Sambro Island commanding the outer approaches to Halifax harbour, but the light was not completed until late in 1758. A chart with sailing directions was then made by Charles Morris, first surveyor general of the province. Sailing directions for Halifax harbour dated 1762 and attributed to Captain Cook name the light as a point of reference in the opening sentence (Hugh F. Pullen, *The Sea Road to Halifax*. Halifax: Nova Scotia Museum, 1980, 18–23).

Evidence for assigning a date to this edition of directions is scant, even contradictory: paper marked 1794, old face type which lingered on in Nova Scotia until at least 1815, and a manuscript date of '1812' in the margin. Perhaps increased navigation and the outbreak of war required the publication of sailing directions in the latter year. Another edition is located in the same collection (**NS120**).

COPY EXAMINED: NSHP: RG1, vol 249, no 1

NS84 Nova Scotia. Adjutant General of Militia

RULES AND ARTICLES | FOR THE BETTER GOVERNMENT OF THE | MILITIA FORCES | OF THIS PROVINCE, | WHILE EMBODIED ON ACTUAL SERVICE. | [swelled rule 39 mm] | HALIFAX: | PRINTED BY JOHN HOWE & SON, | PRINTERS to the KING'S mo*f*t Excellent MAJESTY. | 1812.

COLLATION: 8° (18.7 x 12.6 cm), A^4 [$A2 + \chi 1$] B^4 C^4 [C1 signed], 13 leaves, pp *1–4* [2] *5* 6–24 (incomplete)

CONTENTS: *1* title; *2* blank; *3* proclamation by the lieutenant general, 9 July 1812; *4* blank; [*1*] Militia General Orders signed J. Beckwith, adjutant general militia, 1 August 1812; [*2*] blank; *5*–24 text (ending mid-sentence)

PAPER: Wove, *B* marked 1809, χ marked R | 1807; rest unmarked

TYPOGRAPHY: *Text*: bourgeois, modern face

40 ll., 139 (149) x 80 (103); 67 mm for 20 ll.

NOTES: *Rules and Regulations for the Militia Forces of Nova-Scotia* had been published in 1808 when the province was anticipating war (**NS52**). This incomplete work includes an order clarifying the punishment to which militia men were subject dated 1 August and inserted as a single leaf ahead of the text.

COPY EXAMINED: NSHP

REFERENCES: Akins, Bishop

NS85 Nova Scotia. Deputy Commissary General

DEPUTY COMMISSARY-GENERAL'S OFFICE, | *Halifax, Nova-Scotia, 4th Aug*. 1812. | SIR, | THE Militia being called out, and about to take po*f*t in various | *f*tations on the Coa*f*t within this Province, and it being the wi*f*h | of His Excellency the Lieutenant-General Commanding to furni*f*h them, as | far as may be, with *f*upplies of Provi*f*ions, in the manner that the Regular | Forces are *f*upplied ... | ...

Public notice: 1 leaf (32.6 x 20.2 cm)

CONTENTS: 2 ll. heading; 1 l. salutation; 26 ll. text; 4 ll. closing (to be completed in ms); 4 ll. address (to be completed in ms)

PAPER: Laid, marked [in a circle] KG | 1811; chains vertical 24 mm

TYPOGRAPHY: *Text*: english, old face

210 x 144 mm

NOTES: Prevost's plan for stationing militia forces along the coast required colonels of militia to negotiate local purchase of provisions.

COPY EXAMINED: NSHP: RG 1, vol 440, no 27

NS86 Nova Scotia. Laws (10th Parliament, 1st session: 1812)

[text begins] At the GENERAL ASSEMBLY of the Province of | Nova-Scotia, begun and holden at Halifax, on | Thur*f*day the Sixth day of February, 1812

COLLATION: 2° (29.4 x 21 cm), L3–$Q3^2$ $R3^1$ $S3^2$ $T3^1$ [$1 signed], 16 leaves, pp 679–710 (709 printed with period)

CONTENTS: 679–711 text

PAPER: Wove, M3–O3, Q3, S3 marked D & AC | 1808

TYPOGRAPHY: *Text*: pica, old face

47 ll., 226 (239) x 148 (166); 94 mm for 20 ll.

NOTES: 'A few setts of the Laws' of this session were offered for sale by John Howe, (*Royal Gazette*, 27 May 1812).
COPY EXAMINED: USMH-L

NS87 Nova Scotia. Lieutenant Governor (1811–1816: Sherbrooke)
[royal arms flanked by military emblems 74 x 203 mm] | PROCLAMATION. | By His Excellency Lieutenant General | Sir JOHN COAPE SHERBROOKE, | ... | ... WHEREAS every ſpecies of predatory warfare carried on againſt Defenceleſs In- | habitants, living on the ſhores of the United States, contiguous to this Province | and New Brunſwick, can anſwer no good purpoſe, and will greatly diſtreſs Individuals: | I have therefore thought proper, by and with the advice of His Majeſty's Council, to order | and direct all His Majeſty's Subjects, under my Government, to abſtain from Mo- | leſting the Inhabitants living on the ſhores of the United States, continguous to this Po- | vince and New Brunſwick ... | ... | GIVEN under <my> Hand and Seal at Arms, at Halifax, this | 3d day of July, 1812, in the 52d Year of His Majeſty's Reign. *stet* Po- | vince
Proclamation: 1 leaf (36 x 24 cm)
CONTENTS: royal arms; 7 ll. heading; 16 ll. text; 5 ll. closing signed Sherbrooke and H.H. Cogswell
PAPER: Wove, unmarked
TYPOGRAPHY: *Text*: great primer, transitional face 348 x 207 cm
NOTES: An experienced military commander, John Coape Sherbrooke was appointed to succeed George Prevost as lieutenant governor on 19 August 1811. He arrived in Halifax on 16 October to begin a successful term as civil administrator. Soon after the American declaration of war Sherbrooke issued this proclamation ordering Nova Scotians to keep the peace with their neighbours. He explained his action in a letter to Lord Liverpool, secretary of state for War and the Colonies until his election as prime minister in June of 1812: 'I have further thought it right ... to iſsue a Proclamation of which I transmit a copy No 2, as we hope by these means to encourage and diffuse a friendly disposition, which appears inclined to manifest itself in some of the States in our more immediate neighbourhood.' He went on to say that the American declaration of war was 'very unpopular' in the eastern and northern states (GBPRO: CO 217, vol 89, ff 114–7).

The *Halifax Journal* which was printed by John Howe Jr, son of the king's printer and proprietor of the *Royal Gazette*, reprinted the proclamation 'published at the Gazette Office on Friday last' commending the lieutenant governor: 'We highly applaud the motive that dictated it' (6 July 1812).

Sherbrooke's colleague in New Brunswick, George Stracey Smyth, issued a similar order a week later (**NB39**).
COPY EXAMINED: GBPRO: CO 217, vol 89, f 120

NS88 Nova Scotia. Parliament (10th, 1st session: 1812). House of Assembly
[half title] [thick-thin rule 136 mm] | JOURNAL | AND | PROCEEDINGS | OF | THE HOUSE OF ASSEMBLY, | 1812. | [thin-thick rule 137 mm]
COLLATION: 4° (26.5 x 18.5 cm), *A–B*^{2} C–H^2 χG–H^2 I^2 K–T^2 V–2H^2 [\$1 signed], 68 leaves, pp *1–5* 6–136
CONTENTS: *1* half title; 2 blank; *3–4* proclamations; 5–136 text
PAPER: Laid, marks cropped; chains horizontal 27 mm
TYPOGRAPHY: *Text*: pica, old face. *Display*: royal arms cut 38 x 68 mm
47 ll., 216 (227) x 140; 94 mm for 20 ll.
NOTES: The proclamations for this session were issued on 11 August, 20 September, and 4 November 1811, with the first signed by Prevost, lieutenant governor to 25 August, and the second by Alexander Croke, judge of the Vice-Admiralty Court and administrator of the province until Sherbrooke's arrival on 16 October 1811.
COPY EXAMINED: NSHP

NS89 Nova Scotia. Parliament (10th, 2nd session: 1812). House of Assembly
[half title] [thick-thin rule 144 mm] | JOURNAL | AND | PROCEEDINGS | OF | THE HOUSE OF ASSEMBLY, | 1812. | [thin-thick rule 144 mm]
COLLATION: 4° (26.5 x 18.5 cm), *A*^{2} B–D^2 χD–F^2 [\$1 signed], 14 leaves, pp *1–3* 4–27 *28*
CONTENTS: *1* half title; 2 proclamation; 3–27 text; *28* blank
PAPER: Laid, marks cropped; chains horizontal 27 mm
TYPOGRAPHY: *Text*: pica, old face. *Display*: royal arms cut 38 x 68 mm
45 ll., 222 (234) x 145; 94 mm for 20 ll.
COPIES EXAMINED: NSHL, NSHP

NS90 Nova Scotia and New Brunswick Baptist Association
MINUTES, | OF THE | Nova-Scotia and New-Brunſwick [script] | BAPTIST ASSOCIATION, | HELD AT THE | *Baptiſt Meeting – Houſe* | IN |

UPPER GRANVILLE, | *June* 22 & 23, | 1812; | TOGETHER WITH THEIR | *Circular and Correfponding Letters.* | [thick-thin rule 9 mm] | HALIFAX: | PRINTED BY HOWE & SON, | 1812.
Stet Noufe
COLLATION: 8° (20 x 15.3 cm uncut), *1–2*⁴, 8 leaves, pp *1–3* 4–14 *15–16*
CONTENTS: *1* title; 2 blank; *3–7* text; *8*–12 Circular Letter; 13–14 Corresponding Letter; *15–16* blank
PAPER: Laid, unmarked; chains vertical 28 mm
TYPOGRAPHY: *Text*: english, old face; script for headings and signatures
30 ll., 137 (144) x 108; 92 mm for 20 ll.
BINDING: Stitched (GBL)
NOTES: In their fifteenth resolution his colleagues 'Appointed Brother *Burton* to ſuperintend the printing of the Minutes: four hundred copies to be printed' (p 6). A further resolution required that 'each Church ... raise upon an average ſix-pence for each Member ... for the purpose of defraying the expenſe of printing the Minutes, &c.' (pp 6–7). The minutes listed 1295 members, corrected in manuscript to 1371.
COPIES EXAMINED: NSWA, GBL

1813

NS91 An Almanack for the Year of Our Lord, 1814

[within thick-thin rules with corner ornaments 148 x 85 mm] AN | ALMANACK | FOR | *The Year of Our Lord*, 1814 | BEING THE SECOND AFTER BISSEXTILE OR LEAP YEAR. | Calculated for the Meridian of | *Halifax, in Nova-Scotia,* | BUT WILL SERVE FOR ANY PART OF THE PROVINCE. | CONTAINING: | [8 ll. to left of rule 21 mm] THE ECLIPSES | RISING and SETTING of the | SUN and MOON | TIME of HIGH WATER | FEASTS and FASTS of the | CHURCH | LIST of PROVINCIAL OFFI- | CERS. | [8 ll. to right] SITTINGS of COURTS | OFFICERS of the NAVY on | this STATION | OFFICERS of the ARMY under | Lieutenant-General Sir JOHN | COAPE SHERBROOKE, K.B. | OFFICERS of His Majeſty's NA- | VY-YARD and HOSPITAL, | *With every other matter uſeful or neceſſary.* | [thick-thin rule 75 mm] | *By THEOPHRASTUS.* | [thin-thick rule 75 mm] | HALIFAX: | Printed and ſold by *JOHN HOWE & SON*, at their Office, Barring- | ton-ſtreet, near the Parade.
COLLATION: 8° (20.8 x 12.9 cm), *A*⁸ B⁸ C¹, [B1 signed], 17 leaves, pp *[34]*
CONTENTS: *[1]* title; *[2]* signals; *[3–4]* roads and distances with houses of entertainment; *[4]* Parrsborough packet; holidays; firewards; *[5]* fire engine company; levee days; characters; zodiac; *[6]* man of signs; eclipses; *[7–18]* calendar with verses: 'A Winter's Morning in the Country'; and 'May Day; Or, The Discovery. A Pastoral in the Manner of Cunningham'; *[19–23]* civil list; *[23–24]* courts; *[24–25]* civil list; *[26–27]* freemasons; *[27]* navy yard; Marine Humane Society; *[28]* clergy of established church; King's College; *[29–32]* army; *[33–34]* ships
PAPER: Laid, unmarked; chains horizontal 28 mm, except B marked twice with initials C and E; chains vertical (NSHD)
TYPOGRAPHY: *Text*: bourgeois, old face. *Display*: pages within thick-thin rules some with floral corners (english 4 of 1785 Caslon specimen); man of signs cut (63 x 47 mm) with bellflower frame as **NS3**; long dash of rimmed oval with tapered arrow sides; almanac signs
149 (151) x 84 mm
BINDING: Stitched (NSHD); NSHL with wrapper of dark red leather; laid paste-downs; interleaved
NOTES: Like the previous year's edition this almanac was offered for sale on 23 December in the *Royal Gazette*. A peevish note added with Archibald Cunningham's signature of ownership to the title page of one copy indicates that almanac buyers expected to start the year on time: 'Rec'd not until Sunday the 6th Feb'ry 1814 after having been thro' a great mistake carried back to Halifax, for 4 weeks' (NSHD). Cunningham, whose almanacs are found today in the collections of NSHD and NSWA, may be the 'A. Cunningham' listed in those almanacs as clerk of the Crown at Shelburne.
COPIES EXAMINED: NSHD (2 copies, one lacking pp [33–34]), NSHL, NSHP (lacking pp [1–2], [33–34]), NSWA

NS92 Bromley, Walter, 1775–1838

AN | ADDRESS, [open] | DELIVERED AT THE | FREE-MASON's HALL, | HALIFAX, | *AUGUST 3d*, 1813. | [thick-thin rule 58 mm] | BY WALTER BROMLEY, Esquire, | Late Paymaster of the 23d regiment Welsh Fusiliers. | [thin-thick rule 58 mm] | *ON THE DEPLORABLE STATE OF THE INDIANS.* | [ornamental dash 43 mm] | HALIFAX. | Anthony H. Holland, *Printer.* | 1813.
COLLATION: 8° (21.5 x 13.4 cm), *1–2*⁴, 8 leaves, pp *1–4* 5–16

CONTENTS: *1* title; 2 blank; *3* preface to His Excellency Sir John Coape Sherbrooke dated as Address; 4–16 text; 16 'erata' (6 ll.)
PAPER: Wove, unmarked
TYPOGRAPHY: *Text*: long primer, old face. *Display*: dash is diamond with tapered arrow sides
47 ll., 163 (167) x 95; 64 mm for 20 ll.
BINDING: Disbound, stab holes
NOTES: Retired from his regiment which had served in Nova Scotia in the previous decade Walter Bromley returned to Halifax from England in 1813 as an agent of the British and Foreign Bible Society. During July he exhibited 'Bell and Lancaster's Plan of Education' at the Free-Mason's Hall 'when the attendance of Ladies and Gentlemen, and all friends to the poor' was requested (*Halifax Journal*, 19, 26 July 1813; *Acadian Recorder*, 17 July). By autumn he had founded the Royal Acadian School, a non-sectarian, monitorial school for fee-paying and charity pupils. He had also run headlong into the Church of England establishment represented by Alexander Croke, judge of the Court of Vice-Admiralty, who in an open letter to Bromley refused to be a vice-president of the school because it would allow each student to choose a catechism rather than to subscribe to that of the Church of England (*Acadian Recorder*, 14 August 1813). Bromley replied, Croke countered, and others, including Thomas McCulloch, filled the columns of the *Acadian Recorder* for several months.

With equal enthusiasm but less success Bromley worked to improve the prospects of native people: 'Conſider the poor forlorn ragged Indian, contribute every means in your power to reſcue her from deſtruction, and God will abundantly reward you not only in the next world, but in this one hundred fold. ... Let the year 1813 be ever memorable, and held by the Indians as the anniverſary of the period of their emancipation from a ſtate worſe than ſlavery, and what a glorious idea that the inhabitants of Halifax will have had the ſatisfaction to ſet the example to the other inhabitants of Britiſh America' (p 15).

His *Address* was advertised for sale, priced at 1s 3d, at the Howe, Minns, and Eaton bookstores within the month (*Acadian Recorder*, 23 August 1813; *Chronicle*, 27 August; *Halifax Journal*, 13 September).

Anthony Henry Holland, Bromley's printer, was the namesake, and possibly apprentice, of Anthony Henry, king's printer until his death in 1800. In 1812 Holland returned from Maine where he had been publishing a newspaper to found *The Acadian Recorder*. With his first issue on 16 January 1813 he broke the printing monopoly of the Howe family. John Howe, his brother-in-law William Minns, and his son John Howe Jr had been publishing Halifax's three papers without sustained competition for more than a decade. Holland's reform sympathies and interest in political debate as well as his feuds with rival publishers and brushes with the libel laws transformed journalism in Nova Scotia (*Dictionary of Canadian Biography* VI, s.v. 'Holland, Anthony Henry,' by Gertrude Tratt).
COPY EXAMINED: USMHi

NS93 Church of England
THE | CATECHISM, | OF THE | Church of England, | WITH PARALLEL PASSAGES | FROM THE | CONFESSION OF FAITH, | THE | LARGER AND SHORTER CATECHISMS | OF THE | Church of Scotland. | [thin-thick rule 7 mm] | HALIFAX. | Printed at the ACADIAN RECORDER Office. | 1813.
COLLATION: 12° (18 x 10.6 cm), 1^6, 6 leaves, pp *1–4* 5–12 (pagination underlined with dotted rule)
CONTENTS: *1* title; 2 blank; *3* preface; 4–12 text
PAPER: Wove, unmarked
TYPOGRAPHY: *Text*: brevier, modern face. *Display*: row of stars as nonpareil 1 of 1785 Caslon specimen
50 ll., 135 (149) x 81; 54 mm for 20 ll.
NOTES: The *Catechism* was promised for 'Monday next' on 13 November and offered 'Just Published, And for sale' the following week at the Recorder office and the bookstores of Messrs Minns, Eaton, and Howe. Priced at ninepence, it was advertised for several weeks (*Acadian Recorder*, 13 November–18 December 1813).

Walter Bromley, who was collecting subscriptions for the Royal Acadian School that autumn, may have encouraged the publication of this catechism for his students (NS92). In September, answering a critic in the *Halifax Journal*, he wrote 'I have already in my possession, some of the most elegant printed Church Catechisms ever seen in Nova-Scotia' (20 September 1813).
COPY EXAMINED: NSWA
REFERENCE: Dennis

NS94 Halifax Committee of Trade
The Labradore Fiſhery, | For the Seaſon 1814. | [ornamental dash 43 mm] | THE *Halifax Committee of Trade*, having made application to the | ſeveral Commanders in Chief, on the American and Newfound- | land Stations, to afford Convoy and Protection to the Veſſels expected | to resort to the Coaſt of Labradore, for the purpoſe of fiſhing, in the | Seaſon of 1814, have received an anſwer

from Rea<r> <A>dmiral *Griffith,* | the Port-Admiral at Halifax, of which the following is an extract – | ... | ... they venture to recommend to all Perſons wiſhing to engage in | that valuable Fiſhery, in the summer of 1814, to make preparation for | the ſame accordingly. | *Halifax, November* 10, 1813.
Public notice: 1 leaf (27.5 x 18.5 cm)
CONTENTS: 2 ll. heading; dash; 34 ll. text; 1 l. place and date
PAPER: Laid down
TYPOGRAPHY: *Text*: old faces. *Display*: dash is rimmed oval with tapered arrow sides
250 x 166 mm
NOTES: The convoy was scheduled to leave Saint John about the tenth of May then cross the Bay of Fundy to the Atlantic shore of Nova Scotia calling in at Yarmouth, Shelburne, and Liverpool for vessels assembled in those ports to join the fishery. On 20 May all the ships gathered in Halifax would sail in convoy to Ship-Harbour in the Gut of Canso, the final place of rendezvous. From there on 12 June, 'wind and weather permitting' the vessels would be conducted to the coast of Labrador for the fishing season. On their return voyage protection would be provided back to the Bay of Fundy. As forecast 'that valuable Fiſhery, in the summer of 1814' allowed Nova Scotians, free of competition from American fishermen, to more than double their catch in a prosperous season (G.S. Graham, *Sea Power and British North America, 1783–1820*. Cambridge: Harvard University Press, 1941, 254).
COPY EXAMINED: QMMRB
REFERENCE: Lande S1020

NS95 Inglefield, John Nicholson, 1747–1828
CAPTAIN INGLEFIELD'S | NARRATIVE | OF | The Loss of the Centaur, [script] | IN 1782, | BEING A LITERAL EXTRACT OF HIS LETTER TO | THE ADMIRALTY, WRITTEN FROM | FAYAL IN 1782; | ALSO, | A COPY OF THE SENTENCE OF THE COURT MARTIAL | HELD UPON THE OFFICERS OF | THE CENTAUR. | *Printed by Howe & Son, Halifax.*
COLLATION: 8° (23 x 14.5 cm), A^4 B–C^4 D^1 [$1 signed], 13 leaves, pp *1–4* 5–26 (pagination in ( ))
CONTENTS: *1* title; *2* blank; *3* introduction (11 ll.); *4* blank; *5*–24 text; 24 note (13 ll.); 25 list of officers and men saved in the pinnace; 25–26 verdict of court martial, 25 January 1783
PAPER: Wove, *A* marked R | 1807, B–D unmarked
TYPOGRAPHY: *Text*: english, old face. *Display*: row of bellflower ornaments as long primer 42 of 1790 Fry and Steele specimen; rules and dashes of section marks and colons
31 ll., 156 (169) x 92; 102 mm for 20 ll.
BINDING: Stitched with upper wrapper of bluish greenish gray paper
NOTES: Commissioner of the Navy Yard at Halifax from 1801 to 1811, John Inglefield was an officer of the Royal Navy. In 1782, as captain of the *Centaur*, he abandoned his ship and most of the crew by escaping in a small boat as the storm battered *Centaur* sank. Acquitted by court martial in 1783 Inglefield was still condemned by some of his contemporaries twenty years later. Alexander Croke, judge of the Vice-Admiralty Court, dubbed him 'Britocamp' in 'The Inquisition' his 1805 satire of Halifax society:

There Britocamp, Magnificent, and Proud,
Smiles with complacence on the dunghill Crowd.
To that high emminence by merit raised,
The great he flattered, and their harlots praised;
Unreal vision, formed for empty show,
All pomp above, and meanness all below!
...
Who fears reflection drowns in noisy revels
The stings of conscience and the azure devils.
...
Was it for this, that Heaven's transcendent care
Closed ocean's mouth, and bade the tempest spare?
When from the shipwrecked vessels side he flew,
A bright example to the sinking crew,
And taught old tars, who every danger brave,
That precious thing, a Captain's life to save.

(*Narrative Verse Satire in Maritime Canada*, ed. Thomas B. Vincent. Ottawa: Tecumseh Press, 1978, 168).

The pamphlet exculpating Inglefield is undated but the Howes advertised it in 1813: 'The Centaur. A Few Copies of Captain (late Commissioner) Inglefield's Narrative of the loss of the above ship. May be had of J. & D. Howe' (*Royal Gazette*, 10 May 1813). An edition with the same title was published in England that year (Brentford: P. Norbury) adding to a body of Inglefieldiana which included *Captain Inglefield's Vindication of his Conduct: or, A Reply to a Pamphlet Intitled: "Mrs. Inglefield's Justification"* (1787). This criminal conversation trial was also revived by Croke in 'The Inquisition.' An abridged version of the *Centaur* story entitled *Wonderful Escape from Shipwreck* (1795) had appeared in the English series 'Cheap Repository for Religious and Moral Tracts.'
COPY EXAMINED: NSHD

CAPTAIN INGLEFIELD'S

NARRATIVE

OF

The Loss of the Centaur,

IN 1782,

BEING A LITERAL EXTRACT OF HIS LETTER TO THE ADMIRALTY, WRITTEN FROM FAYAL IN 1782;

ALSO,

A COPY OF THE SENTENCE OF THE COURT MARTIAL HELD UPON THE OFFICERS OF THE CENTAUR.

Printed by Howe & Son, Halifax.

NS95 Courtesy J.J. Stewart Collection, Special Collections Department, Dalhousie University Library, Halifax

NS96 Nova Scotia. Court of Vice-Admiralty
THE | SUBSTANCE OF A | JUDGMENT, [open] | DELIVERED IN THE | COURT OF VICE-ADMIRALTY, | AT | HALIFAX, *(in Nova-Scotia),* | On the 5th February, 1813; | IN THE CASE OF THE | LITTLE-JOE, FAIRWEATHER, MASTER, | UPON SOME QUESTIONS RELATING TO | DROITS OF ADMIRALTY. | [thick-thin rule 28 mm] | *The Independence of Judges is essential to the Impartial Administration* | *of Justice; is one of the best securities of the Rights and Liberties* | *of the Subject, and most conducive to the Honour of the Crown.* | The KING's Speech, 1761. | [thin-thick rule 26 mm] | HALIFAX: | ANTHONY H. HOLLAND, *PRINTER.* | 1813.

COLLATION: 8° (22.9 x 16.2 cm uncut), *1–3*[4], 12 leaves, pp *1–3* 4–24 (pagination flanked by dashes)
CONTENTS: *1* title; 2 blank; *3*–19 text; *20* blank; *21*–24 appendix: A, B
PAPER: Wove, unmarked
TYPOGRAPHY: *Text*: long primer, old face. *Display*: two-line pica open roman; medium dash of rayed oval with tapered sides
47 ll., 157 (165) x 90; 67 mm for 20 ll.
BINDING: Bound with Nova Scotia and London imprints concerning admiralty court decisions on prize cases dated up to 1814. Calf, boards framed blind with leaf and bead roll; spine so divided into six compartments with red lettering piece in second, edges in gilt with rule and leaf and bead roll, lettered TREATISES | ON | PRIZES | . Boards edged with diagonal hatching in blind. Wove endpapers and binder's leaf; armorial book-plate of Richard John Uniacke (NSHP)
NOTES: The schooner *Little Joe* was captured 17 October 1812 by one of the most famous Nova Scotia privateers, the *Liverpool Packet*. Since the seizure was based on Sherbrooke's commission of reprisal rather than the Prince Regent's 'Order for General Reprizals' just issued on 13 October, there were two claimants for the prize when this vessel and cargo were condemned as American property: the privateers and the King. The first decision on 20 January 1813 condemned the ship and cargo as a prize to his Majesty rather than to the privateers; the second on 5 February found for the receiver general of droits rather than the receiver general.

Lieutenant Governor Sherbrooke sent a copy of the judgment to Lord Bathurst with a note: 'Dr Croke ... has transmitted to me the case of the Little Joe which he has had printed' (GBPRO: CO 217, vol 91, ff 61–2).
COPIES EXAMINED: NSHP, GBPRO: CO 217, vol 91, ff 63–74
REFERENCE: Akins

NS97 Nova Scotia [Laws, etc.]
MILITIA LAWS | OF | The Province of Nova-Scotia [script] | IN FORCE IN THE YEAR OF OUR LORD, 1813. | PUBLISHED BY COMMAND OF | HIS EXCELLENCY LIEUTENANT-GENERAL | SIR JOHN COAPE SHERBROOKE, K.B. | LIEUTENANT-GOVERNOR AND COMMANDER IN CHIEF IN AND OVER | HIS MAJESTY'S PROVINCE OF NOVA SCOTIA, | VICE ADMIRAL OF THE SAME, | &c. &c. &c. | WITH AN INDEX AND REFERENCES, | BY H.H. COGSWELL. | [swelled rule 36 mm] | HALIFAX: | PRINTED BY JOHN HOWE AND SON, | PRINTERS TO THE KING'S MOST EXCELLENT MAJESTY. | 1813.

COLLATION: 8° (20.7 x 12.9 cm), π[8] A–I[4] K–L[4] [$1 (+A1) signed], 52 leaves, pp *i–iv* v–xiv *xv–xvi*, *1* 2–84 *85–88*
CONTENTS: *i* title; *ii* blank; *iii* 'Militia Laws'; *iv*–xiv index; *xv–xvi* blank; *1*–84 text; *85–88* blank
PAPER: Wove, unmarked
TYPOGRAPHY: *Text*: english, old face. *Display*: black letter; tail piece (p 84) with FINIS in panel surmounted by urn and palm leaves, swag beneath (86 in Fry and Steele catalogue)
33 ll., 153 (166) x 75 (96); 93 mm for 20 ll.
BINDING: Stitched with lower wrapper of greenish pale blue wove paper
NOTES: Henry Hezekiah Cogswell who prepared this edition of the laws was a lawyer recently appointed deputy provincial secretary. In 1817 after he edited the collected statutes (**NS123**) the House of Assembly voted him a payment of £100 for that work and 'for making an index and superintending the publication' of these 1813 Militia Laws (*Journal* 10:7, 1817, pp 115, 121).
COPY EXAMINED: NSHP
REFERENCES: Bishop, Dennis

NS98 Nova Scotia. Laws (10th Parliament, 3rd session: 1813)
[text begins] At the GENERAL ASSEMBLY of the Province of | Nova-Scotia, begun and holden at Halifax, on | Thurſday the Sixth day of February, 1812, and | continued by ſeveral Prorogations to Thursday the | 13th day of February 1813
COLLATION: 2° (33.6 x 23.8 cm), U3–C4[2] [$1 signed], 18 leaves, pp 711–730 χ730 731–744 *745*

CONTENTS: 711–744 text; *745* blank
PAPER: U3–X3 wove, unmarked; Y3–C4 laid, watermark post horn in crowned shield; countermark AL MASSO; chains vertical 30 mm
TYPOGRAPHY: *Text*: pica, old face
46 ll., 215 (232) x 147 (171); 95 mm for 20 ll.
COPIES EXAMINED: NSHD, NSHP, USMH-L

NS99 Nova Scotia. Parliament (10th, 3rd session: 1813). House of Assembly
[half title] [thick-thin rule 135 mm] | JOURNAL | AND | PROCEEDINGS | OF | THE HOUSE OF ASSEMBLY, | 1813. | [thin-thick rule 135 mm]
COLLATION: 4° (26.5 x 18.5 cm), *A–B*² C–D² χD–I² K–U² χU² W² X¹ [$1 signed], 47 leaves, pp *1–3* 4–94
CONTENTS: *1* half title; 2 proclamation; 3–94 text
PAPER: *A*, G–S wove, unmarked; *B*–F laid, unmarked (NSHL); NSHP copy with *A*, χD, F–R wove, *B*–D, E laid; chains horizontal 28 mm
TYPOGRAPHY: *Text*: pica, old face. *Display*: royal arms cut 85 x 30 mm
45 ll., 210 (219) x 137; 94 mm for 20 ll.
COPIES EXAMINED: NSHL, NSHP (lacking pp 71–94)

NS100 Nova Scotia and New Brunswick. Commander in Chief (1794–1800: Edward Augustus, Duke of Kent and Strathern)
INSTRUCTIONS | TO | BARRACK-MASTERS, [open] | SERVING IN | *Nova-Scotia, New-Brunswick, and their Dependencies.* | [dotted rule 10 mm] | HALIFAX: | PRINTED BY JOHN HOWE AND SON.
COLLATION: 8° (18.4 x 11.1 cm), *1–2*⁸, 16 leaves, pp *1–3* 4–32
CONTENTS: *1* title; 2 blank; *3*–15 text; 16–21 schedule of allowance of Lodging Money and Office Rent (to be completed in ms); 21–26 remarks; 26–32 lists of supplies and charges (to be completed in ms)
PAPER: Laid, watermark post horn in crowned shield; countermark RADWAY | 1813; chains vertical 24 mm
TYPOGRAPHY: *Text*: pica, old face with modern face long primer for schedules and lists. *Display*: modern face open and italic on title
29 ll., 137 (147) x 84; 94 mm for 20 ll.
BINDING: Wrapper of gloster paper, blackish blue with dark pink, orange yellow, and deep blue; paste-downs of laid paper (OTUTF). NSWA with wrapper of spot marbled paper, light grayish yellowish brown
NOTES: The final inventory is headed 'A List of Prices to be charged ... for Barrack Articles, when deficient or damaged ... as established by order of [ ]' (p 28). In the OTUTF copy this caption is completed in manuscript: 'HRH when commander in chief here.' The amounts to be charged to His Majesty's Troops are noted by hand in red ink and range from £8 for a cast iron stove to 3s 6d for a shovel. The list includes chairs, candlesticks, pokers and tongs, six sizes of window glass each priced, as well as doors and latches. 'Tho' H Bailey' whose name is signed on both the title page and wrapper of this copy was barrack master of Fort Anne at Annapolis Royal.

HRH Prince Edward, Victoria's father, was fierce in his obsession with army regulations and brutal in punishment. When he died Lord Dalhousie who had served under him wrote that 'his greatest fault was an overbearing & tyrannical system of military discipline, inconsistent with the nature and feelings of Englishmen. This he pushed to a height that was fatal to his own ambition as a soldier, & the source of all his disagreement with his elder brothers' (*The Dalhousie Journals*, vol 1, ed. Marjorie Whitelaw. Ottawa: Oberon, 1978, 186).

Printed without a date of publication on paper marked 1813 this edition would likely have been required for distribution during the war.
COPIES EXAMINED: NSWA, OTUTF
REFERENCE: Dennis

NS101 Parish, Elijah, 1762–1825
A | DISCOURSE, [open] | DELIVERED AT | BYFIELD, | STATE OF | MASSACHUSETTS, | ON THE | ANNUAL FAST, | APRIL 8, 1813. | [thick-thin rule 58 mm] | BY *ELIJAH PARISH*, D.D. | [thin-thick rule 58 mm] | Printed and for sale at the RECORDER OFFICE. | *Price – One Shilling.*
IMPRINT: ANTHONY H. HOLLAND, *printer*.
COLLATION: 8° (20 x 12.8 cm), *1–2*⁴, 8 leaves, pp *1–3* 4–16
CONTENTS: *1* title; 2 preface; *3*–16 sermon, text: MATT. xxvi. 52; 16 imprint
PAPER: Wove, unmarked
TYPOGRAPHY: *Text*: long primer, old face
46 ll., 158 (162) x 93 mm; 67 mm for 20 ll.
BINDING: Disbound
NOTES: 'Do not, I be*f*eech you, do not move a finger to promote this wicked war' was the theme of Elijah Parish's *Discourse* to his American congregation (p 16). He had published a sermon protesting the war the year before and, again in 1814, denounced it in a discourse which may also have been published in Halifax (Appendix). The publisher Thomas Daniel Cowdell, a Methodist lay preacher, poet, and shopkeeper in Halifax, wrote a preface to the work:

Read, Mark and Learn From an unparalleled Sermon, By Elijah Parish DD Of Byfield Massachusetts, (United States). The Publiſher is well aware, that the above Political Diſcourſe is worthy of the the ſtudy and imitation of every Miniſter, and claims the moſt pious regard of all His Majeſty's Subjects. Every Lover of his King and Country, ſhould certainly poſſeſs and diſſeminate its ſacred principles. It includes all the conſtituent parts which form the accompliſhed and patriotic Orator, ſhewing to his own Countrymen, (our enemies), with all poſſible truth and brevity, the *Cauſe* and *Conſequences* of the preſent unnatural War with Great Britain. If energy of expreſſion – *if* perſpicuity of ſtyle – if elegance of compoſition ever regaled the eye, the ear and the heart of a Britiſh Subject, then this Sermon claims the ſuffrage of every ſoul that loves the beſt of Conſtitutions – namely, that of Old England! In ſhort, it appears to be the moſt Strenuous and grateful ebulition of a Patriotic, Evangelical and Martyr-like Spirit. DIDYMUS. [pointing hand] *To be had at the several Bookstores, and of Mr. McDOUGAL – and of Mr. T.D. COWDELL, the Publisher.*

The *Acadian Recorder* announced on 23 August that Parish's 'unparalleled Political Sermon' was in the press, a notice repeated on 4 September with the promise: 'And will be published on Wednesday next' at the price of one shilling.

COPY EXAMINED: NSHP

1814

NS102 An Almanack for the Year of Our Lord, 1815

[within thick-thin rules 150 x 84 mm] AN | ALMANACK [open] | *For the Year of our Lord,* 1815 | BEING THE THIRD AFTER BISSEXTILE OR LEAP YEAR. | Calculated for the Meridian of | HALIFAX, IN NOVA-SCOTIA, [open] | BUT WILL SERVE FOR ANY PART OF THE PROVINCE. | CONTAINING: | [8 ll. to left of rule 26 mm] THE ECLIPSES. | RISING and SETTING of | the SUN and MOON. | TIME of HIGH WATER. | FEASTS and FASTS of the | CHURCH. | LIST of PROVINCIAL | OFFICERS. | [8 ll. to right] SITTINGS of COURTS. | OFFICERS of the NAVY | on this STATION, | OFFICERS of the ARMY, | under Lieut.-Gen. Sir JOHN | COAPE SHERBROOKE, K.B. | OFFICERS of His Majesty's | NAVY-YARD, & HOSPITAL. | With every other matter useful or necessary. | [double rule 79 mm] | *By THEOPHRASTUS.* | [double rule 79 mm] | HALIFAX: [open] | Printed and Sold by JOHN HOWE and SON, at their | Office, Barrington-Street, near the Parade.

COLLATION: 8° (18.1 x 12.2 cm), *1–2*⁸ *3*⁴, 20 leaves, pp [40]

CONTENTS: [*1*] title; [*2*] signals; [*3–4*] roads and distances with houses of entertainment; [*4*] Parrsborough packet; holidays; firewards; [*5*] fire engine company; levee days; ephemeris, zodiac, cycles, feasts; [*6*] man of signs; eclipses; [*7–18*] calendar; [*19–23*] civil list; [*23–24*] courts; [*24–26*] civil list; [*26–27*] freemasons; [*27–28*] navy yard; [*28*] clergy of established church; [*28–29*] King's College; [*29–32*] army; [*33–37*] ships; [*37*] new buoy; [*38–40*] blank

PAPER: Laid, unmarked; chains horizontal 26 mm

TYPOGRAPHY: *Text*: long primer, modern face. *Display*: pages within thick-thin rules; man of signs cut (63 x 47 mm) with bellflower frame as NS3; medium and long swelled rules; almanac signs 147 x 84 mm

BINDING: Wrapper of gloster paper, interleaved; paste-downs (NSHL, NSWA). OOA copy rebound retaining wrapper, interleaved and used in the Military Secretary's Office to record sailings

NOTES: The new white buoy (p [*37*]) marked 'a rocky shoal, on which H.M.ſhip Superb touched' on 3 December 1814, shortly before publication of this almanac. A notice dated 1 January 1815 offering it for sale appeared in the *Halifax Journal* for 9 January. Archibald Cunningham signed his copy when he received it on the sixteenth (NSWA).

COPIES EXAMINED: NSHD, NSHL, NSHP, NSWA, OOA

NS103 Bromley, Walter, 1775–1838

MR. BROMLEY's | SECOND ADDRESS, | ON THE | *DEPLORABLE STATE OF THE INDIANS,* | DELIVERED | IN THE | *"Royal Acadian School,"* | AT HALIFAX, IN NOVA-SCOTIA, | MARCH 8, 1814. | [swelled rule 15 mm] | "Who shall not fear thee, O Lord, and glorify thy name? | For thou only art holy: | *For all nations shall come and worship before thee."* | REV. 15:4. | [swelled rule 15 mm] | Printed at the RECORDER OFFICE. | 1814.

IMPRINT: A.H. HOLLAND, Printer.

COLLATION: 8° (16.2 x 11.2 cm), *1–7*⁴, 28 leaves, pp *1–3* 4–55 *56*

CONTENTS: *1* title; 2 dedication: 'To His Honor Maj. Gen. Sir Thomas Saumerez, President and

Commander in Chief of the Province of New-Brunswick' signed W. Bromley 'On the half-pay of the Welch Fusiliers'; 3–49 text headed TO THE PUBLIC; *50* blank; *51*–52 'The North American Indian Institution. To the Public'; 53–55 Rules of the North American Indian Institution, established at Fredericton, New-Brunswick, 19 January 1814; 55 'erata' (2 ll.); imprint; *56* blank
STATES: With 'erata' cited p 55 (cemiseration on p 3 and civilzation on p 43) corrected (NSWA, OOA); with only cemiseration corrected (NSHD, NSHL)
PAPER: Laid, unmarked; chains vertical 27 mm
TYPOGRAPHY: *Text*: small pica, modern face (pp *1*–11, 17–26, 33–41, 51–55); long primer, old face (pp 12–16, 27–32, 42–49); notes in modern face brevier
34, 35 ll., 122 (128) x 85; 67, 72 mm for 20 ll.
NOTES: On 30 March John Howe's *Royal Gazette* announced that *Mr Bromley's Second Address* was in the press. The *Acadian Recorder* offered it for sale at 'all the Booksellers in Halifax, and at the Acadian School' for two shillings and three pence (16 April 1814; *Weekly Chronicle* 15 April). A report of the founding meeting of the North American Indian Institution at Fredericton where Walter Bromley served as secretary pro tem was published in the *Halifax Journal* on 7 March 1814 and repeated the next week.
COPIES EXAMINED: NSHD (lacking pp 55–56), NSHL, NSWA, OOA
REFERENCES: Casey 998, Dennis

NS104 Church of England
[within thick-thin rules 160 x 107 mm] A | FORM | OF | PRAYER, | TO BE USED | In all Churches, Chapels, and Places of | PUBLIC WORSHIP, according to the u*ſ*age of the CHURCH | of ENGLAND throughout His Maje*ſ*ty's Province of | NOVA SCOTIA, on FRIDAY, the TWENTY-FIFTH Day of | FEBRUARY, 1814; being the Day appointed by Procla | mation for a GENERAL FAST and HUMILIATION before | ALMIGHTY GOD; to be ob*ſ*erved in the mo*ſ*t devout and | *ſ*olemn manner, by *ſ*ending up our PRAYERS and SUP- | PLICATIONS to the DIVINE MAJESTY: | For obtaining Pardon of our Sins, and for averting tho*ſ*e heavy Judgments | which our manifold Provocations have mo*ſ*t ju*ſ*tly de*ſ*erved; imploring | a continuance of His Ble*ſſ*ing and A*ſſiſ*tance on His Maje*ſ*ty's Arms by | Sea and Land, and on tho*ſ*e of His Maje*ſ*ty's Allies and for re*ſ*toring and | perpetuating Peace, Safety and Pro*ſ*perity, to Him*ſ*elf, and to His Kingdom. | [rule 99 mm] | By Command of His Excellency the Lieutenant-Governor. | [thin-thick rule 100 mm] | HALIFAX: | Printed by JOHN HOWE and SON, Printers to the King's Mo*ſ*t | Excellent MAJESTY. 1814.
COLLATION: 4° (17.8 x 13 cm), *A*[4] B[4] [B1 signed], 8 leaves, pp *1*–*2* 3–11 *12*–*16* (pagination in ( ))
CONTENTS: *1* title; 2 blank; 3–*16* text
PAPER: Laid, unmarked; chains vertical 28 mm
TYPOGRAPHY: *Text*: pica, old face
30 ll., 142 (156) x 104; 93 mm for 20 ll.
NOTES: On this Fast Day ordained by the lieutenant governor to be observed in all churches with worship 'according to the u*ſ*age of the Church of England' Thomas McCulloch the Presbyterian minister at Pictou preached a sermon in his church praising religious cooperation (**NS106**).
COPY EXAMINED: NSHL

NS105 Halifax [Draft of Charter]
THE | DRAFT | OF A | CHARTER, | FOR THE | *INCORPORATION* | OF | The TOWN of HALIFAX, | IN | *The Province of Nova-Scotia.* | [swelled rule 36 mm] | *HALIFAX:* | Printed by JOHN HOWE & SON, | 1814.
COLLATION: 8° (18.8 x 11.6 cm), *A*[4] *B*[2] C[4] [C1 signed], 10 leaves, pp [2] *i* ii, *1* 2–15 *16*
CONTENTS: [1] title; [2] blank; *i*–ii introduction; ii contents; *1*–15 text dated at Halifax, January 1814; 15 notice of meeting on 8 February; *16* blank
PAPER: Laid, unmarked; chains vertical 26 mm
TYPOGRAPHY: *Text*: small pica, old face. *Display*: 42 mm dash of rimmed oval with tapered arrow sides
32 ll., 149 (159) x 98; 84 mm for 20 ll.
NOTES: Halifax was not incorporated until 1841, long after this proposed charter had been greeted with praise, criticism, and even comic verse, in the *Halifax Journal* (7, 14 February 1814).
COPY EXAMINED: NSHP
REFERENCE: Akins

NS106 McCulloch, Thomas, 1776–1843
THE | *Prosperity of the Church in Troublous Times;* | A | SERMON, | *Preached at Pictou, on Friday, February* 25, 1814, | *being the Day appointed for a General Fast,* | BY | THOMAS M'CULLOCH. | [swelled rule 38 mm] | The Lord doth build up Jeru*ſ*alem: he gathereth together the outca*ſ*ts of I*ſ*rael. | [thick-thin rule 96 mm] | *Published by the Congregation.* | [thick-thin rule 96 mm] | HALIFAX: | Printed by JOHN HOWE and SON. | 1814.

COLLATION: 8° (20.3 x 12.7 cm), *A–B*[4] C[4] [C1 signed], 12 leaves, pp *1–3* 4–24
CONTENTS: *1* title; 2 blank; *3*–24 sermon, text: DAN.IX.25.
PAPER: Laid, unmarked (NSHD, NSWA); C marked A (NSHL); *A* marked BA (QMMRB); chains vertical 27 mm
TYPOGRAPHY: *Text*: english, old face. *Display*: dash on wrapper is rimmed oval with tapered arrow sides
31 ll., 143 (153) x 98; 92 mm for 20 ll.
BINDING: Stitched with upper wrapper of bluish greenish gray wove paper printed [ornamental dash 46 mm] | *THE PROSPERITY OF THE CHURCH* | *IN TROUBLOUS TIMES.* | [ornamental dash 49 mm] (NSHD); QMMRB copy bound retaining wrapper
NOTES: A Presbyterian minister at Pictou since 1803, Thomas McCulloch was one of the leading dissenters in the province. He had already founded a school and was working for the establishment of an interdenominational college to serve the majority excluded from King's (**NS26**). He chose this Fast Day to praise the work of religious societies which promoted cooperation rather than division, a reference to the Nova Scotia Bible Society which flourished in 1814 with new branches in Annapolis, Colchester, Cornwallis, Cumberland, Hants, Horton, and Queen's (**NS117**). His support for the non-sectarian Royal Acadian School was already on record (**NS92**).

Notices for the sermon appeared in all four Halifax papers. The *Weekly Chronicle*, the *Acadian Recorder*, and the *Royal Gazette* carried 'in the press' announcements on 6, 7, and 11 May then, along with the *Halifax Journal*, advertised it as 'This day is published – price 1/6' from 16 May.
COPIES EXAMINED: NSHD, NSHL, NSWA, QMMRB
REFERENCES: Bishop, Dennis, Lande S1403

NS107 Nova Scotia. Laws (10th Parliament, 4th session: 1814)
[text begins] At the GENERAL ASSEMBLY of the Province of | Nova-Scotia, begun and holden at Halifax, on | Thurſday the Sixth day of February, 1812, and | continued by ſeveral Prorogations to Thurſday the | 10th day of February, 1814
COLLATION: 2° (33.5 x 23.4 cm), D4–I4[2] K4–M4[2] [$1 signed], 18 leaves, pp 745–763 χ763 764–779
CONTENTS: 745–779 text
PAPER: Laid, unmarked; chains vertical 28 mm
TYPOGRAPHY: *Text*: pica, old face
46 ll., 213 (233) x 147 (169); 92 mm for 20 ll.
COPIES EXAMINED: NSHD, NSHP, USMH-L

NS108 Nova Scotia. Parliament (10th, 4th session: 1814). House of Assembly
[half title] [thick-thin rule 139 mm] | JOURNAL | AND | PROCEEDINGS | OF | THE HOUSE OF ASSEMBLY, | 1814. | [thin-thick rule 139 mm]
COLLATION: 4° (26.5 x 18.5 cm), *A*[2] B–I[2] K–T[2] V–2D[2] [$1 signed], 56 leaves, pp *1–3* 4–112
CONTENTS: *1* half title; 2 proclamation; *3*–112 text
PAPER: Laid, unmarked; chains horizontal 28 mm
TYPOGRAPHY: *Text*: pica, old face. *Display*: royal arms cut 85 x 30 mm
44 ll., 204 (215) x 138; 94 mm for 20 ll.
COPIES EXAMINED: NSHL, NSHP, OOA

NS109 The Nova-Scotia Calendar for 1814
THE | NOVA-SCOTIA CALENDAR, | FOR | TOWN AND COUNTRY. | FOR THE YEAR OF HUMAN REDEMPTION, | 1814. | Being the Second after Bissextile, or Leap Year, | And the 54th of the Reign of his present MAJESTY, | IN WHICH ARE CONTAINED | All THINGS fitting for such a WORK; as | *The Full, Changes, and Quarters of the MOON; Rising and Set-* | *ting of the MOON, and many other Things useful and profitable.* | [rule 84 mm] | By E.W. | [rule 84 mm] | Printed, and for sale at the RECORDER OFFICE, and at the differ- | ent Stores in TOWN and COUNTRY.
COLLATION: 8° (16.1 x 11 cm), *1–6*[4], 24 leaves, pp *1–2* 3–48 (with pp 7, 9, 11 numbered at gutter; 8, 10, 12 at foredge)
CONTENTS: *1* title; 2 common notes, eclipses; 3–14 calendar with court sittings; 15 astrological; King's College; 16 navy yard; street commissioners; horticultural; 17–18 signals; 18–19 freemasons; 19 auctioneers; 20 societies; 20–21 roads and distances with houses of entertainment; 22 Parrsborough packet; civil list; 22–23 sovereigns; 23–25 civil list; 25 holidays, levee days; firewards; 25–26 fire engine company; 26 lieutenant governors; 26–27 courts; 27–33 civil list, clergy of established church; 33–40 militia; 40–44 world chronology (British); 44–46 army; 47–48 navy; 46, 48 with local officers at foot of page
PAPER: Laid, unmarked; chains vertical 28 mm
TYPOGRAPHY: *Text*: long primer, old face, with modern face great primer headings. *Display*: almanac signs
135 (141) x 84 mm
BINDING: One copy at NSHD in gloster paper wrapper, rebacked
NOTES: Although Anthony Holland did not get his first almanac onto the market until more than a month after the Howes (**NS91**) he turned the delay

to his advantage in an announcement: 'IN THE PRESS, And will be Published in the course of this Month, THE NOVA-SCOTIA CALENDAR FOR TOWN AND COUNTRY, To contain (in addition to the one already Published) a complete list of MILITIA OFFICERS, thro' the Province. A CHRONOLOGICAL TABLE of remarkable events, discoveries, &c &c' (*Acadian Recorder* 1, 8, 15 January 1814). In the issue of 22 January he promised the almanac for 'Friday next,' the twenty-eighth.
COPIES EXAMINED: NBSAM (lacking pp 47–8), NSHD (2 copies), NSHL, NSHP, NSWA

NS110 The Nova-Scotia Calendar for 1815
The Nova-Scotia | CALENDAR, | For TOWN and COUNTRY, | For the Year of Human Redemption | 1815, | Being the Third after Bissextile, or Leap Year, | *And the 55th of the Reign of His Majesty;* | IN WHICH ARE CONTAINED | [11 ll. to left of rule 30 mm] The Full, Changes, Quarters, & south- | ing of the MOON, | Rising and setting of the Sun. | Monthly Observations, | The Eclipses, | A remarkable Chronology, | Kings and Queens from the Conquest, | Governors and Lt Governors since the | first settlement of the Province, | The principal Civil Officers in the | Province, | [9 ll. to right] List of the Army in the Province, | Do Do of the Navy, | Do of the Militia of Nova-scotia, | Roads throughout the Province, | Masonic Lodges, under the Jurisdic- | tion of the Grand Lodge of Nova- | scotia, | With a variety of other Useful Infor- | mation. | [thick-thin rule 7 mm] | BY PHILO-URANIÆ. | [thin-thick rule 7 mm] | HALIFAX, Nova-Scotia, | Printed, and for sale at the RECORDER OFFICE, | And at the various stores in Town and Country. | *Price* – 10*s. per dozen, and* 1*s.*3*d. single. Stet* Nova-scotia
COLLATION: 8° (16.3 x 10.8 cm), *1–3*[8] 4[1], 25 leaves, pp *1–2* 3–50
CONTENTS: *1* title; 2 'Addison's 19th Psalm'; 3–14 calendar with court sittings; 15 chronological cycles, feasts; 16 eclipses; levee days, holidays; 17–23 civil list; 23 clergy of established church; Ministers in Halifax: Roman Catholic, Presbyterian, Methodist, and Baptist; auctioneers; 24 governors; 24–25 freemasons; 25–26 firewards; navy yard; poorhouse; 27 King's College; 27–28 signals; 28–29 roads and distances with houses of entertainment; 29 Parrsborough packet; 30–32 chronology (British, to 1813); 33–36 army 'Taken from the Army List for Sept 1814'; 37–43 militia; 43–46 ships; 46–47 sovereigns; 47–50 miscellaneous including remedies (consumption, dysentry), homilies, statistics, and oddities
PAPER: Laid, some sheets marked with crest [?]; chains vertical 28 mm
TYPOGRAPHY: *Text*: modern and old faces. *Display*: almanac signs
135 (138) x 92 mm
NOTES: The simple E.W. of last year's almanac maker (**NS109**) has given way to PHILO-URANIÆ, a properly classical embrace of Urania, the muse of astronomy. Holland's first advertisement printed sideways to catch the eye appeared on page 1 of the *Acadian Recorder* for 26 November 1814: 'This Day Published, And for sale at this Office, and at most of the Stores in Town and Country, – price 10s doz 1s 3d single.'
COPIES EXAMINED: NSHD, NSHL, NSWA, OOA (lacking pp 49–50)

1815

NS111 An Almanack for the Year of Our Lord, 1816
[within thick-thin rules 150 x 84 mm] AN | ALMANACK [open] | *For the Year of Our Lord,* 1816, | BEING BISSEXTILE OR LEAP YEAR, | Calculated for the Meridian of | HALIFAX, IN NOVA-SCOTIA, [open] | BUT WILL SERVE FOR ANY PART OF THE PROVINCE | CONTAINING: | [8 ll. to left of rule 26 mm] The ECLIPSES. | RISING and SETTING of | the SUN and MOON. | TIME of HIGH WATER. | FEASTS and FASTS of the | CHURCH. | LIST of PROVINCIAL | OFFICERS. | [8 ll. to right] SITTING of COURTS. | OFFICERS of the NAVY | on this STATION, | OFFICERS of the ARMY, | under Lieut.-Gen. Sir JOHN | C. SHERBROOKE, K.G.C.B. | OFFICERS of His Majesty's | NAVY-YARD, & HOSPITAL. | With every other matter useful or necessary. | [double rule 80 mm] | *By THEOPHRASTUS.* | [double rule 80 mm] | HALIFAX: [open] | Published by DAVID HOWE, and Sold at his | Stationary Store, George-Street, near the Parade. *Stet* Stationary
COLLATION: 8° (19.4 x 12.8 cm), *1–2*[8] 3[1], 17 leaves, pp [34]
CONTENTS: [1] title; [2] signals; [3–4] roads and distances with houses of entertainment; [4] Parrsborough packet; holidays; firewards; [5–6]

man of signs; eclipses, levee days, ephemeris, zodiac, chronological cycles, feasts; *[7–18]* calendar; *[19–23]* civil list; *[23–24]* courts; *[24–26]* civil list; *[26–27]* freemasons; *[27–28]* navy yard; clergy of established church; *[28–29]* King's College; *[29–33]* army; *[33]* ships; fire engine company; *[34]* blank
PAPER: Laid, unmarked; chains horizontal 26 mm
TYPOGRAPHY: *Text*: long primer, modern face. *Display*: pages within thick-thin rules; man of signs cut (63 x 47 mm) with bellflower frame as **NS3**; swelled rules
150 x 86 mm
BINDING: Stitched (NSHD); NSWA copy in marbled paper wrapper, interleaved; NSHL with wrapper of dark red leather, interleaved
NOTES: From 1812 to 1815 David Howe and his older brother John Jr were partners in a bookbinding and stationery business on the lower side of the Parade. In July of 1815 the partnership was dissolved by mutual consent and David set up his own shop in George Street (*Halifax Journal*, 31 July 1815). The almanac was advertised for sale on 6 November in John Jr's *Halifax Journal* and Archibald Cunningham recorded receipt by signing his copy a week later (NSWA).
COPIES EXAMINED: NSHD (2 copies), NSHL, NSWA

NS112 Hildrith, Isaac, 1741–1807 and Chamberlain, Theophilus, 1737–1824
TO HIS EXCELLENCY [open] | *Sir* JOHN WENTWORTH, *Baronet*. | And the Honourable Commissioners appointed to examine into the Practicability and Expense of | opening an INLAND NAVIGABLE COMMUNICATION between the HARBOUR of HALIFAX and the | BASIN of MINAS, in the Province of NOVA-SCOTIA. | ... | ISAAC HIDRITH, | THOMAS CHAMBERLAIN. | HALIFAX, 15th November, 1797. *Stent* ISAAC HIDRITH, THOMAS CHAMBERLAIN
COLLATION: 2° (43.8 x 27.8 cm), 1^{2}, 2 leaves, pp [4]
CONTENTS: *[1]* text: 5 ll. heading; 1 l. salutation; 57 ll. text; 2 ll. signature with date; [2–4] blank
PAPER: Laid, watermark Strasbourg lily | CW [script]; countermark C WILMOTT | 1815; chains vertical 25 mm
TYPOGRAPHY: *Text*: transitional faces
398 x 235 mm
NOTES: A Shubenacadie canal linking Halifax to the Fundy shore by means of a series of inland waterways was debated by the House of Assembly and Council in 1798 after a report had been prepared for them by the surveyors Hildrith and Chamberlain. Although the commissioners who received the report recommended construction of the canal and the lieutenant governor offered his support the Shubenacadie project lapsed until 1814 when the House voted for another survey. This editon of the 1797 report may be tentatively dated 1815 on the basis of watermarked paper and was probably printed during that renewal of interest in the canal. It was not until 1826 however that a company was incorporated to begin construction. The scheme soon collapsed (*Dictionary of Canadian Biography* V, s.v. 'Hildrith, Isaac,' by M. Susan Whiteside).
COPY EXAMINED: NSHP: RG 1, vol 413, no ^{2}1 (following 66)

NS113 Inglis, John, 1777–1850
A | SERMON [open] | PREACHED IN THE PARISH CHURCH OF ST. PAUL, | AT HALIFAX, | *On Sunday the* 11*th of June*, 1815, | AFTER THE FUNERAL | *Of Mrs. MARY STANSER*, | WIFE OF | *The Revd. ROBERT STANSER, D.D.* | Rector of the Parish. | [dotted rule 67 mm] | *By the Revd. JOHN INGLIS, D.D.* | Ecclesiastical Commissary in the Diocese of | NOVA-SCOTIA. | [dotted rule 68 mm] | *Being dead, she yet speaketh.* | [swelled rule 27 mm] | < >Y JOHN HOWE, SON & < >
COLLATION: 8° (15 x 10 cm), 1^{8}, 8 leaves, pp *1–5* 6–16
CONTENTS: *1* title; 2 blank; *3* dedication: 'To the Churchwardens, Vestry, and Parishioners of the Parish of St. Paul'; *4* blank; *5*–16 sermon, text: Ecclesiastes, Chap 9th, part of Verse 12
PAPER: Laid, watermark Britannia; countermark W TUCKER | 1813; chains vertical 28 mm
TYPOGRAPHY: *Text*: long primer, modern face
31 ll., 102 (111) x 69; 67 mm for 20 ll.
BINDING: Stitched
NOTES: John Inglis, son of Charles Inglis the first bishop of the Church of England in Nova Scotia, followed Robert Stanser as rector of St Paul's in Halifax in 1816 when Stanser was named bishop succeeding Charles Inglis.

The Howe imprint which became 'and Son' in 1804 when John Jr joined his father (**NS31**) was further expanded in 1815 to 'John Howe, Son & Co.' when John took into partnership John Munro (*Royal Gazette*, 28 December 1814). In 1819 Munro was the partner of John Jr at the *Halifax Journal* (4 January 1819); a year later he took it over (3 January 1820).
COPY EXAMINED: NSHP (title partly torn away, imprint covered by label)

NS114 Nova Scotia. Laws (10th Parliament, 5th session: 1815)

[text begins] | At the GENERAL ASSEMBLY of the Province of | Nova-Scotia, begun and holden at Halifax, on | Thurſday the Sixth day of February, 1812, and | continued by ſeveral Prorogations to Thursday the 9th day of February, 1815

COLLATION: 2° (33.3 x 23.5 cm), N4–C5² D5¹ [$1 signed], 33 leaves, pp 780–845

CONTENTS: 780–845 text

PAPER: Laid, unmarked except R4 marked 1815 at the edge of the sheet (NSHD, USMH-L)

TYPOGRAPHY: *Text*: pica, old face

46 ll., 216 (233) x 148 (170); 94 mm for 20 ll.

COPIES EXAMINED: NSHD, NSHP, USMH-L

NS115 Nova Scotia. Lieutenant Governor (1811–1816: Sherbrooke)

(Circular.) [script] | *HALIFAX, 8th March*, 1815. | *SIR*, HIS *Excellency the* LIEUTENANT-GOVERNOR, *has been informed* | *that the Small Pox has made its appearance in several* | *parts of the Province, and as there probably may be persons in the* | [space] *who from poverty, and never having* | *been vaccinated, may be exposed to danger from the spreading of the* | *contagion, and has commanded me to request that you will immediately* | *vaccinate such poor persons* ... | ... | ... *The vaccine matter can be obtained upon* | *application to Dr. W.B. Almon, in Halifax.* | ...

COLLATION: 2° (32 x 19.8 cm), *1*², 2 leaves, pp [4]

CONTENTS: [*1*] Public notice: 1 l. heading; 2 ll. date and salutation; 21 ll. text; 3 ll. signature; [2–4] blank

PAPER: Laid, watermark Britannia; countermark GOLDING | & | SNELGROVE | 1815; chains vertical 26 mm

TYPOGRAPHY: *Text*: english, modern face

228 x 144 mm

NOTES: Doctors vaccinating the poor were required to submit a certificate verifying the patient's inability to pay in order to receive a fee of 2s 6d for each person treated. William Bruce Almon was the second Doctor Almon in Halifax having joined the practice of his father, William James Almon, in 1809 after graduation from the University of Edinburgh. The senior Almon had been using inoculation against smallpox for more than two decades (*Dictionary of Canadian Biography* V, s.v. 'Almon (Allmon) William James,' by Lois K. Kernaghan; VII, s.v. 'Almon, William Bruce,' by Colin D. Howell).

COPY EXAMINED: NSHP: RG 1, vol 288, no 119

NS116 Nova Scotia. Parliament (10th, 5th session: 1815). House of Assembly

[half title] [double rule 136 mm] | *JOURNAL* [fat] | AND | *PROCEEDINGS* | OF THE | *HOUSE of ASSEMBLY*, | 1815. | [double rule 136 mm]

COLLATION: 4° (26.8 x 18.5 cm), *A–B*² C–I² K–T² V–Y² χY–2C² *2D*² [$1 signed], 58 leaves, pp *1–3* 4–115 *116*

CONTENTS: *1* half title; 2 proclamation; *3*–115 text; *116* blank

PAPER: Laid, marked H[?] & I C at the edge of the sheet (NSHL); chains horizontal 28 mm

TYPOGRAPHY: *Text*: pica, old face. *Display*: open romans, script, and modern face italic; long swelled rule; royal arms cut 19 x 54 mm

42 ll., 194 (206) x 134; 94 mm for 20 ll.

COPIES EXAMINED: NSHL, NSHP

NS117 Nova Scotia Bible Society

FIRST [open] | ANNUAL REPORT [open] | OF THE | *NOVA-SCOTIA* | BIBLE SOCIETY. | [swelled rule 28 mm] | *HALIFAX:* | Printed by JOHN HOWE, SON & CO. | PRINTERS TO THE KING'S MOST EXCELLENT MAJESTY. | 1815.

COLLATION: 8° (20 x 12.5 cm uncut), *A*⁴ B⁴ D–F⁴ χF⁴ [$1 signed], 24 leaves, pp *1–3* 4–47 *48*

CONTENTS: *1* title; 2 blank; 3 officers; 4–5 rules and regulations; 5–6 meeting; 7–11 text; 12 treasurer's account; 13–40 subscriptions; 40 'N.B.' note (9 ll.); 41–46 appendix: correspondence 1814, 1815; 47 note headed N.B. (5 ll.); *48* blank

PAPER: Laid, watermark post horn in crowned shield (NSHL); NSHD with same watermark on *A* and E; countermarks RADWAY | 1813 on B and NEWMAN & SON | 1813 on F, χF; chains vertical 23 mm

TYPOGRAPHY: *Text*: long primer, modern face

40 ll., 130 (139) x 82; 67 mm for 20 ll.

BINDING: Stitched (NSHD)

NOTES: Formation late in 1813 of the Nova Scotia Bible Society, an auxiliary of the British and Foreign Bible Society founded in 1804, provided a focus for debate between the Church of England which was the established church in Nova Scotia and dissenters representing the majority of Nova Scotians. Public discussion began when an 'Address to the Inhabitants of Nova-Scotia' was inserted in the *Halifax Journal* outlining the goals and accomplishments of the interdenominational British society, particularly the distribution of bibles. A meeting for the formation of a local auxiliary was announced for 24 November (22 November 1813). The *Weekly Chronicle* of 26

November carried a prompt response from Alexander Croke who urged support for the Church of England Society for Promoting Christian Knowledge (SPCK) rather than the non-sectarian Bible Society. Published in the same issue was a report of the founding meeting of the new society with an appeal for subscriptions (*Weekly Chronicle*, 26 November; *Acadian Recorder*, 4 December). The *Acadian Recorder* of 11 December then published three letters critical of the Bible Society, one from John Inglis saying that another society was not needed since the SPCK would itself distribute bibles, and two disapproving of the membership and policies of societies supported by dissenters which would be sending money out of the province and distributing scriptures printed 'without note or comment' for the proper guidance of readers. Meanwhile the *Halifax Journal* published notice of a meeting for the formation of a local branch of the SPCK with details of their plans for book distribution (13 December).

As both groups organized in 1814 to spread the good word their skirmishes subsided. Local branches of the Bible Society were founded across the province to distribute bibles and testaments in English, French, German, Irish, and Gaelic (**NS106**). The SPCK had a wider range of religious books and tracts for sale and for distribution to jails and the poor-house. All this activity was reported in considerable detail, particularly in the *Halifax Journal* and *Weekly Chronicle*, but both societies published a more permanent record in an annual report (**NS125**). According to this first report of the Bible Society bibles and testaments had been given to American prisoners of war in Melville Island 'who expressed an anxious desire to receive them' (p 47).

COPIES EXAMINED: NSHD (lacking pp 47–*48*), NSHL

NS118 The Nova-Scotia Calendar for 1816

THE | *NOVA-SCOTIA* [open] | CALENDAR, [open] | For TOWN and COUNTRY, | FOR THE | YEAR OF HUMAN REDEMPTION | 1816, | Being Bissextile or Leap Year, | *And the 56th of the Reign of His Majesty*, | In which are Contained | [10 ll. to left of rule 27 mm] The Full, Changes, Quarters & south- | ing of the Moon, | Rising and setting of the Sun, | Monthly Observations, | The Eclipses, | A remarkable Chronology, | Kings and Queens from the Conquest | Governors and Lt. Governors since | the first settlement of the Prov- | ince. | [10 ll. to right] List of the Army in the Province | Do do of the Navy, | The principal Civil Officers in | the Province, | Roads throughout the Province, | Masonic Lodges, under the Jur- | isdiction of the Grand Lodge | of Nova-Scotia, | With a variety of other Useful | Information. | [rule 56 mm] | *BY PHILO-URANIÆ*. | [rule 58 mm] | HALIFAX: | Printed, and for Sale at the Recorder Office.

IMPRINT: A.H. HOLLAND, *Publisher*, | Corner of Duke and Water-Streets,

COLLATION: 8° (16.2 x 11.3 cm uncut), 1^8 2–5^4, 24 leaves, pp *1–3* 4–48

CONTENTS: *1* title; 2 levee days, holidays; 3–14 calendar with court sittings; 15 ephemeris, zodiac, cycles, moveable feasts; 16 eclipses; 17–22 civil list; 22 governors and lieutenant governors; 23–24 freemasons; 24 firewards, fire engine company; 24–25 King's College; 25 clergy of established church; 25–26 signals; 26–28 roads and distances with houses of entertainment; Parrsborough packet; 28 postmasters; 28–29 sovereigns; 29–31 civil list; 31 the Falls; 32–35 army; 35–36 militia; 36 ships; 36–41 chronology (to 8 August 1815, including Canadian events); 41 tides; 41–48 anecdotes, miscellany including customs of 'the English in Ancient Times'; 'Effects of Music'; anecdotes of the Parish of Cramford in Scotland; 'Algiers'; and a story about Dr Ogilvie in Italy 'on authority of Lady Hamilton' which was 'To be concluded in the next Calendar'; 48 'Price of the Nova-Scotia Calendar: By the Dozen, 8s. – Single, 1s.'; imprint

PAPER: Laid, marked coat of arms with scroll frame; chains vertical 27 mm

TYPOGRAPHY: *Text*: old and modern faces, much long primer. *Display*: swash italic on title; almanac signs

36 ll., 130 (134) x 89 mm

BINDING: Stitched (NSHP)

NOTES: The notice announcing 'This Day Published' in the *Acadian Recorder* offered interleaved almanacs for an extra sixpence or 1s 6d per copy (11 November 1815).

COPIES EXAMINED: NSHD, NSHL, NSHP (2 copies, one lacking pp 47–48), OOA

NS119 A Poetical Account of the American Campaigns

A | POETICAL ACCOUNT [open] | OF THE | AMERICAN CAMPAIGNS [open] | OF | 1812 *and* 1813; | WITH SOME SLIGHT SKETCHES | *RELATING TO THE PARTY POLITICS* | WHICH GOVERNED | THE UNITED STATES, [open] | DURING THE WAR, AND AT ITS COMMENCEMENT. | [rule 81 mm] |

A

POETICAL ACCOUNT

OF THE

AMERICAN CAMPAIGNS

OF

1812 *and* 1813;

WITH SOME SLIGHT SKETCHES

RELATING TO THE PARTY POLITICS

WHICH GOVERNED

THE UNITED STATES,

DURING THE WAR, AND AT ITS COMMENCEMENT.

DEDICATED TO THE PEOPLE OF CANADA,

BY THE PUBLISHER.

HALIFAX:

PRINTED BY JOHN HOWE, JUN.

1815.

NS119 Courtesy Metropolitan Toronto Reference Library

DEDICATED TO THE PEOPLE OF CANADA, | *BY THE PUBLISHER.* | [rule 81 mm] | HALIFAX: | PRINTED BY JOHN HOWE, JUN. | 1815.

COLLATION: 8° (19.5 x 12.5 cm), *A*[4] B–I[4] K–R[4] S[2] [$1 signed], 70 leaves, pp *1–5* 6–139 *140*

CONTENTS: *1* title; 2 blank; *3–4* dedication: 'TO the brave and loyal Canadians, as a tribute of respect for the noble manner in which they have defended a Colony so distant from the Mother Country, and so weak in points of resources compared to their late enemy' signed AN ACADIAN at Halifax; *5*–139 text: five letters in verse, each with notes, dated May to December 1812, and four more letters headed SECOND CAMPAIGN, each with notes, dated May to December 1813, the final one with dateline: 'United States of America'; *140* blank

PAPER: Laid, watermark Strasbourg lily | JB [script]; countermark J BUDGEN | 1813; chains vertical 28 mm

TYPOGRAPHY: *Text*: long primer, modern face. *Display*: english and great primer open romans 30 ll., 135 (144) x 68; 67 mm for 20 ll. prose, 89 mm for verse

BINDING: Quarter light yellowish brown paper and greenish gray wove paper boards. Laid endpapers (QMMRB)

NOTES: The traditional attribution of authorship of this work to Thomas Daniel Cowdell has been twice disputed by Thomas B. Vincent: 'Nova Scotia Bibliography: Two Notes,' *Papers of the Bibliographical Society of Canada/Cahiers de la Société bibliographique du Canada* XVI (1977): 58; *Dictionary of Canadian Biography* VI, s.v. 'Cowdell, Thomas Daniel'. Perhaps Cowdell's connection with *A Poetical Account* was not as author but as publisher. Two years earlier he had published Elijah Parish's equally vigorous condemnation of the war (**NS101**).

Priced at 7s 6d the *Poetical Account* was published on 13 September and advertised in the *Royal Gazette* (13 September 1815) and the *Halifax Journal* (18 September *et seq.*).

COPIES EXAMINED: NBSAM, NSHL, NSHP, OOA, OTMCL, QMMRB

REFERENCES: Akins, Casey 1015, Lande S556, TPL 1041

1816

NS120 Directions for Avoiding the Sambro Ledges

DIRECTIONS, [fat] | For avoiding the Ledges lying to the Eastward and Westward of *Sambro-Island*, whereon is now erected a Light- | House; for entering the Harbour of HALIFAX, in NOVA-SCOTIA. | ...

Notice: 1/2° (32 x 19.5 cm)

CONTENTS: 1 l. heading; 30 ll. text

PAPER: Laid, marked Britannia; chains vertical 26 mm

TYPOGRAPHY: *Text*: bourgeois, modern face 168 x 144 mm

NOTES: These undated sailing directions were probably not printed before 1816 when modern and fat face types are commonly found in Halifax imprints. In that year the first commissioners of lighthouses were appointed.

COPY EXAMINED: NSHP: RG1, vol 249, no 2

NS121 James, William

AN | INQUIRY | INTO THE MERITS | OF THE | PRINCIPAL NAVAL ACTIONS, | BETWEEN | GREAT-BRITAIN | AND THE | UNITED STATES; | COMPRISING | AN ACCOUNT OF | ALL BRITISH AND AMERICAN SHIPS OF WAR, | RECIPROCALLY CAPTURED AND DESTROYED, | SINCE THE 18th OF JUNE 1812. | BY | WILLIAM JAMES. | [ornamental dash 40 mm] | "TRUTH came from above, FALSEHOOD from below." | JOHNSON. | [ornamental dash 32 mm] | HALIFAX, N.S. | PRINTED FOR THE AUTHOR, | BY ANTHONY H. HOLLAND, | ACADIAN RECORDER OFFICE. | 1816. [UNITED STATES; with italic semicolon and N.S. with wf S]

COLLATION: 4° (21 x 15 cm), *1–2*[4] (21 + χ1) *3–9*[4] (91 + 2χ1) *10*[2] *11–13*[4] 3χ1 *14*[4], 57 leaves, pp *i–v* vi, *1* 2–3 *4* [2] *5* 6–60 [2][2] 61–94 [3][2] 95–102 (vi printed with period); STATE: 8, 9 mispaged 14, 15; [χ1, 2χ1, 3χ1 folded tables 38 x 34 cm, 19.5 x 30 cm, 43 x 15.8 cm]

CONTENTS: *i* title; *ii* blank; *iii* dedication: TO THE | LOYAL INHABITANTS | OF | HIS MAJESTY'S | North-American Provinces, | ... signed *THE AUTHOR* at Halifax, 9 March 1816; *iv* errata (12 ll.); advertisement (about Table 7); *v*–vi preface; *1*–3 introduction; *4* blank; *5*–101 text: Notes A to Z, Aa to Hh with [*1*] Table 1; [2] blank; 59 Table 2; [2][*1*] Table 3; [2][2] blank; [3][*1*] Table 4; [3][2] blank; 99–101 Tables 5 to 7; 102 conclusion

PAPER: Laid, marked eagle in crowned shield | GIOR MAGNANI [or] GM (505, 507 in Gravell and Miller, *Foreign*); chains horizontal 28 mm; χ1 wove unmarked except NSHP, OTMCL copies laid, marked coat of arms with scroll frame and initials GFM | GEORGE SMI[ ]; 2χ1, 3χ1 as text paper or laid, greenish, marked AL MASSO.

AN

INQUIRY

INTO THE MERITS

OF THE

PRINCIPAL NAVAL ACTIONS,

BETWEEN

GREAT-BRITAIN

AND THE

UNITED STATES;

COMPRISING

AN ACCOUNT OF

ALL BRITISH AND AMERICAN SHIPS OF WAR,

RECIPROCALLY CAPTURED AND DESTROYED,

SINCE THE 18th OF JUNE 1812.

BY

WILLIAM JAMES.

"TRUTH came from above, FALSEHOOD from below."

JOHNSON

HALIFAX, N. S.

PRINTED FOR THE AUTHOR,

BY ANTHONY H. HOLLAND,

ACADIAN RECORDER OFFICE.

1816.

NS121 Courtesy Metropolitan Toronto Reference Library

TYPOGRAPHY: *Text*: modern faces; gatherings *1–4*, *10* with mixed use, page by page, of long primer and small pica except pp 6–10 with changes on each page; *5* with outer forme small pica, inner long primer; *6–9*, *11–14* with outer forme long primer, inner small pica. *Display*: long ornamental dashes; wrapper with Greek key a more rectangular version of two lines great primer 1 of Vincent Figgins specimen and acorns as long primer 13 of 1785 Caslon
48, 50 ll., 171 (178) x 105; 67, 72 mm for 20 ll.
ILLUSTRATION: Woodcut (p 74) of seven weapons with printed reference a to g [73 x 48 mm]
BINDING: Wrapper of bluish gray wove paper the upper printed [within 9 mm Greek key rules with corner rosettes and acrons midway head and foot 184 x 110 mm] as title except ... ACTIONS | ... | ... RECIPROCALLY CAPTURED AND | DESTROYED, SINCE THE | ... [with both wf of title]. Lower printed within same rules with woodcut illustrations of six weapons (as p 74 but lacking 'd,' the Patent Porcupine hand-grenade); [below caption] American dismantling shot. | Laid endpapers (NSHD, OTUTF). Rebound retaining wrapper (QMMRB, GBL, USMWA, USMH-H)
NOTES: With the working title 'An Account of all the British and American National Ships, Taken and Destroyed during the Late War' William James, motivated by 'the cause of Truth, and the British Navy,' announced that his 'little work' would be published 'shortly.' He added a request: 'Any gentleman acquainted with a material fact respecting either of the actions, not supposed to be generally known, will confer a favor, by communicating it, on paper' (*Acadian Recorder*, 5 August 1815). Under a new title 'A Full and Impartial Account of the Naval Actions, between Great-Britain, and the United-States' it was advertised as 'In the Press' with a request that 'the Editors of the New-Brunswick City Gazette, the Montreal Herald, and Quebec Gazette' give the notice six insertions and transmit their accounts to the Acadian Recorder Printing Office (11 December 1815).

Finally, on 18 March, *An Inquiry*, by then called simply 'James' Naval Actions,' was ready for delivery at the Recorder office and at the bookstores of George Eaton and David Howe. Subscribers to the work were invited to pick up their copies from Mr Eaton (*Halifax Journal*, 25 March 1816). Just five days after publication an editorial note in the *Acadian Recorder* reported that upwards of eight hundred copies had already been disposed of (23 March).

When James went on to publish *A Full and Correct Account of the Chief Naval Occurrences of the Late War between Great Britain and the United States of America* in London in 1817 he referred to the success of his preliminary Halifax pamphlet: 'The colonial public, however, gave the work a most flattering reception: in the short space of two months, nearly 2000 copies went off; and the remainder, about 500 in number, the author brought with him to England' (pp vi–vii). The London edition includes an engraved plate of American dismantling shot signed 'James del' which is similar to the woodcut illustration used in this imprint. The *Free Press* published a review of *A Full and Correct Account* noting its 'high reputation ... deservedly acquired' (28 October 1817).
COPIES EXAMINED: NBSAM, NSHD (3 copies), NSHL (title page photomechanical reproduction), NSHP, OTMCL, OTUTF, QMBM, QMMRB, GBL, USMH-H
REFERENCES: Akins, Dennis, Gagnon I 1774, Lande 466, TPL 1056

NS122 The Nova-Scotia Calendar for 1817
[upper wrapper printed] [within 9 mm Greek key rules with rosette corners and flowers and stars midway head and foot 152 x 90 mm] THE | NOVA-SCOTIA | CALENDAR, [fat, open] | *For Town and Country*; | For the Year of Human Redemption | 1817; | Being the First after Bissextile or Leap Year, | AND | the 57th of the Reign of His Majesty GEORGE III. | *In which are Contained*, | THE Full, Changes, Quarters and Southing of the Moon – | Rising and setting of the Sun – Monthly Observations – The | Eclipses – A remarkable Chronology – Kings and Queens | from the Conquest – Governors and Lt. Governors since the | first settlement of the Province – list of the Army, Navy, | and Militia Officers in the Province – The Principal Civil | Officers – Post Roads throughout the Province – Officers | of His Majesty's Customs, and Excise – Ditto of the Dock- | Yard, Hospital, and Ordinance Departments – Masonic In- | formation – With a variety of other Matter, both Useful and | Entertaining. | [rule 70 mm] | *By W. Fairweather*; | [rule 68 mm] | HALIFAX N.S.: Printed, and for Sale at the Office of the | ACADIAN RECORDER, Corner of Duke & Water-sts. | *Price – 8s. doz. 1s. single.*
COLLATION: 12° (18.5 x 11.8 cm), *1–4*^{6}, 24 leaves, pp *1–12* 13–48
CONTENTS: printed wrapper: upper as transcribed; verso printed with eclipses, planets, zodiac, common notes, feasts; lower blank; verso printed with 'Alterations, &c.'; *1–12* calendar with court

sittings; 13–19 civil list including levee days, holidays, King's College, clergy of established church; firewards, fire engine company; 20 freemasons; 20–21 governors and lieutenant governors; 21 signals; 22 sovereigns; 23–24 roads and distances with houses of entertainment; Parrsborough packet; sheriffs; 25–28 army; 29–35 militia; 35–36 ships; 37–40 chronology (1066 to 8 August 1815, no Canadian events); 40 story concluded from 1816 Calendar; 41–48 stories and verse including 'The Miser and the Mouse'; 'London Inscriptions'; 'The Cockney's Journal of the First of September'; epitaphs; 'Highwayman Reclaimed'

PAPER: Wove, unmarked

TYPOGRAPHY: *Text*: old and modern faces, much long primer. *Display*: thickened modern faces, title with Greek key a more rectangular version of two lines great primer 1 of Vincent Figgins 1815 specimen and pansies as Figgins great primer 10 with flower heads only; stars (nonpareil 1) of 1785 Caslon specimen; almanac signs
45 ll., 150 (156) x 92 mm

BINDING: Wrapper of laid paper, greenish, with cloth spine. Printed as transcribed with title on upper, astronomical and annual information on verso. Lower wrapper blank, verso printed with additional information

NOTES: The addenda inside the lower wrapper are headed 'The following Alterations, &c. were received after the first 48 pages of the Calendar was put to Press.' There are additions to the civil list, to roads and distances, and to the section of freemasons, most notably the name of Anthony H. Holland, Grand Marshall of the Provincial Grand Lodge, and founder of the *Acadian Recorder* where this Calendar was published.

W. Fairweather, the third almanac maker (or perhaps third pseudonym) at the *Nova-Scotia Calendar*, may have been inspired by the popular Abraham Weatherwise series in the United States.

COPIES EXAMINED: NSHD, NSHP

NS123 Nova Scotia. Laws (8th Parliament, 6th session: 1805 to 10th Parliament, 6th session: 1816)
THE | STATUTES AT LARGE, | PASSED IN THE SEVERAL | GENERAL ASSEMBLIES | HELD IN | HIS MAJESTY's PROVINCE OF NOVA-SCOTIA: | FROM | The SIXTH SESSION of the EIGHTH GENERAL ASSEMBLY, | Which met at HALIFAX, the twenty-eighth Day of November, in | the forty-ſixth year of His Majeſty's Reign, A.D. 1805, | being the fifty-fifth Seſſion of the GENERAL ASSEMBLY; | TO | The fifty-ſixth year of His Majeſty's Reign, incluſive; | WITH AN INDEX. [open] | PUBLISHED BY ORDER OF THE GOVERNOR, COUNCIL AND HOUSE OF ASSEMBLY. | *VOL. II.* | BY | HENRY H. COGSWELL. | [royal arms 40 x 90 mm] | HALIFAX: | PRINTED by JOHN HOWE, SON & CO. Printers to the KING's Moſt Excellent Majeſty. | 1816.

COLLATION: 4° (28.4 x 22.8 cm) πA² B–F² G¹, A–I² K–T² V–2I² 2K–2T² 2V–3G² [$1 (–πE, F, R, X, 2G) signed], 123 leaves, pp *i–iii* iv–xxv *xxvi*, 1–220

CONTENTS: *i* title; *ii* blank; *iii*–xiii titles of the statutes; *xiv* index to the expired laws; *xv*–xxv index to the statutes; *xxvi* blank; 1–220 text

PAPER: Unmarked, laid, chains vertical 27 mm except some sections of wove in all copies, usually H–L, N–P

TYPOGRAPHY: *Text*: pica, old face roman with modern face italic. *Display*: long swelled rule
46 ll., 214 (228) x 158 (182); 92 mm for 20 ll.

BINDING: Dark green leather, probably roan, spine lettered between gilt rules NOVA | SCOTIA | LAWS | 2 ; upper board lettered J. PRYOR ESQ[R] on NSHD copy, name cut away (NSHP). Quarter dark green roan and marbled paper in stormont, gloster, spotted, or shell pattern. Spine lettered 2 in some copies. Laid endpapers and binder's leaf (NSHD, NSWA, OONL, OTMCL)

NOTES: Three hundred 'Sets of the Statutes at Large' were printed with £100 voted to H.H. Cogswell for preparing the statutes, superintending the publication, correcting the press, and making an index for this and an earlier work (**NS97**); £225 to John Howe, Son and Company for printing; and £95 to David Howe 'upon his completing the binding in calf of 80 Sets and alſo half binding 220 Sets' (*Journal*, 10:7, 1817, pp 115–6, 121).

COPIES EXAMINED: NSHD (2 copies), NSHP, NSWA (2 copies), OOA, OONL, OTMCL, USMH-L

REFERENCES: Bishop, TPL 4830

NS124 Nova Scotia. Parliament (10th, 6th session: 1816). House of Assembly
[half title] [thick-thin rule 130 mm] | *JOURNAL* [fat] | AND | *PROCEEDINGS* | OF THE | *HOUSE of ASSEMBLY*, | 1816. | [thin-thick rule 130 mm]

COLLATION: 4° (26.8 x 18.5 cm), *A*² B–I² K–U² W–2C² [$1 signed], 54 leaves, pp *1–3* 4–107 *108*

CONTENTS: *1* half title; 2 proclamation; 3–107 text; *108* blank

PAPER: Laid, unmarked; chains horizontal 28 mm (NSHP); NSHL copy with *A*–E wove, unmarked

TYPOGRAPHY: *Text*: pica, old face with modern face numbers. *Display*: script, modern face italics, and open romans; medium swelled rule; royal arms cut 20 x 58 mm
46 ll., 212 (226) x 134; 92 mm for 20 ll.
NOTES: Soon after this session ended Lieutenant Governor Sherbrooke was commissioned governor-in-chief of British North America and left Halifax for Quebec. His successor was George Ramsay, 9th Earl of Dalhousie.
COPIES EXAMINED: NSHL, NSHP

NS125 Society for Promoting Christian Knowledge. Halifax Diocesan Committee
ANNUAL REPORT | OF THE | HALIFAX DIOCESAN COMMITTEE | OF THE | SOCIETY | FOR | PROMOTING CHRISTIAN KNOWLEDGE | FOR | 1815. | [swelled rule 14 mm] | HALIFAX, | Anthony H. Holland, printer.
COLLATION: 8° (14.9 x 10.7 cm), *1*⁸, 8 leaves, pp *1–3* 4–16
CONTENTS: *1* title; 2 blank; 3–10 text dated at Halifax, January 1816; 10–11 statement of books dispersed; 11–16 members
PAPER: Laid, marked eagle in crowned shield | GIOR MAGNANI (505, 507 in Gravell and Miller, *Foreign*); chains vertical 29 mm
TYPOGRAPHY: *Text*: bourgeois, transitional face
33 ll., 113 (118) x 77; 67 mm for 20 ll.
NOTES: Although the Society for the Propagation of the Gospel had assisted missionaries of the established church, distributed tracts, and sponsored charity schools in Nova Scotia since the previous century it was not until 1813 when the non-sectarian Nova Scotia Bible Society was established that a diocesan committee of the Society for Promoting Christian Knowledge was organized to involve members of the established church in more active dissemination of religious literature (**NS117**).
COPY EXAMINED: NSHL

1817

NS126 An Almanack for the Year of Our Lord, 1817
[within thick-thin rules 149 x 85 mm] AN | ALMANACK [open] | *For the Year of Our Lord*, 1817, | BEING THE FIRST AFTER BISSEXTILE OR LEAP YEAR, | Calculated for the Meridian of | HALIFAX, IN NOVA-SCOTIA, [open] | BUT WILL SERVE FOR ANY PART OF THE PROVINCE | CONTAINING: | [8 ll. to left of rule 25 mm] The ECLIPSES. | RISING and SETTING of | the SUN and MOON. | TIME of HIGH WATER. | FEASTS and FASTS of the | CHURCH. | LIST of PROVINCIAL | OFFICERS. | [8 ll. to right] SITTINGS of COURTS. | OFFICERS of the NAVY | on this STATION, | OFFICERS of the ARMY, | under Lieut. Gen. GEORGE, | Earl of Dalhousie, G.C.B. | OFFICERS of His Majesty's | NAVY-YARD, & HOSPITAL. | With every other matter useful or necessary. | [double rule 80 mm] | *By THEOPHRASTUS*. [double rule 80 mm] | HALIFAX: [open] | Published by DAVID HOWE, and Sold at his | Stationary Store. *Stet* Stationary
COLLATION: 8° (20.5 x 13.2 cm), *1–2*⁸, 16 leaves, pp [32]
CONTENTS: [*1*] title; [*2*] signals; [*3*] man of signs; eclipses, cycles, feasts, zodiac; [*4*] levee days; commissioners for the poor; equation table; remedy for cattle swelled by eating green clover; [*5–16*] calendar; [*17–21*] civil list; [*21–22*] courts; [*23–24*] civil list; [*24–25*] freemasons; [*25–26*] navy yard; [*26*] clergy of established church; [*26–27*] King's College; [*27–31*] army; [*31*] ships; fire engine company; [32] roads and distances with houses of entertainment
PAPER: Wove, unmarked
TYPOGRAPHY: *Text*: long primer, modern face, with old faces. *Display*: pages within thick-thin rules; man of signs cut (63 x 47 mm) with bellflower frame as **NS3**; almanac signs
148 x 86 mm
BINDING: Stitched
NOTES: A notice in the *Weekly Chronicle* of 3 January that almanacs for 1817 would be available the following day at the Gazette office and David Howe's store is corroborated by Archibald Cunningham who received his copy on 12 January and noted 'Published the 4th Jan.y' with his signature.
COPY EXAMINED: NSHD

NS127 An Almanack for the Year of Our Lord, 1818
[within thick-thin rules 151 x 85 mm] AN | ALMANACK [open] | *For the Year of Our Lord*, 1818, | BEING THE SECOND AFTER BISSEXTILE OR LEAP YEAR, | Calculated for the Meridian of | HALIFAX, IN NOVA-SCOTIA, [open] | BUT WILL SERVE FOR ANY PART OF THE PROVINCE | CONTAINING: | [8 ll. to left of rule] The ECLIPSES. | RISING and SETTING of |

the SUN and MOON. | TIME of HIGH WATER. | FEASTS and FASTS of the | CHURCH. | LIST of PROVINCIAL | OFFICERS. | [8 ll. to right] SITTING of COURTS. | OFFICERS of the NAVY | on this STATION, | OFFICERS of the ARMY, | under Lieut. Gen. GEORGE | Earl of Dalhousie, G.C.B. | OFFICERS of His Majesty's | NAVY-YARD, & HOSPITAL. | With every other matter useful or necessary. | [double rule 80 mm] | *By THEOPHRASTUS.* | [double rule 80 mm] | HALIFAX: [open] | Published by DAVID HOWE, and Sold at his | Stationary Store, George-Street, and at the Gazette Office. *Stet* Stationary

COLLATION: 8° (21 x 14.2 cm), *1–2*[8] *3*[4], 20 leaves, pp [*40*]

CONTENTS: [*1*] title; [*2–3*] signals; [*3*] man of signs; moveable feasts; [*4*] eclipses, cycles, levee days; commissioners of the poor; [*5–16*] calendar with seasonal health hints: 'Old Parr's Maxims of Health'; [*17–21*] civil list; [*21–22*] courts; [*23–24*] civil list; [*24–25*] freemasons; [*25–26*] navy yard; [*26*] clergy of established church; [*26–27*] King's College; [*27–30*] army; [*31*] ships; mail coach; [*32–33*] roads and distances with houses of entertainment; [*33*] Parrsborough packet; holidays; firewards; [*34–37*] chronology (to 1816, no Canadian events); [*37*] hints, remedies: 'potatoe' tops, warts or corns, whooping cough, asthma, orchards; [*38–40*] 'On Drunkenness'; [*40*] discount tables; cholera; anecdote

PAPER: Wove, unmarked

TYPOGRAPHY: *Text*: long primer, modern face, with other faces in old and modern. *Display*: pages within thick-thin rules; man of signs cut (63 x 47 mm) with bellflower frame as **NS3**; almanac signs 151 x 85 mm

BINDING: Stitched

NOTES: David Howe's entry into the now crowded almanac market was announced in his uncle's *Weekly Chronicle* on 10 October with copies advertised for sale in his brother's *Halifax Journal* (20 October 1817).

COPY EXAMINED: NSHD

NS128 Heart and Hand Fire-Company (Halifax)

THE | RULES [open] | OF THE | *Heart and Hand Fire-Company,* | FORMED AT | HALIFAX, NOVA-SCOTIA, [open] | THE 3D APRIL, 1810; | REVISED, | AND ORDERED TO BE RE-PRINTED, | AT AN EXTRA MEETING, | HOLDEN ON THE 31ST DECEMBER, 1816. | [swelled rule 38 mm] | HALIFAX: PRINTED BY JOHN HOWE, SON AND CO. | 1817.

COLLATION: 8° (16.4 x 11.6 cm), *1*[8], 8 leaves, pp *1–3* 4–14 *15–16*

CONTENTS: *1* title; 2 blank; 3–13 text, I to IX; 14 list of members (40); *15–16* blank

PAPER: Laid, marked [crest] | N & S | 18[?]5; chains vertical 24 mm

TYPOGRAPHY: *Text*: pica, modern face 25 ll., 117 (126) x 75 (94); 95 mm for 20 ll.

BINDING: Stitched

NOTES: Each member was required to have two bags of raven's duck, one and a half yards long, a leather cap, and two buckets of three gallon capacity, black in colour with the owner's name marked in white. Buckets and cap were to bear the figure of Heart and Hand 'the Heart to be painted red, the hand flesh colour, and reclining on the heart' (p 9). The society would furnish '6 Lanthorns and 6 Bed Keys' numbered and marked Heart and Hand (p 9).

COPY EXAMINED: NSWA

REFERENCE: Dennis

NS129 McCulloch, Thomas, 1776–1843

WORDS OF PEACE: | BEING AN | ADDRESS, | DELIVERED TO THE CONGREGATION OF HALIFAX IN | CONNEXION WITH THE PRESBYTERIAN CHURCH OF | NOVA-SCOTIA, IN CONSEQUENCE OF SOME CON- | GREGATIONAL DISPUTES WHICH REQUIRED | THE INTERFERENCE OF PRESBYTERY. | *By THOMAS M'CULLOCH,* | PICTOU. | [thick-thin rule 28 mm] | *Now I beseech you, brethren, by the name of our* | *Lord Jesus Christ, that ye all speak the same* | *things, and that there be no divisions among* | *you; but that ye be perfectly joined together in* | *the same mind and in the same judgment.* 1. *Cor.* | 1. 10. | [rule 12 mm] | PUBLISHED BY A MEMBER OF THE CONGREGATION. | [double rule 69 mm] | HALIFAX: | Printed by *EDMUND WARD,* at his Office, No. 15 | Barrington Street. | 1817. STATE: WORDS OF PEACE.

COLLATION: 8° (16.6 x 10.4 cm), *1*[8], 8 leaves, pp *1–3* 4–16 (pagination in [ ])

CONTENTS: *1* title; 2 blank; 3–16 text

PAPER: Laid, marked Vryheyt | 1809 | [?]TE; chains vertical 28 mm

TYPOGRAPHY: *Text*: bourgeois, modern face 39 ll., 129 (136) x 69; 67 mm for 20 ll.

BINDING: Stitched (NSHD); wrapper of bluish gray wove paper (NSHL)

NOTES: Summoned from Pictou to mediate a dispute in the Halifax congregation McCulloch

offered a stern warning: 'Brethren, there is something among you which cannot abide the day of Christ's coming; and now is the time to have the evil rectified' (p 15). The *Free Press* announced that McCulloch's address would be 'ready for delivery tomorrow' (15 April 1817).
COPIES EXAMINED: NSHD (2 copies), NSHL, NSWA
REFERENCE: Dennis

NS130 Methodist Missionary Society (Nova Scotia District)
A REPORT | OF THE | *FORMATION OF A* | METHODIST | Missionary Society, | FOR THE | NOVA-SCOTIA DISTRICT, | *At a Public Meeting held at the Methodist Chapel,* | *HALIFAX:* | *On the third of June,* 1817. | With the RESOLUTIONS which were proposed and carried. – Toge- | ther with a short | ADDRESS, | TO the INHABITANTS of NOVA-SCOTIA, NEW-BRUNSWICK, and | PRINCE-EDWARD ISLAND. | [thick-thin rule 20 mm] | *TO WHICH ARE ADDED:* | *Important and interesting Extracts from a* | REPORT | Recently published in England, and a LIST of the | FOREIGN STATIONS, of the METHODIST MISSIONARIES, &c. | [thick-thin rule 66 mm] | *HALIFAX:* | PRINTED BY EDMUND WARD, 1817.
COLLATION: 8° (19.6 x 12 cm), *1–2*[4] *3*[3], 11 leaves, pp *1–3* 4-22 (pagination in [ ])
CONTENTS: *1* title; 2 blank; *3*–6 text; 7–9 address; 9–15 extract from the report of the Methodist Missionary Society recently formed in Manchester; 15–19 Address to the Public; 19–22 'A List of the Stations of the Methodist Missionaries in Foreign Parts'; 22 conclusion by the Nova-Scotia Committee
PAPER: Wove, *1* marked 1815 (OTMCL); 2, 3 and NSHP copy unmarked
TYPOGRAPHY: *Text*: long primer, modern face
48 ll., 160 (167) x 100; 67 mm for 20 ll.
BINDING: Rebound
NOTES: The Nova Scotia Committee concluded: 'Though the success of the Methodist Missionaries in this District, has not been equal to their wishes, yet, they have cause to rejoice, that their labours have not been as water spilt on the ground' (p 22). Fifteen circuits and stations had been established with 'upwards of 30 chapels' served by eighteen regular preachers ministering to two thousand communicants. Publication of this report was noted in the *Free Press* on 1 July 1817.
COPIES EXAMINED: NSHP, OTMCL
REFERENCES: Akins, TPL 1121

NS131 Nova Scotia. Laws (10th Parliament, 7th session: 1817)
[text begins] At the GENERAL ASSEMBLY of the Province of | Nova-Scotia, begun and holden at Halifax, on Thurſday | the 6th day of February, 1812, and continued by ſeve- | ral Prorogations to Thurſday the Thirteenth day of Fe- | bruary, 1817
COLLATION: 4° (28.4 x 22.5 cm), 3H–3I[2] 3K–3T[2] 3V–3Y[2] [$1 signed], 32 leaves, pp 221–284 (mispaging 275 as 274)
CONTENTS: 221–284 text
PAPER: Wove, unmarked
TYPOGRAPHY: *Text*: pica, old face with modern face italics; mixed use of comma from a script fount; long swelled rule
45 ll., 210 (225) x 157 (180); 94 mm for 20 ll.
NOTES: This was the first session of the Assembly in Lord Dalhousie's term as lieutenant governor.
COPIES EXAMINED: NSHP, OOA, USMH-L

NS132 Nova Scotia. Parliament (10th, 7th session: 1817). House of Assembly
[half title] [thick-thin rule 130 mm] | *JOURNAL* [fat] | AND | *PROCEEDINGS* | OF THE | *HOUSE of ASSEMBLY,* | 1817. | [thin-thick rule 130 mm]
COLLATION: 4° (26.8 x 18.5 cm), *A*[2] B–I[2] K–T[2] V–2H[2] [$1 signed], 64 leaves, pp *1–3* 4–128
CONTENTS: *1* half title; 2 proclamation; 3–128 text
PAPER: Laid, marks cropped at fore-edge (NSHL); chains horizontal 27 mm
TYPOGRAPHY: *Text*: pica, old face with modern face. *Display*: royal arms cut 19 x 54 mm
41 ll., 189 (205) x 134; 92 mm for 20 ll.
COPIES EXAMINED: NSHL, NSHP, OOA

NS133 The Nova-Scotia Almanack for the Year of Our Lord, 1817
THE | *NOVA-SCOTIA* | ALMANACK, | *FOR THE YEAR OF OUR LORD* 1817, | BEING THE FIRST AFTER BISSEXTILE OR LEAP YEAR. | *Calculated for the Meridian of* | HALIFAX IN NOVA-SCOTIA, | *But will serve for any part of the Provinee.* | [dotted rule 75 mm] | *HALIFAX:* | Published by EDMUND WARD, at his Office, No. 15 | Barrington Street. *Stet Provinee*
COLLATION: 8° (18.4 x 11.5 cm), *1–3*[8], 24 leaves, pp [*48*]
CONTENTS: [*1*] title; [2] blank; [3] levee days, holidays; [4–7] Halifax harbour, signals; [*8–10*] 'Regulations in the United States on Commerce. Extracted from Blunt's American Coast Pilot'; [*10–12*] roads and distances with houses of

entertainment; [12–13] ships; [13] Parrsborough packet; [14–15] Nova Scotia Bible Society, Acadian School Society, Trustees of Pictou Academy; mail coaches; miscellaneous: 'Precaution to avoid the effect of Lightning'; [16–20] army; [20] note on postal service; [21–32] calendar; [33–38] farmer's calendar; [38–39] civil list; [39–44] courts, justices; [44] King's College; [45] freemasons; [46] clergy of established church; [46–47] civil list; [47] firewards; [47–48] fire engine company; [48] navy yard, hospital; the Falls

PAPER: Laid, unmarked; chains horizontal 28 mm

TYPOGRAPHY: *Text*: long primer, modern face. *Display*: almanac signs

140 x 80 mm

BINDING: Wrapper of marbled paper; interleaved (NSWA)

NOTES: A native of Halifax, Edmund Ward had apprenticed with William Minns at the *Weekly Chronicle* before moving in 1809 to Bermuda where he was appointed king's printer. His dismissal from that office in 1815 was reported in the *Acadian Recorder* (10 June 1815). He returned to Halifax and in March of the following year published the prospectus of a new weekly, *The Free Press*, which was established in April (*Weekly Chronicle*, 29 March 1816).

Ward's notice for his new almanac claimed that it contained 'in addition to what is usually inserted in the Halifax Almanacks, Directions for coming into the Harbour, Private Signals of the Merchants of the Place, Regulations in the United States on Commerce, the Farmers calendar, with many other articles useful and entertaining' (*Free Press*, 14 January 1817).

COPIES EXAMINED: NSHD (2 copies), NSHL, NSWA

NS134 The Nova-Scotia Almanack for the Year of Our Lord, 1818

[within lattice rules] THE | NOVA-SCOTIA | ALMANACK, | *FOR THE YEAR OF OUR LORD 1818.* | BEING THE SECOND AFTER BISSEXTILE OR LEAP YEAR. | CALCULATED FOR THE MERIDIAN OF | HALIFAX IN NOVA-SCOTIA. | *WILL SERVE FOR ANY PART OF THE PROVINCE.* | [thick-thin rule 27 mm] | BY PYTHAGORAS. | [thin-thick rule 27 mm] | [dotted rule 85 mm] | *HALIFAX.* | Printed by EDMUND WARD, at his Office, No. 15, Barrington | Street; where PRINTING of every description is executed.

COLLATION: 8° (18.5 x 12.2 cm), *1–4*⁴, 18 leaves, pp [36]

CONTENTS: [*1*] title; [*2*] levee days, holidays; [*3–6*] Halifax harbour, signals; [*7*] Parrsborough packet; the Falls; [*7–8*] astronomical, cycles, feasts, eclipses; [*9–20*] calendar; [*21–28*] civil list, courts; King's College; firewards, fire engine company; mail coach; [*29*] freemasons; [*30*] Nova Scotia Bible Society, Acadian School Society; lighthouse commissioners; [*31*] navy yard, hospital; [*31–32*] roads and distances with houses of entertainment; [*32*] tides; [*33–36*] army; ships; [*36*] errata (2 ll.)

PAPER: Wove, unmarked

TYPOGRAPHY: *Text*: modern faces. *Display*: pages within lattice rules as long primer 10 of 1790 Fry and Steele specimen; almanac signs

140 x 80 mm

NOTES: Ward advertised this almanac as he had the one for the previous year noting information 'in addition to what is usually inserted in the Halifax Almanacks' (*Free Press*, 7 October 1817). His price was six shillings per dozen. Pythagoras, newly cited as almanac maker, turned to the history of Greek philosophy for a pseudonym with classical credentials as impressive as the Howes' Theophrastus.

COPY EXAMINED: NSHD

NS135 Nova Scotia Bible Society

THE | SECOND | REPORT | OF THE | *NOVA-SCOTIA BIBLE SOCIETY.* | [dotted rule 75 mm] | *HALIFAX, NOVA-SCOTIA.* | Printed by EDMUND WARD, No. 15 Barrington Street, | next door to the Post Office. | 1817.

COLLATION: 8° (17.4 x 11.4 cm), *1–4*⁴ *5*¹, 17 leaves, pp *1–4* 5–34 (pagination in [ ])

CONTENTS: *1* title; 2 blank; 3 officers; 4 blank; 5 meeting; 6 laws and regulations; 7–9 text; 10 treasurer's account; 11–15 appendix I to III: branch societies; 16–34 subscriptions and donations; 34 'NB' note (6 ll.)

PAPER: Laid, *1*, *4* marked 1813; *2*, *3* marked Vryheyt (NSHL); USMBAt with *1*, *3* as 1813; *2*, *4* Vryheyt; chains vertical 27 mm

TYPOGRAPHY: *Text*: long primer, modern face

38 ll., 127 (134) x 76; 67 mm for 20 ll.

NOTES: Since the founding of the provincial society in 1814 subscriptions, donations, and collections totalled almost £1680. After expenses were deducted the balance was sent to the parent society in England. In a little over two years the Nova Scotia branch had distributed more than 2600 of the British society's bible and testaments.

COPIES EXAMINED: NSHL, USMBAt

NS136 The Nova-Scotia Calendar for 1818
[within 9 mm Greek key rules with rosette corners, flowers and stars midway at head and to right at foot, acorns at base of sides 183 x 91 mm] THE | NOVA-SCOTIA | CALENDAR, [open] | *For Town and Country;* | *For the Year of Human Redemption,* | 1818: | Being the Second after Leap Year, | AND | The 58th of the Reign of His Majesty GEORGE III. | *In which are Contained,* | THE Full, Changes, Quarters and Southing of the Moon – | Rising and sitting of the Sun – Monthly Observations – The | Eclipses – A remarkable Chronology – Kings and Queens | from the Conquest – Governors and Lt. Governors since the | first settlement of the Province – List of the Army, Navy, | and Militia Officers in the Province – The Principal Civil | Officers – Post Roads throughout the Province – Officers | of His Majesty's Customs, and Excise – Ditto of the Dock- | Yard, Hospital, and Ordnance Departments – Masonic In- | formation – With a variety of other Matter, both Useful and | Entertaining. | [rule 69 mm] | By PHILO-URANIÆ. | [rule 67 mm] | HALIFAX N.S.: | Printed, and for Sale by A.H. HOLLAND, at the | ACADIAN RECORDER Office, | Corner of Duke and Water-streets. | [thick-thin rule 17 mm] | *Price* – 8*s. doz.* 1*s. single. Stet* Rising and sitting
COLLATION: 8° (21.3 x 12.9 cm), *A–C*^{4} D^4 E^1 [D1 signed], 17 leaves, pp *1–14* 15–34
CONTENTS: *1* title; *2* astronomical characters, eclipses, cycles, feasts; *3–14* calendar with seasonal verses opening 'Though hills and dales are clad in snow' for January, 'The ploughman hails the kindlier skies' for May, and 'Now Winter in unwelcome haste' for November; 15–20 civil list, courts, Halifax officials, fire engine company; 20 King's College; clergy of established church; governors and lieutenant governors; levee days; 21 holidays; 21–22 freemasons; 22 signals; 22–23 roads and distances with the names of innkeepers; Parrsborough packet; 23–24 sovereigns; 24–26 chronology (1066 to August 1816, no Canadian events); 26–28 army; 28–32 militia; 33 ships; 33–34 remedies and hints including hooping cough, smoky chimneys, and 'The Use of Garlic against Moles, Grubs, and Snails'
PAPER: Wove, unmarked
TYPOGRAPHY: *Text*: modern and old faces, much brevier. *Display*: title with Greek key a more rectangular version of two lines great primer 1 of Vincent Figgins 1815 specimen and pansies as Figgins great primer 10 with flower heads only; stars (nonpareil 1) and acorns (long primer 13) as 1785 Caslon specimen; almanac signs
66 ll., 180 (184) x 90 mm
NOTES: The *Free Press* noted publication on 7 October.
COPIES EXAMINED: NBS, NSHD (2 copies, one lacking pp 33–34), NSHL, NSHP

NS137 Orders and Instructions for the Signal Duty at Halifax
[text begins] *HEAD QUARTERS,* | HALIFAX, NOVA-SCOTIA, | 1st January, 1817. | NO copy to be made from this Signal Book, nor any part of its contents made known | to any person not entitled to be instructed in the Signal Duty. No writing to be put into | it, or alteration made, except at Head Quarters.
COLLATION: Broad 8° (9.3 x 15.4 cm), *1–4*^{4} *5–7*^{2}, 22 leaves, pp *1* 2–43 *44*
CONTENTS: *1* preliminaries; 2–3 plan of the Halifax Telegraph; 3–39 'Orders and Instructions for the Signal Duty at Halifax' with *6, 14, 15* blank; *40–41* blank; 42–43 tables; *44* blank
PAPER: Laid, marked Britannia; chains horizontal 28 mm
TYPOGRAPHY: *Text*: long primer, modern face
70 (76) x 124 printed parallel to head
117 (123) x 59 printed parallel to spine
NOTES: In addition to the printed signals there are pennants and flags in manuscript as well as a note requiring the book to be 'ret'd to Deputy Quarter Master General's Office.' A name added by hand on the first page may be that of John Starr, a Halifax resident.
COPY EXAMINED: NBSM

NS138 Perro, B
ABECEDAI<RE> | *RELIGIEUX, MORAL, INSTRUCTIF et AM<USANT>* | Fondé sur des Subjets tirés de l'ancien et du no<uveau> | Testament. | Suivi d'Elémens d'Arithmétique à la portée des < > | Francais. | PAR UN ANCIEN PROFESSEUR. | *Seconde édition, revue et corrigée: Augmentée d'un Sup-* | *plément en Anglais pour l'usage de ce livre. Par* | B. PERRO. | [rule 32 mm] | *PARIS:* | A la librairie Economique, rue de la Harpe, No. 34, ancien | College d'Harcourt. | [rule 35 mm] | M DCCC VII. | [double rule 82 mm] | *HALIFAX, N.S.* | *Printed by* EDMUND WARD, *at his Office, No.* 15, *Bar-* | *rington Street.* | 1817.
COLLATION: 8° (18.4 x 12.4 cm), *1–5*^{4} (–5 3, 4), 18 leaves, pp *1–7* 8–38 (incomplete); (pagination in [ ] with period to 16.)

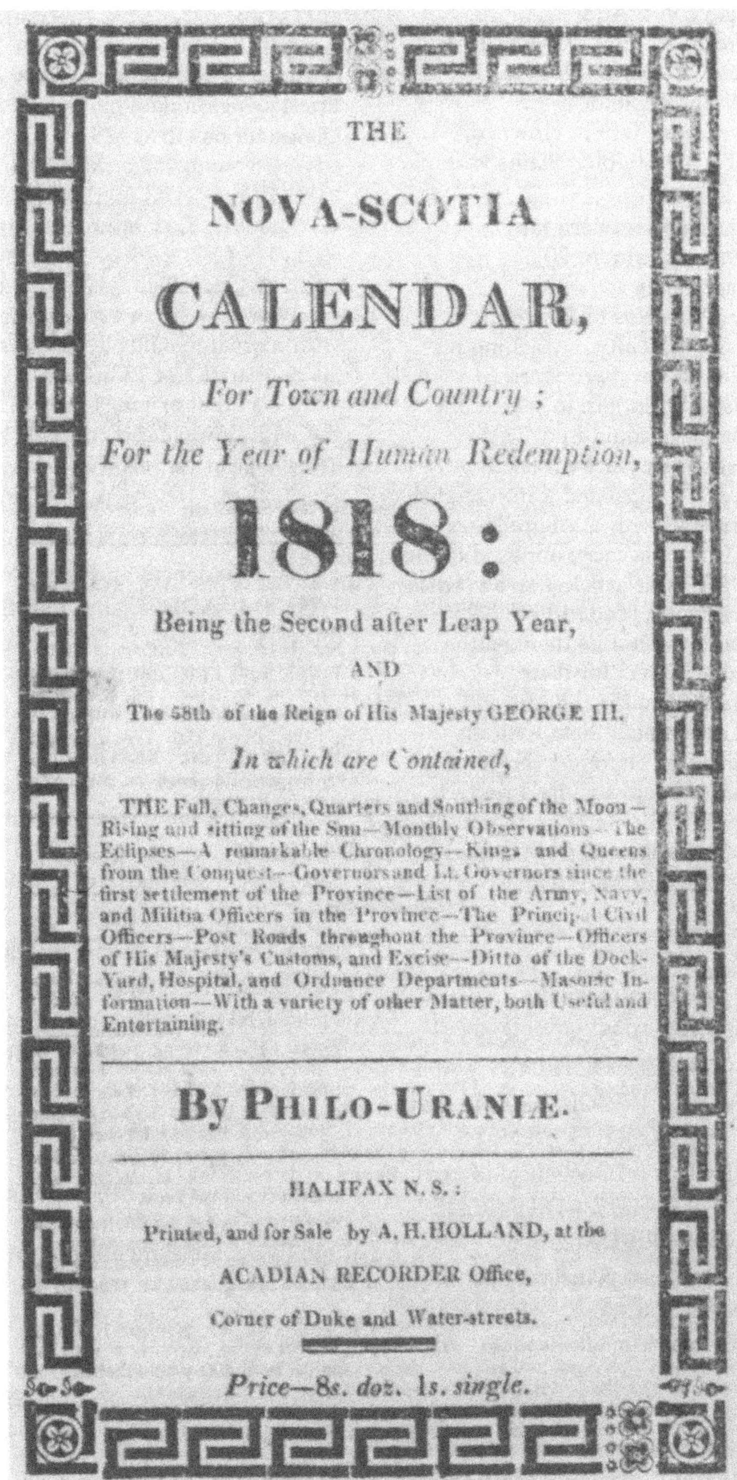

THE

NOVA-SCOTIA

CALENDAR,

For Town and Country ;

For the Year of Human Redemption,

1818:

Being the Second after Leap Year,

AND

The 58th of the Reign of His Majesty GEORGE III.

In which are Contained,

THE Full, Changes, Quarters and Southing of the Moon—Rising and sitting of the Sun—Monthly Observations—The Eclipses—A remarkable Chronology—Kings and Queens from the Conquest—Governors and Lt. Governors since the first settlement of the Province—List of the Army, Navy, and Militia Officers in the Province—The Principal Civil Officers—Post Roads throughout the Province—Officers of His Majesty's Customs, and Excise—Ditto of the Dock-Yard, Hospital, and Ordnance Departments—Masonic Information—With a variety of other Matter, both Useful and Entertaining.

By PHILO-URANIÆ.

HALIFAX N. S. :

Printed, and for Sale by A. H. HOLLAND, at the

ACADIAN RECORDER Office,

Corner of Duke and Water-streets.

Price—8s. doz. 1s. single.

NS136 Courtesy J.J. Stewart Collection, Special Collections Department, Dalhousie University Library, Halifax

CONTENTS: *1* title; 2 blank; *3–4* 'Address to the Public' signed B. Perro, at Halifax, 1 March 1816; *5* 'Instruction'; *6* blank; *7–34* text, articles I to LIII; 35–38 'Lecture Suivie' (incomplete)
PAPER: Laid, watermark post horn in crowned shield; countermark L TOVIL | 1808; chains vertical 24 mm
TYPOGRAPHY: *Text*: bourgeois, modern face 33 ll., 117 (124) x 82 mm; 65 mm for 20 ll.
BINDING: Disbound, stab holes
NOTES: In his prefatory 'Address to the Public' Perro explained that the difficulty of teaching his native language 'in this country' without appropriate textbooks induced him to search out the best French grammar he could find. This *ABECEDAIRE*, published ten years earlier in France, was his choice. He translated it into English then had both texts printed with his 'Supplément en Anglais' (missing from this copy) annexed to the French, complete in fifty-three articles. To advertise the work he inserted a notice headed FRENCH TEACHER in the *Free Press*. In it he thanked the ladies and gentlemen of Halifax for their encouragement, assured them that he was still teaching French, and acquainted them with his 'valuable Book ... which will be found very useful to such persons as may wish to acquire a perfect knowledge of the pronunciation and grammatical principles of that elegant language' (*Free Press*, 10 June 1817 with notice dated 27 May).
COPY EXAMINED: NSHP

NS139 Priestley, James
THE | THEOLOGICAL COMPENDIUM, | CONTAINING | SEVERAL DISSERTATIONS | ON SOME OF THE | GREAT DOCTRINES | AND | DUTIES OF RELIGION, | WHICH ARE MADE PLAIN | BY THEIR | PRIMARY EVIDENCES AND DEMONSTRATIONS: | TO WHICH IS ADDED, | A SKETCH | OF THE | DIFFERENT DENOMINATIONS OF CHRISTIANS | IN THE | KNOWN WORLD; | Designed principally for the Benefit of Young Persons, and those | who have not Money to Purchase, nor Time to Read | elaborate and voluminous Works. | BY JAMES PRIESTLEY. | [rule 21 mm] | "*In every work regard the writer's end.*" | "*Be ready always to give an answer to every man that asketh you* | *a reason of the hope that is in you, with meekness and fear.*" | PETER. | [thin-thick rule 20 mm] | HALIFAX, (N.S.) | Printed for the Author, | BY ANTHONY H. HOLLAND. | 1817.

COLLATION: 12° (16.5 x 10.3 cm), *A*[6] B–G[12] [$1 signed], 78 leaves, pp *i–iii* iv, *1* 2–150 *151–152*
CONTENTS: *i* title; *ii* blank; *iii*–iv preface signed J. Priestley at Halifax, November 1817; *1*–127 Dissertations I to X; 128–150 Sketch; *151* advertisement; *152* errata (18 ll. and 3 ll. note)
PAPER: Wove, *A*, G marked 1816; B–F unmarked
TYPOGRAPHY: *Text*: bourgeois, modern face 39 ll., 129 (137) x 78; 67 mm for 20 ll.
BINDING: Quarter grayish brown paper and greenish gray paper boards, the upper printed within ornamental rules of stars at head and foot (as nonpareil 1 of 1785 Caslon specimen) and pansy sides (as great primer 10 of 1815 Figgins specimen but with flower heads only) [139 x 90 mm] A | Theological Compendium, | containing | *Ten Dissertations,* | OF SOME OF THE | *Great Doctrines of Religion,* | which are made plain | BY THEIR | Primary Evidences and Demonstrations: | TO WHICH IS ADDED, | A COMPENDIOUS VIEW | OF THE | *Principal Christian Sects in the World,* | DESIGNED PRINCIPALLY | For the benefit of young persons, and those who | have not money to purchase, nor time to | read elaborate and voluminous works | By J. PRIESTLEY. | The lower printed with same rules "*In every work regard the writer's end.*" | "*Be ready always to give an answer to every man* | *that asketh you a reason of the hope that is in you,* | *with meekness and fear.*" | PETER. | [ornamental dash 24 mm] | HALIFAX, (N.S.) | Printed for the Publisher, | By ANTHONY H. HOLLAND, | *And for Sale at the Book-Store of* | *Mr. George Eaton.* | [pointing hand] The same may be had of all the METHODIST | Ministers in *Nova-Scotia, New-Brunswick,* | and *Prince Edward Island.* | *Price Five Shillings, in boards.* | 1817. | Endpapers laid, marked C (NSHD). NSHP copy treed calf gilt, the boards framed with rope roll, the spine divided into five compartments, each with flower (10 x 10 mm). Endpapers of french shell marbled paper with moderate pink spots
NOTES: Mr Priestley, a Methodist who later served in New Brunswick (**NB93**), was replaced as chairman of the Nova Scotia District in 1824 after a scandal about his excessive use of alcohol (W.S. MacNutt, *The Atlantic Provinces*. Toronto: McClelland and Stewart, 1965, 153; *Dictionary of Canadian Biography* VII, s.v. 'Bamford, Stephen,' by G.S. French).

An 'In the Press' notice appeared in Holland's *Acadian Recorder* citing conditions of sale: 'As the number of copies to be printed are not large, those

who wish to become purchasers are requested to leave their names *immediately* with any of the persons whose names are here subjoined' (11 October 1817).
COPIES EXAMINED: NSHD, NSHP
REFERENCE: Dennis

NS140 Society for Promoting Christian Knowledge. Halifax Diocesan Committee
ANNUAL REPORT | OF THE | *HALIFAX DIOCESAN COMMITTEE* | OF THE SOCIETY | *FOR PROMOTING CHRISTIAN KNOWLEDGE,* | FOR 1816. | [rule 39 mm] | *HALIFAX:* | *Printed by EDMUND WARD, at his Office, No. 15. Bar-* | *rington Street, next door north of the Post-Office.*
COLLATION: 8° (18.8 x 12 cm), 1^8, 8 leaves pp *1–3* 4–14 *15–16* (pagination in [ ])
CONTENTS: *1* title; 2 blank; *3*–9 text dated at Halifax, January 1817; 9–14 members; *15–16* blank
PAPER: Laid, watermark post horn in crowned shield | 180[?]; countermark J LARKING; chains vertical 25 mm
TYPOGRAPHY: *Text*: bourgeois, modern face. *Display*: thickened modern faces
41 ll., 136 (143) x 89; 66 mm for 20 ll.
BINDING: Wrapper of gloster marbled paper in reddish orange, bluish gray, and black. Paste-downs and free endpapers conjugate, the latter leaf marked HOOKE | 1812
COPY EXAMINED: NSHL

1818

NS141 An Almanack for the Year of Our Lord, 1819
[within thick-thin rules 151 x 84 mm] AN | ALMANACK [open] | *For the Year of Our Lord,* 1819, | BEING THE THIRD AFTER BISSEXTILE OR LEAP YEAR, | Calculated for the Meridian of | HALIFAX, IN NOVA-SCOTIA, [open] | BUT WILL SERVE FOR ANY PART OF THE PROVINCE | CONTAINING: | [8 ll. to left of rule 26 mm] The ECLIPSES. | RISING and SETTING of | the SUN and MOON. | TIME of HIGH WATER. | FEASTS and FASTS of the | CHURCH. | LIST of PROVINCIAL | OFFICERS. | [8 ll. to right] SITTINGS of COURTS. | OFFICERS of the NAVY | on this STATION, | OFFICERS of the ARMY, | under Lieut. Gen. GEORGE, | Earl of Dalhousie, G.C.B. | OFFICERS of His Majesty's | NAVY-YARD & HOSPITAL. | With every other matter useful or necessary. | [double rule 80 mm] | *By THEOPHRASTUS.* | [double rule 80 mm] | HALIFAX: [open] | Published by JOHN HOWE, & SON, at the | Gazette Office.
COLLATION: 8° (22 x 12.5 cm), *1–2*^{8} 3^2, 18 leaves, pp [36]
CONTENTS: [1] title; [2–3] signals; [3] man of signs; moveable feasts; [4] eclipses, cycles for 1818, astronomical characters, levee days; [*5–16*] calendar with seasonal health hints: 'Old Parr's Maxim of Health'; [*17–21*] civil list; [21–22] courts; [23–24] civil list; [24–25] freemasons; [25–26] navy yard; [26] clergy of established church; [26–27] King's College; [27–30] army; [30–31] ships; [31] Presbyterian and Methodist clergy; mail coach; [32–34] roads and distances with houses of entertainment; Parrsborough packet; [34] holidays; firewards; 'Hint to the Fair Sex'; [35–36] Nova Scotia Bible Society, Acadian School Society, Halifax officials; hint about lustre of silver plate; fire engine company; 'From the Life of Augustus Von Kotzebue'
PAPER: Wove, unmarked
TYPOGRAPHY: *Text*: bourgeois and other old and modern faces. *Display*: pages within thick-thin rules; man of signs cut (63 x 47 mm) with bellflower frame as NS3; almanac signs
150 x 85 mm
COPY EXAMINED: NSHD

NS142 An Almanack for the Year of Our Lord, 1819
STATE: [within thick-thin rules 151 x 84 mm] AN | ALMANACK [open] | *For the year of Our Lord,* 1819, | [title as transcribed] | Published by JOHN MUNRO, at the | Journal Office.
BINDING: Stitched
COPY EXAMINED: NSHD (lacking pp [*35–36*])
NOTES: For the previous three years David Howe had published the customary Howe almanac with calculations by Theophrastus and Anthony Henry's eighteenth century man of signs cut. This year the almanac appeared with two states of the title page, one with the imprint 'John Howe & Son,' which had not been used since the 1815 edition, and the other with the imprint of John Munro who was the partner of John Howe Jr at the *Halifax Journal* during 1819. Copies were offered for sale in *Free Press* (8 December 1818).

NS143 Halifax
RULES | AND | REGULATIONS | FOR THE | *ESTABLISHMENT and GOVERNMENT* | OF A | WATCH AND PATROL | IN THE | TOWN OF HALIFAX. | [dotted rule 81 mm] | *HALIFAX:* | Printed by EDMUND WARD, No. 15, Barrington-Street. | 1818.
COLLATION: 8° (20.8 x 13 cm uncut), 1^4 2^2, 6 leaves, pp *1–3* 4–12
CONTENTS: *1* title; 2 blank; *3*–12 text, 1 to 18
PAPER: Laid, marked J LARKING; chains vertical 25 mm
TYPOGRAPHY: *Text*: pica, transitional
27 ll., 127 (135) x 82 mm; 93 mm for 20 ll.
BINDING: Stitched
NOTES: According to the second rule those eligible for service in the Watch had to be at least 18 years of age and 'not House Servants, Daily Laborers or People of Color'; they had moreover 'to be proper persons for watching and patroling or capable by their circumstances to find substitutes' (p 3). Only clergymen were excepted from this responsibility.
COPIES EXAMINED: NSHP, NSWA
REFERENCE: Dennis

NS144 Halifax Committee of Trade
[text begins] Halifax, N.S. December 31, 1817. | THE HALIFAX COMMITTEE OF TRADE, having requested | the attendance of the MERCHANTS, TRADERS, and | other persons interested in *Trade* and *Commerce*, at the | New Court-House, for the purpose of considering the | situation of the FISHERIES of the Province
IMPRINT: [double rule 35 mm] | A.H. HOLLAND, Printer.
COLLATION: 8° (22.8 x 14.5 cm), 1^8, 8 leaves, pp *1–2* 3–15 *16*
CONTENTS: *1* meeting and resolutions signed by the chairman, Joseph Allison, and Lewis E. Piers; 2–15 text headed MEMOIR | *On the COD and SMALL FISH- | ERIES of Nova-Scotia.* |; 15 imprint; *16* blank
PAPER: Laid, unmarked
TYPOGRAPHY: *Text*: long primer, transitional face
45 ll., 153 (160) x 91; 67 mm for 20 ll.
NOTES: Founded in 1804 the Committee of Trade represented the interests of merchants and traders to local and imperial governments. At this meeting a committee was appointed to draw up a report to the lieutenant governor 'stating the decayed situation of the Cod Fisheries' and suggesting means to encourage Nova Scotia fishermen (p *1*). Their *Memoir* summarized the development of that industry and the renewed encroachment of Americans on the West Indian trade.
COPY EXAMINED: NSHP: RG 1, vol 305, no 113

NS145 Methodist Missionary Society (Nova Scotia District)
THE | FIRST ANNUAL REPORT, | OF THE | *Methodist Missionary Society,* | FOR THE | *Nova-Scotia District,* | INCLUDING | *Nova-Scotia, New-Brunswick & Pr. Edw. Island,* | AT A | PUBLIC MEETING, | HELD AT THE METHODIST CHAPEL, | HALIFAX, | *On the 2d of June,* 1818. | Together with a short | Address to the Public: | To which are added, | THE | *Foreign Stations of the Methodist Missionaries,* | &c. &c. | [ornamental dash 32 mm] | A.H. HOLLAND, *Printer.*
COLLATION: 8° (22.5 x 14.2 cm), A^4 B^4 $B2^4$ C^4 [$1 signed], 16 leaves, pp *1–3* 4–32
CONTENTS: *1* title; 2 blank; 3–11 text; 11–14 Address to the Public; 14–19 appendix; 19–22 foreign stations; 22–25 proceedings; 25–31 subscriptions and donations; 32 abstract of the cash account
PAPER: Wove, C marked 1817, *A*–B2 unmarked
TYPOGRAPHY: *Text*: small pica, modern face
41 ll., 141 (152) x 89; 72 mm for 20 ll.
BINDING: Stitched (NSHD)
COPIES EXAMINED: NSHD, NSHP
REFERENCE: Akins

NS146 Nova Scotia. Court of Vice-Admiralty
THE | SUBSTANCE | OF A | JUDGMENT, | DELIVERED IN THE | *COURT OF VICE-ADMIRALTY,* | AT | HALIFAX IN NOVA SCOTIA, | ON THE TWENTY-FOURTH DAY OF AUGUST, 1818; | *In the Case of the* | SCHOONER NABBY, THOMAS STANDLEY MASTER; | BY | *CROFTON UNIACKE, ESQ.* | JUDGE OF THAT COURT. | [thick-thin rule 66 mm] | "Every deviation from this system, whether voluntary or from irre- | sistible necessity, every licence to admit *foreign vessels into British* | *ports,* is a nail driven into the coffin of the British empire." | SIR ALEXANDER CROKE. | [dotted rule 88 mm] | *HALIFAX:* | Printed by EDMUND WARD, at his Office, No. 41, corner of Up- | per Water and Jacobs streets. STATE: MASTER |
COLLATION: 8° (19.1 x 14.5 cm uncut), 1^8 2^4, 12 leaves, pp *1–3* 4–23 *24* (pagination in [ ])
CONTENTS: *1* title; 2 blank; 3–23 text; *24* blank

PAPER: Laid, unmarked; chains horizontal 28 mm
TYPOGRAPHY: *Text*: long primer, modern face. *Display*: thickened romans
42 ll., 137 (144) x 90; 65 mm for 20 ll.
NOTES: There was contradictory evidence about why the *Nabby* entered Pope's Harbour in Halifax County and what the crew did there. Was it a matter of taking on water? And did they do a bit of trading? For Judge Uniacke the answer was both clear and consistent with the judgments of his predecessor Alexander Croke whose opinion was invoked on the title page. Uniacke declared the incident 'a violation of the laws of trade and navigation' and pronounced the *Nabby* and her cargo liable to confiscation (p 23). Uniacke's father, Richard John, was advocate general of the Vice-Admiralty Court and one of his brothers, also Richard John, published a report of this case (NS154).

Delivered on 24 August, the *Judgment* was rushed into print and advertised 'This Day Published and for Sale' at Ward's office within the week (*Acadian Recorder*, 29 August 1818).
COPIES EXAMINED: OOA, QMBM, QMMRB, OTMCL, GBL, USMWA
REFERENCES: Casey 1054, Gagnon I 3599, Lande 2270, MTL 7021

NS147 Nova Scotia. Laws (10th Parliament, 8th session: 1818)
[text begins] At the GENERAL ASSEMBLY of the Province of | Nova-Scotia, begun and holden at Halifax, on Thurſday | the Sixth day of February, 1812, and continued by | ſeveral Prorogations to Thurſday the Fifth day of | February 1818
COLLATION: 4° (28 x 22.5 cm), A^2 B–I^2 χI^2 K–Q^2 [$1 signed], 34 leaves, pp 285–352 (mispaging 304 as 303)
CONTENTS: 285–352 text
PAPER: Wove, unmarked; pale greenish blue
TYPOGRAPHY: *Text*: pica, old face with modern face italics; mixed use of comma from a script fount
45 ll., 214 (228) x 151 (174); 92 mm for 20 ll.
COPIES EXAMINED: NSHP, OOA, USMH-L

NS148 Nova Scotia. Parliament (10th, 8th session: 1818). House of Assembly
[half title] [thick-thin rule 154 mm] | *JOURNAL* [fat] | AND | *PROCEEDINGS* | OF THE | *HOUSE OF ASSEMBLY,* | 1818. | [thin-thick rule 148 mm]
COLLATION: 4° (26.8 x 18.5 cm cropped), *A*–B^2 C–I^2 K–T^2 V–$2A^4$ [$1 signed], 50 leaves, pp 1–3 4–99 *100*
CONTENTS: *1* half title; 2 proclamation; *3*–99 text; *100* blank
PAPER: Laid, unmarked; chains horizontal 27 mm
TYPOGRAPHY: *Text*: pica, old face with modern face italics. *Display*: long swelled rule; royal arms cut 20 x 58 mm
51 ll., 237 (250) x 153; 93 mm for 20 ll.
NOTES: On 5 February Lord Dalhousie noted the start of the session: 'This being the day fixed for opening the General Assembly, I went down *in State*, in my sleigh with 4 horses as a Post chaise.' He prorogued the session on 28 March, 'preparatory to a dissolution in May next' since an election was due, then recorded his opinions in a journal entry for that day:

> It is expected that a very general change of Representatives over the Province will take place, a number of the present Members (being illiterate working farmers, tho' sensible men) are not fit persons for public affairs. ... Altho' the annual meeting of the Parliament of Nova Scotia has little other business to do than appropriate the disposable revenue towards public works & purposes, the amount of which for some years has been about £40,000, the Session has generally been protracted to six weeks. This has been more talkative than usual, & on the whole the business treated in a less liberal manner, the country members evidently working for popularity, & their known sentiments on public matters struggling under the apprehension of the approaching dissolution' (*The Dalhousie Journals*, vol 1, ed. Marjorie Whitelaw. Ottawa: Oberon, 1978, 76–8).

COPIES EXAMINED: NSHL, NSHP, OOA

NS149 The Nova-Scotia Almanack for 1819
[within 4 mm bead and garland rules 177 x 88 mm] THE | NOVA-SCOTIA | ALMANACK, | FOR TOWN AND COUNTRY. | FOR THE YEAR OF OUR LORD | 1819; | BEING THE THIRD AFTER LEAP YEAR. | AND | Fifty-ninth of the Reign of His Majesty GEORGE III | IN WHICH IS CONTAINED | THE Full, Changes, Quarters and Southing of the Moon, | Rising and Setting of the Sun, Monthly Observations, E- | clipses, Merchants' Private Signals, Lists of the Army, Na- | vy, and Militia Officers in the Province, His Majesty's Mi- | nisters, the Principal Civil Officers, Post Roads, throughout | the Province, Officers of His Majesty's Customs and Ex- | cise, Ditto of the Dock Yard, Hospital and Ordnance De- |

partments, Masonic Information, with a variety of other | Matter, both useful and entertaining. | [rule 73 mm] | BY PYTHAGORAS. | [rule 73 mm] | *HALIFAX:* | Printed and for Sale by EDMUND WARD, | At the FREE PRESS Office, No. 76 Argyle-street, up- | per side of the Parade. | *PRICE.* – 6 *Shillings per Doz. and* 9 *Pence single.*
COLLATION: 12° (21.5 x 12.2 cm), *1–2*^{6} *3*^{4} *4*^{1}, 17 leaves, pp *1–2* 3–34
ISSUE as **NS151** *The Nova-Scotia Calendar* for 1819, pp 2–34
CONTENTS: *1* title; 2 levee days, holidays; 3–5 Halifax harbour, signals; 5 Parrsborough packet, the Falls; epigram on Love; 6–7 roads and distances with the names of innkeepers; 7 Nova Scotia Bible Society, Acadian School Society; lighthouse commissioners; 8 astronomical, zodiac, cycles, feasts, eclipses; *9–20* calendar with seasonal verses opening 'Welcome kindred gloom!' for February and 'Ripening the latent seeds of gold,' for August; 21–25 civil list; courts; firewards; 25 clergy of established church; 25–26 King's College; 26 fire engine company; 26–27 freemasons; 27–28 army; 28–32 militia; 32 mail coach; 33 British officers of state; 33–34 Presbyterian and Methodist clergy with 'Numbers in Society'; 34 ships
PAPER: Wove, unmarked except *1*, 2 marked AP | 1816 (NSHL)
TYPOGRAPHY: *Text*: modern faces, much bourgeois. *Display*: thickened romans; title with bead and garland rule and foliage corner, pica 1 and 2 from 1812 Binny and Ronaldson specimen; almanac signs 178 (181) x 90 mm
BINDING: Marbled paper wrapper, interleaved (NSWA)
NOTES: Except for their title pages this almanac and the *Nova-Scotia Calendar* (**NS151**) were printed from the same setting of type. Although technically states I have called them issues since this collaboration which was repeated the following year (**NS164, 166**) interrupted for both Ward and Holland an established series of almanacs.

A notice quoting much of the title, dated 5 October and headed 'This Day is Published,' was printed in the *Acadian Recorder* (24 October 1818), the *Free Press* (8 December), and in the Thursday edition of the *Free Press* which was called the *Commercial Advertiser* (11 February 1819).
COPIES EXAMINED: NSHD, NSHL, NSWA

NS150 Nova Scotia Bible Society
THE | THIRD [open] | REPORT | OF THE | *NOVA-SCOTIA BIBLE SOCIETY.* | [thick-thin rule 14 mm] | *HALIFAX:* | Printed by JOHN HOWE & SON, | 1818.
COLLATION: 8° (15.2 x 9.6 cm), *1–4*^{4} *5*^{2}, 18 leaves, pp *1–3* 4–35 *36*
CONTENTS: *1* title; 2 blank; *3* officers; 4 laws and regulations; 5–6 meeting; 7–9 text; 10 treasurer's account; 11–15 appendix; 16–35 subscriptions and donations; *36* blank
PAPER: Laid, watermark Britannia; countermark W TUCKER | 1815; chains vertical 27 mm
TYPOGRAPHY: *Text*: long primer, modern face 37 ll., 118 (125) x 73; 67 mm for 20 ll.
NOTES: Of £418 collected for the year, £376 remained for the parent society after expenses were paid. More than seven hundred bibles and testaments in English, French, and German had been distributed.
COPY EXAMINED: NSHL

NS151 The Nova-Scotia Calendar for 1819
[within 9 mm Greek key rules at head and sides with corner rosettes; flowers and stars midway at head; foot with 3 mm row of acorns 173 x 90 mm] THE | NOVA-SCOTIA | CALENDAR, [open] | FOR TOWN AND COUNTRY, | *For the Year of Human Redemption* | 1819: | Being the Third after Leap Year, | and | Fifty-ninth of the Reign of His Majesty | GEORGE III. | *In which is contained,* | THE Full, Changes, Quarters and Southing of the Moon; | Rising and sitting of the Sun; Monthly Observations; | The Eclipses; List of the Army, Navy, and Mil- | itia Officers in the Province; The Principal Civil | Officers; Officers of His Majesty's Customs, | and Excise; Ditto of the Dock-Yard, Hospit- | al, and Ordnance Departments; Gover- | nors and Lt. Governors since the first | settlement of the Province; Post | Roads throughout the Province; | Masonic Information, with a var- | iety of other Matter, both Use- | ful and Entertaining. | [rule 69 mm] | By PHILO-URANIÆ. | *Menses et Sidera Serva. Virg.* [rule 67 mm] | HALIFAX N.S.: | Printed, and for Sale by A.H. HOLLAND, at the | ACADIAN RECORDER Office, | Corner of Duke and Water-streets. | [thick-thin rule 17 mm] | *Price* – 6s. *dozen. Stet* Rising and sitting
COLLATION: 12° (19.8 x 12.4 cm), *1*^{1} 2–3^2 4–5^6, 17 leaves, pp *1–2* 3–34
ISSUE as (**NS149**) *The Nova-Scotia Almanack* for 1819, pp 2–34
CONTENTS: *1* title; 2 levee days, holidays; 3–5 Halifax harbour, signals; 5 Parrsborough packet, the Falls; epigram on Love; 6–7 roads and distances

with the names of innkeepers; 7 Nova Scotia Bible Society, Acadian School Society; lighthouse commissioners; 8 astronomical, zodiac, cycles, feasts, eclipses; *9–20* calendar with seasonal verses opening 'Welcome kindred gloom!' for February and 'Ripening the latent seeds of gold,' for August; 21–25 civil list; courts; firewards; 25 clergy of established church; 25–26 King's College; 26 fire engine company; 26–27 freemasons; 27–28 army; 28–32 militia; 32 mail coach; 33 British officers of state; 33–34 Presbyterian and Methodist clergy with 'Numbers in Society'; 34 ships
PAPER: Wove, unmarked
TYPOGRAPHY: *Text*: modern faces, much bourgeois. *Display*: thickened romans; title with Greek key a more rectangular version of two lines great primer 1 of Vincent Figgins 1815 specimen and pansies as Figgins great primer 10 with flower heads only; stars (nonpareil 1) and acorns (long primer 13) as 1785 Caslon specimen; almanac signs
178 (181) x 90 mm
NOTES: The *Acadian Recorder* ran a 'Just Published' notice on 24 October. Holland's price of six shillings per dozen and nine pence single was the same as Ward's (**NS149**).
COPY EXAMINED: NSHD

NS152 Presbyterian Church of Nova Scotia
THE | REPORT [open] | OF A | *COMMITTEE*, | APPOINTED BY THE SYNOD OF THE PRESBYTERIAN CHURCH | OF NOVA-SCOTIA, TO PREPARE A STATEMENT OF | MEANS FOR PROMOTING RELIGION IN THE | CHURCH, SECURING THE PERMA- | NENCE OF THE CHURCH, | AND ENLARGING | ITS BOUNDS. | AND ALSO, | THE SUBSEQUENT RESOLUTIONS AND ARRANGEMENTS | OF THE SYNOD. | [thick-thin rule 58 mm] | *The God of Heaven he will prosper us; therefore we* | *his servants will arise and build:* [9 mm dotted rule] NEHEMIAH. | [thin-thick rule 58 mm] | *HALIFAX:* | PRINTED BY JOHN HOWE & SON, | 1818.
COLLATION: 8° (22.9 x 15.8 cm uncut), π^2 A^8 B^8 (B7 + C^2) [B1, C1 signed], 20 leaves, pp [4] *1* 2–34 *35–36*
CONTENTS: [*1*] title; [*2*] blank; [*3*] note about synod meeting and publication signed at Truro, Court-House, 9 October 1817, by James Robson, synod clerk; [*4*] blank; *1*–26 text; 27–30 abstract, no 1 to 15; *31*–34 appendix: 'Formula of Questions to be put to all who are ordained to the office of the holy ministry'; *35–36* blank
PAPER: Wove, unmarked except π marked [?] ELL | [?] 1 in OTMCL copy
TYPOGRAPHY: *Text*: pica, old face with modern face english, italic, and numbers
29 ll., 137 (149) x 82; 92 mm for 20 ll.
BINDING: Stitched in wrapper of light grayish blue wove paper (NSHD)
NOTES: The Synod of the Presbyterian Church of Nova Scotia was formed in July of 1817 by the union of the two secessionist branches of the Church of Scotland. James Drummond MacGregor was chosen first moderator of the synod. Resolutions drawn from this report, which was prepared by Thomas McCulloch, recommended the promotion of religion through fellowship meetings and by means of educational improvements such as congregational libraries and the establishment of a printing press to disseminate religious materials. One resolution encouraged all congregations to support the academy at Pictou (**NS159**).
COPIES EXAMINED: NSHD (2 copies), NSHL (lacking pp *31–36*), OTMCL, USMH-H
REFERENCES: Dennis, TPL 4851

NS153 Priestley, James
A | CHARITY SERMON, | DELIVERED IN THE | Methodist Chapel, | HALIFAX, (NOVA-SCOTIA,) | ON THE EVENING OF | CHRISTMAS-DAY, | By JAMES PRIESTLEY. | [ornamental dash 24 mm] | *Published by request, for the Benefit of the Poor.* | [ornamental dash 31 mm] | I was hungry, and ye gave me meat; I was thirsty, and ye gave | me drink; I was a stranger, and ye took me in: naked, | and ye clothed me; I was sick, and ye visited me; I was | in prison, and ye came unto me. | JESUS CHRIST. | [thin-thick rule 41 mm] | A.H. HOLLAND, PRINTER. | 1818.
COLLATION: 8° (20.3 x 12.4 cm), $1–2^4$, 8 leaves, pp *1–3* 4–16
CONTENTS: *1* title; 2 advertisement signed The Author at Halifax, December 1817; *3*–16 sermon, text: Proverbs XIX. 17
PAPER: Wove, unmarked
TYPOGRAPHY: *Text*: small pica, modern face, moderate cut. *Display*: medium and long ornamental dashes with diamond and open beads
44 ll., 158 (164) x 92; 72 mm for 20 ll.
NOTES: James Priestley's Christmas sermon was advertised as 'IN THE PRESS,' priced at one shilling, six pence, early in January. The notice continued: 'As the entire profits arising from the sale of this publication, will be given to the POOR, it is hoped that the Benevolent of every denomination, will further its circulation' (*Acadian Recorder*, 10 January 1818).

COPY EXAMINED: QMBM
REFERENCE: Gagnon I 2809

NS154 Uniacke, Richard John, 1789–1834
A | REPORT | OF THE | CASE OF THE NABBY, THOS. STANDLEY, MASTER. | *ARGUED AND DETERMINED* | IN THE | *COURT OF VICE ADMIRALTY,* | AT | HALIFAX IN NOVA SCOTIA. | BEFORE | *CROFTON UNIACKE, ESQ.* | ON THE TWENTY FOURTH DAY OF AUGUST 1818. | BY | *RICHARD JOHN UNIACKE, JUN. ADVOCATE* | [dotted rule 88 mm] | HALIFAX: | Printed by EDMUND WARD, at his Office, No. 41, corner of Up- | per Water and Jacobs streets.
COLLATION: 4° (17.6 x 12 cm), A^4 B^4 C^4 [B1 signed, B underlined], 12 leaves, pp *1–3* 4–24 (pagination in [ ])
CONTENTS: *1* title; 2 blank; *3*–24 text
PAPER: Laid, unmarked; chains horizontal 28 mm
TYPOGRAPHY: *Text*: long primer, modern face
42 ll., 138 (150) x 89; 65 mm for 20 ll.
NOTES: Son of Richard John Uniacke (1753–1830), attorney general and advocate general of the Vice-Admiralty Court, Uniacke junior was practising law in Halifax after serving as attorney general of Cape Breton for several years. Crofton Uniacke, whose judgment appeared in another *Nabby* pamphlet, was an older brother (**NS146**). In 1819 Richard John succeeded his father as advocate general of this court (*Dictionary of Canadian Biography* VI, s.v. 'Uniacke, Richard John,' by B.C. Cuthbertson).
COPY EXAMINED: GBL

1819

NS155 Freemasons. United Grand Lodge (Nova Scotia)
CONSTITUTION | OF THE | *ANCIENT FRATERNITY* | OF | FREE AND ACCEPTED MASONS, | WITH THE | Charges of a Free Mason. | EXTRACTED FROM | THE ANCIENT RECORDS OF LODGES BEYOND SEA, AND | OF THOSE IN ENGLAND, SCOTLAND, AND IRELAND. | FOR THE USE OF LODGES. | [thick-thin rule 10 mm] | *To be read at the making of New Brethren, or when the Master* | *shall order it.* | [thick-thin rule 8 mm] | REPUBLISHED BY ORDER OF THE GRAND LODGE OF NOVA-SCOTIA. | [dotted rule 80 mm] | *HALIFAX:* | Printed by EDMUND WARD, at his Office, No. 4, Cheap Side, | 1819.
COLLATION: 8° (20 x 11.8 cm), A^4 B^8 C–H^4 [$1 signed], 36 leaves, pp *1–3* 4–72
CONTENTS: *1* title; 2 blank; *3*–4 preface; *5*–8 'Rise and Progress of Free Masonry in Nova-Scotia, &c. &c. &c.'; *9*–20 'The Charges of a Free Mason'; 21–68 General Regulations; 69 form for Return of the Members of a Lodge; 70 Lodges in Nova-Scotia; 71–72 'An Ode to Masonry'
PAPER: Wove, unmarked
TYPOGRAPHY: *Text*: pica, transitional face. *Display*: Masonic vignette (p 20) is ornament 38 in Fry and Steele catalogue
33 ll., 155 (165) x 82 (98); 93 mm for 20 ll.
BINDING: Sprinkled calf. Wove endpapers (QMMRB)
NOTES: The progress of freemasonry in Nova Scotia can be measured both numerically and politically: twenty-seven lodges established since 1750, and the membership of most governors including Cornwallis, Lawrence, Parr, and John Wentworth.
COPIES EXAMINED: NSHP, QMMRB
REFERENCE: Lande 1780

NS156 Halifax Methodist Female Benevolent Society
THE | THIRD REPORT, | OF THE | *HALIFAX METHODIST FEMALE* | BENEVOLENT SOCIETY. | [thick-thin rule 37 mm] | *It is more blessed to give than to receive. – Jesus Christ.* | *Only they would that we should remember the Poor; the same* | *which I also was forward to do. – St. Paul.* | [rule 27 mm] | *Thy mind throughout my life be shewn,* | *While listening to the wretches cry,* | *The widow and the orphan's groan,* | *On mercy's wings I swiftly fly* | *The poor and helpless to relieve. – Wesley's Hymns.* | [dotted rule 75 mm] | *HALIFAX:* | Printed by EDMUND WARD, at his Office, No. 4 Cheap- | side, near the Province Building. | 1819.
COLLATION: 8° (17 x 10.9 cm), 1^4, 4 leaves, pp *[8]*
CONTENTS: [*1*] title; [*2*] blank; [*3*–*6*] report; [*7*] meeting, 7 October 1819; [*8*] treasurer's account
PAPER: Laid, marked Britannia; chains vertical 26 mm
TYPOGRAPHY: *Text*: long primer, modern face
30 ll., 126 x 76; 67 mm for 20 ll.
NOTES: A similar report may have been printed the year before since the treasurer reported an expenditure of £2 10 for printing on 24 November 1818 (p [*8*]).
COPY EXAMINED: NSHP
REFERENCE: Akins

ARTICLES OR RULES

FOR THE

GOVERNMENT

OF THE

LUNENBURG FARMER SOCIETY,

INSTITUTED DEC. 28, 1818.

PREAMBLE.

WHEREAS, at a public meeting of Land Proprietors and Farmers, of the County of Lunenburg, held at Lunenburg on the 28th of December, in the year 1818, for the purpose of deliberating on the present state of Agriculture in the County, and devising means for its improvement, they were unanimously of opinion, that though the Grain produced in this County has never been sufficient for the subsistence of the inhabitants, there is as much land cleared, or may very soon be cleared and brought under culture, as, under an improved system of husbandry, may be made to produce not only a sufficiency of food for the inhabitants of the County, but an abundance that will admit of some supply being carried to other markets: THEREFORE, in order to attain this important end, the Land Proprietors and Farmers aforesaid did FORM, and do hereby FORM themselves into an Agricultural Society, to be called the LUNENBURG FARMER SOCIETY; and they did, and do hereby AGREE, and bind and pledge themselves one to another, to adopt, and to submit to, the following ARTICLES or RULES, as the Laws by which the said Society shall be governed, until the same shall be revised, altered and amended, in the manner to be hereafter mentioned:

ARTICLE I. The objects of this Society shall be,

1. To instruct its members in the most approved methods of *Dividing, Clearing, Draining, Cultivating, Manuring, and Cropping*, their farms;

NS158 Courtesy J.J. Stewart Collection, Special Collections Department, Dalhousie University Library, Halifax

NS157 Knowlan, James, 1779–1845
A SERMON, [fat] | PREACHED IN THE METHODIST CHAPEL, AT THE FUNERAL OF | *THE LATE* | MRS. ABIGAIL NEWTON, | *WIFE OF* | JOSHUA NEWTON, Esquire, | *OF LIVERPOOL, NOVA SCOTIA,* | Eldest Daughter of the Late Colonel PERKINS. | [rule 24 mm] | DELIVERED ON THE 12th SEPTEMBER 1819. | *BY JAMES KNOWLAN,* | WESLEYAN METHODIST MISSIONARY. | [dotted rule 94 mm] | *HALIFAX:* | Printed by EDMUND WARD, at his Office, No. 4 Cheapside, near the | Province Building. | 1819.
COLLATION: 8° (21 x 13.1 cm), *1–3*[4], 12 leaves, pp *1–5* 6–21 *22–24*
CONTENTS: *1* title; 2 blank; 3 advertisement dated at Liverpool, 6 November; *4* blank; *5*–20 sermon, text: Proverbs 11 c. 16 v.; 21 'Hymn Sung at the Funeral'; *22–24* blank
PAPER: Wove, unmarked
TYPOGRAPHY: *Text*: long primer, modern face, with great primer for hymn. *Display*: short ornamental dash
39 ll., 156 (164) x 95; 79 mm for 20 ll.
BINDING: Stitched (NSHP)
NOTES: A zealous Methodist, Abigail Newton was a daughter of Simeon Perkins, one of the founders of Liverpool.
COPIES EXAMINED: NSHP, OTMCL
REFERENCE: MTL 7030

NS158 Lunenburg Farmer Society
[caption title] ARTICLES OR RULES [shadowed] | FOR THE | GOVERNMENT [contra italic] | OF THE | LUNENBURG FARMER SOCIETY, [contra italic] | INSTITUTED DEC. 28, 1818. | [notched french rule 16 mm]
COLLATION: 8° (20.5 x 13.3 cm), *1*[4] *2*[1], 5 leaves, pp *1* 2–9 *10*
CONTENTS: *1* 'Preamble'; *1*–7 articles I to XVIII; 8 appendix 1: form for 'Return of crop, 1819' to be completed in ms with name and place of residence; 9 appendix 2: blank for payment to the treasurer of the Lunenburg Farmer Society; 9 board of directors for 1819, and committee; *10* blank
PAPER: Wove, unmarked
TYPOGRAPHY: *Text*: small pica, modern face. *Display*: swash A, M, N in contra italic of title; open two-line pica drop letter; medium french rules with beads and notches
46 ll., 166 (169) x 86; 72 mm for 20 ll.
BINDING: Stitched in wrapper of grayish blue wove paper
NOTES: Originally an Acadian community Lunenburg was populated by the British government in 1753 with nearly 1500 'Foreign Protestants' of Germanic origin, recruited to balance the French and Catholic Acadians. By the end of that century Lunenburg, a major fishing port, supplied the Halifax market with agricultural products as well. Organization of a farmer society here in December was a prompt response to John Young's call for provincial agricultural reform in his Agricola letters in the *Acadian Recorder* (**NS167**). The first, on 25 July, had suggested the formation of local societies. Lord Dalhousie, a keen amateur of agriculture, took up Agricola's cause, first recording approval of the letters in his journal, then proposing a toast to Agricola at a Saint Andrew's day banquet, and before the year ended, attending the founding meeting of the provincial Agricultural Society. (*The Dalhousie Journals*, vol 1, ed. Marjorie Whitelaw. Ottawa: Oberon, 1978, pp 104–5).
COPY EXAMINED: NSHD

NS159 McCulloch, Thomas, 1776–1843
The Nature and Uses of a Liberal [contra italic] | Education illustrated, [contra italic] | BEING A | LECTURE, | DELIVERED | AT THE | OPENING OF THE BUILDING, | ERECTED FOR THE | ACCOMMODATION OF THE CLASSES | OF THE | *Pictou Academical Institution.* | BY THOMAS M'CULLOCH. | [dotted rule 7 mm] | Wisdom is the principal thing; therefore get wisdom: and with | all thy getting get understanding. | PROVERBS. | [dotted rule 7 mm] | PUBLISHED BY THE TRUSTEES OF THE INSTITUTION. | [dotted rule 7 mm] | HALIFAX: | A.H. HOLLAND, PRINTER. | 1819
COLLATION: 8° (20.6 x 13.2 cm), *A*[4] B–C[4] [$1 signed], 12 leaves, pp *1–3* 4–24
CONTENTS: *1* title; 2 note about publication; *3*–24 text
PAPER: Wove, unmarked; coarse and speckled
TYPOGRAPHY: *Text*: small pica, modern face
42 ll., 147 (156) x 87; 72 mm for 20 ll.
BINDING: Stitched in wrapper of grayish blue wove paper (NSWA)
NOTES: In answer to the religious exclusiveness of King's College (**NS26**) the Presbyterian minister Thomas McCulloch, a teacher and supporter of nonsectarian education (**NS92**), had been working for the establishment of an institution of higher education open to all. The Pictou Academy Bill passed the House of Assembly in 1816 but was stalled in Council until a compromise was achieved

requiring trustees of the Academy to be members of the Church of England or to declare adherence to the Westminster Confession of Faith. Although the Reverend McCulloch was chosen president and classes began in 1817 a new building was not opened until November of 1818 when McCulloch delivered this inaugural lecture defining a liberal education (B. Anne Wood, 'Thomas McCulloch's Use of Science in Promoting a Liberal Education,' *Acadiensis* 17, no 1 (Autumn 1987): 56–73).
COPIES EXAMINED: NSHP, NSWA, QMMRB
REFERENCES: Akins, Dennis, Lande S1401

NS160 Native of the Province
A | PATRIOTIC CALL [shadowed] | TO PREPARE IN A SEASON OF | PEACE, | FOR ONE OF | POLITICAL DANGER; | SUGGESTED BY | REFLECTIONS ON THE POLICY AND DESIGNS | OF THE | Government of the United States, [contra italic] | TOWARDS | Great Britain and her American Colonies. [contra italic] | ALSO, | A BRIEF VIEW | OF SOME OF THE PRINCIPAL ADVANTAGES | POSSESSED BY THE | *Province of Nova-Scotia.* | WITH | AN INQUIRY | INTO THE CAUSES WHICH HAVE HITHERTO | RETARDED ITS PROSPERITY; | AND | OBSERVATIONS | UPON THE MEANS WHICH CAN MOST EFFEC- | TUALLY BE EMPLOYED, FOR ITS AD- | VANCEMENT TO A WEALTHY AND | FLOURISHING CONDITION. | [dotted rule 8 mm] | BY A NATIVE OF THE PROVINCE. | [dotted rule 8 mm] | HALIFAX, N.S. | PRINTED BY A.H. HOLLAND, FOR THE AUTHOR. | 1819.
COLLATION: 8° (22.7 x 14.2 cm uncut), π^4 A^4 B–I^4 K–S^4 [$1 signed], 76 leaves, pp *i–iii* iv–vii *viii*, *1* 2–144
CONTENTS: *i* title; *ii* blank; *iii*–vii introduction dated February 1819; *viii* blank; *1*–144 text
PAPER: Wove, most sheets marked in corner 1817
TYPOGRAPHY: *Text*: small pica, modern face. *Display*: thickened romans; contra italic with swash A 40 ll., 142 (154) x 88; 72 mm for 20 ll.
BINDING: Stitched in grayish blue wrapper with conjugate free endpapers (USMH-H); NSHD stitched
NOTES: Attributed to John George Marshall, a lawyer and member of the House of Assembly in the tenth parliament, but defeated in 1818 for the eleventh, the *Patriotic Call* was widely advertised. According to the *Acadian Recorder* it was in the press on 13 February and 'This Day Published' and for sale at 2s 6d single a week later. The four other Halifax papers inserted a notice promptly (*Weekly Chronicle*, 19 February 1819; *Halifax Journal*, 22 February; *Free Press*, 23 February; *Royal Gazette*, 3 March). In March the *Acadian Recorder* listed agents who had copies for sale in nine other Nova Scotia towns.
COPIES EXAMINED: NSHD (2 copies), NSHP, OTMCL, USMH-H
REFERENCES: Akins, MTL 7032 and p *128*

NS161 Nova Scotia. Laws (11th Parliament, 1st session: 1819)
[text begins] At the GENERAL ASSEMBLY of the Province of | Nova-Scotia, begun and holden at Halifax on Thurſ- | day, the Eleventh Day of February, 1819
COLLATION: 4° (28.4 x 21.5 cm), A–I^2 K^2 L–S^2 T^1 [$1 (+A1) signed], 37 leaves, pp 353–426
CONTENTS: 353–426 text
PAPER: Wove, unmarked
TYPOGRAPHY: *Text*: pica, old face with modern face long primer and english. *Display*: long swelled rule 44 ll., 201 (220) x 156 (179); 92 mm for 20 ll.
COPIES EXAMINED: NSHP, OOA, USMH-L

NS162 Nova Scotia. Legislature. Joint Committee Appointed to Consider the Convention Lately Concluded between His Majesty and the Government of the United States of America
PROVINCE OF N. SCOTIA. [open] | [royal arms 16 x 38 mm] | PROCEEDINGS | OF THE | GENERAL ASSEMBLY [open] | UPON THE | CONVENTION, [open] | CONCLUDED BETWEEN HIS MAJESTY AND THE | UNITED STATES OF AMERICA. | *PUBLISHED BY ORDER OF BOTH HOUSES, IN GENERAL* | *SESSION AT HALIFAX, IN APRIL,* 1819. | [swelled rule 28 mm] | HALIFAX, NOVA-SCOTIA; | FROM THE CHRONICLE PRINTING OFFICE, | JUNE, 1819.
COLLATION: 8° (22.5 x 13.5 cm uncut), 1^2 2–6^4 7–16^2, 42 leaves, pp [12] *1* 2–29 *30* ²[42]
CONTENTS: [*1*] title; [*2–4*] blank; [*5*] formation of select committee, 15 February 1819; [*6*] blank; [*7*] message to Earl of Dalhousie presenting address and report signed S.S. Blowers, president of Council and S.B. Robie, speaker, House of Assembly; [*8*] blank; [*9–11*] address to Prince of Wales, Prince Regent; [*12*] blank; *1*–9 report dated 30 March 1819, signed by committees; *10* blank; 11–29 collation of answers to 53 questions included in 'a circular letter to the principal merchants and inhabitants throughout the Province'; *30* blank; ²[*1–41*] appendix: trade statistics A to G; ²[*42*] blank

PAPER: Wove, 2 marked C | 1816 (OOA); *3* so marked (NBSM, NSHP), *4* (NSHD, OOA), *16* marked 1815 (OOA); rest unmarked
TYPOGRAPHY: *Text*: long primer, modern face 48 ll., 162 (165) x 94; 67 mm for 20 ll.
BINDING: Stitched (NSHD)
NOTES: By the Convention of 1818 the Americans won back many of the fishing rights lost during the War of 1812. They were granted the right to fish part of the southern shore of Newfoundland, along the Gulf of St Lawrence and the Labrador coast, and around the Magdalen Islands. Although American vessels were excluded from the inshore fishery of the British colonies by a three mile limit they were allowed to take shelter there and to land for repairs, wood, or water.

Describing the Convention as ruinous the joint committee concluded with a warning that if no measures were taken for the relief and security of British America the result would be 'most serious and fatal injury to the Commercial, Maritime and Financial Interests of Great Britain' (p 9). Discussion of these issues reached other parts of British America when the text was reprinted the following year at the office of the *Upper Canada Gazette* in York (Patricia Fleming, *Upper Canadian Imprints*. Toronto: University of Toronto Press, 1988, 43).

On 25 May Lord Dalhousie noted in his journal: 'I have also transmitted an Address from the Assembly on the late Convention ... this treaty with America has laid open the fisheries to them, & admits them to come freely into all our harbours to wood & water when they please – it is to license to them a free smuggling trade into the Province ... This address is accompanied by a Report by a Joint Committee of the two Houses, embracing the general interests of British America; very ably drawn up & expressed in very strong language. If it does not, nothing will open the eyes of our present Government to the falling state of these colonies ...' (*The Dalhousie Journals*, vol 1, ed. Marjorie Whitelaw. Ottawa: Oberon, 1978, 111). Dalhousie's more circumspect note of transmittal to Bathurst suggested 'that your Lordship will give them that serious attention which their peculiarly interesting nature so well deserves' (GBPRO: CO 217, vol 102, ff 57–8).

The account for printing the report was £64 1s 6d (Laws, 11:2, 1820, p 451).
COPIES EXAMINED: NBSM, NSHD, NSHL (lacking pp ²[*39–42*]), NSHP, NSWA, OOA, GBPRO: CO 217, vol 102, ff 63–104; USMWA
REFERENCES: Akins, Bishop, Dennis

NS163 Nova Scotia. Parliament (11th, 1st session: 1819). House of Assembly
[half title] [thick-thin rule 148 mm] | JOURNAL [fat] | AND | PROCEEDINGS | OF | The House of Assembly, | 1819. | [thin-thick rule 148 mm]
COLLATION: 4° (26.8 x 18.5 cm), *A*² B–I² K–T² Y–2I² [$1 signed], 66 leaves, pp *1–3* 4–131 *132*
CONTENTS: *1* half title; *2* proclamations; *3*–131 text; *132* blank
PAPER: Unmarked, mixed lot of wove and laid, chains horizontal 26 mm
TYPOGRAPHY: *Text*: pica, old face with modern face italics, numbers, and display; printing *L* for £. *Display*: royal arms cut 19 x 54 mm
52 ll., 238 (250) x 151; 91 mm for 20 ll.
NOTES: This session met in the newly completed Province House but, despite the harmony and symmetry of that Palladian building, it was a session of 'much party spirit' according to Lord Dalhousie on the day he prorogued it. There was 'much difference of opinion ... everyone opposing or resisting the proposals as they touched his own personal interests.' Claims by dissenters to share the Church of England's monopoly on marriage licences was a focus of dispute but there were other issues: 'I was compelled to censure lightly their voting an increase of pay to themselves at a time when they debated the inadequacy of the Revenue to meet the wants of the State. We parted however very good friends, many of the opulent and independent members & all the Council publicly approving the reprimand' (*The Dalhousie Journals*, vol 1, ed. Marjorie Whitelaw. Ottawa: Oberon, 1978, 109–10).
COPIES EXAMINED: NSHL, NSHP

NS164 The Nova-Scotia Almanack for 1820
[within 4 mm bead and garland rules 177 x 88 mm] THE | NOVA-SCOTIA | ALMANACK, [fat] | FOR TOWN AND COUNTRY. | *FOR THE YEAR OF OUR LORD* | 1820; [fat] | BEING A LEAP YEAR. | AND | Sixtieth of the Reign of His Majesty GEORGE III. | IN WHICH IS CONTAINED | THE Full, Changes, Quarters and Southing of the Moon, | Rising and Setting of the Sun, Monthly Observations, E- | clipses, Merchants' Private Signals, Lists of the Army | and Navy, in the Province, His Majesty's Ministers, the | Principal Civil Officers, Post Roads throughout the Pro- | vince, Officers of His Majesty's Customs and Excise, Ditto | of the Dock Yard, Hospital and Ordnance Departments, | Masonic Information, *a*

Collection of highly approved and | *valuable Receipts, for Domestic Economy*, with a variety of | other Matter, both useful and entertaining. | [rule 76 mm] | BY PYTHAGORAS. | [rule 76 mm] | *HALIFAX:* | Printed and for Sale by EDMUND WARD, | At the FREE PRESS Office, No. 4, Cheapside, oppo- | site the Province Building. | *PRICE. – 6 Shillings per Doz. and 9 Pence single.*
COLLATION: 8° (22 x 14 cm uncut), 1^4 2^8 $3–4^4$, 20 leaves, pp [40]
ISSUE as **NS166** *The Nova-Scotia Calendar* for 1820, pp [2–32]
CONTENTS: [*1*] title; [*2*] levee days, holidays; [*3–5*] Halifax harbour, signals; [*5*] Parrsborough packet, the Falls; [*6–7*] roads and distances with the names of innkeepers; [*7*] Nova Scotia Bible Society, Acadian School Society; commissioners for lighthouses; [*8*] astronomy, zodiac, cycles, feasts, eclipses; [*9–20*] calendar with seasonal verses opening 'See Smiling Spring with modest mien,' for April and 'In the thick City's smoke can Beauty find' for September; [*21–25*] civil list, courts; [*25–26*] clergy of established church, King's College, Roman Catholic, Presbyterian, and Methodist clergy; fire engine company, firewards; [*27*] freemasons; [*27–28*] British officers of state; [*28–29*] army; [*29*] mail coach; [*30*] ships; [*30–32*] story: 'Sir Robert Maxwell of Orchardston'; errata (4 ll.); [*33–40*] 'Collection of Highly Approved and Valuable Receipts for Domestic Economy' including recipes (soup, wine, cake, preserves, and pickles), remedies (insect stings, burns), domestic hints (lavender water, stains, cleaning, ink), and garden notes
STATE: p [32] with 'FINIS' at end of story and no errata
PAPER: Wove, unmarked
TYPOGRAPHY: *Text*: bourgeois, modern face. *Display*: title with bead and garland rule and foliage corner, pica 1 and 2 from 1812 Binny and Ronaldson specimen
54 ll., 176 x 88 mm
BINDING: Wrapper of marbled paper, spot or shell. Wove endpapers, interleaved (NSHD, NSHP)
NOTES: Published on 19 October this year's edition, printed from the same setting of type as the *Calendar* (**NS166**), was priced at the established rate of six shillings per dozen and nine pence single (*Acadian Recorder*, 16 October 1819; *Free Press*, 19 October).
COPIES EXAMINED: NSHD (3 copies), NSHL, NSHP, NSWA (2 copies, one lacking pp [1–2] [39–40])

NS165 Nova Scotia Bible Society
THE | FOURTH [open] | REPORT, | OF THE | *NOVA-SCOTIA BIBLE SOCIETY.* | [thick-thin rule 13 mm] | *HALIFAX:* | Printed by JOHN HOWE & SON, | 1819.
COLLATION: 8° (15.3 x 9.6 cm), 1^8 4^4, 12 leaves, pp *1–3* 4–23 *24*
CONTENTS: *1* title; 2 blank; 3 officers; 4 laws; 5–6 annual meeting, 11 March 1819; 7–9 text; 10 treasurer's account; 11–12 'Appendex'; 13–23 subscriptions and donations; 24 blank
PAPER: Laid, watermark Britannia; countermark COLES | 1818; chains vertical 26 mm
TYPOGRAPHY: *Text*: long primer, modern face; printing *L* for £
37 ll., 123 (133) x 74; 67 mm for 20 ll.
NOTES: The Society was pleased to report that despite a commercial decline for several years and 'a great influx of distressed strangers' to care for, a total of £468 15s 11d was collected with £413 sent on to the parent society. From that society the Nova Scotia branch had received 870 bibles and testaments of which more than five hundred had been distributed. Stock on hand included almost four hundred volumes, nearly all in Irish and Gaelic. The following year's account noted '£20 were paid for printing our last Report' (*The Fifth Report*, 1820, p 7).
COPIES EXAMINED: NSHL, NSHP (lacking pp 17–24), USMBAt
REFERENCE: Akins

NS166 The Nova-Scotia Calendar for 1820
[within 9 mm Greek key rules with corner rosettes; flowers midway head and foot and at base of sides 173 x 87 mm] THE | NOVA-SCOTIA [shadowed] | CALENDAR, [shadowed] | *FOR TOWN AND COUNTRY,* | *FOR THE YEAR OF HUMAN REDEMPTION,* | 1820: | BEING BISSEXTILE OR LEAP YEAR. | *In the Sixtieth of the Reign of His Majesty* | *GEORGE III* | IN WHICH IS CONTAINED, | The Full, Changes, Quarters and Southing of the Moon; | Rising and sitting of the Sun; Monthly Observations; | the Eclipses; List of the Army and Navy Of- | ficers in the Province; the Principal Civil Officers; | Officers of His Majesty's Customs, and Excise; | Do. of the Dock-Yard, Hospital, and Ordnance | Departments; Governors and Lt. Governors | since the first settlement of the Province; | Post Roads throughout the Province; | Masonic Information, with a variety | of other Matter, both Useful | and

Entertaining. | [rule 67 mm] | By PHILO-URANIÆ. | [dash 11 mm] *assidua vapitur vertigine cœtum* | *Sideraque alta trahit, ceterique volumine torquex.* | Ovid. | [rule 66 mm] | HALIFAX, N.S. | Printed and for Sale by A.H. HOLLAND, at the | ACADIAN RECORDER OFFICE, | Corner of Duke and Water-streets. | [thick-thin rule 14 mm] | *Price – 6s. dozen. Stet* Rising and sitting
COLLATION: 8° (21.7 x 13 cm), 1^{1} 2^{4} 3^{8} 4^{2} 5^{1}, 16 leaves, pp [32]
ISSUE as **NS164** *The Nova-Scotia Almanack* for 1820, pp [2–32]
CONTENTS: [*1*] title; [*2*] levee days, holidays; [*3–5*] Halifax harbour, signals; [*5*] Parrsborough packet, the Falls; [*6–7*] roads and distances with the names of innkeepers; [*7*] Nova Scotia Bible Society, Acadian School Society; commissioners for lighthouses; [*8*] astronomy, zodiac, cycles, feasts, eclipses; [*9–20*] calendar with verses opening 'See Smiling Spring with modest mien,' for April and 'In the thick City's smoke can Beauty find' for September; [*21–25*] civil list, courts; [*25–26*] clergy of established church, King's College, Roman Catholic, Presbyterian, and Methodist clergy; fire engine company, firewards; [*27*] freemasons; [*27–28*] British officers of state; [*28–29*] army; [*29*] mail coach; [*30*] ships; [*30–32*] story: 'Sir Robert Maxwell of Orchardston' [*32*] 'FINIS' and no errata
PAPER: Wove, unmarked
TYPOGRAPHY: *Text*: bourgeois, modern face. *Display*: title with Greek key a more rectangular version of two lines great primer 1 of Vincent Figgins 1815 specimen and pansies as Figgins great primer 10 with flower heads only
54 ll., 176 x 88 mm
NOTES: Not surprisingly the *Calendar* was advertised along with the *Almanack* (**NS164**) in the *Free Press* at the same price (19 October 1819).
COPIES EXAMINED: NSHD, OTMCL
REFERENCE: TPL 1204 and p *265*

NS167 Young, John, 1773–1837
AGRICOLA [open] | TO HIS | READERS. [shadowed] | [ornamental dash 24 mm] | I am again under the necessity of in- | termitting the series of these letters, till | my tour through the Western and East- | ern districts of the Province is complet- | ed ... | ... | ... as it is the | wish of many that they should be pub- | lished in a distinct volume, I mean to | devote the winter to their revisal ... | ... | Subscriptions shall be received in | town at the Office of the Acadian Re- | corder, and in the country by the Se- | cretaries only of the different Agricul- | tural Societies. The lists shall be clos- | ed, and transmitted to me by the 15th | of November next; and I shall then | have the materials before me to deter- | mine, whether the publication shall | take place or not ... | ... | JOHN YOUNG, Sec'y. | Halifax, Oct. 1, 1819.
Prospectus: $1/4^{\circ}$ (22.6 x 18.4 cm)
CONTENTS: 3 ll. heading; rule; 101 ll. in 2 cols; 2 ll. signature
PAPER: Laid, marked J WHATMAN | 1817; chains vertical 22 mm
TYPOGRAPHY: *Text*: long primer, modern face 203 x 119 mm
NOTES: An enterprising Scottish merchant, John Young had been in Halifax little more than four years when he began to publish in the *Acadian Recorder* a series of letters on agricultural reform. As Agricola he called for the establishment of local agricultural societies and a central board to encourage, inform, and reward the province's farmers. Addressing his readers about a collected edition of the letters with this prospectus, printed here as a handbill and in the newspapers (*Halifax Journal*, 11 October 1819; *Acadian Recorder*, 16 October), he explained that he would publish the volume only when enough copies were subscribed to cover the cost of printing a 'full sized' octavo. He promised, moreover, to contribute the first fifty pounds of profit from the book to the fund for agricultural premiums. *The Letters of Agricola* was published in 1822.
COPIES EXAMINED: NSHP (2 copies): RG 8, vol 2, no 13, 14

1820

NS168 An Almanack for the Year of Our Lord, 1821
[within thick-thin rules 152 x 84 mm] AN | ALMANACK, | *For the Year of Our Lord* 1821, | BEING THE FIRST AFTER BISSEXTILE OR LEAP YEAR, | Calculated for the Meridian of | HALIFAX, NOVA-SCOTIA, [open] | BUT WILL SERVE FOR ANY PART OF THE PROVINCE, | CONTAINING: | [8 ll. to left of rule 26 mm] The ECLIPSES. | RISING and SETTING of | the SUN and MOON. | TIME of HIGH WATER, | FEASTS and FASTS of the | CHURCH. | LIST OF

PROVINCIAL | OFFICERS. | [8 ll. to right] SITTINGS of COURTS. | OFFICERS of the ARMY | under Lieut. General Sir | JAMES KEMPT, G.C.B. | OFFICERS of the NAVY | on this STATION. | OFFICERS of His Majesty's | Navy Yard. | With every other matter usefnl or necessary. | [double rule 79 mm] | *By THEOPHRASTUS.* | [double rule 79 mm] | HALIFAX: [open] | Printed by JOHN MUNRO, and for Sale at the | JOURNAL OFFICE. *Stet* usefnl
COLLATION: 8° (21.7 x 14.5 cm uncut), *1–2*[8] *3*[2], 18 leaves, pp *[36]*
CONTENTS: *[1]* title; *[2–3]* signals; *[3]* man of signs; moveable feasts; *[4]* eclipses, cycles; commissioners of the poor; firewards; *[5–16]* calendar with seasonal health hints: 'Old Parr's Maxims of Health'; *[17–21]* civil list; *[21–22]* courts; *[22–23]* civil list; *[24]* clergy of established church; King's College; *[25–26]* freemasons; *[26–29]* army; *[29–30]* ships; *[30–31]* Church of Scotland, Roman Catholic, Presbyterian, and Methodist clergy; *[31]* Nova Scotia Bible Society; *[31–32]* Acadian School Society; *[32]* local officers; fire engine company; holidays; *[33–35]* roads and distances with houses of entertainment; *[35]* Parrsborough packet; Halifax harbour; *[36]* signals; hint about lustre of silver
PAPER: Wove, unmarked
TYPOGRAPHY: *Text*: modern faces. *Display*: pages within thick-thin rules; man of signs cut (63 x 47 mm) with bellflower frame as **NS3**; almanac signs 150 x 93 mm
BINDING: Stitched (NSHD, NSHP)
COPIES EXAMINED: NSHD, NSHL, NSHP, OOA

NS169 An Almanack for the Year of Our Lord, 1821

STATE: [within thick-thin rules 148 x 81 mm] AN | ALMANACK, | *For the Year of our Lord* 1821, | [title as transcribed] | [double rule 78 mm] | *By THEOPHRASTUS.* | [double rule 75 mm] | HALIFAX: [open] | Printed by WILLIAM MINNS, and for Sale at the | CHRONICLE OFFICE.
BINDING: One copy stitched, another in wrapper of spot marbled paper, interleaved
COPIES EXAMINED: NSHD (2 copies)
NOTES: Again, as in 1818, the extended Howe family printed an almanac with two states of the title page, one for John Munro at the *Halifax Journal*, the other for William Minns, publisher of the *Weekly Chronicle* and John Howe's brother-in-law. It is possible that there was a third state with the 'John Howe & Son' imprint since the *Halifax Journal* noted 'Just Published, And for sale by John Howe & Son, An Almanack for the year 1821' a characteristically terse Howe almanac announcement (31 October 1820). In the *Royal Gazette* the Howes advertised almanacs for sale at their own office and at the Halifax Journal (1, 15 November 1820).

William Minns advertised his almanac much more aggressively than Munro or the Howes showing an entreprenurial spirit not notable during his more than thirty years as a newspaper publisher. He offered it first 'by the Gross, dozen, or Single.' Two weeks later he assured retailers of a 'large allowance.' The following week he announced that 'a few dozen interleaved with fine hot-pressed paper, will be sold very low' (*Weekly Chronicle*, 3–24 November 1820).

NS170 Barrow, George

CRITICAL | OBSERVATIONS | ON A | *PAMPHLET* | ENTITLED | CRIM. CON. | [thin-thick rule 12 mm] | WILLIAM HENRY HALL, | PLAINTIFF, | AGAINST | *MAJOR GEORGE BARROW*, | DEFENDANT, | *For Criminal Conversation with the Plaintiff's Wife.* | [rule 13 mm] | TOGETHER WITH | A PLAN OF THE HOUSES | OCCUPIED BY THE | *PLAINTIFF, DEFENDANT, AND Mr. HAVERSTOCK.* | [rule 13 mm] | TO WHICH WILL BE ADDED | *EXTRACTS FROM OPINIONS ON CASES*, | *Which have taken place in Ingland*, | UPON THE SAME SUBJECT. *Stet Ingland*
COLLATION: 8° (21 x 13.2 cm), *A*[4] B–D[4] [$1 signed], 16 leaves, pp *1–3* 4–32
CONTENTS: *1* title; 2 blank; 3–5 preface; *6* blank; 7–32 text
PAPER: Wove, unmarked
TYPOGRAPHY: *Text*: small pica, modern face 42 ll., 150 (164) x 94; 72 mm for 20 ll.
ILLUSTRATION: Engraved 'plan of the houses occupied by the plaintiff, defendant, and Mr. Haverstock' with features such as distances, windows, a door, and a ladder identified and lettered A to I. Beneath the scene is the scale '1/20 of an Inch to a Yard' and 'Reference' (9 ll. text, 8 in 2 cols). Plate mark 12 x <21.5> cm; sheet size 12.9 x 22.5 cm; paper laid, marked NEWMAN & SON; chains vertical 24 mm
BINDING: Rebound with engraving
NOTES: Major Barrow, a member of His Majesty's 15th regiment serving in Nova Scotia, was the defendant in a notorious adultery, or criminal conversation, trial in Halifax. Found guilty, he was ordered to pay damages of £400 to Mr Hall, the

injured husband, on 20 July 1820. Details of the case were published soon after in two pamphlets as well as in newspaper reports (**NS174, 175**). Barrow's illustrated response was for sale by the end of August although one merchant promptly dissociated himself from it: 'Notice: E.J. Hobson, having observed in the FREE PRESS of yesterday, That he is designated in an advertisement as the Vender of a pamphlet entitled "*Critical Observations* on a Pamphlet entitled Crim Con. – WM HENRY HALL, plaintiff, against Major GEORGE BARROW;" respectfully intimates to the Public, That he was unwarily drawn in to promise to sell it, before he had examined its contents; but that having so examined the pamphlet, he is determined not to vend or dispose of any of them' (*Weekly Chronicle*, 1 September 1820).

'Vindex' challenged Barrow's version of the case in letters published in the *Acadian Recorder* on 16 and 23 September. The latter issue also contains a deposition from William Hall denying that he is Vindex. A similar reply to Barrow was published by 'Julius' in the *Halifax Journal* on 18 September.

COPY EXAMINED: USMBAt

NS171 Bromley, Walter, 1775–1838

AN | APPEAL | TO THE | VIRTUE AND GOOD SENSE | OF THE | *INHABITANTS OF GREAT BRITAIN, &c.* | IN BEHALF OF THE | Indians of North America. | [thick-thin rule 13 mm] | BY WALTER BROMLEY, | LATE PAYMASTER OF THE 23D REGIMENT, OR ROYAL WELCH | FUSILIERS, SUPERINTENDANT OF THE LANCASTERIAN | OR ROYAL ACADIAN INSTITUTION, | HALIFAX, NOVA-SCOTIA. | [thin-thick rule 13 mm] | *Now if the fall of them* be *the riches of the world, and the* | *diminishing of them be the riches of the Gentiles; how much* | *more their fulness.* – Rom. c. xi, v. 12. | "*For their original I am ready to believe them of the Jewish* | "*race, I mean of the stock of the Ten Tribes.*" | WILLIAM PENN. | [ornamental dash 24 mm] | *Halifax*: | PRINTED BY EDMUND WARD, | At his Office, No. 4. Cheapside, near the Province Building. | [rule 11 mm] | 1820.

COLLATION: 12° (19.5 x 12 cm), *A*[6] B–E[6] [$1 signed], 30 leaves, pp *1–3* 4–57 *58–60*

CONTENTS: *1* title; 2 blank; *3*–51 text including extracts of correspondence, speeches, memorial, petition, etc.; *52* blank; *53*–57 appendix, No I, II; *58* errata (8 ll.); *59–60* blank

STATE: errata (p 58) with Duponsceau corrected (NSHD, USMBAt); spelled Duponssceau (NSHD, NSHL, NSHP, NSWA, QMMRB)

PAPER: Wove, unmarked

TYPOGRAPHY: *Text*: long primer, modern face 40 ll., 131 (142) x 79; 67 mm for 20 ll.

BINDING: Half sheep edged in blind with cross and diamond roll and spot marbled paper in greenish gray, pink, yellow, and black. Endpapers replaced (NSWA). QMMRB copy stitched

NOTES: Once again Mr Bromley appealed to Nova Scotians on behalf of the native population (**NS92, 103**). An assessment of Bromley's work is found in Judith Fingard's 'English Humanitarianism and the Colonial Mind: Walter Bromley in Nova Scotia, 1813–25,' (*Canadian Historical Review* 54, no 2 (1973): 123–51).

The announcement of publication cited as 'N.B.' the inclusion by Bromley of letters addressed to him by 'several pious and benevolent persons' on this important subject (*Halifax Journal*, 28 February 1820; *Acadian Recorder*, 4 March). Copies were available at Mr Eaton's book store for a price of 1s 3d.

COPIES EXAMINED: NSHD (2 copies), NSHL, NSHP, NSWA, QMMRB, GBL (lacking pp *59–60*), USMBAt, USMWA

REFERENCES: Akins, Lande S265

NS172 Cleland, John, 1709–1789

THE | MEMOIRS [double shadowed] | OF | *Fanny Hill*, [open] | A | WOMAN OF PLEASURE. [egyptian] | WITH PLATES, | *Engraved by a Member of the Royal Academy.* | [ornamental dash 12 mm] | *Written by Herself.* | [ornamental dash 12 mm] | HALIFAX, (*Novia Scotia.*) | Printed by G. Fendon, for W.H.S. Fillman. | 1820. *Stet Novia*

COLLATION: 16° (12.6 x 8.5 cm), A–E[16] (–E[16]), [$1 (+ A2, 3, 4, 5, 6, 7, 8) signed], 79 leaves, pp *1–3* 4–158 (pagination in ( ); misprinting 64 as 34); plate facing E2v

CONTENTS: *1* title; 2 preface; *3*–158 text

PAPER: Wove, unmarked

TYPOGRAPHY: *Text*: brevier, modern face 36 ll., 104 (108) x 66; 56 mm for 20 ll.

ILLUSTRATION: Wood engraving of erotic scene (rule frame 83 x 54 mm) with text | *Page* 132 | below frame to left

NOTES: First published as *Memoirs of a Woman of Pleasure* in London in 1749 by Ralph Griffiths, and his shadowy brother Fenton Griffiths, with the imprint 'Printed for G. FENTON in the *Strand*,' *Fanny Hill* was not legally available in the United States until 1963 or in England until 1970.

This clandestine printing, with Nova Scotia as Novia Scotia and Fenton as Fendon on the title

page, would not have been printed at any shop in Halifax in 1820. Nor is it likely to be one of the celebrated New England copies of *Fanny Hill* associated with Isaiah Thomas of Worcester, Massachusetts. Sheets of this edition were discovered soon after printing and turned into marbled paper used for binding sermons, textbooks, and files of Thomas's own newspaper. Isaiah Thomas senior would have been familiar with 'Halifax, Nova Scotia' as an imprint, having lived there in 1765 as an apprentice to Anthony Henry, but the *Fanny Hill* tentatively attributed to Thomas's shop was printed earlier than this 1820 'Novia Scotia' volume, possibly in 1805 (Henry Spencer Ashbee, *Bibliography of Prohibited Books*, vol III. New York: Jack Brussel, 1962, 60–91; John Cleland, *Memoirs of a Woman of Pleasure*, ed. with an introduction and notes by Peter Sabor. Oxford: Oxford Univeristy Press, 1985; William H. Epstein, *John Cleland: Images of a Life*. New York: Columbia University Press, 1974; David Foxon, *Libertine Literature in England, 1660–1745*. New York: University Books, 1965, 52–63; Marcus A. McCorison, 'Fanny Hill,' *Proceedings of the American Antiquarian Society* 82 (1972): 65–6; —. 'Memoirs of a Woman of Pleasure or Fanny Hill in New England,' *American Book Collector* 1, no 3 (May/June 1980): 29–30; —. 'Two Unrecorded American Printings of "Fanny Hill,"' *Vermont History* 40 (Winter 1972): 64–6; Ralph Thompson, 'Deathless Lady,' *The Colophon* ns 11, no 2 (1935): 207–20).
COPY EXAMINED: USMWA

NS173 Halifax Poor Man's Friend Society
THE | REPORT | OF THE | Halifax Poor Man's Friend | SOCIETY; | 1820. [shadowed] | [thick-thin rule 27 mm] | HALIFAX: | *PRINTED FOR THE SOCIETY*, | BY | EDMUND WARD, | *Cheapside.* | [rule 7 mm] | 1820.
COLLATION: 12° (16.5 x 10.2 cm), *1*[12], 12 leaves, pp *1–3* 4–21 22–24
CONTENTS: *1* title; 2 auditor's report dated 6 December 1820, signed M. Tobin, John Starr; 3–4 proceedings of meeting, 20 December 1820; 5–6 laws; 7 committee; 8–16 text; 16–21 contributions; 22–23 'summary of relief granted from 17th Feb to 6th Dec 1820'; 24 treasurer's accounts
PAPER: Wove, marked J A [script] | 1816 (NSHP); NSHL unmarked
TYPOGRAPHY: *Text*: small pica, modern face 39 ll., 141 (147) x 60; 72 mm for 20 ll.
NOTES: The work of this benevolent association has been analyzed by George Hart in 'The Halifax Poor Man's Friend Society, 1820–1827: An Early Social Experiment,' (*Canadian Historical Review* 34, no 2 (1953): 109–23).
COPIES EXAMINED: NSHL, NSHP

NS174 Hall, William Henry, plaintiff
Crim. Con. | [swelled rule 46 mm] | A | TRIAL. | [thick-thin rule 24 mm] | WILLIAM HENRY HALL, Plaintiff, | AGAINST | MAJOR GEORGE BARROW, Defendant, | FOR | *Criminal Conversation* | WITH THE | Plaintiff's Wife. | [beaded french rule 24 mm] | SUPREME COURT, | AT HALIFAX, NOVA-SCOTIA, | 20th JULY, 1820. | [swelled rule 45 mm] | PRINTED, AND FOR SALE AT THE | RECORDER OFFICE.
COLLATION: 8° (22.8 x 14 cm), *1*[8], 8 leaves, pp *1–3* 4–16
CONTENTS: *1* title; 2 blank; 3–16 text
PAPER: Wove, unmarked; dark and soft
TYPOGRAPHY: *Text*: brevier, modern face 2 cols., 71 ll., 195 (199) x 113; 55 mm for 20 ll.
NOTES: Although the action against Major Barrow was not heard in court until July, letters about the case were published as early as April when Hall identified himself as 'a too deeply injured and persecuted man' (*Acadian Recorder*, 1 April 1820). An officer at the Barrack Department, Hall had been jailed several weeks for debt. Major Barrow abused his friendship and took advantage of this and other absences from home to visit Mrs Hall. According to testimony from the servants he gave her a golden necklace and got her 'as drunk as an owl' (p 16). The summary of evidence given by Mr Haverstock, a watchful neighbour, was slyly put: 'When Mr. Hall went to his office, Major Barrow mounted guard at his house, and filled the vacancy until his return' (p 15). The jury found for the plaintiff and awarded him not the £5000 claimed but £400.

Two days later the *Acadian Recorder* announced 'In the Press; Shortly to be published in a pamphlet, and for sale at the Acadian Recorder Office, THE TRIAL of W.H. Hall versus Major George Barrow' (22 July 1820). The issue of 12 August carried the text of the pamphlet on the first two pages with an explanation from the editor on page three: 'We understand that the Reporter of the case Hall against Barrow has sold the entire number of pamphlets originally struck off. This trial is of an interesting kind; and for the sake of example, the result cannot be too widely known. We have, therefore, republished it in today's paper.' The *Halifax Journal* had already reported on the decision soon after the case was heard (24 July) while the *Weekly Chronicle* printed a letter deploring publication of the trial (4 August).

Another edition was printed, probably by Edmund Ward (**NS175**). Major Barrow responded before the end of the summer (**NS170**).
COPY EXAMINED: OTMCL
REFERENCE: TPL 1196

NS175 Hall, William Henry, plaintiff
CRIM. CON. | [thick-thin rule 22 mm] | A | TRIAL. | [ornamental dash 24 mm] | WILLIAM HENRY HALL, – *Plaintiff,* | AGAINST | MAJOR GEORGE BARROW, – *Defendant,* | FOR | *CRIMINAL CONVERSATION* | WITH THE | PLAINTIFF'S WIFE. | [rule 11 mm] | *DAMAGES LAID AT* £5,000. | [rule 11 mm] | SUPREME COURT, | AT HALIFAX, NOVA-SCOTIA, | 20th JULY, 1820.
COLLATION: 8° (21.2 x 12.4 cm uncut), *A*[4] B–D[4] E[2] [$1 signed], 18 leaves, pp *1–3* 4–36
CONTENTS: *1* title; 2 blank; *3*–36 text
PAPER: Wove, *A* marked C | 1819; B–E unmarked (NSHP: Akins, USMBAt); second copy unmarked (NSHP)
TYPOGRAPHY: *Text*: small pica with long primer pp 18–24. *Display*: dash is asterisk with tapered sides
42 (46) ll., 151 (162) x 94; 72 (67) mm for 20 ll.
BINDING: Stitched in wrapper of stiffened moderate greenish blue paper
NOTES: Although this edition of the trial was published without an imprint the USMBAt copy is inscribed: 'Presented Boston Athæneum | Mr Edmund Wild | of Halifax (N.S.) | Sept <?>.' The name 'Wild' is an error in the transcription of 'Ward,' correctly added in manuscript to other Ward imprints presented to the same institution. One of the copies at NSHP has a manuscript note on the title page: 'Edwd Brown – Reporter.'
COPIES EXAMINED: NSHP (2 copies), USMBAt
REFERENCE: Akins

NS176 Nova Scotia. Laws (11th Parliament, 2nd session: 1820)
[text begins] At the GENERAL ASSEMBLY of the Province of | Nova-Scotia, begun and holden at Halifax on Thurſ- | day, the Eleventh Day of February, 1819; and | continued by ſeveral Prorogations until Thursday, | the Tenth Day of February, 1820
COLLATION: 4° (28 x 21.2 cm), A–G[2] [$1 (+A1) signed], 14 leaves, pp 427–453 *454*
CONTENTS: 427–453 text; *454* blank
PAPER: Wove, unmarked
TYPOGRAPHY: *Text*: pica, old face with modern face italic
47 ll., 220 (233) x 155 (178); 93 mm for 20 ll.
COPIES EXAMINED: NSHP, OOA, USMH-L

NS177 Nova Scotia. Parliament (11th, 2nd session: 1820). House of Assembly
[half title] [thick-thin rule 149 mm] | JOURNAL | AND | PROCEEDINGS | OF | The House of Assembly, | 1820. | [thin-thick rule 149 mm]
COLLATION: 4° (30.5 x 19.3 cm cropped), *A*[2] B–I[2] K–T[2] χ[2] 2χ[2] X–Y[2] χY–2D[2], 58 leaves, pp *132–134* 135–247 (mispaging 247 as 243)
CONTENTS: *132* half title; *133* proclamation; *134*–247 text
PAPER: Mixed lot, laid with some wove; unmarked except R, χY marked BA (NSHD); chains horizontal 26 mm
TYPOGRAPHY: *Text*: pica, old face with modern face notes and italics. *Display*: thickened and fat romans; royal arms cut 19 x 54 mm
51 ll., 240 (252) x 154; 92 mm for 20 ll.
NOTES: This Assembly sat for only two sessions because of the death of George III. An election for the twelfth parliament was held later in 1820.
COPIES EXAMINED: NSHD, NSHL, NSHP

NS178 The Nova-Scotia Almanack for the Year of Our Lord, 1821
[within bead and garland rules 176 x 86 mm] THE | NOVA-SCOTIA | ALMANACK, [fat] | FOR TOWN AND COUNTRY. | *FOR THE YEAR OF OUR LORD* | 1821; [fat] | BEING THE FIRST YEAR AFTER BISSEXTILE OR | LEAP YEAR, | AND | First of the Reign of His Majesty, GEORGE IV. | IN WHICH IS CONTAINED | THE Full, Changes, Quarters and Southing of the | Moon, Rising, and Setting of the Sun, Monthly Observa- | tions, Eclipses, Merchants' Private Signals, Lists of the | Army and Navy, in the Province, His Majesty's Minis- | ters, the Principal Civil Officers, Post Roads throughout | the Province, Officers of His Majesty's Customs and Ex- | cise, Ditto of the Dock Yard, Hospital and Ordnance De- | partments, Masonic Information, *a Collection of highly ap-* | *proved and valuable Receipts, for Domestic Economy,* with | a variety of other Matter, both useful and entertaining. | [rule 76 mm] | BY PYTHAGORAS. | [rule 77 mm] | *HALIFAX:* | Printed and for Sale by EDMUND WARD, | At the

FREE PRESS Office, No. 4, Cheapside, op- | posite the Province building, and at the Book | Store of Mr. GEORGE EATON. | *PRICE. – 6 Shillings per Doz. and 9 Pence single.*
COLLATION: 8° (20.3 x 13 cm), *1–4*[4], 16 leaves, pp [32]
CONTENTS: [*1*] title; [*2–4*] Halifax harbour, signals; [*4*] Parrsborough packet, the Falls; [*5–6*] roads and distances with the names of innkeepers; [*6*] Nova Scotia Bible Society, Acadian School Society; commissioners for lighthouses; [*7–8*] courts; [*8*] recipes for wines, punch, and jelly; [*9*] ships; [*10*] astronomical, zodiac, cycles, feasts, eclipses; [*11–22*] calendar; [*23–24*] army; merchants' signals; [*25–30*] civil list; King's College; clergy of established church and Presbyterians; firewards; freemasons; fire engine company; [*31–32*] story entitled 'Superstition' about the Duc de Berri
PAPER: Wove, unmarked
TYPOGRAPHY: *Text*: long primer, modern face. *Display*: title with bead and garland rule and foliage corner, pica 1 and 2 from 1812 Binny and Ronaldson specimen; almanac signs
56 ll., 178 x 91 mm
BINDING: Wrapper of marbled paper with wove endpapers, interleaved (NSHP, NSWA); stitched (NSHD)
COPIES EXAMINED: NSHD (2 copies), NSHL, NSHP

NS179 Nova Scotia Bible Society
THE | FIFTH [shadowed] | REPORT, [open] | OF THE | NOVA-SCOTIA BIBLE SOCIETY. [contra italic] | [swelled rule 34 mm] | HALIFAX: | PRINTED BY HOLLAND & CO. | 1820. [contra italic]
COLLATION: 8° (18.4 x 11.2 cm), *1–3*[4], 12 leaves, pp *1–3* 4–24
CONTENTS: *1* title; *2* blank; *3* officers; 4 laws; 5–14 annual meeting, 24 March 1820; 15 treasurer's account; 16–17 appendix 1, 2; 17–24 subscriptions and donations
PAPER: Wove, unmarked
TYPOGRAPHY: *Text*: brevier, modern face. *Display*: swash A, N in contra italic on title
55 ll., 150 (156) x 88; 54 mm for 20 ll.
BINDING: Bound retaining wrapper of bluish gray wove paper (NSHL)
NOTES: By the time of this meeting contributions to the Society totalled £2783 (p 7).
COPIES EXAMINED: NSHL, NSHP, USMBAt
REFERENCE: Akins

NS180 The Nova-Scotia Calendar for 1821
[within 9 mm Greek key rules with corner rosettes and flowers midway head and foot 180 x 89 mm] THE | NOVA-SCOTIA [shadowed] | CALENDAR, | *FOR TOWN AND COUNTRY;* | *FOR THE YEAR OF HUMAN REDEMPTION,* | 1821: | BEING THE FIRST AFTER BISSEXTILE. | *In the First Year of the Reign of His Majesty* | *GEORGE IV.* | IN WHICH IS CONTAINED, | The Full, Changes, Quarters and Southing of the Moon; | Rising and sitting of the Sun; Monthly Observations; the | Eclipses; Merchants' Private Signals, List of the Army | and Navy in the Province; His Majesty's Ministers, the | Principal Civil Officers; Post Roads throughout the Pro- | vince, Officers of His Majesty's Customs, and Excise; | Commissary, &c. Do. of the Dock-Yard, Hospital and | Ordnance Departments; Clergy of the Established | Churches throughout the Province; a Table of the Sun's | Declination, for the years 1821, 1825 and 1829; a List of | the Masonic Lodges, &c. with a great variety of other | Matter, both Useful and Entertaining. | [rule 68 mm] | By PHILO-URANIÆ.. | *Coeli enarrant Glorium Dei.* Psalm 19th. | [rule 67 mm] | HALIFAX, N.S. | Printed, and for Sale by HOLLAND & CO. at the | ACADIAN RECORDER OFFICE, | Corner of Duke and Water-streets. | [thick-thin rule 15 mm] | *Price – 6s. dozen. Stet* Rising and sitting
COLLATION: 8° (22 x 13.5 cm uncut), *A–B*[4] C–D[4] [$1 signed], 16 leaves, pp [32]
CONTENTS: [*1*] title; [*2*] sun's declination; [*3–4*] astronomical, zodiac, chronological cycles, feasts, eclipses, 'The Fixed Stars'; [*5–16*] calendar with seasonal verses, 8 ll., opening 'Hail welcome guest, propitious May' and 'Autumn is o'er – a feeble span' for October; [*17–19*] Halifax harbour, signals; [*19–20*] roads and distances with the names of innkeepers; [*20–21*] Parrsborough packet, the Falls; British officers of state; Nova Scotia Bible Society, Acadian School Society; [*21*] freemasons; [*22–27*] civil list; fire engine company; [*27–28*] King's College; clergy of established church, Methodist, Presbyterian, and Roman Catholic; [*28*] ships; [*29–30*] army; [*30*] holidays; [*31–32*] 'Story of Two Highlanders'
PAPER: Wove, unmarked
TYPOGRAPHY: *Text*: modern faces, much brevier. *Display*: title with Greek key a more rectangular version of two lines great primer 1 of Vincent Figgins 1815 specimen and pansies as Figgins great

primer 10 with flower heads only; almanac signs
66 ll., 179 (182) x 93 mm
BINDING: Stitched (NSHD)
NOTES: This year's edition was promised from 28 October until publication on 25 November (*Acadian Recorder*).
COPIES EXAMINED: NSHD, NSHL (lacking pp [31–32])

NS181 Temple, Isaac
TWO | SERMONS, | PREACHED IN ST. MATTHEW'S CHURCH, | HALIFAX, N.S. | ON SUNDAY THE 9TH AND SUNDAY THE 16TH OF APRIL 1820. | ON THE DEATH OF HIS LATE MOST GRACIOUS | MAJESTY | *GEORGE III.* | AND THE ACCESSION OF HIS MOST GRACIOUS | MAJESTY | *GEORGE IV.* | [thick-thin rule 63 mm] | *BY THE REV. ISAAC TEMPLE, A.B.* | OF QUEEN'S COLLEGE, CAMBRIDGE, DOMESTIC CHAPLAIN TO THE | RIGHT HON. GEORGE, EARL OF DALHOUSIE. | [thin-thick rule 63 mm] | *HALIFAX:* | PRINTED BY JOHN MUNRO. | [ornamental rule 13 mm] | 1820.
COLLATION: 8° (17.5 x 11.6 cm), 1^8 2^4, 12 leaves, pp *1–5* 6–24
CONTENTS: *1* title; 2 blank; *3* dedication to the congregation of St Matthew's Church signed Isaac Temple at Halifax, 6 June 1820; *4* blank; *5*–12 sermon, text: Genesis, 25th Chap. 8th v.; *13–14* blank; *15*–24 sermon, text: 2d Kings, 11th Chap. lat. pt. 12 v.
PAPER: Wove, unmarked
TYPOGRAPHY: *Text*: bourgeois, modern face. *Display*: ornamental rule on title and in text using *o*
42 ll., 126 (133) x 77; 59 mm for 20 ll.
BINDING: Stitched (NSHD)
NOTES: Perhaps the first of these two sermons, which was preached by Lord Dalhousie's chaplain before the Church of Scotland congregation at St Matthew's, was superior to the one John Inglis preached that same day at St Paul's. Lord Dalhousie wrote afterwards in his journal for 9 April that St Paul's was crowded with 'the congregation in the deepest mourning' but he found Dr Inglis's funeral sermon 'rather a weak & poor production' (*The Dalhousie Journals*, vol 1, ed. Marjorie Whitelaw. Ottawa: Oberon, 1978, 190).
John Munro had taken over the *Halifax Journal* in January after publishing the paper in partnership with John Howe Jr the year before. Several years earlier he had been the partner of the elder John Howe.
COPIES EXAMINED: NSHD, NSHL, NSHP

NS182 The Triumphale
THE | TRIUMPHALE, | A | POETICAL HISTORY | OF THE | *SUCCESSIVE TRIUMPHS* | OF THE | RECORDER [contra italic] | OVER THE | FREE PRESS; | IN FOUR CANTOS. | [thick-thin rule 53 mm] | Arma virumque cano. – *Virgil.* | [thin-thick rule 54 mm] | Halifax, N.S. [contra italic] | PRINTED AND FOR SALE AT THE | RECORDER OFFICE, | 1820. [contra italic]
COLLATION: 12° (17.3 x 9.2 cm), 1^{12}, 12 leaves, pp *i–iii* iv–v *6* 7–21 *22–24*
CONTENTS: *i* title; *ii* blank; *iii*–v preface signed The Author, 17 February 1820; *6*–21 text; *22–24* blank
PAPER: Wove, unmarked
TYPOGRAPHY: *Text*: brevier, modern face
47 ll., 136 (142) x 60; 54 mm for 20 ll.
NOTES: Notices announcing *The Triumphale* were published in three other Halifax papers but not in the *Free Press* which was the target of this satire and, according to the poet represented 'an envious, snarling and dangerous faction' (p *iii*) (*Royal Gazette*, 16 February 1820; *Acadian Recorder*, 19 February; *Halifax Journal*, 28 February).
Although the work was published anonymously, both in the newspaper and here in pamphlet form, the author did deny one possible attribution: 'In justice to myself and in compliance with a request of my printer, I shall therefore make this one specific explanation – that I am neither Mr. Young; nor am I personally connected, in any way whatsoever, with him or his family' (p v). Mr Young was Agricola (**NS184**).
COPY EXAMINED: NSHP

NS183 Wilkie, William, fl. 1820
A | LETTER [shadowed] | TO THE | *PEOPLE OF HALIFAX,* | CONTAINING | STRICTURES | *On the conduct of the Magistrates with regard to the* | *Police Office, Court of Quarter Session, Work* | *House, Poor House, Jail, &c.* | ALSO, | STRICTURES | *On the Court of Commissioners, Supreme Court, &c.* | ALSO, | STRICTURES | *On his Majesty's Council and House of Assembly,* | *Bank Bill, Militia, issuing Tickets for Flats,* | *Digby Election, Raising* | *the Pay, &c. &c.* | [thick-thin rule 8 mm] | BY A NOVA-SCOTIAN. | [thin-thick rule 8 mm] | PRINTED FOR THE AUTHOR. | [dotted rule 10 mm] | 1820.
COLLATION: 8° (23.3 x 14 cm uncut), 1^4 2–3^4 [$1 signed], 12 leaves, pp *1–3* 4–20 *21* 21 23–24 (misnumbering 22 as 21)
CONTENTS: *1* title; 2 letter addressed 'The People of the Town of Halifax' headed 'Gentlemen,' signed

The Author; 3–20 text; 21–21 General Remarks; 23–24 blank
PAPER: Wove, unmarked
TYPOGRAPHY: *Text*: pica, modern face
39 ll., 166 (178) x 92; 85 mm for 20 ll.
NOTES: Mr Wilkie was blunt about the target of his strictures:

So many complaints have arisen ... and as I know these complaints to be founded on facts, I have taken the task of displaying in a very small compass, how woefully and wilfully the taxes have been misapplied. In doing this, I have been actuated by no malice or vindictive feelings against any man or set of men, but on the contrary, to give them their merits, if they possess any. But on the perusal of these sheets it will appear they possess none. I conceive I have therefore done justice ... (p 2).

Having done justice Wilkie was soon doing time. His next letter, addressed like the *Strictures* to the people of Halifax, was written while he was 'in confinement' with trial 'fast approaching' (*Acadian Recorder*, 25 March 1820). Within a month he was found guilty of 'publishing a scandalous, seditious, and unlawful libel against almost all the conſtituted authorities in this province' and sentenced to two years hard labour (*Acadian Recorder*, 22 April; *Halifax Journal*, 24 April; *Weekly Chronicle*, 21 April). Wilkie seems to have served at least part of the sentence and was not heard from again (*Dictionary of Canadian Biography* V, s.v. 'Wilkie, William,' by D.A. Sutherland).

A biographer of Anthony Henry Holland states that Holland 'apparently printed' Wilkie's libellous pamphlet (*Dictionary of Canadian Biography* VI, s.v. 'Holland, Anthony Henry,' by Gertrude Tratt). Not surprisingly the issue of the *Acadian Recorder* which carried Wilkie's prison letter added a note on the same page: 'Reports having circulated that a pamphlet, entitled a "Letter to the people of Halifax," was printed in this town, we think it proper to state that it did not proceed from this office, nor, as we have reason to think from any other here' (25 March).

By that time Anthony Holland had taken his brother Philip and Edward Moody into partnership at the *Acadian Recorder* and was busy himself with the Acadian Paper Mill at Hammond Plains. He had announced his intention to erect a mill early in 1819 and began then to advertise for linen and cotton rags. By November of that year he was offering wrapping paper for sale and in January of 1820 both the *Acadian Recorder* (22 January) and the *Halifax Journal* (24 January) were being printed on Nova Scotia-made paper.

COPIES EXAMINED: NSHL, NSHP
REFERENCE: Akins

NS184 Young, John, 1773–1837

Agricultural Prizes for 1820. | THE plan which has been this year | adopted, differs somewhat from | that of the last ... | ... | I have this day republished the appro- | priation of the £1000 granted last ses- | sion in support of the agricultural insti- | tutions ... | ... | Most part of the information, and in- | deed all the material points, in the pre- | ceding statement appeared before in the | Recorder, and particularly in that of | the 8th April last; yet some of the | Directors have been apprehensive, least | the agricultural body should not have | been fully apprised of the great ends | ... | ... In obedience to their wishes | the present details have been prepared, | and presented in the present form. – | ... | In addition, I have been requested to | print 300 copies of this scheme, in the | shape of handbills, for general distri- | bution ... | ... | JOHN YOUNG, Sec'y. | Willowpark, June 9, 1820.
Prize notice: 1 leaf (38 x 30.2 cm)
CONTENTS: 1 l. heading; text in 4 cols
PAPER: Wove, unmarked
TYPOGRAPHY: *Text*: long primer, modern face. *Display*: thickened two-line double pica
371 x 227 mm
NOTES: Prompted by Young's Agricola letters in the *Acadian Recorder* (NS167), and with the enthusiastic leadership of Lord Dalhousie, a provincial agricultural society was formed late in 1819 and incorporated the following year with a grant of £1500. Young became secretary and treasurer. His farm 'Willow Park' was used as a model farm. Between 1819 and 1826 when the House of Assembly voted not to renew the charter of the Central Board of Agriculture more than £2500 had been distributed in agricultural prizes and premiums (*Dictionary of Canadian Biography* VII, s.v. 'Young, John,' by R.A. MacLean).

This notice was also published in the *Acadian Recorder* (10 June 1820) and the *Weekly Chronicle* (23 June).

COPIES EXAMINED: NSHP (3 copies): RG 8, vol 2, no 142, 262, 263

Prince Edward Island

1804

PEI1 Address to Lieutenant Governor Fanning (Acadians)
[caption title] ADDRESS | *To his Excellency the Lieutenant General Edmund Fanning,* | &c. &c. &c. | AS ſoon as the Acadiens who have their ſettlements in Malpec, Caſcum- | pec and Tagniſh ...
COLLATION: 1/2° (31.7 x 20 cm), 1 leaf, pp [2]
CONTENTS: [*1*–2] address signed with 142 names and certified De Coloune; [2] answer signed EDMUND FANNING
PAPER: Laid, marked Britannia; chains vertical 26 mm
TYPOGRAPHY: *Text*: pica, old face
45 ll., 271 x 129; 140 mm for 20 ll.
NOTES: When Lieutenant Governor Fanning's retirement from office became known loyal addresses were prepared across the Island (**PEI1–8**). The second, and arguably most successful of the early governors, Fanning continued to live in Charlottetown for some years. These Acadians from the north shore (forty-seven of them named Arſenau and eighteen Galland) explained: 'As the moſt part of us can't wright, the Abbe de Coloune is commiſſioned to inſcribe all our names.' Their scribe, Jacques-Ladislas-Joseph de Calonne, formerly Abbé of Saint-Pierre in Melun and brother to the King's controller of finance, was a Royalist emigré who came to Prince Edward Island in 1799 (*Dictionary of Canadian Biography* VI, s.v. 'Calonne, Jacques-Ladislas-Joseph de' by Claude Galarneau). In his reply Fanning commended the 'orderly, peaceable, and meritorious behaviour' of the Acadians and his 'highly reſpected and much eſteemed friend L'Abbe de Coloune.'
The addresses to Fanning are among the first imprints of young James Bagnall. His brother-in-law and master William Alexander Rind had come to the Island of Saint John (Prince Edward Island) in 1788 as a journeyman printer in the office of James Robertson, founder of the first press in 1787. Rind took over the office after Robertson's departure in 1789 and was king's printer by 1791. He returned home to Virginia in 1798 leaving the Island without a press for six years. Bagnall, his former apprentice, was appointed king's printer by Lieutenant Governor Fanning in December of 1804.
COPY EXAMINED: GBPRO: CO 226, vol 21, f 268

PEI2 Address to Lieutenant Governor Fanning (Charlottetown and Queen's County)
[caption title] ADDRESS | *To His Excellency* EDMUND FANNING ... | ... | MAY IT PLEASE YOUR EXCELLENCY. | WE His Majeſty's Dutiful and Loyal Subjects the Inhabitants of Char- | lotte Town and Queen's County ...
COLLATION: 2° (31.7 x 20 cm), *1*², 2 leaves, pp [4]
CONTENTS: [*1*–2] address signed with eighty-four names, dated at Charlotte-Town, 12 August 1804; [2–3] answer signed Edmund Fanning; [4] blank
PAPER: Laid, watermark Britannia; countermark A BLACKWELL | 1800; chains vertical 26 mm
TYPOGRAPHY: *Text*: pica, old face. *Display*: ornamental dash of rimmed oval with tapered arrow sides.
39 ll., 273 x 129; 130 mm for 20 ll.
COPY EXAMINED: GBPRO: CO 226, vol 21, ff 258–9

PEI3 Address to Lieutenant Governor Fanning (Great Rustico)
[caption title] ADDRESS | *To the Lieutenant General Fanning.* | ALTHOUGH, we the inhabitants of Great Ruſtico ...
COLLATION: 2° (31.2 x 19.8 cm), *1*², 2 leaves, pp [4]

CONTENTS: [1–2] address signed with 102 names and dated 2 September; [2–3] answer addressed to Abbe De Coloune and Captain J. Galland who are requested to interpret and explain it, signed EDMUND FANNING at Charlotte-Town, 4 September 1804; [4] blank
PAPER: Laid, marked circles; chains vertical 28 mm
TYPOGRAPHY: *Text*: pica, old face
40 ll., 268 x 130; 138 mm for 20 ll.
NOTES: The French origin of these inhabitants of Great Rustico, north of Charlottetown, is manifest not only in their names but also in French constructions throughout the text. They explained that their address might be among the last received by Fanning because they 'were waiting the coming of one, who well informed of our true ſentiments, could interpret them worthily.'
COPY EXAMINED: GBPRO: CO 226, vol 21, ff 265–6

PEI4 Address to Lieutenant Governor Fanning (King's County)
[caption title] ADDRESS | *To His Excellency* EDMUND FANNING ... | MAY IT PLEASE YOUR EXCELLENCY. | WE His Majeſty's Dutiful and Loyal Subjects the Inhabitants of King's | County ... [Inhabitants amended possibly by erasure and stamping ts over t]
COLLATION: 2° (31.7 x 20 cm), *1*², 2 leaves, pp [4]
CONTENTS: [1–2] address signed with 129 names; [2–3] answer signed EDMUND FANNING; [4] blank
PAPER: Laid, watermark Britannia; countermark A BLACKWELL | 1800; chains vertical 26 mm
TYPOGRAPHY: *Text*: pica, old face. *Display*: ornamental dash of rimmed oval with tapered arrow sides
38 ll., 268 x 129; 144 mm for 20 ll.
COPY EXAMINED: GBPRO: CO 226, vol 21, ff 262–3

PEI5 Address to Lieutenant Governor Fanning (Prince County)
[caption title] ADDRESS | *To His Excellency* EDMUND FANNING ... | MAY IT PLEASE YOUR EXCELLENCY. | WE the Inhabitants of Prince County ...
COLLATION: 2° (31.7 x 20 cm), *1*², 2 leaves, pp [4]
CONTENTS: [1–2] address signed with 107 names, dated at Prince-Town, 30 July 1804; [3] fifty additional signatures; [3–4] answer signed Edmund Fanning
PAPER: Laid, marked Britannia; countermark A BLACKWELL | 1800 | : chains vertical 26 mm
TYPOGRAPHY: *Text*: pica, old face. *Display*: ornamental dash of rimmed oval with tapered arrow sides
37 ll., 256 x 129; 139 mm for 20 ll.
NOTES: This is the earliest of the dated addresses, allowing Fanning to use 'very prompt' to describe their 'affectionate Address' in his response. He characterize others as handsome, obliging, and flattering.
COPY EXAMINED: GBPRO: CO 226, vol 21, ff 260–261

PEI6 Address to Lieutenant Governor Fanning (Tryon River)
[caption title] ADDRESS | *To His Excellency* EDMUND FANNING ... | ... | THE ADDRESS OF THE MAGISTRATES AND INHABITANTS OF TRYON RIVER SET- | TLEMENT AND ITS VICINITY. | MAY IT PLEASE YOUR EXCELLENCY. | ...
COLLATION: 1/2° (31.7 x 20 cm), 1 leaf, pp [2]
CONTENTS: [1] address signed with fifty-eight names; [2] answer signed EDMUND FANNING
PAPER: Laid, marked Britannia; chains vertical 26 mm
TYPOGRAPHY: *Text*: pica, old face
42 ll., 267 x 129; 128 mm for 20 ll.
COPY EXAMINED: GBPRO: CO 226, vol 21, f 264

PEI7 Prince Edward Island. Executive Council
[caption title] ADDRESS | Of His Majeſty's Council to Lieutenant General Fanning, | on receiving information of his having obtained the King's | permission to return to England, on the arrival of his Suc- | cessor in the Government of Prince Edward Iſland, who | was daily expected.
COLLATION: 2° (32.5 x 19.7 cm), *1*², 2 leaves, pp [4]
CONTENTS: [1–2] address dated at Charlotte-Town, 4 September 1804; [2–3] Fanning's answer; [4] blank
PAPER: Laid, watermark Britannia; countermark of name and date unreadable; chains vertical 26 mm
TYPOGRAPHY: *Text*: pica, old face. *Display*: two long dashes, solid with tapered sides
42 ll., 248 x 143; 118 mm for 20 ll.
NOTES: Fanning's successor, the amazing octogenarian Joseph Frederick Wallet DesBarres, although appointed in May 1804 and 'daily expected,' did not arrive in Charlottetown until July of the following year.
COPY EXAMINED: GBPRO: CO 226, vol 21, ff 256–7

1805

PEI8 Prince Edward Island. Grand Jury
[caption title] ADDRESS | *To His Excellency* EDMUND FANNING ... | ... | MAY IT PLEASE YOUR EXCELLENCY. | WE His Majeſty's moſt dutiful and loyal Subjects, the Grand-Jury of this | Iſland ...
COLLATION: 1/2° (31.7 x 20 cm), 1 leaf, pp [2]
CONTENTS: [*1*] address signed by foreman and seventeen jurors at the Grand-Jury Room, 20 February 1805; [*1–2*] answer signed EDM. FANNING
PAPER: Laid marked A BLACKWELL | 1800; chains vertical 26 mm
TYPOGRAPHY: *Text*: pica, old face. *Display*: ornamental dash of rimmed oval with tapered arrow sides
40 ll., 266 x 129; 144 mm for 20 ll.
NOTES: In this instance there is an edge to Fanning's note accepting 'this very obliging, but after ſo many which have already been received, unexpected Addreſs.'
COPY EXAMINED: GBPRO: CO 226, vol 21, f 267

PEI9 Prince Edward Island. Lieutenant Governor (1787–1805: Fanning)
A | LETTER | FROM THE | *RIGHT HONORABLE J.H. ADDINGTON, Esq.* | TO | LIEUT. GENERAL FANNING, | LIEUT. GOVERNOR OF PRINCE EDWARD ISLAND, | AND | *HIS ANSWER:* | ENCLOSING A | MEMORIAL | AND SUNDRY PAPERS AND DOCUMENTS | TO WHICH THEY REFER. | ALSO A | *SUBSEQUENT LETTER.* | FROM HIM TO MR. ADDINGTON ON RECEIVING NO | ANSWER TO THE FORMER.
COLLATION: 4° (19 x 15 cm), *A–C*[2] D–G[2] *H–I*[2] *K–N*[2] [$1 signed], 26 leaves, pp *1–2* 3–52 (pagination in ( ))
CONTENTS: *1* title; *2* note about contents and purpose of the work dated at Prince Edward Island, 27 February 1805; 3 letter to Fanning from J.H. Addington reporting decision of Lords Commissioners of His Majesty's Treasury not to revise Fanning's claim for compensation for loss of office as Surveyor General of Lands in New York, dated 13 January 1802; 3–11 Fanning's answer dated 20 September 1803; 12–27 Fanning's Memorial; 27 note headed N.B. (15 ll.); 28–29 second letter from Fanning dated 25 August 1803; 29 note with pointing hand (3 ll.); 30–52 appendix, numbers 1 to 18
PAPER: Laid, watermark Britannia; countermark 1797 on *H*; W DA[?]E | 1803 on *M*; chains horizontal 25 mm
TYPOGRAPHY: *Text*: pica, old face. *Display*: ornamental dash of rimmed oval with tapered arrow sides
33 ll., 153 (164) x 90; 92 mm for 20 ll.
NOTES: Before the American Revolution Edmund Fanning had been surveyor general of New York. During that war he raised and commanded a loyalist regiment. In 1783 he became lieutenant governor of Nova Scotia; three years later he accepted the appointment as lieutenant governor of Prince Edward Island, assuming control of that government the following year. This collection of documents indicates that Fanning, like many of his compatriots, was not yet satisfied with British compensation paid to loyalists for their losses. As he explained, he had it 'printed in order to perpetuate the humble Pretentions of Lieutenant General Fanning, in common with other loyal American Sufferers' (p 2). (*Dictionary of Canadian Biography* V, s.v. 'Fanning, Edmund' by J.M. Bumsted).
COPY EXAMINED: GBPRO: CO 226, vol 21, ff 269–94

PEI10 Prince Edward Island. Lieutenant Governor (1805–1812: DesBarres)
[caption title] SPEECH | *Of His Excellency Lt. Governor* DES BARRES, *to both Houses of the General* | *Assembly, Convened at Charlotte-Town, Prince Edward Island:*
COLLATION: 2° (30 x 18.3 cm), *1*[2], 2 leaves, pp [4]
CONTENTS: [*1–2*] speech of DesBarres dated 12 November 1805; [*2–3*] address of the Council in reply signed Thomas DesBrisay, president of Council, 14 November; [*3*] His Excellency's reply; [*4*] blank
PAPER: Laid, watermark arms of England; countermark S FINE; chains vertical 24 mm
TYPOGRAPHY: *Text*: pica, old face. *Display*: long ornamental dash of rimmed oval with tapered arrow sides
42 ll., 252 x 128; 117 mm for 20 ll.
NOTES: As a preliminary to the business of the session the new governor and the Islanders exchanged greetings.
COPY EXAMINED: GBPRO: CO 226, vol 20, ff 67–8

PEI11 Prince Edward Island. Parliament. House of Assembly
Assembly-Room, Prince Edward Iſland, November 20th, 1805. | *Resolved,* That the proceedings of the Legiſlature of this Iſland in | paſſing the Two

Acts, namely, "For enforcing the due and regular pay- | ment of the Quit-Rents, and For reveſting His Majeſty's with the unſet- | tled Lands in this Iſland," were in direct conformity with his Majeſty's | Royal Pleaſure ſignified by his Secretary of State to the late Governor | *Lieutenant General Fanning*. | ... | *Resolved*, That the Committee of Correſpondence do tranſmit the ſame | ... | ... to get the grievance | complained of, removed, and obtain the ſignification of His Majeſty's | Royal Will and Pleaſure on this important Subject.

Resolutions: 1/2° (30 x 18 cm)

CONTENTS: 1 l. heading; 44 ll. text of eight resolutions

PAPER: Laid, marked S FINE; chains vertical 24 mm

TYPOGRAPHY: *Text*: pica, old face, mixed fount; using J for j and a cut j for i

267 x 127 mm

NOTES: The land question which dominated Prince Edward Island politics from 1767 until the middle of the next century was once again the central issue with members concerned that royal assent might be withheld 'by means of unfounded representations of interested individuals in England' (Francis W.P. Bolger, 'Land and Politics, 1787–1824,' in *Canada's Smallest Province: A History of P.E.I.*, ed. F.W.P. Bolger. Charlottetown, 1973, 66–94).

COPY EXAMINED: GBPRO: CO 226, vol 20, f 96

PEI12 Prince Edward Island. Parliament (7th, 2nd session: 1805). House of Assembly

JOURNAL | OF THE | HOUSE OF ASSEMBLY | *OF HIS MAJESTY'S* | ISLAND PRINCE EDWARD. | ANNO QUADRAGESIMO SEXTO. | *REGIS GEORGII III.* | [ornamental dash 89 mm] | SECOND SESSION OF THE SEVENTH GENERAL ASSEMBLY. | [ornamental dash 89 mm] | [rule 124 mm] | [royal arms 44 x 63 mm] | [thick-thin rule 129 mm] | CHARLOTTE-TOWN, PRINCE EDWARD ISLAND: | [swelled rule 35 mm] | PRINTED BY JAMES BAGNALL, | PRINTER TO THE KING'S MOST EXCELLENT MAJESTY. | [swelled rule 19 mm] | 1805.

COLLATION: 2° (30.2 x 18.5 cm), *A–B*[2] C[2] *D–E*[2] *F*[1] [C1 signed], 11 leaves, pp [2] *1–3* 4–20

CONTENTS: [*1–2*] blank; *1* title; 2 blank; 3–20 text

PAPER: Laid, watermark arms of England; countermark T SIMMONS | 1803; chains vertical 25 mm

TYPOGRAPHY: *Text*: pica, old face. *Display*: ornamental dash of rimmed oval with tapered arrow sides

41 ll., 243 (253) x 127; 118 mm for 20 ll.

NOTES: Because the Island had been without a press since Rind's departure in 1798 this 1805 Journal was the first printed since 1797 (Tremaine 1066).

COPY EXAMINED: GBPRO: CO 226, vol 20, ff 81–90

1806

PEI13 Prince Edward Island. Parliament (8th, 1st session: 1806). House of Assembly

JOURNAL | OF THE | HOUSE OF ASSEMBLY | *OF HIS MAJESTY'S* | ISLAND PRINCE EDWARD. | ANNO QUADRAGESIMO SEPTIMO | *REGIS GEORGII III.* | [ornamental dash 89 mm] | FIRST SESSION OF THE EIGHTH GENERAL ASSEMBLY. | [ornamental dash 89 mm] | [rule 128 mm] | [royal arms 44 x 63 mm] | [thick-thin rule 129 mm] | CHARLOTTE-TOWN, PRINCE EDWARD ISLAND. | [swelled rule 35 mm] | PRINTED BY JAMES BAGNALL, | PRINTER TO THE KING'S MOST EXCELLENT MAJESTY. | [swelled rule 20 mm] | 1806. [ISLAND in title with wf A]

COLLATION: 2° (31 x 18.7 cm), *1*[2] 2[1] *3–8*[2] χ^2, 17 leaves, pp *1–3* 4–30 [4]

CONTENTS: *1* title; 2 blank; 3–30 text; [*1–2*] stub; [*3–4*] errata (12 ll.)

PAPER: Laid, watermark Britannia; countermark 1803 | 2; chains vertical 26 mm

TYPOGRAPHY: *Text*: pica, old face. *Display*: ornamental dash of rimmed oval with tapered arrow sides

42 ll., 247 (252) x 127; 117 mm for 20 ll.

NOTES: By 1806 James Bagnall had become involved in politics. In November of that year he was elected to the House of Assembly for Prince-Town along with fellow members of the Loyal Electors. With an annual allowance of £150 as 'the Printer of Government' he was now well established in his trade (PCA: RG3: ms Journal of the House of Assembly, 13 December 1806). He had advertised the year before: 'A Smart active Boy, between the age of ten and fifteen, of a mild and tractable dispositon, will be taken as an apprentice to the ART OF PRINTING, by making immediate application at this Office (*Royal Herald*, 11, 22 May, 6 June, 6 July 1805). Certainly this title page with rules off-centre suggests the work of an apprentice rather than a master printer.

COPY EXAMINED: GBPRO: CO 226, vol 24, ff 94–109

1812

PEI14 Letters on the DesBarres-Colclough Controversy
[caption title] PRINCE EDWARD ISLAND. | The following is a Letter from the late Lieutenant Governor | Des Barres, to the Houſe of Assembly, denying his having | given his assent to the obtaining certain Affidavits from the | Council Office as is therein mentioned, to which are added | two Letters from the Assistant Judges in contradiction there- | to ... together with Depoſitions made by the ſeveral Sheriffs, | who have ſerved for the last five years, in conſequence of | aſpersions thrown out by seven Members of the House of | Assembly with intent to injure Chief Justice Colclough, who | are also Members of the Democratic Club of Loyal Electors:
COLLATION: 4° (27.5 x 20 cm), 1^2, 2 leaves, pp *1* 2–4 (pagination in [ ])
CONTENTS: *1*–2 DesBarres's letter dated at Government House, 25 September 1812; 2–4 two letters to Cæsar Colclough from James Curtis and Robert Gray both dated at Charlotte-Town, 2 October; 4 affadavit supporting Colclough signed by four former high sheriffs at Charlotte-Town, 19 October
PAPER: Laid, marked L & B | ; chains horizontal 28 mm
TYPOGRAPHY: *Text*: pica, modern face. *Display*: ornamental dash of rimmed oval with tapered arrow sides
47 ll., 192 (203) x 142; 84 mm for 20 ll.
NOTES: Appointed chief justice in 1805, Cæsar Colclough did not arrive in Charlottetown until 1807. He soon allied himself with the 'cabal' in opposition to DesBarres and the Loyal Electors who supported him. Proving a rule about big politics in small places the conflict churned on, not without assistance from 'the proprietors,' the British owners of most of the Island. It ended with DesBarres suspending Colclough and Lord Bathurst dismissing DesBarres. Colclough was transferred to Newfoundland in 1813 (**PEI17**) while DesBarres moved to Nova Scotia and lived to be 102.
COPY EXAMINED: GBPRO: CO 226, vol 28, ff 46–47

PEI15 Prince Edward Island. Grand Jury
[caption title] *ADDRESS*. [open] | [swelled rule 14 mm] | To the Honorable CÆSAR COLCLOUGH, his Majesty's Chief | Juſtice of Prince Edward Island.
COLLATION: 4° (25.5 x 20.2 cm), 1^2, 2 leaves, pp *1* 2–4 (pagination in [ ])
CONTENTS: *1*–2 address signed by foreman and twenty-two jurors at Grand Jury Room, Hilary Term, 1812; 2–4 reply signed CÆSAR COLCLOUGH, Ch.J. at Charlotte-Town, 29 February 1812
PAPER: Laid, marked T STAINES (copy 1, vol 26; vol 29); marked post horn in crowned shield | 1810 (copy 3, vol 26); chains horizontal 23 mm
TYPOGRAPHY: *Text*: pica, modern face. *Display*: medium and long ornamental dashes including the rimmed oval with tapered arrow sides; open italic is fat and swash
47 ll., 194 (209) x 144; 83 mm for 20 ll.
NOTES: In their address the foreman and jurors praised Colclough for supporting the regularity, dignity, and decorum of the court. His reply condemned the 'evil tendencies' of political clubs, a comment no doubt on the Loyal Electors. One copy of this pamphlet in the Public Record Office is accompanied by an affadavit sworn in October by James Bagnall and James Haszard, his apprentice and nephew, that Cæsar Colclough ordered the address to be printed in the *Weekly Recorder* (16 March 1812) and also in pamphlet form but not before he deleted the five words 'greatly to be deprecated and' from the newspaper text (vol 28, ff 161–2).
COPIES EXAMINED: GBPRO (5 copies): CO 226, vol 26, ff 60–61, 64–5, 70–1; vol 28, ff 159–60; vol 29, ff 131–2

PEI16 Prince Edward Island. Parliament. House of Assembly
[caption title] To the Honorable WILLIAM TOWNSHEND, President and Com- | mander in Chief in and over his Majeſty's Iſland Prince | Edward, and Territories thereunto belonging, &c. &c. &c.
COLLATION: 4° (25 x 20 cm), 1^2, 2 leaves, pp [4]
CONTENTS: [*1*] address thanking Townshend for 'frustrating the late unjustifiable and unprecedented attempt to deprive the country of the highly meritorious services of the Honorable Chief Justice Colclough' signed by the speaker and ten members of the House of Assembly; [2] letter congratulating Colclough signed as address; [3–4] blank
PAPER: Wove, marked [?] A & H [script] | 1810
TYPOGRAPHY: *Text*: pica, modern face
28 ll., 205 x 143; 144 mm for 20 ll.
NOTES: William Townshend, a member of the Island Council, was named temporary commander following the dismissal of DesBarres. He reinstated Colclough in October prompting members of the House who were not among the Loyal Electors to issue this address.
COPY EXAMINED: GBPRO: CO 226, vol 29, ff 133–4

ACTS

OF THE

GENERAL ASSEMBLY

OF

PRINCE EDWARD ISLAND.

PART THE SECOND.

From the Thirty-Ninth to the Fifty-Fourth Year of the Reign of King George the Third.

Charlotte-Town:

PRINTED BY JAMES BAGNALL, PRINTER TO THE KNG'S MOST EXCELLENT MAJESTY.

::::::::::

1814.

PEI19 Courtesy, National Library of Canada, Ottawa

1813

PEI17 Prince Edward Island. Executive Council
[caption title] To the Honorable CÆSAR COLCLOUGH, Chief Justice of his | Majesty's Supreme Court of Judicature, in Prince Edward | Ifland, &c. &c. &c. | *The Address of his Majefty's Council*
COLLATION: 4° (23.3 x 18.2 cm), *1*², 2 leaves, pp *1* 2–3 *4* (pagination in [ ])
CONTENTS: *1*–2 letter congratulating Colclough on his appointment as chief justice of Newfoundland signed by six members at Charlotte-Town, 6 August 1813; 2–3 Colclough's response; *4* blank
PAPER: Wove, marked IVY MILL | 1810 | (CO 226, vol 29)
TYPOGRAPHY: *Text*: pica, modern face
24 ll., 175 (184) x 142; 148 mm for 20 ll.
NOTES: In the first month of his term in Newfoundland Colclough sent this message, along with a similar one from the grand jury (**PEI18**), to the Colonial Office as part of his request for an increase in salary.
COPIES EXAMINED: GBPRO (2 copies): CO 194, vol 54, ff 264–5; CO 226, vol 29, ff 137–8

PEI18 Prince Edward Island. Grand Jury
[caption title] To the Honorable CÆSAR COLCLOUGH, Efquire, Chief Juftice | of Prince Edward Island, &c. &c. &c. | *The ADDRESS of the Grand Jury, Trinity Term* 1813.
COLLATION: 4° (24.7 x 20 cm), *1*², 2 leaves, pp *1* 2–3 *4* (pagination in ( ))
CONTENTS: *1*–2 address wishing Colclough prosperity in 'a more important and lucrative appointment' signed by foreman and sixteen jurors at the Grand Jury Room, Charlotte-Town, Trinity Term, 1813; 2–3 Colclough's reply; *4* blank
PAPER: Wove, marked [?] A & H [script] | 1810
TYPOGRAPHY: *Text*: pica, modern face. *Display*: ornamental dash of rimmed oval with tapered arrow sides
24 ll., 178 (188) x 143; 140 mm for 20 ll.
COPY EXAMINED: GBPRO: CO 226, vol 29, ff 135–6

1814

PEI19 Prince Edward Island. Laws (6th Parliament, 7th session: 1798 to 9th Parliament, 2nd session: 1814)
ACTS | OF THE | *GENERAL ASSEMBLY* [open] | OF | PRINCE EDWARD ISLAND. | [swelled rule 20 mm] | *PART THE SECOND.* | [swelled rule 20 mm] | *From the Thirty-Ninth to the Fifty-Fourth Year of the Reign of* | *King George the Third.* | [rule 140 mm] | [royal arms 30 x 87 mm] | [rule 140 mm] | *Charlotte-Town*: | PRINTED BY JAMES BAGNALL, PRINTER TO THE KNG'S MOST | EXCELLENT MAJESTY. | [double dotted rule 10 mm] | 1814.
Stet KNG'S
COLLATION: 4° (25.7 x 20.2 cm), π¹ *A*² B–I² K–N² O³ P¹ [$1 (-M) signed], 31 leaves, pp *1–3* 4–62
CONTENTS: *1* title; 2 blank; *3*–62 text
PAPER: Wove, mixed lot of unmarked and marked D & AC | 1810 | 10 | ; CT | 1808; H | 1809; and H | 1808
TYPOGRAPHY: *Text*: pica, transitional. *Display*: swash A, M, N in open italic of title; old face english and open modern; ornamental rules and dashes
46 ll., 195 (205) x 117 (147); 83 mm for 20 ll.
NOTES: Collecting and printing the laws was a burden during much of Bagnall's chaotic tenure as king's printer, particularly after 1812 when William Townshend discontinued his salary, a penalty continued by the new governor Charles Douglass Smith. The Treasurer's Warrant Book records the final allowance of £75 to Bagnall as government printer on 15 December 1812 (PCA: RG8, vol 22, #16). Subsequent payments to him were by contract and by demand, often repeated for several years. For these laws he received a first installment of £33 on 6 November 1813 and £30 a month later (#72-8, 84-9).
The collection includes acts passed since the publication of William Alexander Rind's final volume in 1797 (Tremaine 1067).
COPIES EXAMINED: OONL, PCL, PCU, GBL

PEI20 Prince Edward Island. Laws (9th Parliament, 2nd session: 1814)
ACTS | OF THE | *GENERAL ASSEMBLY* [open] | OF HIS MAJESTY'S | ISLAND PRINCE EDWARD. | *ANNO QUINQUAGESSIMO QUARTO* | REGIS GEORGII III. | [ornamental dash 88 mm] | *Seconv Session of the Ninth General* Assembly | [ornamental dash 54 mm] | [rule 141 mm] | [royal arms 31 x 86

mm] | [rule 140 mm] | CHARLOTTE-TOWN PRINCE EDWARD ISLAND: | PRINTED BY JAMES BAGNALL, | PRINTER TO THE KING'S MOST EXCELLENT MAJESTY. | [double dotted rule 15 mm] | 1814. *Stet Seconv*
COLLATION: 4° (28.5 x 20.5 cm), 1^4, 4 leaves, pp *1–3* 4–8
CONTENTS: *1* title; 2 blank; *3*–8 text
PAPER: Wove, marked CT | 1808
TYPOGRAPHY: *Text*: pica, modern face. *Display*: swash A, M, N in open italic of title; ornamental dash of rimmed oval with tapered arrow sides
183 (193) x 106 (137); 83 mm for 20 ll.
NOTES: Only two acts, one about fire prevention and the other about printing and acts, were passed before Lieutenant Governor Smith prorogued the assembly on 13 January. Bagnall printed them promptly since the Colonial Office copy was certified in manuscript by Thomas Desbrisay on 21 February 1814.
COPY EXAMINED: GBPRO: CO 226, vol 29, ff 13–16

PEI21 Prince Edward Island. Lieutenant Governor (1813–1824: Smith)
MILITIA ADJUTANT GENERAL'S OFFICE, | [two lines braced] *Charlotte-Town, Prince Edward* | *Island*, 1st *May* 1814. | MILITIA [open] | *GENERAL ORDER.* | [swelled rule 24 mm] | HIS EXCELLENCY THE LIEUT. GOVERNOR | IS PLEASED TO DIRECT THAT THE FOLLOWING | Orders, Rules, and Regulations, | IN WHICH IS ALSO CONTAINED | An Abstract of the MILITIA LAW, | Be strictly observed by the Militia throughout Prince | Edward Island, and continue in force | until further Orders. | *J.F. HOLLAND*, | Colonel & Adjutant General Militia. | [ornamental dash 23 mm] | *Charlotte-Town*, | *PRINTED BY JAMES BAGNALL, PRINTER TO THE KING'S* | *MOST EXCELLENT MAJESTY.* | [rule 11 mm] | 1814.
COLLATION: 8° (23 x 14.8 cm), *1*–2^4, χ1 2χ1, 10 leaves, pp *1–3* 4–16 [2] ^{2}[2] (pagination in ( )) [χ1, 2χ1 folded leaves 26.7 x 45 cm]
CONTENTS: *1* title; 2 blank; 3–15 text headed STANDING ORDERS, | *RULES AND REGULATIONS*, | TO BE OBSERVED BY THE MILITIA, | *And Abstract of the Militia Law*; 15–16 Militia Almanack [*1*] Form of Militia Summons; [2] Form of Company Quarterly Return; ^{2}[*1*] blank; ^{2}[2] Form of General Return of 'Inhabitans'
PAPER: Wove, marked CT | 1808 (OOA); GBPRO copy unmarked except 2χ marked D & AC | 1810
TYPOGRAPHY: *Text*: pica, modern face. *Display*: dash is oval with tapered sides
39 ll., 163 (174) x 96; 84 mm for 20 ll.
NOTES: Remembered as an autocrat and a tyrant Lieutenant Governor Charles Douglass Smith arrived in 1813 convinced that the Island was full of enemies. Having detected them in the Assembly which he summoned reluctantly, prorogued abruptly, and did not convene again till 1817, he set about reforming the militia with these regulations. Instead he drove officers and men to disobedience and, with his meddling (**PEI23**) prompted John Coape Sherbrooke to withdraw all but twenty-two men from the Island garrison (*Dictionary of Canadian Biography* VIII, s.v. 'Smith, Charles Douglass' by Phillip Buckner).
COPIES EXAMINED: OOA (lacking χ1, 2χ1), GBPRO: CO 226, vol 30, ff 56–65
REFERENCES: Bishop, Casey 1000

1815

PEI22 Prince Edward Island. Lieutenant Governor (1813–1824: Smith)
[royal arms flanked by military emblems 74 x 202 mm] | BY HIS EXCELLENCY | *CHARLES DOUGLASS SMITH*, | ... | A PROCLAMATION. | WHEREAS an Act of the General Affembly of this Ifland was | paffed in the Year 1776, and in the Sixteenth Year of His Ma- | jefty's Reign, intituled "An Act for regulating Fees," and the faid Act | having never been repealed, but remains ftill in full force ... | ... | Given under My Hand, and Seal at Arms, at Charlotte-Town, this Ninth day | of May, one thoufand eight hundred and Fifteen ... | ... | GOD SAVE THE KING.
Proclamation: 1 leaf (44 x 25 cm)
CONTENTS: royal arms; 6 ll. heading; 24 ll. text; 7 ll. closing
PAPER: Wove, marked CT | 1808
TYPOGRAPHY: *Text*: double pica, old face. *Display*: open two-line pica and four-line pica
384 x 207 mm
COPY EXAMINED: GBPRO: CO 226, vol 30, f 41

PEI23 Prince Edward Island. Lieutenant Governor (1813–1824: Smith)
[royal arms flanked by military emblems 74 x 202 mm] | BY HIS EXCELLENCY | *CHARLES*

DOUGLASS SMITH, | ... | A PROCLAMATION. | WHEREAS it appears that the following Officers ... | ... | ... gave permiſſion to ſeveral of | the Non-Commiſſioned Officers and privates belonging to their reſpective | Companies, to enroll themſelves in other Companies ... | ... | And I do further ſtrictly charge and command all His Majeſty's loyal | Subjects within this Government, to abſtain from propagating falſe and | injurious Reports, as they ſhall anſwer the ſame at their peril. | Given under my Hand, and Seal at Arms, at Charlotte-Town, this Eleventh day | of November, in the Year of Our Lord one thouſand eight hundred and Fif- | teen ... | ... | GOD SAVE THE KING.
Proclamation: 1 leaf (44.7 x 27.2 cm)
CONTENTS: royal arms; 6 ll. heading; 25 ll. text; 7 ll. closing
PAPER: Wove, marked CT | 1808
TYPOGRAPHY: *Text*: double pica, old face. *Display*: open two-line pica and four-line pica
392 x 205 mm
COPY EXAMINED: GBPRO: CO 226, vol 30, f 146

1816

PEI24 Prince Edward Island. Lieutenant Governor (1813–1824: Smith)
[royal arms flanked by military emblems 74 x 202 mm] | BY HIS EXCELLENCY | *CHARLES DOUGLASS SMITH,* | ... A PROCLAMATION. | WHEREAS it having been ſignified to Me by *The Right Honorable* | *Earl* BATHURST, His Majesty's principal Secretary of State for the | Colonial Department, that it is intended on the Part of the Crown, to ex- | tend to the Proprietors of Land in this Colony immunity from certain | Forfeitures, to which they were liable by the Conditions of their original | Grants, and alſo to grant the remission of certain Arrears of Quit Rent, | and fix a Scale for Future Payment of ſuch Quit Rent. | ... | Given under my Hand and Seal, at Arms, at Charlotte-Town, this Firſt day of | October, in the Year of our Lord One thouſand Eight hundred and Sixteen | ... | GOD SAVE THE KING.
Proclamation: 1 leaf (39.3 x 27.5 cm)
CONTENTS: royal arms; 9 ll. heading including *L.S.* in a square of type ornaments [23 mm]; 15 ll. text; 6 ll. closing signed Thomas Desbrisay, secretary
PAPER: Wove, unmarked
TYPOGRAPHY: *Text*: double pica, old face. *Display*: leaf and sunburst ornaments and lattice (long primer 11 of 1785 Caslon specimen)
349 x 224 mm
NOTES: Without waiting for the 'Scale for Future Payment' of quit rents promised in Bathurst's dispatch Smith published this proclamation. The proprietors ignored it. Early in 1818 Smith's son-in-law, John Edward Carmichael, acting receiver general of quit rents, threatened legal action against the landowners (PEI32). Their protests to Bathurst resulted in a rebuke to Smith prefacing the long-awaited schedule of rates and payments of quit rent issued in May of that year (PEI30). Smith enclosed this copy of his proclamation as part of his response to Bathurst's censure.
COPIES EXAMINED: GBPRO: (2 copies): CO 226, vol 34, f 110, f 276

1817

PEI25 Prince Edward Island. Laws (1st Parliament, 1st session: 1773 to 9th Parliament, 3rd session: 1817)
ACTS | OF THE | *GENERAL ASSEMBLY* [open] | OF | PRINCE EDWARD ISLAND; | COMPRISING | *PARTS FIRST AND SECOND,* | *From the First Establishment of the Legislature to the Fifty-Seventh* | *Year of the Reign of King George the Third.* | [swelled rule 20 mm] | WITH AN INDEX. | [swelled rule 20 mm] | [rule 113 mm] | [royal arms 30 x 88 mm] | [rule 108 mm] | *Charlotte-Town,* | PRINTED BY JAMES BAGNALL, | PRINTER TO THE KING'S MOST EXCELLENT MAJESTY. | [double dotted rule 16 mm] | 1817.
COLLATION: 4° (25.8 x 19.5 cm) π^2 A^2 B–I^2 K–U^2 χU–2I^2 2K^2 χ2K–2S^2 2T^1, 1^2 2^1, ^{21}–2^2 [$1 (-H) signed], 100 leaves, pp *1–5* 6–185 *186*, 63–68, *i* ii–viii (185 in ( ))
CONTENTS: *1–2* blank; *3* title; *4* blank; *5*–185 text; *186* blank; 63–68 acts of 9th Parliament, 3rd session, paged in continuation of 1814 consolidation; *i*–viii index; 1773 to 1817
PAPER: Mixed lot, wove except I laid, marked F H & C (PCL); wove unmarked or marked D & AC | 1810 | 10 | ; R | 1807; CT | 1808; H | 1806; H | 1815; and H | 1816
TYPOGRAPHY: *Text*: pica, modern face with old face for headings. *Display*: open romans, plume ornament (long primer 45 of 1790 Fry and Steele specimen), and ornamental rules and dashes
49 ll., 206 (213) x 127 (157); 82 mm for 20 ll.

COPIES EXAMINED: OONL (lacking pp *1–2*, vii–viii), PCL, PCU (both lacking pp *1–2*), GBL
REFERENCE: Bishop

PEI26 Prince Edward Island. Laws (9th Parliament, 3rd session: 1817)
ACTS | OF THE | *GENERAL ASSEMBLY* [open] | OF | PRINCE EDWARD ISLAND; | *ANNO QUINQUAGESSIMO SEPTIMO.* | REGIS GEORGII III. | [swelled rule 20 mm] | *Third Session of Ninth General Assembly.* | [swelled rule 18 mm] | [rule 110 mm] | [royal arms 31 x 86 mm] | [rule 106 mm] | *Charlotte-Town,* | PRINTED BY JAMES BAGNALL, | PRINTER TO THE KING'S MOST EXCELLENT MAJESTY. | [double dotted rule 16 mm] | 1817.
COLLATION: 4° (27.4 x 19.5 cm), *1*[4], 4 leaves, pp *1–2* 3–8 (3 in ( ))
CONTENTS: *1* title; 2 blank; 3–8 text
PAPER: Wove, marked 1816
TYPOGRAPHY: *Text*: pica, modern face with old face great primer for caption titles. *Display*: swash A, M, N in open italic of title; ornamental dashes and dot and arrow rule (brevier 28 of 1790 Fry and Steele specimen)
49 ll., 200 (212) x 125 (154); 83 mm for 20 ll.
NOTES: Smith prorogued this Assembly, the first since 1814, on 14 August; he sent the printed Acts to Lord Bathurst on the first of October.
COPY EXAMINED: GBPRO: CO 226, vol 32, ff 129–32

PEI27 Prince Edward Island. Lieutenant Governor (1813–1824: Smith)
[caption title] PRINCE EDWARD ISLAND. [open] | [swelled rule 19 mm] | Speech of His Excellency Lieut. Governor CHARLES DOU- | GLASS SMITH, at the opening of the General Affembly of | Prince Edward Ifland, upon the 8th July, 1817, with the | Addrefses of His Majefty's Council and Houfe of Affembly, | in anfwer, and His Excellency's Replies thereto.
COLLATION: 2° (31.5 x 19.6 cm), *1*[2], 2 leaves, pp [4]
CONTENTS: [*1*–2] Smith's speech; [2–3] Council's address followed by Smith's thanks; [3–4] House of Assembly address followed by Smith's thanks
PAPER: Laid, watermark Britannia; countermark DUSAUTOY & CO | 1815
TYPOGRAPHY: *Text*: pica, modern face. *Display*: open double pica roman and swelled rules
58 ll., 256 x 140; 84 mm for 20 ll.
NOTES: Only a week after the opening Smith sent a printed copy of his speech and the addresses to Lord Bathurst: 'I do myself the Honour to inclose ...' (f68). In a letter he explained that the disposition of the lower House towards him had improved. He went on to remind the colonial secretary that he had succeeded in discharging £2000 of the province's debt during his term. A draft reply added in manuscript to his letter in London expressed Lord Bathurst's satisfaction with the news and his approval of Smith's rewarding himself by an appropriation for his own use of £200 from the funds he controlled.
COPY EXAMINED: GBPRO: CO 226, vol 32, ff 70–71

PEI28 Prince Edward Island. Parliament (9th, 3rd session: 1817). House of Assembly
JOURNAL | OF THE | *HOUSE OF ASSEMBLY* [open] | OF HIS MAJSTY'S | ISLAND PRINCE EDWARD. | *ANNO QUINQUAGESSIMO SEPTIMO* | REGIS GEORGII III. | [rule 113 mm] | *Third Session of the Ninth General Assembly.* | [rule 108 mm] | [ornamental dash 91 mm] | [royal arms 31 x 88 mm] | [ornamental dash 89 mm] | CHARLOTTE-TOWN, PRINCE EDWARD ISLAND: | PRINTED BY JAMES BAGNALL, | PRINTER TO THE KINGS MOST EXCELLENT MAJESTY. [double dotted rule 16 mm] | 1817. *Stet* KINGS
COLLATION: 2° (29.7 x 18.5 cm), *1*[2] (*1* 1 + 2–8[2]), 16 leaves, pp *1–3* 4–32
CONTENTS: *1* title; 2 blank; 3–32 text
PAPER: Laid, watermark arms of England; countermark SKEATS | 1816 | ; chains vertical 26 mm
TYPOGRAPHY: *Text*: pica, old and modern faces alternating by paragraphs. *Display*: open italic with swash A, M; ornamental dash of rimmed oval with tapered arrow sides
58 ll., 247 (254) x 139; 85 mm for 20 ll.
NOTES: The record of this session, which lasted from 8 July to 14 August, was printed and away to Lord Bathurst on 1 September.
COPY EXAMINED: GBPRO: CO 226, vol 32, ff 97–112

1818

PEI29 Prince Edward Island. Lieutenant Governor (1813–1824: Smith)
[caption title] PRINCE EDWARD ISLAND. [open] | [swelled rule 33 mm] | SPEECH of His Excellency Lt. Governor CHARLES DOUGLASS | SMITH, at the opening of the General Affembly of Prince | Edward Island, upon the 3d November 1818; with

the | Addre*f*s of His Maje*f*ty's Council in an*f*wer, and His Excel- | lency's Reply thereto; al*f*o, His Excellency's Me*ff*age and | the Communications of the Hou*f*e of A*ff*embly upon the | Subject of His Excellency's declining to receive its Addre*f*s in | an*f*wer to his Speech at the opening of the Se*ff*ion, viz.
COLLATION: 2° (32.8 x 19.7 cm), 1^2, 2 leaves, pp *1* 2–3 *4* (pagination in [ ])
CONTENTS: *1*–2 Smith's speech; 2 Council's address with Smith's thanks; 2–3 proceedings of the House of Assembly and correspondence with the lieutenant governor about the address refused on 6 and 9 November; *4* blank
PAPER: Laid, watermark Britannia; countermark BROOK MILL | 1818 | ; chains vertical 26 mm
TYPOGRAPHY: *Text*: pica, modern face
2 cols., 64 ll., 265 (273) x 140; 84 mm for 20 ll.
NOTES: The session began badly when the lieutenant governor refused to receive the Assembly's address claiming that it contained 'unconstitutional animadversion.' During the disputes which followed one of Smith's sons broke the window of the Assembly room while the House was sitting with closed doors. Smith prorogued the legislature early in the new year.
COPY EXAMINED: GBPRO: CO 226, vol 35, ff 5–6

PEI30 Prince Edward Island. Lieutenant Governor (1813–1824: Smith)
[royal arms flanked by military emblems 74 x 202 mm] | BY HIS EXCELLENCY | *CHARLES DOUGLASS SMITH*, | ... | A PROCLAMATION. | WHEREAS by my Proclamation i*ff*ued on the fir*f*t day of October, 1816, it was no- | tified that it was intended on the part of the Crown to fix a Scale for future pay- | ment of *Quit Rents* ... | ... | And Whereas the Right Honorable the Secretary of State for the Colonial Department | has, in a De*f*patch bearing date, Downing Street, 30th May la*f*t, communicated to me | that His Royal Highne*f*s the Prince Regent has been bountifully and graciously plea*f*ed to | alter the rate of *Quit Rent* ... | ... | It is the further pleasure of His Royal Highne*f*s that an additional indulgence *f*hall be | granted ... | ... | The further plea*f*ure of his Royal Highne*f*s is ... | ... | Given under my Hand, and Seal, at Arms, at Charlotte-Town, this Twenty-Eighth | day of July in the Year of our Lord One thou*f*and Eight hundred and | Eighteen ... | ... | GOD SAVE THE KING.
Proclamation: 1 leaf (53.3 x 25 cm)
CONTENTS: royal arms; 9 ll. heading including *L.S.* in a square of type ornaments [24 mm]; 35 ll. text; 6 ll. closing signed Fade Goff, deputy provincial secretary
PAPER: Wove, unmarked
TYPOGRAPHY: *Text*: great primer, old face. *Display*: leaf and sunburst ornaments and lattice (long primer 11 of 1785 Caslon specimen)
445 x 224 mm
NOTES: Almost two years after Smith's quit rent proclamation (**PEI24**) and as he was proceeding against proprietors who were in arrears (**PEI32**), Lord Bathurst's contradictory dispatch arrived for proclamation. A notice of the new rules was published the same day (**PEI31**).
COPY EXAMINED: GBPRO: CO 226, vol 34, f 111

PEI31 Prince Edward Island. Receiver General of Quit Rent
Quit Rent Office, July 28th, 1818. | PUBLIC NOTICE. | [ornamental dash 46 mm] | WHEREAS His Royal Highne*f*s the Prince Regent | has been graciously plea*f*ed to grant the following | Indulgence to | CERTAIN PROPRIETORS | ...
Public notice: 1/2° *(33.4 x 20.7 cm)*
CONTENTS: 2 ll. heading; dash; 3 ll. text; 2 ll. signature J.E. Carmichael, R.G. of Quit Rent
PAPER: Laid, marked Britannia; chains vertical 26 mm
TYPOGRAPHY: *Text*: double pica, old face with letter R from a two-line pica fount. *Display*: long dashes with sunburst and bellflower ornaments; dot and arrow rule (brevier 28 of 1790 Fry and Steele specimen)
292 x 165 mm
COPY EXAMINED: GBPRO: CO 226, vol 34, f 112

PEI32 Prince Edward Island. Receiver General of Quit Rent
SPECIAL NOTICE | TO THE | LAND-HOLDERS, | *And Refident AGENTS of LANDHOLDERS,* | IN PRINCE EDWARD ISLAND. | [ornamental dash 55 mm] | Receiver General of Quit Rent's | Office, January 5th, 1818. | JT being the intention of his Maje*f*ty's Govern- | ment to prevent any further accumulation in the | Arrears of Quit Rent, and the Proprietors having | failed to pay due attention to the Proclamation ... [Rent's with wf R] Public notice: 1 leaf (44.2 x 19 cm)
CONTENTS: 8 ll. heading including dash; 17 ll. text; 1 l. heading; 25 ll. scale of fees in tabular form; 3 ll.

Vastator Perditus.

THE SUBSTANCE

OF A

SERMON,

DELIVERED FEBRUARY 21st, 1819,

AT THE

WESLEYAN METHODIST CHAPEL, CHARLOTTE-TOWN,

PRINCE EDWARD ISLAND, ON THE OCCASION OF

THE LAMENTED DEATH

OF

Her Majesty Queen Charlotte.

By ROBERT ALDER,

METHODIST MISSIONARY.

PRINTED BY REQUEST.

"Awake and sing ye that dwell in dust, for thy dew is as the dew of herbs, and the Earth shall cast out the Dead."—*Isa.* xxvi. 19.

CHARLOTTE-TOWN, PRINCE EDWARD ISLAND,

PRINTED BY JAMES BAGNALL,

1819.

PEI33 Courtesy, J.J. Stewart Collection, Special Collections Department, Dalhousie University Library, Halifax

text; 2 ll. signature J.E. Carmichael, acting receiver general of Quit Rent
PAPER: Wove, unmarked
TYPOGRAPHY: *Text*: double pica, old face with wf R. *Display*: four-line pica and ornamental dash of rimmed oval with tapered arrow sides
406 x 143 mm
COPY EXAMINED: GBPRO: CO 226, vol 34, f 277

1819

PEI33 Alder, Robert, 1796–1873
Vastator Perditus. | [double rule 34 mm] | THE SUBSTANCE | OF A | *SERMON,* [open] | DELIVERED FEBRUARY 21st, 1819, | *AT THE* | WESLEYAN METHODIST CHAPEL, CHARLOTTE-TOWN, | PRINCE EDWARD ISLAND, ON THE OCCASION OF | THE LAMENTED DEATH | OF | *Her Majesty Queen Charlotte.* | [thick-thin rule 28 mm] | BY ROBERT ALDER, | METHODIST MISSIONARY. | [thin-thick rule 28 mm] | *PRINTED BY REQUEST.* | [rule 82 mm] | "Awake and sing ye that dwell in dust, for thy dew is as the dew | of herbs, and the Earth shall cast out the Dead." – *Isa.* xxvi.19. | [rule 82 mm] | CHARLOTTE-TOWN, PRINCE EDWARD ISLAND, | *PRINTED BY JAMES BAGNALL.* | [double dotted rule 11 mm] | 1819.
COLLATION: 8° (19.7 x 13.6 cm uncut), *1–5*[4] *6*[1], 21 leaves, pp *i–iii* iv *5* 6–41 *42*
CONTENTS: *i* title; *ii* dedication: 'To the Society and Congregation Assembling in the Wesleyan Methodist Chapel Charlotte-town'; *iii*–iv advertisement; *5*–41 sermon, text: I Cor.xv.26; *42* blank
PAPER: Wove, unmarked
TYPOGRAPHY: *Text*: pica, modern face. *Display*: swash M, N in open italic of title
30 ll., 137 (144) x 93; 91 mm for 20 ll.
BINDING: Stitched (NSHD)
NOTES: In the advertisement to his sermon Mr Alder explained that 'he had not the least expectation ... that it would ever appear in print' (p *iii*) and that 'the substance of this discourse was not committed to paper till after it was delivered' (p iv).
COPIES EXAMINED: NSHD, NSHP, NSWA (with gathering *3* lacking and *4* duplicated)
REFERENCES: Akins, MacFarlane

PEI34 Prince Edward Island. Laws (10th Parliament, 1st session: 1818–1819)
[caption title] (1) | [ornamental rule 115 mm] | Anno Quinquage*ſſ*imo Nono GEORGII III. | 1818 [above marginal notes] | At the GENERAL ASSEMBLY of His Maje*ſ*ty's | ISLAND OF PRINCE EDWARD, begun and holden | at CHARLOTTE-TOWN on the Third Day of No- | vember ANNO DOMINI One thou*ſ*ad Eight hun- | dred and Eighteen ... *Stet* thou*ſ*ad
COLLATION: 4° (28 x 20.5 cm), *1–5*[2] *6*[1], 11 leaves, pp 1–22
CONTENTS: 1–22 text
PAPER Wove, unmarked
TYPOGRAPHY: *Text*: pica, modern face. *Display*: dashes with sunburst ornament and lattice (long primer 11 of 1785 Caslon specimen); dot and arrow rule (brevier 28 of 1790 Fry and Steele)
46 ll., 195 (203) x 115 (144); 83 mm for 20 ll.
COPY EXAMINED: GBPRO: CO 226, vol 35, ff 79–89
ISSUE paged in continuation of 1814 consolidation and 1817 Acts as 69–90 with [caption title] (69) | ...
PAPER: Wove, unmarked except *6* marked 1815 (or 1813) in PCU copy
COPIES EXAMINED: OONL, PCL (2 copies), PCU

PEI35 Prince Edward Island. Lieutenant Governor (1813–1824: Smith)
[royal arms flanked by military emblems 74 x 202 mm] | BY HIS EXCELLENCY | CHARLES DOUGLASS SMITH, | ... | A PROCLAMATION. | WHEREAS by a return from the Regi*ſ*ter's Office it appears that the following Town and Pa*ſ*ture Lots in the | *ſ*everal Towns and Royalties of this I*ſ*land, remain ungranted and are now the property of the Crown, to wit: | ... | AND WHEREAS it is apprehended, that many of the *ſ*aid Town and Pa*ſ*ture Lots *have been, and now are, under im-* | *provement, and occupied by various Persons,* and it being deemed highly expedient that the mo*ſ*t correct information ... | ... | Given under my Hand, and Seal at Arms at Charlotte-Town, in the *ſ*aid Island, this | Sixth day of April in the Year of our Lord one thou*ſ*and Eight hundred and | Nineteen ... | ... | GOD SAVE THE KING.
Proclamation: 1 leaf (54 x 25 cm)
CONTENTS: royal arms; 9 ll. heading including *L.S.* in a square of type ornaments [24 mm]; 63 ll. text, part in 2 and 3 cols; 6 ll. closing signed Fade Goff, deputy provincial secretary
PAPER: Wove, unmarked

TYPOGRAPHY: *Text*: old faces including open double pica and four-line pica with modern face headings. *Display*: leaf ornament and lattice (long primer 11 of 1785 Caslon specimen)
522 x 224 mm
NOTES: Lieutenant Governor Smith sent his proclamation to London on 15 May with the assertion, 'I cannot but anticipate Lord Bathurst's approbation.' A draft response added by hand in London reads: 'previous to adopting any measure for dispossessing the actual occupiers of the lots specified he should communicate further information with respect to the nature of the claims advanced by the several occupiers' (ff 147–8).
COPY EXAMINED: GBPRO: CO 226, vol 35, f 149

PEI36 Prince Edward Island. Parliament (10th, 1st session: 1818–1819). House of Assembly
JOURNAL | OF THE | *HOUSE OF ASSEMBLY* [open] | OF HIS MAJESTY'S | ISLAND PRINCE EDWARD. | Anno Quinquage*ſſ*imo Nono, | REGIS GEORGII III. | [ornamental dash 86 mm] | *First Session of the Tenth General Assembly.* | [ornamental dash 86 mm] | [royal arms 26 x 78 mm] | [thick-thin rule 123 mm] | CHARLOTTE-TOWN, PRINCE EDWARD ISLAND: | PRINTED BY JAMES BAGNALL, | PRINTER TO THE KING'S MOST EXCELLENT MAJESTY. | [bead rule 17 mm] | 1819.
COLLATION: 2° (31.2 x 19 cm), 1^2 (*1* 1 + 2–13^2), 28 leaves, pp *1–3* 4–55 *56*
CONTENTS: *1* title; 2 blank; 3–55 text; *56* blank
PAPER: Laid, watermark Britannia; countermark C BALL | 1816 except *4–9* countermark A | 1815 in OOA copy; chains vertical 27 mm
TYPOGRAPHY: *Text*: pica, modern face. *Display*: long dashes with sunburst and bellflower ornaments; dot and arrow rule (brevier 28 of 1790 Fry and Steele specimen); dash of rimmed oval with tapered arrow sides
NOTES: On 27 February the lieutenant governor sent the Journal to London with extensive notes about this rancorous session.
COPIES EXAMINED: OOA, GBPRO: CO 226, vol 35, ff 35–77

1820

PEI37 Alder, Robert, 1796–1873
THE SUBSTANCE | OF A | SERMON, | DELIVERED IN THE WESLEYAN CHAPEL, | *Charlotte-Town, Prince Edward Island,* | *ON THE OCCASION OF THE LAMENTED DEATH OF* | *HIS LATE MAJESTY* | GEORGE III. | *OF BLESSED MEMORY.* | [thick-thin rule 32 mm] | BY ROBERT ALDER, | *METHODIST MISSIONARY.* | [thin-thick rule 32 mm] | *Printed by Request.* | [rule 80 mm] | "God is our refuge and strength, a very present help in trouble." | Psalm 46, 1. | [rule 75 mm] | CHARLOTTE-TOWN PRINCE EDWARD ISLAND, | *PRINTED BY JAMES BAGNALL.* | [double dotted 14 mm] | 1820. *stet Eharlotte*
COLLATION: 8° (23 x 14.1 cm), *1–3*^{4} 4^2, 14 leaves, pp *1–5* 6–28 pagination in ( ))
CONTENTS: *1* title; 2 blank; *3* dedication: 'To the Hon. Robert Gray, signed The Author; *4* advertisement; 5–28 sermon, text: Psalm cii.26, 27
PAPER: Wove, unmarked; speckled with brown and grey
TYPOGRAPHY: *Text*: pica, modern face. *Display*: open italic and long swelled rule
40 ll., 167 (175) x 90; 84 mm for 20 ll.
NOTES: The final paragraph of the advertisement reads: 'The Author begs leave to apologize to the Subscribers for the length of time which has elapsed between the preaching and publishing of the following Sermon. The fault is not to be attributed to him, as the manuscript has long been ready. The delay has been occasioned by the want of suitable paper, which could not be obtained earlier in consequence of local circumstances' (p 4).
A notice headed 'SPEEDILY WILL BE PUBLISHED by Request' had appeared in the *Prince Edward Island Gazette* on 22 July 1820 naming agents for subscriptions at Charlotte-Town and Bedeque. An editorial note in the issue of 16 August explained the delay: 'We deem it our duty to state to the Public, that the reason why Mr Alder's sermon is not yet published, is, our having been disappointed of Paper, which we expected from Halifax. We shall do all in our power to obtain it as speedily as possible, and in the mean time, the Subscribers may rest assured, that there will be no unnecessary delay either on the part of the author or our own.' Perhaps the paper 'expected from Halifax' was being made at Anthony Holland's Acadian Paper Mill (**NS183**).
COPIES EXAMINED: NSHD, OTMCL
REFERENCE: MacFarlane

PEI38 Prince Edward Island. Laws (11th Parliament, 1st session: 1820)
[caption title] Anno Primo Regis GEORGII IV. | At the GENERAL ASSEMBLY of His Maje*ſ*ty's ISLAND | PRINCE EDWARD, begun and holden at CHARLOTTE- | TOWN, on the Twenty-Fifth day of JULY, ANNO | DOMINI, one thou*ſ*and eight hundred and twenty ...
COLLATION: 2° (32 x 19.5 cm), *1*², 2 leaves, pp [4]
CONTENTS: [1–3] text; [4] blank
PAPER: Laid, watermark Britannia; countermark J SNELGROVE | 181[?] | ; chains vertical
TYPOGRAPHY: *Text*: pica, modern face
58 ll., 246 x 127; 85 mm for 20 ll.
NOTES: The Acts of this session, like those of 1819 (**PEI34**), were paged both in continuation of previous years and as a separate publication. This year however the type was reset producing two editions (**PEI39**). When the lieutenant governor reported to the Colonial Office he noted that '3 Acts were passed of no importance' (CO 226, vol 36, f 60ʳ).
COPY EXAMINED: GBPRO: CO 226, vol 36, ff 96–97

PEI39 Prince Edward Island. Laws (11th Parliament, 1st Session: 1820)
[caption title] (91) | Anno Primo Regis GEORGII IV. | [in margin] 1820. | At the GENERAL ASSEMBLY of His Maje*ſ*ty's ISLAND | PRINCE EDWARD, begun and holden at CHAR- | LOTTE- TOWN, on the Twenty-Fifth day of | JULY, ANNO DOMINI, one thou*ſ*and eight hun- | dred and twenty ...
COLLATION: 4° (25 x 19.5 cm), *1*², 2 leaves, pp 91–94 (91 in ( ))
CONTENTS: 91–94 text
PAPER: Wove, unmarked
TYPOGRAPHY: *Text*: pica, modern face
47 ll., 201 (212) x 115 (145); 84 mm for 20 ll.
COPY EXAMINED: PCL

PEI40 Prince Edward Island. Lieutenant Governor (1813–1824: Smith)
[caption title] PRINCE EDWARD ISLAND. [open] | SPEECH of His Excellency Lt. Governor CHARLES DOUGLASS | SMITH, at the opening of the General A*ſſ*embly, on the 9th | May, 1820.
COLLATION: 4° (25.4 x 20 cm), *1*², 2 leaves, pp [4]
CONTENTS: [*1*] blank; [2] Smith's speech; [3] two extracts from letters received by Smith from Earl Bathurst; [4] blank
PAPER: Laid, marked post horn in crowned shield; chains vertical 25 mm
TYPOGRAPHY: *Text*: pica, modern face with great primer old face for headings
2 cols., 49 ll., 195 (226) x 143; 84 mm for 20 ll.
NOTES: Smith dissolved the Assembly and called an election for June. All but four of the members were returned for a session which the lieutenant governor prorogued more promptly than ever before.
COPY EXAMINED: GBPRO (2 copies): CO 226, vol 36, ff 42–43, 108–109

PEI41 Prince Edward Island. Lieutenant Governor (1813–1824: Smith)
[caption title] PRINCE EDWARD ISLAND. [open] | [swelled rule 15 mm] | SPEECH of His Excellency Lt. Governor CHARLES DOUGLASS | SMITH, at the opening of the General A*ſſ*embly of Prince | Edward I*ſ*land, upon the 25th July, 1820; with the | Addre*ſ*s of His Maje*ſ*ty's Council in an*ſ*wer, and His Excel- | lency's Reply thereto:
COLLATION: 2° (32.5 x 20.7 cm), *1*², 2 leaves, pp [4]
CONTENTS: [*1*] Smith's speech; [2] Council's address with Smith's thanks; [3–4] blank
PAPER: Laid, watermark Britannia; countermark S SHARP | 1815 | ; chains vertical 25 mm
TYPOGRAPHY: *Text*: pica, modern face with great primer old face for headings
2 cols., 59 ll., 251 x 141; 84 mm for 20 ll.
COPY EXAMINED: GBPRO: CO 226, vol 36, ff 62, 65

PEI42 Prince Edward Island. Lieutenant Governor (1813–1824: Smith)
PRINCE EDWARD ISLAND. [open] | [swelled rule 15 mm] | The Addre*ſ*s of the Lower Hou*ſ*e of A*ſſ*embly, in an*ſ*wer to His | Excellency's SPEECH at the opening of the General A*ſſ*em- | bly, and His Excellency's Reply. | ...
Address: 1/2° (32 x 19.7 cm)
CONTENTS: 5 ll. heading including dash; 101 ll. of text in 2 cols including the address of the House of Assembly dated 26 July and Smith's reply, 28 July
PAPER: Laid, marked Britannia; chains vertical 27 mm
TYPOGRAPHY: *Text*: pica, modern face with great primer old face for headings
255 x 143 mm
COPY EXAMINED: GBPRO: CO 226, vol 36, f 63

PEI43 Prince Edward Island. Lieutenant Governor (1813–1824: Smith)
SPEECH of His Excellency Lt. Governor CHARLES DOUGLASS | SMITH, at the closing of the Se*ſſ*ion. | ... | "Under any circumstances my hearty | and earnest desire to promote the public | welfare will continue undiminished, | feeling as I trust I ever

shall, superior | to all party politics, and necessarily re- | garding with both regret and wonder, | those who allow themselves to be hurried | away by them. | "C. DOUGLASS SMITH, | "Lt. Govr. | "August 10th, 1820."
Speech: 1/2° (30.7 x 18.5 cm)
CONTENTS: 2 ll. heading; 72 ll. text in 2 cols including 4 ll. saluation and 3 ll. closing
PAPER: Laid, marked arms of England; chains vertical 26 mm
TYPOGRAPHY: *Text*: pica, modern face with great primer old face for headings
167 x 144 mm
COPY EXAMINED: GBPRO: CO 226, vol 36, f 64

PEI44 Prince Edward Island. Parliament (11th, 1st session: 1820). House of Assembly
JOURNAL | OF THE | *HOUSE OF ASSEMBLY* [open] | OF HIS MAJESTY'S | ISLAND PRINCE EDWARD. | Anno Primo | REGIS GEORGII IV. | [ornamental dash 90 mm] | *First Session of the Eleventh General Afsembly.* | [ornamental dash 86 mm] | [royal arms 27 x 80 mm] | [thick-thin rule 125 mm] | CHARLOTTE-TOWN, PRINCE EDWARD ISLAND: | PRINTED BY JAMES BAGNALL, | PRINTER TO THE KING'S MOST EXCELLENT MAJESTY. | [bead rule 18 mm] | 1820.

COLLATION: 2° (31 x 19.5 cm), *1*[1] 2–5[2], 11 leaves, pp *1–3* 4–22
CONTENTS: *1* title; 2 blank; 3–22 text
PAPER: Laid, watermark Britannia; countermark T EDMONDS | 1819 | ; chains vertical 26 mm
TYPOGRAPHY: *Text*: pica, modern face. *Display*: old faces for headings; open italic with swash A, M; long dash is rimmed oval with tapered arrow sides; bead rule as long primer 14 of 1785 Caslon specimen
2 cols., 63 ll., 268 (277) x 142; 85 mm for 20 ll.
NOTES: After proroguing the legislature on 10 August the lieutenant governor sent copies of the speeches and addresses to London (**PEI41–43**) on 15 August explaining that 'The Lower House were in their usual state of ill temper' (CO 226, vol 36, f 60v). In his opinion 'The holding a Sefsion at all was a necefsary evil, I got it over as quickly & as quietly as I could, & having succeeded in so doing, there is now no necefsity for calling a General Afsembly for Years' (f 61r).
COPY EXAMINED: GBPRO: CO 226, vol 36, ff 105–125

APPENDIX
Imprints Not Located

Acadian Recorder Handbill. Halifax: 1814
'Immediately after the arrival of the Swift sure packet, we published a Hand-Bill (thinking it would be acceptable to such of our readers as have not access to the Coffee-Room), with all the intelligence time would allow us to collect' (*Acadian Recorder*, 26 March 1814).

An Almanack for the Year 1810. Halifax: James Bagnall, 1810
'Will be published and sold at this Office in the course of a few days' (*Novator*, 1 January 1810). A list of contents follows the announcement. Bagnall's 1809 almanac is **NS49**.

Bates, Walter. The Mysterious Stranger; or, The Memoirs of Henry More Smith, alias Henry Frederick Moon, alias William Newman, Containing an account of his extraordinary conduct during his confinement in the Gaol of King's County, Province of New Brunswick, where he was under sentence of Death; With a statement of his succeeding conduct, before and since his confinement in Newgate, State of Connecticut. Halifax: Acadian Recorder, 1817
'This day published and for sale at the Office of the Acadian Recorder' (7 June 1817). MacFarlane lists British, American, and later New Brunswick editions. The Connecticut edition, published at New Haven in 1817, differs in the wording of its subtitle from this *Acadian Recorder* notice. Walter Bates (1760–1842), sheriff of King's County, was a loyalist, long settled at Kingston, New Brunswick.

Beardsley, John. A Sermon Delivered in Trinity Church, at Saint John, the 24th of June 1803, to the Free Masons, Met to Celebrate the Memory of St John the Baptist. Saint John: Jacob Mott, 1803. 8 pages
MacFarlane

Campbell, Donald. The Confession of Donald Campbell, Who was executed at Pictou, on the 22d of last month, for the Murder of his Father and Mother. Halifax: Acadian Recorder, 1819
'Will be published, this afternoon, and for sale at the Recorder Office, – price 1s' (*Free Press*, 5 October 1819; *Weekly Chronicle*, 8 October; *Acadian Recorder*, 9 October).

Church of England. A Form of Prayer to be used in all Places of Public Worship throughout this Province, on Friday Next, the 17th inst., the day appointed by Proclamation for a General Fast, &c. Saint John: John Ryan, 1801
'A few copies' (*Royal Gazette*, 14 July 1801); MacFarlane

Church of England. Form of Prayer for Fast Day. Saint John: John Ryan, 1804
'A few copies may be had' (*Royal Gazette*, 4 January 1804).

Church of England. A Form of Prayer to be Used in all Churches and Chapels within the Province of New Brunswick, on Wednesday the 27th day of August, being the day appointed by Proclamation for a General Fast and Humiliation. By his Honor the President's Command. Fredericton, printed by Mr Ryan, at his office near the church, Front Street, 1806. 16 pages
MacFarlane. The printer would be Michael Ryan, son of John Ryan and proprietor of Fredericton's first paper, the short-lived *Fredericton Telegraph* (**NB55**).

Church of England. Form of Prayer to be used on Wednesday the Seventh of March 1810; being appointed the Day by Proclamation for a General Fast and Humiliation. Saint John: Jacob Mott, 1810

'For sale at this office. A few copies' (*Royal Gazette*, 5 March 1810).

Church of England. Form of Prayer to be used in all Churches and Chapels in this Province on Wednesday, the 6th of March, being the day appointed by Proclamation, for a Public Fast, &c. Saint John: Jacob Mott, 1811

'For sale at this office, a few copies' (*Royal Gazette*, 4 March 1811).

A Circumstantial, True and Impartial History of the Rise and Progress of the Interesting Town of St Andrews, in New Brunswick, from its original settlement to the present era, containing a biographical sketch of the most eminent characters, whether legislative, judicial, magisterial, commercial, legal or medical, interspersed with hints for the improvement and other regulation of the timber trade. Saint John: Courier office, 1818

MacFarlane

Connolly, Joseph. An Essay on Universal Telegraphic Communication, in which a plan is laid down for Reciprocal Intercourse between the Different Nations of the World, in their Respective Languages; on a principle the most simple and economical. By Joseph Conolly, Telegraphist. Halifax: Acadian Recorder, 1817

'Just published, and for sale at this Office' (*Acadian Recorder*, 27 December 1817). In May of the previous year the *Acadian Recorder* had announced a plan to print by subscription 'A Telegraphic Dictionary, and Code of Signals, On New Principles, calculated for the various Numerical Symbols used by Sea and Land' (18 May 1816). One hundred subscriptions were required for the work to be published 'on a good paper, with a new type' and comprising 'about 40 large octavo pages' to be delivered to subscribers at 20 shillings. The next month officers of the Army and Navy were 'respectfully acquainted' that the subscription list was 'nearly filled up' (22 June 1816). In November the *Acadian Recorder* analyzed the superiority of the code of signals proposed for publication by Mr Connolly, the local telegraphist, compared to the system developed by Sir Home Popham which had recently been adopted by the Admiralty at a cost of £30,000. According to the *Recorder* Connolly now planned to 'solicit proof at the Admiralty previous to publishing the work' (2 November 1816).

The following year a London publisher, W. Lewis of St John's Square, published *The Acadian Code of Signals, On New Principles, Calculated for the Various Numerical and Alphabetical Symbols Used at Sea and by Land* ... by 'A Practical Telegraphist' (copy seen at QMMRB). In his preface dated at London, 18 February 1817, the author identified himself as a plain, unlettered man who first projected the plan for his code in the Island of Guadeloupe in 1811 and then finished it on a desolate island fifteen leagues east of Halifax. He concluded: 'From repeated trials, the Author flatters himself the result of further proof will be equally satisfactory, whether it be by Flags, or any other Symbols ...' This 'Practical Telegraphist' is almost certainly Joseph Connolly of Halifax and *The Acadian Code of Signals* is the work proposed by the *Acadian Recorder* in 1816. Connolly's 'Essay on Universal Telegraphic Communication' advertised in that same paper late in 1817 would seem to be another aspect of his plan.

Mrs Cuff. Catalogue of Subscription Library. Halifax, 1813

'Catalogues are ready to deliver to such subscribers as please to favor her with their custom' (*Halifax Journal*, 6 December 1813, *et seq.*).

Cumberland Agricultural Society. Handbill advertising a meeting on 5 January 1819. Halifax, 1818

In a letter dated County of Cumberland, 22 December 1818, 'A Farmer' criticizes the Cumberland Agricultural Society as a clique who have named themselves founders and executive without the participation of farmers and community leaders: 'And then to stop the complaints of the inhabitants for so gross an insult offered them, a number of printed handbills, dated the 4th inst. advertising a meeting of their sham Society ... have been struck off and circulated, in which handbills, the author, after making a puff of what he will do as a member of the Legislature, gives the finishing stroke with a little Latin borrowed from Agricola' (*Free Press*, 5 January 1819).

Elder, William. Thoughts on the Divine Perfections. Halifax, 1818

'This day published and may be had at the Recorder Office' (*Acadian Recorder*, 7 March 1818). William Elder (1784–1848) was ordained a Baptist preacher early in 1820. His best known work, *Infant Sprinkling Weighed in the Balance of the Sanctuary and Found Wanting* (Halifax, 1823), prompted a torrent of baptism literature (*Dictionary of Canadian Biography* VII, s.v. 'Elder, William,' by Franklyn H. Hicks).

Election Notice. Halifax, 1819
'Notice was given, by a handbill, issued on Friday last, that a Poll is to be opened for the election of a Member to serve in the Provincial Assembly, in place of E. Mortimer, deceased, at the County Court-House in this town, on Tuesday next, the 23d inst' (*Weekly Chronicle*, 19 November 1819).

An Extract from an Officer's Journal on the 10th January 1817. Together with some observations humbly and affectionately addressed to the Inhabitants of St John's, Newfoundland. Recommended by the Rev David Rowland. St John's: Lewis K. Ryan, 1817
'In the press and will be speedily published for the benefit of the Society for Improving the Condition of the Poor' (*Royal Gazette*, 18 March 1817). The adjoining column of the *Royal Gazette* carried notices for a charity sermon at the Methodist chapel and a benefit performance of *The Fair Penitent*. Rev Rowland was rector of St John the Baptist in St John's from 1810 to 1817.

Field Officer. Drill and Instructions of the 104th, or New Brunswick Regiment of Foot; grounded upon, and explaining the Rules and Regulations for the Formation, Field Exercise and Movements of the Infantry, and the Regulations for the Exercise of Light Infantry. Saint John, 1814
'For sale at the City Gazette Office ... price 2s' (3 May 1814).

Gotze, Charles Gotfried. A Narrative of the Past Life. Halifax: Acadian Recorder, 1816
'In the press and will be published on Monday next, price 1s 3d each, A Narrative of the Past Life of Charles Gotfried Gotze, Private in H.M. 3d Battalion, 60th Regiment of Foot, now under Sentence of Death, for the Murder of Sergeant John Glass, of the same regiment. Written by himself and faithfully translated from the German' (*Acadian Recorder*, 12 October 1816). An extract from Gotze's narrative was printed with this notice. He was tried on 10 October and sentenced to be executed on the fourteenth. The execution was reported on 19 October.

Grand Exhibition at Mason's Hall, 8 December in the year of Masonry 5813. Halifax, 1813
'The Entertainment had been for many days announced by splendid hand-bills' (*Acadian Recorder*, 11 December 1813).

Hudibras Minimus. A Gentle Scourge, a Poem in Two Cantos. Saint John, 1814
'In the press' (*Royal Gazette*, 25 July 1814); 'Just published ... price 1s' (8 August).

Journeymen Shoemakers, a publication on their strike. Halifax, 1820
From a coment on the 'local scribblers': 'Such must have been the case with the worthy gentleman who lately undertook to eulogize the conduct of the Journeymen Shoemakers in "striking work" for an increase in wages. Allowing that he got but one solitary guinea for the job, wrung from the scanty pockets of his poor clients, it was far beyond the merits of his publication' (*Weekly Chronicle*, 21 July 1820).

Kirk, Abdiel. Prospectus for a Reading Room at the New Circulating Library. Halifax, 1814
'A Reading Room will be opened, as an appendage to the Library, as soon as a number of subscribers have offered sufficient to defray the principal expences. Gentlemen who may wish to forward the Institution will be presented with a Prospectus at the Library or at Mr Geo. Eaton's' (*Acadian Recorder*, 17 September 1814).

Kirk, Abdiel. Catalogue of the New Circulating Library. Halifax, 1815
'A second part of the Catalogue is now published by desire of the subscribers' (*Acadian Recorder*, 6 May 1815; *Halifax Journal*, 15 May).

Nova Scotia and New Brunswick. Commander in Chief (1794–1800: Edward Augustus, Duke of Kent and Strathern). Military Regulations and Orders. Halifax, 1804
'Military Regulations and Orders, published in November last, by order of H.R.H. the Commander in Chief. A few copies may be had of W. Minns' (*Weekly Chronicle*, 29 June 1805). Although Prince Edward left Halifax in 1800 his regulations and instructions continued in use (**NS100**).

Nova Scotia Militia Officers. Halifax, 1811
'Just published and for sale at the Gazette Office, lists of the N.S. Militia Officers' (*Halifax Journal*, 15 April 1811).

An Ode Descriptive of the Awful Catastrophe by Fire, in St John's, Newfoundland, on the 7th of November 1817; With Illustrative Notes and Comments. St John's: Lewis K. Ryan, 1818

'In the press and shortly will be published, price 2s' (*Royal Gazette*, 9 December 1817); 'Just published' (13 January 1818). Although 'the major part of our Printing Materials' were destroyed in this fire Lewis Kelly Ryan continued to publish the *Royal Gazette* at the office of the *Mercantile Journal* which was offered to him 'with great kindness' by the proprietor, Robert Lee Jr (*Royal Gazette*, 11 November 1817).

Parish, Elijah. A Discourse Delivered at Byfield, Massachusetts, on the Public Fast, April 7, 1814. Halifax: Acadian Recorder, 1814

'In the press and will be published on Friday next' (*Acadian Recorder*, 6 August 1814); 'to be published on Tuesday next and will be for sale at this office, also, by Thomas D. Cowdell, and at the various bookstores in town. Price 1s 3d single' (13, 20 August); 'This day published' (27 August). Parish's discourse, based on Exodus 5, 17, 18 was also printed in the United States. His 1813 Fast day sermon had been published in Halifax by Cowdell the year before (**NS101**).

Presbyterian Church of Nova Scotia. Treasurer's Account for 1818. Halifax

A report of the 1819 meeting of the Synod at Truro includes 'Disbursements ... Paid for printing 300 copies of the Treasurer's account last year £1' (*Halifax Journal*, 26 July 1819).

The Prince Edward Island Calendar for the Year of Our Lord, 1815. Charlottetown: Printed and for sale at the Prince Edward Island Gazette Office. 32 pages

A detailed description of the contents taken from a copy in hand was printed in a Charlottetown paper, *The Patriot*, on 25 September 1879.

Reis, Edmund. A Short Account of the Life, Conversion, and Death of Michael McComb ... an Unhappy Youth Who Was Executed for the Crime of Murder, on the 13th Day of April, 1814, in the City of St John, New Brunswick ... Saint John: Henry Chubb, 1814. 16 pages

Dennis, p 16: NSWA copy not available

Society for Promoting Christian Knowledge. Halifax Diocesan Committee. Catalogue of Books. Halifax, 1815

'The books ... are now numerically arranged at the shop of Mr Thomas Heaviside. Printed Catalogues with the price of every article may be obtained gratuitously upon application at Mr Heaviside's, and at all the Booksellers' shops in Halifax, and also throughout the diocese by application to the clergy' (*Acadian Recorder*, 18 November 1815).

Society for Promoting Christian Knowledge. Halifax Diocesan Committee. Catalogue of Books. Halifax, 1819

'a new Catalogue of the Books on sale by the Committee, including the numerous additions which have lately been made to its stock, will soon be ready for distribution' (*Weekly Chronicle*, 3 December 1819).

Uniacke, Richard John, defendant. The Trial of Richard J. Uniacke for Murder. Halifax: Acadian Recorder, 1819

'The above sketch will be published in pamphlet form' (*Acadian Recorder*, 31 July 1819); 'We regret several errors in the Report of Mr Uniacke ... It has since been carefully revised and corrected and published in a Pamphlet to be had at this office' (7 August). A lawyer and former attorney general of Cape Breton, Uniacke was acquitted of the charge of murdering William Bowie in Nova Scotia's last recorded fatal duel (*Dictionary of Canadian Biography* VI, s.v. 'Uniacke, Richard John,' by B.C. Cuthbertson).

The Union Harmony; or, British America's Sacred Vocal Music. Containing, 1st, the principals of vocal music in a plain and concise manner; 2nd, a large collection of psalms and hymn tunes, many of which are original, suitable to all the metres now in use in these provinces. Saint John, 1801

MacFarlane; *Royal Gazette* (8 September 1801). A second edition was published in 1816 (**NB59**).

Warren, William. A Wonderful Dream. Halifax, 1810

'Just published, and for sale by Mr Spurr, at Annapolis, Mr Fuller, Horton, at the Novator-Office and by the subscriber in Halifax, a small poem entitled A Wonderful Dream [signed] William Warren' (*Novator*, 14 May 1810).

Wesley, John. Hymns. Saint John: Jacob Mott, 1802

'Now in the press and shortly to be published, by Jacob S. Mott, a handsome edition of Wesley's Hymns; with additions' (*Saint John Gazette*, 4 December 1802).

Imprint Not Seen

Important and Interesting Intelligence: Defeat and Capture of the Danish Fleet, Death of the Emperor Paul, and Dissolution of the Boasted Northern Confederacy. Printed by John Howe, printer to the King's Most Excellent Majesty

Extracts dated February to April 1801, from newspapers brought to Halifax in the brig *Tyger*, published as a broadside (57 x 46 cm)
COPY LOCATED: USMWA (not seen)

Name Index

Acadian. *A poetical account of the American campaigns*, 1815 **NS119**

Agricola. *Agricola to his readers*, 1819 **NS167**

Alder, Robert. *The substance of a sermon delivered in the Wesleyan Chapel*, 1820 **PEI37**; *Vastator perditus*, 1819 **PEI33**

Ancien professeur. *Abécédaire religieux, moral, instructif, et amusant*, 1817 **NS138**

Andrews, Samuel. *The necessity, the certainty, and the sufficiency of revealed religion*, 1801 **NB1**; *Sermon preached in Trinity Church, Kingston*, 1809 **NB33**

Aplin, Joseph. *Opinions of several gentlemen of the law*, 1802 **NB14**

Barrow, George. *Critical observations on a pamphlet entitled Crim. con. William Henry Hall, plaintiff, against Major George Barrow, defendant*, 1820 **NS170**

Benevolent Irish Society (St John's). *Appendix to the foregoing report*, 1808 **Nfld3**; *A report of the members names*, 1807 **Nfld1**; *Rules and constitution*, 1807 **Nfld2**

Bermuda. The substance of a decision ... upon a petition from the deputy to the treasurer of Greenwich Hospital, 1811 **NS75**

Bermuda. Court of Vice-Admiralty. *The case of the Legal Tender*, 1812 **NS80**

Botsford, William. *The question respecting the right of the United States of America to the islands in Passamaquoddy-Bay*, 1805 **NB21**

British North America. Commander of British Forces (1811-1815: Prevost). *Circular ... His Excellency the commander in chief ... is now pleased to express his intention to call out and embody*, 1812 **NS81**

Bromley, Walter. *An address delivered at the Free-Mason's Hall, Halifax, August 3d, 1813*, 1813 **NS92**; *An appeal to the virtue and good sense of the inhabitants of Great Britain, &c. in behalf of the Indians of North America*, 1820 **NS171**; *Mr Bromley's second address on the deplorable state of the Indians*, 1814 **NS103**

Burke, Edmund. *Continuation of the first principles of Christianity*, 1810 **NS69**; *Letter of instruction to the Catholic missionaries of Nova Scotia and its dependencies*, 1804 **NS29**; *Remarks on a pamphlet entitled Popery condemned*, 1809 **NS60**; *Remarks on the Rev Mr Stanser's Examination of the Rev Mr Burke's Letter of instruction*, 1805 [1806] **NS36**; *A treatise on the first principles of Christianity*, 1808 **NS50**

Burns, George. *Active goodness recommended and enforced*, 1819 **NB78**; *Lectures and sermons delivered in the Scots Church of Saint John*, 1820 **NB85**; *Letter addressed to the Rev James Milne, A.M.*, 1818 **NB70**; *A sermon preached at Saint John before the Saint John's and Union Lodges of free and accepted ancient Masons*, 1820 **NB86**; *A view of the principles and forms of the Church of Scotland*, 1817 **NB61**

Carrier. *The news-carrier's address ... to the patrons of the Royal Gazette*, 1805 **NB25**

Carrier of the Times; or, True Briton. *Address of the carrier of the Times; or, True Briton*, 1809 **NB32**

Catholic Church. Diocese of Quebec. Vicar General of Nova Scotia (1801-1817: Burke). *Letter of instruction to the Catholic missionaries of Nova Scotia and its dependencies*, 1804 **NS29**

Chamberlain, Theophilus. *To His Excellency Sir John Wentworth, baronet, and the honourable commissioners appointed to examine into the practicability and expense of opening an inland navigable communication*, [1815] **NS112**

Charles the Carrier. *The news-carrier's address to the customers of the Royal Gazette*, 1803 **NB18**

Chipman, Ward. *At a meeting of a respectable number of the electors, both for the city and county of Saint*

John, 1802 **NB6**; *A fair and candid review of the proceedings of the House of Assembly*, 1802 **NB15**
Church of England. *The catechism of the Church of England with parallel passages*, 1813 **NS93**; *A form of prayer*, 1804 **NB20**; *A form of prayer*, 1813 **NB43**; *A form of prayer*, 1814 **NB48**; *A form of prayer*, 1807 **NS43**; *A form of prayer*, 1812 **NS82**; *A form of prayer*, 1814 **NS104**; *A form of prayer and thanksgiving*, 1802 **NB7**; *A form of prayer and thanksgiving*, [1802] **NS14**
Church of England. Diocese of Nova Scotia. Bishop (1787-1816: Inglis). *A charge delivered to the clergy of the diocess of Nova Scotia*, 1804 **NS30**
Cleland, John. *The memoirs of Fanny Hill*, 1820 **NS172**
Cochran, Andrew William. *Report of the trial of Edward Jordan and Margaret Jordan his wife for piracy & murder*, 1810 **NS70**
Cogswell, Henry Hezekiah. *Militia laws of the province of Nova-Scotia in force in the year of Our Lord, 1813.*, 1813 **NS97**; *The statutes at large*, 1816 **NS123**
Copernicus. *An almanack for the year of Our Lord, 1819*, [1818] **NB68**
Cowdell, Thomas Daniel. *A poetical account of the American campaigns*, 1815 **NS119**
Creon. *A statement of facts relative to the proceedings of the House of Assembly*, 1802 **NB8**
Croke, Alexander *The rights and powers of captors and prize agents*, 1808 **NS53**; *The substance of a decision ... upon a petition from the deputy to the treasurer of Greenwich Hospital*, 1811 **NS75**; *The substance of a judgment in the case of the Little Joe*, 1813 **NS96**
Cubit, George. *Jesus Christ the supreme governor and only foundation of the Christian church*, 1818 **Nfld13**; *Observations on the nature, evidences, and authority of the Christian religion*, 1818 **Nfld14**

E.W. *The Nova-Scotia calendar for 1814*, [1814] **NS109**

Fairbanks, Charles Rufus. *Report of the trial of Edward Jordan and Margaret Jordan his wife for piracy & murder*, 1810 **NS70**
Fairweather, W. *The Nova-Scotia calendar for 1817*, [1816] **NS122**
Falmouth. *The question respecting the right of the United States of America to the islands in Passamaquoddy-Bay*, 1805 **NB21**
Freemasons. Solomon's Lodge, No XXII (Fredericton). *By-laws of Solomon's Lodge, no XXII*, 1819 **NB79**
Freemasons. United Grand Lodge (Nova Scotia). *Constitution of the ancient fraternity of free and accepted Masons*, 1819 **NS155**

George. *The news-carrier's address to the customers of the Royal Gazette*, 1808 **NB31**
Gray, Archibald. *A sermon preached on 10th August 1804*, 1804 **NS31**

Halifax. *Rules and regulations for the establishment and government of a watch and patrol*, 1818 **NS143**
Halifax [Draft of Charter]. *The draft of a charter for the incorporation*, 1814 **NS105**
Halifax Committee of Trade. *The Halifax Committee of Trade, having requested the attendance of the merchants, traders, and other persons ... for the purpose of considering the situation of the fisheries*, 1818 **NS144**; *The Labradore fishery for the season 1814*, 1813 **NS94**
Halifax Methodist Female Benevolent Society. *The third report*, 1819 **NS156**
Halifax Poor Man's Friend Society. *The report*, 1820 **NS173**
Hall, William Henry. *Crim. con. A trial. William Henry Hall, plaintiff, against Major George Barrow, defendant*, 1820 **NS174, NS175**
Hand in Hand Fire Company (Halifax). *Rules and articles*, 1802 **NS15**
Hay-Drummond, George William Auriol. *Select portions of the new version of Psalms*, 1818 **NB71**
Heart and Hand Fire-Company (Halifax). *The rules of the Heart and Hand Fire-Company*, 1817 **NS128**
Herkimer. *The rights and powers of captors and prize agents*, 1808 **NS53**
Hildrith, Isaac. *To His Excellency Sir John Wentworth, baronet, and the honourable commissioners appointed to examine into the practicability and expense of opening an inland navigable communication*, [1815] **NS112**
Humbert, Stephen. *Union harmony*, 1816 **NB59**

Inglefield, John Nicholson. *Captain Inglefield's narrative of the loss of the Centaur*, 1813 **NS95**
Inglis, Charles. *A charge delivered to the clergy of the diocess of Nova Scotia*, 1804 **NS30**; *A sermon on confirmation*, 1801 **NS6**
Inglis, John. *A sermon preached in the parish church of St Paul at Halifax on Sunday the 11th of June 1815*, 1815 **NS113**

James, William. *An inquiry into the merits of the principal naval actions between Great-Britain and the United States*, 1816 **NS121**
Job Creon. *A statement of facts relative to the standfasts and the runaways*, 1802 **NB11**
Jordan, Edward. *Report of the trial of Edward Jordan and Margaret Jordan his wife for piracy & murder*, 1810 **NS70**

Jordan, Margaret. *Report of the trial of Edward Jordan and Margaret Jordan his wife for piracy & murder*, 1810 **NS70**

Kelly, John. *Report of the trial of Edward Jordan and Margaret Jordan his wife for piracy & murder*, 1810 **NS70**

Kiernan, Bernard. *An almanack for the year of Our Lord, 1812*, [1811] **NB36**; *An almanack for the year of Our Lord, 1813*, [1812] **NB38**; *An almanack for the year of Our Lord, 1818*, [1817] **NB60**; *An almanack for the year of Our Lord, 1819*, [1818] **NB69**; *An almanack for the year of Our Lord, 1820*, [1819] **NB77**; *An almanack for the year of Our Lord, 1821*, [1820] **NB84**

Knowlan, James. *A review of Edmund J. Reis's Short account of Michael McComb, &c.*, 1814 **NB49**; *A sermon preached in the Methodist Chapel*, 1819 **NS157**

Legal Tender. *The case of the Legal Tender*, 1812 **NS80**

Little Joe. *The substance of a judgment in the case of the Little Joe*, 1813 **NS96**

Lockwood, Anthony. *Report on the projected canal across the istmus*, 1820 **NB87**

Loyal British Hero. *A new song on peace and conquered Bonaparte*, 1814 **NB50**

Lugrin, George. *The news-carrier's address to the customers of the Royal Gazette*, 1808 **NB31**

Lunenburg Farmer Society. *Articles or rules for the government of the Lunenburg Farmer Society*, 1819 **NS158**

McCulloch, Thomas. *The nature and uses of a liberal education*, 1819 **NS159**; *The prosperity of the Church in troublous times*, 1814 **NS106**; *Words of peace*, 1817 **NS129**

Madras School. *Annual report*, 1820 **NB88**

Marshall, John George. *A patriotic call to prepare in a season of peace for one of political danger*, 1819 **NS160**

Methodist Missionary Society (Nova Scotia District). *The first annual report*, 1818 **NS145**; *A report of the formation*, 1817 **NS130**

Milne, James. *A friendly address to the congregation of Christ's Church, Fredericton*, 1819 **NB80**; *Remarks on Dr Burns's View of the principles and forms of the Presbyterian Kirk*, 1818 **NB72**

Monro, James. *A treatise on baptism*, 1811 **NS73**

Mountain, George Jehoshaphat. *A sermon preached in the parish church of Fredericton*, 1816 **NB55**; *A valedictory sermon*, 1817 **NB62**

Nabby. *The substance of a judgment ... in the case of the schooner Nabby*, 1818 **NS146**

Native. *An almanack for the year of Our Lord, 1809*, [1808] **NS49**

Native of the Province. *A patriotic call to prepare in a season of peace for one of political danger*, 1819 **NS160**

New Brunswick [Agricultural Export Prohibition Act]. *An act to prohibit the exportation of corn, meal, flour, and potatoes*, 1817 **NB63**

New Brunswick. Administrator (1812-1813: Smyth). *A proclamation. Whereas the government of the United States of America ... has declared war*, 1812 **NB39**

New Brunswick. Court of Vice-Admiralty. *The question respecting the right of the United States of America to the islands in Passamaquoddy-Bay*, 1805 **NB21**

New Brunswick. Executive Council. *At a council holden in the city of Saint John on the 10th day of July 1812 ... securing the neutrality of those Indians*, 1812 **NB40**

New Brunswick. Laws (1st Parliament, 1st session: 1786 to 4th Parliament, 2nd session: 1805). *The acts*, 1805 **NB22**

New Brunswick. Laws (4th Parliament, 3rd session: 1807 to 6th Parliament, 1st session: 1817). *The acts*, 1817 **NB64**

New Brunswick. Laws (3rd Parliament, 5th session: 1801). *Acts*, 1801 **NB3**

New Brunswick. Laws (3rd Parliament, 6th session: 1802). *Acts*, 1802 **NB12**

New Brunswick. Laws (4th Parliament, 1st session: 1803). *Acts*, 1803 **NB16**

New Brunswick. Laws (4th Parliament, 2nd session: 1805). *Acts*, 1805 **NB23**

New Brunswick. Laws (4th Parliament, 3rd session: 1807). *Acts*, 1807 **NB27**

New Brunswick. Laws (4th Parliament, 4th session: 1808). *Acts*, 1808 **NB29**

New Brunswick. Laws (5th Parliament, 1st session: 1810). *Acts*, 1810 **NB34**

New Brunswick. Laws (5th Parliament, 2nd session: 1812). *Acts*, 1812 **NB41**

New Brunswick. Laws (5th Parliament, 3rd session: 1813). *Acts*, 1813 **NB44**

New Brunswick. Laws (5th Parliament, 4th session: 1814). *Acts*, 1814 **NB51**

New Brunswick. Laws (5th Parliament, 5th session: 1816). *Acts*, 1816 **NB56**

New Brunswick. Laws (6th Parliament, 1st session: 1817). *Acts*, 1817 **NB65**

New Brunswick. Laws (6th Parliament, 2nd session: 1818). *Acts*, 1818 **NB73**

New Brunswick. Laws (6th Parliament, 3rd session: 1819). *Acts*, 1819 **NB81**

New Brunswick. Laws (7th Parliament, 1st session: 1820). *Acts*, 1820 **NB89**

New Brunswick. Parliament (3rd, 3rd session: 1798). House of Assembly. *Journal*, 1801 **NB2**

New Brunswick. Parliament (3rd, 4th session: 1799). House of Assembly. *Journal*, 1801 **NB4**

New Brunswick. Parliament (3rd, 5th session: 1801). House of Assembly. *Journal*, 1801 **NB5**

New Brunswick. Parliament (3rd, 6th session: 1802). House of Assembly. *Journal*, 1802 **NB13**

New Brunswick. Parliament (4th, 1st session: 1803). House of Assembly. *Journal*, 1803 **NB17**

New Brunswick. Parliament (4th, 2nd session: 1805). House of Assembly. *Journal*, 1805 **NB24**

New Brunswick. Parliament (4th, 3rd session: 1807). House of Assembly. *Journal*, 1807 **NB28**

New Brunswick. Parliament (4th, 4th session: 1808). House of Assembly. *Journal*, 1808 **NB30**

New Brunswick. Parliament (5th, 1st session: 1810). House of Assembly. *Journal*, 1810 **NB35**

New Brunswick. Parliament (5th, 2nd session: 1812). House of Assembly. *Journals*, 1812 **NB42**

New Brunswick. Parliament (5th, 3rd session: 1813). House of Assembly. *Journals*, 1813 **NB45**

New Brunswick. Parliament (5th, 4th session: 1814). House of Assembly. *Journal*, 1814 **NB52**

New Brunswick. Parliament (5th, 5th session: 1816). House of Assembly. *Journal*, 1816 **NB57**

New Brunswick. Parliament (6th, 1st session: 1817). House of Assembly. *Journal*, 1817 **NB66**

New Brunswick. Parliament (6th, 2nd session: 1818). House of Assembly. *Journal*, 1818 **NB74**

New Brunswick. Parliament (6th, 3rd session: 1819). House of Assembly. *Journal*, 1819 **NB82**

New Brunswick. Parliament (7th, 1st session: 1820). House of Assembly. *Journal*, 1820 **NB90**

New Brunswick Central Society for Promoting the Rural Economy of the Province. *At a meeting held in Fredericton ... promoting the agricultural interests of the province*, 1820 **NB91**

Newfoundland. Governor (1810-1813: Duckworth). *Conditions for leasing by public auction certain lots of ground heretofore fishing ships' rooms*, 1811 **Nfld7**; *I do hereby declare that the said wharf has been erected at the government expence*, 1812 **Nfld11**; *Whereas it has been found requisite that certain alterations should take place in the table of fees*, 1810 **Nfld5**; *Whereas it is the intention of His Majesty's government that the wharf ... should be used for the general accommodation of the town*, [1812] **Nfld12**; *Whereas the great want of specie in this island is continuing to increase*, 1811 **Nfld9**

Norris, Robert. *A candid discussion of the principal tenets of the Roman faith*, 1806 **NB26**

Nova Scotia. [Billeting Act], 1808 **NS51, NS52**

Nova Scotia [Laws, etc.] *Militia laws of the province of Nova-Scotia in force in the year of Our Lord, 1813*, 1813 **NS97**; *Province of Nova Scotia. Revenue laws in force in 1802*, 1802 **NS17**

Nova Scotia. [Militia Act], 1808 **NS52**

Nova Scotia. [School Act] *School act*, 1811 **NS74**

Nova Scotia. Adjutant General of Militia. *Rules and articles for the better government of the militia forces*, 1812 **NS84**; *Rules and regulations for the militia forces of Nova-Scotia*, 1808 **NS52**

Nova Scotia. Court of Vice Admiralty. *A report of the case of the Nabby*, 1818 **NS154**; *The rights and powers of captors and prize agents*, 1808 **NS53**; *The substance of a judgment ... in the case of the Little Joe*, 1813 **NS96**; *The substance of a judgment ... in the case of the schooner Nabby*, 1818 **NS146**; *The substance of a decision ... upon a petition from the deputy to the treasurer of Greenwich Hospital*, 1811 **NS75**

Nova Scotia. Deputy Commissary General. *The militia being called out and about to take post in various stations on the coast*, 1812 **NS85**

Nova Scotia. Laws (1st Parliament, 1st session: 1758 to 8th Parliament, 5th session, 1804). *The statutes at large*, 1805 **NS37**

Nova Scotia. Laws (8th Parliament, 6th session: 1805 to 10th Parliament, 6th session: 1816). *The statutes at large*, 1816 **NS123**

Nova Scotia. Laws (8th Parliament, 2nd session: 1801). *At the general assembly of the province of Nova Scotia begun ... on the ninth day of June 1801*, 1801 **NS7**

Nova Scotia. Laws (8th Parliament, 2nd session: 1801). *At the general assembly of the province of Nova Scotia begun ... on the ninth day of June 1801*, 1801 **NS8**

Nova Scotia. Laws (8th Parliament, 3rd session: 1802). *At the general assembly of the province of Nova Scotia begun ... on Thursday the twenty-fifth day of February 1802*, 1802 **NS16**

Nova Scotia. Laws (8th Parliament, 4th session: 1803). *At the general assembly of the province of Nova Scotia begun ... on Wednesday the first day of June 1803*, 1803 **NS22**

Nova Scotia. Laws (8th Parliament, 4th session: 1803). *At the general assembly of the province of Nova Scotia begun ... on Wednesday the first day of June 1803*, 1803 **NS23**

Nova Scotia. Laws (8th Parliament, 6th session: 1805-1806). *At the general assembly of the province of Nova Scotia begun ... on the twentieth day of February Anno Domini 1800*, 1806 **NS39**

Nova Scotia. Laws (9th Parliament, 1st session: 1806-1807). *At the general assembly of the province of Nova-Scotia begun ... on the eighteenth day of November 1806,* 1807 **NS44**

Nova Scotia. Laws (9th Parliament, 2nd session: 1807-1808). *At the general assembly of the province of Nova-Scotia begun on Tuesday the eighteenth day of November Anno Domini 1806,* 1808 **NS54**

Nova Scotia. Laws (9th Parliament, 3rd session: 1808). *At the general assembly of the province of Nova-Scotia begun on Tuesday the eighteenth day of November Anno Domini 1806,* 1808 **NS55**

Nova Scotia. Laws (9th Parliament, 4th session: 1808-1809). *At the general assembly of the province of Nova-Scotia begun ... on Tuesday the eighteenth day of November Anno Domini 1806,* 1809 **NS61**

Nova Scotia. Laws (9th Parliament, 5th session: 1809). *At the general assembly of the province of Nova-Scotia begun ... on Tuesday the eighteenth day of November Anno Domini 1806,* 1809 **NS62**

Nova Scotia. Laws (9th Parliament, 6th session: 1809). *At the general assembly of the province of Nova-Scotia begun ... on Tuesday the eighteenth day of November Anno Domini 1806,* 1809 **NS63**

Nova Scotia. Laws (9th Parliament, 7th session: 1811). *At the general assembly of the province of Nova-Scotia begun ... on Tuesday the eighteenth day of November Anno Domini 1806,* 1811 **NS76**

Nova Scotia. Laws (10th Parliament, 1st session: 1812). *At the general assembly of the province of Nova-Scotia begun ... on Thursday the sixth day of February 1812,* 1812 **NS86**

Nova Scotia. Laws (10th Parliament, 3rd session: 1813). *At the general assembly of the province of Nova-Scotia begun ... on Thursday the sixth day of February 1812,* 1813 **NS98**

Nova Scotia. Laws (10th Parliament, 4th session: 1814). *At the general assembly of the province of Nova-Scotia begun ... on Thursday the sixth day of February 1812,* 1814 **NS107**

Nova Scotia. Laws (10th Parliament, 5th session: 1815). *At the general assembly of the province of Nova-Scotia begun ... on Thursday the sixth day of February 1812,* 1815 **NS114**

Nova Scotia. Laws (10th Parliament, 7th session: 1817). *At the general assembly of the province of Nova-Scotia begun ... on Thursday the 6th day of February 1812,* 1817 **NS131**

Nova Scotia. Laws (10th Parliament, 8th session: 1818). *At the general assembly of the province of Nova-Scotia begun ... on Thursday the sixth day of February 1812,* 1818 **NS147**

Nova Scotia. Laws (11th Parliament, 1st session: 1819). *At the general assembly of the province of Nova-Scotia begun ... on Thursday the eleventh day of February 1819,* 1819 **NS161**

Nova Scotia. Laws (11th Parliament, 2nd session: 1820). *At the general assembly of the province of Nova-Scotia begun ... on Thursday the eleventh day of February 1819,* 1820 **NS176**

Nova Scotia. Legislature. Joint Committee Appointed to Consider the Convention Lately Concluded between His Majesty and the Government of the United States of America. *Proceedings of the general assembly upon the convention concluded between His Majesty and the United States of America,* 1819 **NS162**

Nova Scotia. Legislature. Joint Committee on the Indians. *In performance of the duty assigned to us by the two houses of the general assembly ... to form some plan for the settlement of the Indians,* 1801 **NS9**

Nova Scotia. Lieutenant Governor (1792-1808: Wentworth). *His Excellency the lieutenant-governor has ordered me to desire that you will immediately assemble the magistrates,* 1807 **NS45**; *I have it in command from his Excellency the lieutenant-governor to acquaint you that in the event of the negociation now pending ... not terminating amicably,* 1808 **NS56**

Nova Scotia. Lieutenant Governor (1808-1811: Prevost). *Proclamations ... and I do order ... that no trade or intercourse whatsoever shall be carried on between this province and the United States of America,* 1809 **NS64**

Nova Scotia. Lieutenant Governor (1811-1816: Sherbrooke). *(Circular) ... His Excellency the lieutenant-governor has been informed that the small pox has made its appearance,* 1815 **NS115**; *Proclamation ... whereas every species of predatory warfare carried on against defenceless inhabitants,* 1812 **NS87**

Nova Scotia. Parliament (8th, 2nd session: 1801). House of Assembly. *Journal,* 1801 **NS10**

Nova Scotia. Parliament (8th, 3rd session: 1802) House of Assembly. *Journal,* 1802 **NS18**

Nova Scotia. Parliament (8th, 4th session: 1803). House of Assembly. *Journal,* 1803 **NS24**

Nova Scotia. Parliament (8th, 5th session: 1804). House of Assembly. *Journal,* 1804 **NS32**

Nova Scotia. Parliament (8th, 6th session: 1805-1806). House of Assembly. *Journal,* 1806 **NS40**

Nova Scotia. Parliament (9th, 1st session: 1806-1807). House of Assembly. *Journal,* 1807 **NS46**

Nova Scotia. Parliament (9th, 2nd session: 1807-1808). House of Assembly. *Journal,* 1808 **NS57**

Nova Scotia. Parliament (9th, 3rd session: 1808). House of Assembly. *Journal,* 1808 **NS58**

Nova Scotia. Parliament (9th, 4th session: 1808-1809). House of Assembly. *Journal,* 1809 **NS65**

Nova Scotia. Parliament (9th, 5th session: 1809). House of Assembly. *Journal*, 1809 **NS66**
Nova Scotia. Parliament (9th, 6th session: 1809). House of Assembly. *Journal*, 1809 **NS67**
Nova Scotia. Parliament (9th, 7th session: 1811). House of Assembly. *Journal*, 1811 **NS77**
Nova Scotia. Parliament (10th, 1st session: 1812). House of Assembly. *Journal*, 1812 **NS88**
Nova Scotia. Parliament (10th, 2nd session: 1812). House of Assembly. *Journal*, 1812 **NS89**
Nova Scotia. Parliament (10th, 3rd session: 1813). House of Assembly. *Journal*, 1813 **NS99**
Nova Scotia. Parliament (10th, 4th session: 1814). House of Assembly. *Journal*, 1814 **NS108**
Nova Scotia. Parliament (10th, 5th session: 1815). House of Assembly. *Journal*, 1815 **NS116**
Nova Scotia. Parliament (10th, 6th session: 1816). House of Assembly. *Journal*, 1816 **NS124**
Nova Scotia. Parliament (10th, 7th session: 1817). House of Assembly. *Journal*, 1817 **NS132**
Nova Scotia. Parliament (10th, 8th session: 1818). House of Assembly. *Journal*, 1818 **NS148**
Nova Scotia. Parliament (11th, 1st session: 1819). House of Assembly. *Journal*, 1819 **NS163**
Nova Scotia. Parliament (11th, 2nd session: 1820). House of Assembly. *Journal*, 1820 **NS177**
Nova Scotia and New Brunswick. Commander in Chief (1794-1800: Edward Augustus, Duke of Kent and Strathern). *Instructions to barrack-masters serving in Nova-Scotia, New-Brunswick, and their dependencies*, [1813] **NS100**
Nova Scotia and New Brunswick Baptist Association. *Minutes*, 1810 **NS71**; *Minutes*, 1811 **NS78**; *Minutes*, 1812 **NS90**; *Minutes*, 1813 **NB46**; *Minutes*, 1814 **NB53**; *Minutes*, 1815 **NB54**; *Minutes*, 1816 **NB58**; *Minutes*, 1818 **NB75**; *Minutes*, 1819 **NB83**; *Minutes*, 1820 **NB92**

Nova Scotia Bible Society. *First annual report*, 1815 **NS117**; *The second report*, 1817 **NS135**; *The third report*, 1818 **NS150**; *The fourth report*, 1819 **NS165**; *The fifth report*, 1820 **NS179**
Nova-Scotian. *A letter to the people of Halifax*, 1820 **NS183**

Odell, Jonathan. *On seeing the address to the ship America*, [1803] **NB19**

Parish, Elijah. *A discourse delivered at Byfield, state of Massachusetts*, 1813 **NS101**
Perro, B. *Abécédaire religieux, moral, instructif, et amusant*, 1817 **NS138**
Philo-Uraniæ. *The Nova-Scotia calendar for 1815*, [1814] **NS110**; *The Nova-Scotia calendar for 1816*, [1815] **NS118**; *The Nova-Scotia calendar for 1818*, [1817] **NS136**; *The Nova-Scotia calendar for 1819*, [1818] **NS151**; *The Nova-Scotia calendar for 1820*, [1819] **NS166**; *The Nova-Scotia calendar for 1821*, [1820] **NS180**
Presbyterian Church of Nova Scotia. *The report of a committee appointed by the synod*, 1818 **NS152**
Priestley, James. *A charity sermon delivered in the Methodist Chapel, Halifax*, 1818 **NS153**; *A sermon occasioned by the lamented demise of His late Majesty George III*, 1820 **NB93**; *The theological compendium*, 1817 **NS139**
Prince Edward Island. Executive Council. *Address of His Majesty's Council to Lieutenant General Fanning*, 1804 **PEI7**; *To the honorable Caesar Colclough ... the address of His Majesty's Council*, 1813 **PEI17**
Prince Edward Island. Grand Jury. *Address to His Excellency Edmund Fanning*, 1805 **PEI8**; *Address to the honorable Caesar Colclough*, 1812 **PEI15**; *To the honorable Caesar Colclough ... the address of the grand jury*, 1813 **PEI18**
Prince Edward Island. Laws (1st Parliament, 1st session: 1773 to 9th Parliament, 3rd session: 1817). *Acts*, 1817 **PEI25**
Prince Edward Island. Laws (6th Parliament, 7th session: 1798 to 9th Parliament, 2nd session: 1814). *Acts*, 1814 **PEI19**
Prince Edward Island. Laws (9th Parliament, 2nd session: 1814). *Acts*, 1814 **PEI20**
Prince Edward Island. Laws (9th Parliament, 3rd session: 1817). *Acts*, 1817 **PEI26**
Prince Edward Island. Laws (10th Parliament, 1st session: 1818-1819). *At the general assembly of His Majesty's Island of Prince Edward begun ... on the third day of November Anno Domini one thousad eight hundred and eighteen*, 1819 **PEI34**
Prince Edward Island. Laws (11th Parliament, 1st session: 1820). *At the general assembly of His Majesty's Island Prince Edward begun ... on the twenty-fifth day of July Anno domini one thousand eight hundred and twenty*, 1820 **PEI38, PEI39**
Prince Edward Island. Lieutenant Governor (1787-1805: Fanning). *A letter from the Right Honorable J.H. Addington, Esq to Lieut. General Fanning*, 1805 **PEI9**
Prince Edward Island. Lieutenant Governor (1805-1812: DesBarres). *Speech of His Excellency Lt. Governor Des Barres*, 1805 **PEI10**
Prince Edward Island. Lieutenant Governor (1813-1824: Smith). *The address of the lower house of assembly in answer to His Excellency's speech*, 1820 **PEI42**; *Militia general order. His Excellency the Lieut. Governor is pleased to direct that the following orders, rules, and regulations ... be strictly observed*, 1814 **PEI21**; *A proclamation. Whereas an act of the*

general assembly of this Island was passed ... intituled 'An act for regulating fees,' 1815 **PEI22**; *A proclamation. Whereas by my proclamation issued on the first day of October 1816,* 1818 **PEI30**; *A proclamation. Whereas by a return from the register's office,* 1819 **PEI35**; *A proclamation. Whereas it appears that the following officers ... gave permission,* 1815 **PEI23**; *A proclamation. Whereas it having been signified to me ... that it is intended on the part of the crown to extend to the proprietors of land in this colony immunity from certain forfeitures,* 1816 **PEI24**; *Speech of His Excellency Lt. Governor Charles Douglass Smith at the closing of the session,* 1820 **PEI43**; *Speech of His Excellency Lieut. Governor Charles Douglass Smith at the opening of the general assembly ... 8th July 1817,* 1817 **PEI27**; *Speech of His Excellency Lt. Governor Charles Douglass Smith at the opening of the general assembly ... 3d November 1818,* 1818 **PEI29**; *Speech of his Excellency Lt. Governor Charles Douglass Smith at the opening of the general assembly on the 9th May 1820,* 1820 **PEI40**; *Speech of his Excellency Lt. Governor Charles Douglass Smith at the opening of the general assembly ... upon the 25th July 1820,* 1820 **PEI41**

Prince Edward Island. Parliament. House of Assembly. *Resolved that the proceedings of the legislature of this Island in passing the two acts ... were in direct conformity with His Majesty's royal pleasure,* 1805 **PEI11**; *To the honourable William Townshend,* 1812 **PEI16**

Prince Edward Island. Parliament (7th, 2nd session: 1805). House of Assembly. *Journal,* 1805 **PEI12**

Prince Edward Island. Parliament (8th, 1st session: 1806). House of Assembly. *Journal,* 1806 **PEI13**

Prince Edward Island. Parliament (9th, 3rd session: 1817). House of Assembly. *Journal,* 1817 **PEI28**

Prince Edward Island. Parliament (10th, 1st session: 1818-1819). House of Assembly. *Journal,* 1819 **PEI36**

Prince Edward Island. Parliament (11th, 1st session: 1820). House of Assembly. *Journal,* 1820 **PEI44**

Prince Edward Island. Receiver General of Quit Rent. *Public notice. Whereas His Royal Highness the Prince Regent has been graciously pleased to grant the following indulgence,* 1818 **PEI31**; *Special notice to the landholders and resident agents of landholders,* 1818 **PEI32**

Pythagoras. *The Nova-Scotia almanack for the year of Our Lord, 1818,* [1817] **NS134**; *The Nova-Scotia almanack for 1819,* [1818] **NS149**; *The Nova-Scotia almanack for 1820,* [1819] **NS164**; *The Nova-Scotia almanack for the year of Our Lord, 1821,* [1820] **NS178**

Ratford, Jenkin. *The trial of John Wilson alias Jenkin Ratford,* 1807 **NS47**

Sabine, James. *A sermon in commemoration of the benevolence of the citizens of Boston,* 1818 **Nfld15**

Saint John. *Laws and ordinances,* 1817 **NB67**; *Laws and ordinances,* 1820 **NB94**

Saint John [Charter]. *The charter of the city of Saint John,* 1811 **NB37**

Saint John. Town Major. *Notice is hereby given that all persons having any business to transact with the commandant,* 1813 **NB47**

Shoemaker, Abraham. *An almanack for the year of Our Lord, 1804,* [1803] **NS20**; *An almanack for the year of Our Lord, 1805,* [1804] **NS27, NS28**; *An almanack for the year of Our Lord, 1806,* [1805] **NS34**; *Astronomical calculations for the year 1801,* [1800] **NS2**

Shreve, Thomas. *A sermon preached at St Paul's Church in Halifax before the Provincial Grand Lodge of free and accepted ancient Masons,* 1803 **NS25**

Society for Improving the Condition of the Poor (St John's). *An account of the rise, progress, and establishment of the society,* 1808 **Nfld4**

Society for Promoting Christian Knowledge. Halifax Diocesan Committee. *Annual report,* 1816 **NS125**; *Annual report,* 1817 **NS140**

Spectator. *A fair and candid review of the proceedings of the House of Assembly,* 1802 **NB15**

St George's Society (Saint John). *Rules for the Saint Georges' Society,* 1820 **NB95**

St Peter's Church (Halifax). *Resolves of the delegates,* 1801 **NS11**

Stanser, Robert. *An examination of the Reverend Mr Burke's Letter of instruction to the Catholic missionaries of Nova Scotia and its dependencies,* 1804 **NS33**

Street, Samuel Denny. *A statement of facts relative to the proceedings of the House of Assembly,* 1802 **NB8**

Temple, Isaac. *Two sermons preached in St Matthew's Church, Halifax,* 1820 **NS181**

Theophrastus. *An almanack for the year of Our Lord, 1801,* [1800] **NS1**; *An almanack for the year of Our Lord, 1802,* [1801] **NS4, NS5**; *An almanack for the year of Our Lord, 1803* , [1802] **NS12, NS13**; *An almanack for the year of Our Lord, 1804,* [1803] **NS21**; *An almanack for the year of Our Lord, 1806,* [1805] **NS35**; *An almanack for the year of Our Lord, 1807,* [1806] **NS38**; *An almanack for the year of Our Lord, 1808,* [1807] **NS42**; *An almanack for the year of Our Lord, 1809,* [1808] **NS48**; *An almanack for the year of Our Lord, 1810,* [1809]

NS59; *An almanack for the year of Our Lord, 1811*, [1810] **NS68**; *An almanack for the year of Our Lord, 1812*, [1811] **NS72**; *An almanack for the year of Our Lord, 1813*, [1812] **NS79**; *An almanack for the year of Our Lord, 1814*, [1813] **NS91**; *An almanack for the year of Our Lord, 1815*, [1814] **NS102**; *An almanack for the year of Our Lord, 1816*, [1815] **NS111**; *An almanack for the year of Our Lord, 1817*, [1817] **NS126**; *An almanack for the year of Our Lord, 1818*, [1817] **NS127**; *An almanack for the year of Our Lord, 1819*, [1818] **NS141, NS142**; *An almanack for the year of Our Lord, 1821*, [1820] **NS168, NS169**

Uniacke, Crofton. *A report of the case of the Nabby*, 1818 **NS154**; *The substance of a judgment ... in the case of the schooner Nabby*, 1818 **NS146**

Uniacke, Richard John. *The statutes at large*, 1805 **NS37**

Uniacke, Richard John, Jr. *A report of the case of the Nabby*, 1818 **NS154**

University of King's College (Windsor). *The statutes, rules, and ordinances*, 1803 **NS26**

Violet, Edmund. *Remarks upon the life and manners of the Rev John Jones*, 1810 **Nfld6**

Wilkie, William. *A letter to the people of Halifax*, 1820 **NS183**

Wilson, John. *The trial of John Wilson alias Jenkin Ratford*, 1807 **NS47**

Winslow, Edward. *A statement of facts relative to the standfasts and the runaways*, 1802 **NB11**

Young, John. *Agricola to his readers*, 1819 **NS167**; *Agricultural prizes for 1820*, 1820 **NS184**

Title Index

Abécédaire religieux, moral, instructif et amusant, 1817. Perro, B. **NS138**

An abridgement of the statutes, 1805. Nova Scotia. Laws (1st Parliament, 1st session: 1758 to 8th Parliament, 5th session: 1804) **NS37**

An account of the rise, progress, and establishment of the society, 1808. Society for Improving the Condition of the Poor (St John's) **Nfld4**

An act to prohibit the exportation of corn, meal, flour, and potatoes, 1817. New Brunswick [Agricultural Export Prohibition Act] **NB63**

Active goodness recommended and enforced, 1819. Burns, George **NB78**

The acts, 1805. New Brunswick. Laws (1st Parliament, 1st session: 1786 to 4th Parliament, 2nd session: 1805) **NB22**

The acts, 1817. New Brunswick. Laws (4th Parliament, 3rd session: 1807 to 6th Parliament, 1st session: 1817) **NB64**

Acts, 1801. New Brunswick. Laws (3rd Parliament, 5th session: 1801) **NB3**

Acts, 1802. New Brunswick. Laws (3rd Parliament, 6th session: 1802) **NB12**

Acts, 1803. New Brunswick. Laws (4th Parliament, 1st session: 1803) **NB16**

Acts, 1804. New Brunswick. Laws (4th Parliament, 2nd session: 1805) **NB23**

Acts, 1807. New Brunswick. Laws (4th Parliament, 3rd session: 1807) **NB27**

Acts, 1808. New Brunswick. Laws (4th Parliament, 4th session: 1808) **NB29**

Acts, 1810. New Brunswick. Laws (5th Parliament, 1st session: 1810) **NB34**

Acts, 1812. New Brunswick. Laws (5th Parliament, 2nd session: 1812) **NB41**

Acts, 1813. New Brunswick. Laws (5th Parliament, 3rd session: 1813) **NB44**

Acts, 1814. New Brunswick. Laws (5th Parliament, 4th session: 1814) **NB51**

Acts, 1816. New Brunswick. Laws (5th Parliament, 5th session: 1816) **NB56**

Acts, 1817. New Brunswick. Laws (6th Parliament, 1st session: 1817) **NB65**

Acts, 1818. New Brunswick. Laws (6th Parliament, 2nd session: 1818) **NB73**

Acts, 1819. New Brunswick. Laws (6th Parliament, 3rd session: 1819) **NB81**

Acts, 1820. New Brunswick. Laws (7th Parliament, 1st session: 1820) **NB89**

Acts, 1814. Prince Edward Island. Laws (6th Parliament, 7th session: 1798 to 9th Parliament, 2nd session: 1814) **PEI19**

Acts, 1817. Prince Edward Island. Laws (1st Parliament, 1st session: 1773 to 9th Parliament, 3rd session: 1817) **PEI25**

Acts, 1814. Prince Edward Island. Laws (9th Parliament, 2nd session: 1814) **PEI20**

Acts, 1817. Prince Edward Island. Laws (9th Parliament, 3rd session: 1817) **PEI26**

An address delivered at the Free-Mason's Hall, Halifax, August 3d, 1813, 1813. Bromley, Walter **NS92**

Address of His Majesty's Council to Lieutenant General Fanning, 1804. Prince Edward Island. Executive Council **PEI7**

Address of the carrier of the Times; or, True Briton, 1809. **NB32**

The address of the lower house of assembly in answer to His Excellency's speech, 1820. Prince Edward Island. Lieutenant Governor (1813-1824: Smith) **PEI42**

Address to His Excellency Edmund Fanning, 1804 **PEI2, PEI4, PEI5, PEI6**

Address to His Excellency Edmund Fanning, 1805. Prince Edward Island. Grand Jury **PEI8**

Address to His Excellency the Lieutenant General Edmund Fanning, 1804 **PEI1**

[Address to Lieutenant Governor Fanning (Acadians)], 1804 **PEI1**

[*Address to Lieutenant Governor Fanning (Charlottetown and Queen's County)*], 1804 **PEI2**
[*Address to Lieutenant Governor Fanning (Great Rustico)*], 1804 **PEI3**
[*Address to Lieutenant Governor Fanning (King's County)*], 1804 **PEI4**
[*Address to Lieutenant Governor Fanning (Prince County)*], 1804 **PEI5**
[*Address to Lieutenant Governor Fanning (Tryon River)*], 1804 **PEI6**
Address to the honorable Caesar Colclough, 1812. Prince Edward Island. Grand Jury **PEI15**
Address to the Lieutenant General Fanning, 1804 **PEI3**
Agricola to his readers, 1819. Young, John **NS167**
Agricultural prizes for 1820, 1820. Young, John **NS184**
An almanack for the year of Our Lord, 1801, [1800] **NS1**
An almanack for the year of Our Lord, 1802, [1801] **NS4, NS5**
An almanack for the year of Our Lord, 1803, [1802] **NS12, NS13**
An almanack for the year of Our Lord, 1804, [1803] **NS20, NS21**
An almanack for the year of Our Lord, 1805, [1804] **NS27, NS28**
An almanack for the year of Our Lord, 1806, [1805] **NS34, NS35**
An almanack for the year of Our Lord, 1807, [1806] **NS38**
An almanack for the year of Our Lord, 1808, [1807] **NS42**
An almanack for the year of Our Lord, 1809, [1808] **NS48, NS49**
An almanack for the year of Our Lord, 1810, [1809] **NS59**
An almanack for the year of Our Lord, 1811, [1810] **NS68**
An almanack for the year of Our Lord, 1812, [1811] **NB36**
An almanack for the year of Our Lord, 1812, [1811] **NS72**
An almanack for the year of Our Lord, 1813, [1812] **NB38**
An almanack for the year of Our Lord, 1813, [1812] **NS79**
An almanack for the year of Our Lord, 1814, [1813] **NS91**
An almanack for the year of Our Lord, 1815, [1814] **NS102**
An almanack for the year of Our Lord, 1816, [1815] **NS111**
An almanack for the year of Our Lord, 1817, [1817] **NS126**
An almanack for the year of Our Lord, 1818, [1817] **NB60**
An almanack for the year of Our Lord, 1818, [1817] **NS127**
An almanack for the year of Our Lord, 1819, [1818] **NB68, NB69**
An almanack for the year of Our Lord, 1819, [1818] **NS141, NS142**
An almanack for the year of Our Lord, 1820, [1819] **NB77**
An almanack for the year of Our Lord, 1821, [1820] **NB84**
An almanack for the year of Our Lord, 1821, [1820] **NS168, NS169**
Annual report, 1820. Madras School **NB88**
Annual report, 1816. Society for Promoting Christian Knowledge. Halifax Diocesan Committee **NS125**
Annual report, 1817. Society for Promoting Christian Knowledge. Halifax Diocesan Committee **NS140**
An appeal to the virtue and good sense of the inhabitants of Great Britain, &c. in behalf of the Indians of North America, 1820. Bromley, Walter **NS171**
Appendix to the foregoing report, 1808. Benevolent Irish Society (St John's) **Nfld3**
Articles or rules for the government of the Lunenburg Farmer Society, 1819. Lunenburg Farmer Society **NS158**
Astronomical calculations for the year 1801, [1800] **NS2**
At a council holden in the city of Saint John on the 10th day of July 1812 ... securing the neutrality of those Indians, 1812. New Brunswick. Executive Council **NB40**
At a general meeting (St John's) ... for the purpose of petitioning the Prince Regent, 1811 **Nfld8**
At a meeting held in Fredericton ... promoting the agricultural interests of the province, 1820. New Brunswick Central Society for Promoting the Rural Economy of the Province **NB91**
At a meeting of a respectable number of the electors, both for the city and county of Saint John, 1802. Chipman, Ward **NB6**
At the general assembly of His Majesty's Island of Prince Edward begun ... on the third day of November Anno Domini one thousad eight hundred and eighteen, 1819. Prince Edward Island. Laws (10th Parliament, 1st session: 1818-1819) **PEI34**
At the general assembly of His Majesty's Island Prince Edward begun ... on the twenty-fifth day of July Anno domini one thousand eight hundred and twenty, 1820. Prince Edward Island. Laws (11th Parliament, 1st session: 1820) **PEI38, PEI39**
At the general assembly of the province of Nova Scotia

begun ... on the ninth day of June 1801, 1801. Nova Scotia. Laws (8th Parliament, 2nd session: 1801) **NS7**

At the general assembly of the province of Nova Scotia begun ... on the ninth day of June 1801, 1801. Nova Scotia. Laws (8th Parliament, 2nd session: 1801) **NS8**

At the general assembly of the province of Nova Scotia begun ... on Thursday the twenty-fifth day of February 1802. 1802. Nova Scotia. Laws (8th Parliament, 3rd session: 1802) **NS16**

At the general assembly of the province of Nova Scotia begun ... on Wednesday the first day of June 1803, 1803. Nova Scotia. Laws (8th Parliament, 4th session: 1803) **NS22**

At the general assembly of the province of Nova Scotia begun ... on Wednesday the first day of June 1803, 1803. Nova Scotia. Laws (8th Parliament, 4th session: 1803) **NS23**

At the general assembly of the province of Nova Scotia begun ... on the twentieth day of February Anno Domini 1800, 1806. Nova Scotia. Laws (8th Parliament, 6th session: 1805-1806) **NS39**

At the general assembly of the province of Nova-Scotia begun ... on the eighteenth day of November 1806, 1807. Nova Scotia. Laws (9th Parliament, 1st session: 1806-1807) **NS44**

At the general assembly of the province of Nova-Scotia begun ... on Tuesday the eighteenth day of November Anno Domini 1806, 1808. Nova Scotia. Laws (9th Parliament, 2nd session: 1807-1808) **NS54**

At the general assembly of the province of Nova-Scotia begun ... on Tuesday the eighteenth day of November Anno Domini 1806, 1808. Nova Scotia. Laws (9th Parliament, 3rd session: 1808) **NS55**

At the general assembly of the province of Nova-Scotia begun ... on Tuesday the eighteenth day of November Anno Domini 1806, 1809. Nova Scotia. Laws (9th Parliament, 4th session: 1808–1809) **NS61**

At the general assembly of the province of Nova-Scotia begun ... on Tuesday the eighteenth day of November Anno Domini 1806, 1809. Nova Scotia. Laws (9th Parliament, 5th session: 1809) **NS62**

At the general assembly of the province of Nova-Scotia begun ... on Tuesday the eighteenth day of November Anno Domini 1806, 1809. Nova Scotia. Laws (9th Parliament, 6th session: 1809) **NS63**

At the general assembly of the province of Nova-Scotia begun ... on Tuesday the eighteenth day of November Anno Domini 1806, 1811. Nova Scotia. Laws (9th Parliament, 7th session: 1811) **NS76**

At the general assembly of the province of Nova-Scotia begun ... on Thursday the sixth day of February 1812, 1812. Nova Scotia. Laws (10th Parliament, 1st session: 1812) **NS86**

At the general assembly of the province of Nova-Scotia begun ... on Thursday the sixth day of February 1812, 1813. Nova Scotia. Laws (10th Parliament, 3rd session: 1813) **NS98**

At the general assembly of the province of Nova-Scotia begun ... on Thursday the sixth day of February 1812, 1814. Nova Scotia. Laws (10th Parliament, 4th session: 1814) **NS107**

At the general assembly of the province of Nova-Scotia begun ... on Thursday the sixth day of February 1812, 1815. Nova Scotia. Laws (10th Parliament, 5th session: 1815) **NS114**

At the general assembly of the province of Nova-Scotia begun ... on Thursday the 6th day of February 1812, 1817. Nova Scotia. Laws (10th Parliament, 7th session: 1817) **NS131**

At the general assembly of the province of Nova-Scotia begun ... on Thursday the sixth day of February 1812, 1818. Nova Scotia. Laws (10th Parliament, 8th session: 1818) **NS147**

At the general assembly of the province of Nova-Scotia begun ... on Thursday, the eleventh day of February 1819, 1819. Nova Scotia. Laws (11th Parliament, 1st session: 1819) **NS161**

At the general assembly of the province of Nova-Scotia begun ... on Thursday, the eleventh day of February 1819, 1820. Nova Scotia. Laws (11th Parliament, 2nd session: 1820) **NS176**

By-laws of Solomon's Lodge, no XXII, 1819. Freemasons. Solomon's Lodge, No XXII (Fredericton) **NB79**

A candid discussion of the principal tenets of the Roman faith, 1806. Norris, Robert **NB26**

Captain Inglefield's narrative of the loss of the Centaur, 1813. Inglefield, John Nicholson **NS95**

The case of the Legal Tender, 1812. Bermuda. Court of Vice-Admiralty **NS80**

The catechism of the Church of England with parallel passages, 1813. Church of England **NS93**

A charge delivered to the clergy of the diocess of Nova Scotia, 1804. Church of England. Diocese of Nova Scotia. Bishop (1787-1816: Inglis) **NS30**

A charity sermon delivered in the Methodist Chapel, Halifax, 1818. Priestley, James **NS153**

The charter of the city of Saint John, 1811. Saint John [Charter] **NB37**

Circular ... His Excellency the commander in chief ... is now pleased to express his intention to call out and embody, 1812. British North America. Commander of British Forces (1811-1815: Prevost) **NS81**

(Circular) ... His Excellency the lieutenant-governor has been informed that the small pox has made its

appearance, 1815. Nova Scotia. Lieutenant Governor (1811-1816: Sherbrooke) **NS115**
Conditions for leasing by public auction certain lots of ground heretofore fishing ships' rooms, 1811. Newfoundland. Governor (1810-1813: Duckworth) **Nfld7**
Constitution of the ancient fraternity of free and accepted Masons, 1819. Freemasons. United Grand Lodge (Nova Scotia) **NS155**
Continuation of the first principles of Christianity, 1810. Burke, Edmund **NS69**
Crim. con. A trial. William Henry Hall, plaintiff, against Major George Barrow, defendant, 1820. Hall, William Henry **NS174, NS175**
Critical observations on a pamphlet entitled Crim. con. William Henry Hall, plaintiff, against Major George Barrow, defendant, 1820. Barrow, George **NS170**

[*Directions for avoiding the Sambro ledges*], [1812] **NS83**
[*Directions for avoiding the Sambro ledges*], [1816] **NS120**
A discourse delivered at Byfield, state of Massachusetts, 1813. Parish, Elijah **NS101**
A dissertation on the thirteenth and seventeenth chapters of the book of St John's Revelation, 1802 **NB9**
The draft of a charter for the incorporation, 1814. Halifax [Draft of Charter] **NS105**

The elector's mirror, 1802 **NB10**
An examination of the Reverend Mr Burke's Letter of instruction to the Catholic missionaries of Nova Scotia and its dependencies, 1804. Stanser, Robert **NS33**
Extracts from provincial acts relative to the marching of His Majesty's troops, 1808. Nova Scotia. [Billeting Act] **NS51**

A fair and candid review of the proceedings of the House of Assembly, 1802. Spectator **NB15**
The fifth report, 1820. Nova Scotia Bible Society **NS179**
The first annual report, 1818. Methodist Missionary Society (Nova Scotia District) **NS145**
First annual report, 1815. Nova Scotia Bible Society **NS117**
A form of prayer, 1804. Church of England **NB20**
A form of prayer, 1813. Church of England **NB43**
A form of prayer, 1814. Church of England **NB48**
A form of prayer, 1807. Church of England **NS43**
A form of prayer, 1812. Church of England **NS82**
A form of prayer, 1814. Church of England **NS104**
A form of prayer and thanksgiving, [1802]. Church of England **NB7**
A form of prayer and thanksgiving, 1802. Church of England **NS14**
The fourth report, 1819. Nova Scotia Bible Society **NS165**
A friendly address to the congregation of Christ's Church, Fredericton, 1819. Milne, James **NB80**

The Halifax Committee of Trade, having requested the attendance of the merchants, traders, and other persons ... for the purpose of considering the situation of the fisheries, 1818. Halifax Committee of Trade **NS144**
His Excellency the lieutenant-governor has ordered me to desire that you will immediately assemble the magistrates, 1807. Nova Scotia. Lieutenant Governor (1792-1808: Wentworth) **NS45**

I do hereby declare that the said wharf has been erected at the government expence, 1812. Newfoundland. Governor (1810-1813: Duckworth) **Nfld11**
I have it in command from His Excellency the lieutenant-governor to acquaint you that in the event of the negociation now pending ... not terminating amicably, 1808. Nova Scotia. Lieutenant Governor (1792-1808: Wentworth) **NS56**
In performance of the duty assigned to us by the two houses of the general assembly ... to form some plan for the settlement of the Indians, 1801. Nova Scotia. Legislature. Joint Committee on the Indians **NS9**
An inquiry into the merits of the principal naval actions between Great-Britain and the United States, 1816. James, William **NS121**
Instructions to barrack-masters serving in Nova-Scotia, New-Brunswick, and their dependencies, [1813]. Nova Scotia and New Brunswick. Commander in Chief (1794-1800: Edward Augustus, Duke of Kent and Strathern) **NS100**

Jesus Christ the supreme governor and only foundation of the Christian church, 1818. Cubit, George **Nfld13**
Journal, 1801. New Brunswick. Parliament (3rd, 3rd session: 1798). House of Assembly **NB2**
Journal, 1801. New Brunswick. Parliament (3rd, 4th session: 1799). House of Assembly **NB4**
Journal, 1801. New Brunswick. Parliament (3rd, 5th session: 1801). House of Assembly **NB5**
Journal, 1802. New Brunswick. Parliament (3rd, 6th session: 1802). House of Assembly **NB13**
Journal, 1803. New Brunswick. Parliament (4th, 1st session: 1803). House of Assembly **NB17**
Journal, 1805. New Brunswick. Parliament (4th, 2nd session: 1805). House of Assembly **NB24**

Journal, 1807. New Brunswick. Parliament (4th, 3rd session: 1807). House of Assembly **NB28**
Journal, 1808. New Brunswick. Parliament (4th, 4th session: 1808). House of Assembly **NB30**
Journal, 1810. New Brunswick. Parliament (5th, 1st session: 1810). House of Assembly **NB35**
Journal, 1814. New Brunswick. Parliament (5th, 4th session: 1814). House of Assembly **NB52**
Journal, 1816. New Brunswick. Parliament (5th, 5th session: 1816). House of Assembly **NB57**
Journal, 1817. New Brunswick. Parliament (6th, 1st session: 1817). House of Assembly **NB66**
Journal, 1818. New Brunswick. Parliament (6th, 2nd session: 1818). House of Assembly **NB74**
Journal, 1819. New Brunswick. Parliament (6th, 3rd session: 1819). House of Assembly **NB82**
Journal, 1820. New Brunswick. Parliament (7th, 1st session: 1820). House of Assembly **NB90**
Journal, 1801. Nova Scotia. Parliament (8th, 2nd session: 1801). House of Assembly **NS10**
Journal, 1802. Nova Scotia. Parliament (8th, 3rd session: 1802) House of Assembly **NS18**
Journal, 1803. Nova Scotia. Parliament (8th, 4th session: 1803). House of Assembly **NS24**
Journal, 1804. Nova Scotia. Parliament (8th, 5th session: 1804). House of Assembly **NS32**
Journal, 1806. Nova Scotia. Parliament (8th, 6th session: 1805-1806). House of Assembly **NS40**
Journal, 1807. Nova Scotia. Parliament (9th, 1st session: 1806-1807). House of Assembly **NS46**
Journal, 1808. Nova Scotia. Parliament (9th, 2nd session: 1807-1808). House of Assembly **NS57**
Journal, 1808. Nova Scotia. Parliament (9th, 3rd session: 1808). House of Assembly **NS58**
Journal, 1809. Nova Scotia. Parliament (9th, 4th session: 1808-1809). House of Assembly **NS65**
Journal, 1809. Nova Scotia. Parliament (9th, 5th session: 1809). House of Assembly **NS66**
Journal, 1809. Nova Scotia. Parliament (9th, 6th session: 1809). House of Assembly **NS67**
Journal, 1811. Nova Scotia. Parliament (9th, 7th session: 1811). House of Assembly **NS77**
Journal, 1812. Nova Scotia. Parliament (10th, 1st session: 1812). House of Assembly **NS88**
Journal, 1812. Nova Scotia. Parliament (10th, 2nd session: 1812). House of Assembly **NS89**
Journal, 1813. Nova Scotia. Parliament (10th, 3rd session: 1813). House of Assembly **NS99**
Journal, 1814. Nova Scotia. Parliament (10th, 4th session: 1814). House of Assembly **NS108**
Journal, 1815. Nova Scotia. Parliament (10th, 5th session: 1815). House of Assembly **NS116**
Journal, 1816. Nova Scotia. Parliament (10th, 6th session: 1816). House of Assembly **NS124**
Journal, 1817. Nova Scotia. Parliament (10th, 7th session: 1817). House of Assembly **NS132**
Journal, 1818. Nova Scotia. Parliament (10th, 8th session: 1818). House of Assembly **NS148**
Journal, 1819. Nova Scotia. Parliament (11th, 1st session: 1819). House of Assembly **NS163**
Journal, 1820. Nova Scotia. Parliament (11th, 2nd session: 1820). House of Assembly **NS177**
Journal, 1805. Prince Edward Island. Parliament (7th, 2nd session: 1805). House of Assembly **PEI12**
Journal, 1806. Prince Edward Island. Parliament (8th, 1st session: 1806). House of Assembly **PEI13**
Journal, 1817. Prince Edward Island. Parliament (9th, 3rd session: 1817). House of Assembly **PEI28**
Journal, 1819. Prince Edward Island. Parliament (10th, 1st session: 1818-1819). House of Assembly **PEI36**
Journal, 1820. Prince Edward Island. Parliament (11th, 1st session: 1820). House of Assembly **PEI44**
Journals, 1812. New Brunswick. Parliament (5th, 2nd session: 1812). House of Assembly **NB42**
Journals, 1813. New Brunswick. Parliament (5th, 3rd session: 1813). House of Assembly **NB45**

The Labradore fishery for the season 1814, 1813. Halifax Committee of Trade **NS94**
Laws and ordinances, 1817. Saint John **NB67**
Laws and ordinances, 1820. Saint John **NB94**
Lectures and sermons delivered in the Scots Church of Saint John, 1820. Burns, George **NB85**
Letter addressed to the Rev James Milne, A.M., 1818. Burns, George **NB70**
A letter from the Right Honorable J.H. Addington, Esq to Lieut. General Fanning, 1805. Prince Edward Island. Lieutenant Governor (1787-1805: Fanning) **PEI9**
Letter of instruction to the Catholic missionaries of Nova Scotia and its dependencies, 1804. Catholic Church. Diocese of Quebec. Vicar-General of Nova Scotia (1801–1817: Burke) **NS29**
A letter to the people of Halifax, 1820. Wilkie, William **NS183**
[*Letters on the DesBarres-Colclough controversy*], 1812 **PEI14**

Memoir on the cod and small fisheries of Nova-Scotia, 1818. Halifax Committee of Trade **NS144**
The memoirs of Fanny Hill, 1820. Cleland, John **NS172**
The militia being called out and about to take post in

various stations on the coast, 1812. Nova Scotia. Deputy Commissary General **NS85**
Militia general order. His Excellency the Lieut. Governor is pleased to direct that the following orders, rules, and regulations ... be strictly observed, 1814. Prince Edward Island. Lieutenant Governor (1813-1824: Smith) **PEI21**
Militia laws of the province of Nova-Scotia in force in the year of Our Lord, 1813, 1813. Nova Scotia [Laws, etc.] **NS97**
Minutes, 1810. Nova Scotia and New Brunswick Baptist Association **NS71**
Minutes, 1811. Nova Scotia and New Brunswick Baptist Association **NS78**
Minutes, 1812. Nova Scotia and New Brunswick Baptist Association **NS90**
Minutes, 1813. Nova Scotia and New Brunswick Baptist Association **NB46**
Minutes, 1814. Nova Scotia and New Brunswick Baptist Association **NB53**
Minutes, 1815. Nova Scotia and New Brunswick Baptist Association **NB54**
Minutes, 1816. Nova Scotia and New Brunswick Baptist Association **NB58**
Minutes, 1818. Nova Scotia and New Brunswick Baptist Association **NB75**
Minutes, 1819. Nova Scotia and New Brunswick Baptist Association **NB83**
Minutes, 1820. Nova Scotia and New Brunswick Baptist Association **NB92**
Mr Bromley's second address on the deplorable state of the Indians, 1814. Bromley, Walter **NS103**

The nature and uses of a liberal education, 1819. McCulloch, Thomas **NS159**
The necessity, the certainty, and the sufficiency of revealed religion, 1801. Andrews, Samuel **NB1**
Der Neu-schottländische calender, 1801, [1800] **NS3**
A new song on peace and conquered Bonaparte, 1814. Loyal British Hero **NB50**
The news-carrier's address ... to the patrons of the Royal Gazette, 1805. **NB25**
The news-carrier's address to the customers of the Royal Gazette, 1803. **NB18**
The news-carrier's address to the customers of the Royal Gazette, 1808. **NB31**
Notice is hereby given that all persons having any business to transact with the commandant, 1813. Saint John. Town Major **NB47**
The Nova-Scotia almanack for the year of Our Lord, 1817, [1817] **NS133**
The Nova-Scotia almanack for the year of Our Lord, 1818, [1817] **NS134**
The Nova-Scotia almanack for 1819, [1818] **NS149**
The Nova-Scotia almanack for 1820, [1819] **NS164**
The Nova-Scotia almanack for the year of Our Lord, 1821, [1820] **NS178**
The Nova-Scotia and New-Brunswick magazine, 1806 **NS41**
The Nova-Scotia calendar for 1814, [1814] **NS109**
The Nova-Scotia calendar for 1815, [1814] **NS110**
The Nova-Scotia calendar for 1816, [1815] **NS118**
The Nova-Scotia calendar for 1817, [1816] **NS122**
The Nova-Scotia calendar for 1818, [1817] **NS136**
The Nova-Scotia calendar for 1819, [1818] **NS151**
The Nova-Scotia calendar for 1820, [1819] **NS166**
The Nova-Scotia calendar for 1821, [1820] **NS180**

Observations on the nature, evidences, and authority of the Christian religion, 1818. Cubit, George **Nfld14**
On seeing the address to the ship America, [1803]. Odell, Jonathan **NB19**
Opinions of several gentlemen of the law, 1802. **NB14**
Order of procession for the funeral of ... Jonathan Odell, 1818 **NB76**
Orders and instructions for the signal duty at Halifax, 1817 **NS137**

A patriotic call to prepare in a season of peace for one of political danger, 1819. Native of the Province **NS160**
[*Petition of inhabitants of St John's*], 1811 **Nfld10**
A poetical account of the American campaigns, 1815 **NS119**
Prince Edward Island. The following is a letter from the late Lieutenant Governor Des Barres to the House of Assembly, 1812 **PEI14**
Proceedings of the general assembly upon the convention concluded between His Majesty and the United States of America, 1819. Nova Scotia. Legislature. Joint Committee Appointed to Consider the Convention Lately Concluded between His Majesty and the Government of the United States of America **NS162**
A proclamation. Whereas an act of the general assembly of this Island was passed ... intituled 'An act for regulating fees', 1815. Prince Edward Island. Lieutenant Governor (1813-1824: Smith) **PEI22**
A proclamation. Whereas by a return from the register's office, 1819. Prince Edward Island. Lieutenant Governor (1813-1824: Smith) **PEI35**
A proclamation. Whereas by my proclamation issued on the first day of October 1816, 1818. Prince Edward Island. Lieutenant Governor (1813-1824: Smith) **PEI30**
Proclamation ... whereas every species of predatory warfare carried on against defenceless inhabitants, 1812. Nova Scotia. Lieutenant Governor (1811-1816: Sherbrooke) **NS87**
A proclamation. Whereas it appears that the following

officers ... gave permission, 1815. Prince Edward Island. Lieutenant Governor (1813-1824: Smith) **PEI23**

A proclamation. Whereas it having been signified to me ... that it is intended on the part of the crown to extend to the proprietors of land in this colony immunity from certain forfeitures, 1816. Prince Edward Island. Lieutenant Governor (1813-1824: Smith) **PEI24**

A proclamation. Whereas the government of the United States of America ... has declared war, 1812. New Brunswick. Administrator (1812-1813: Smyth) **NB39**

Proclamations ... and I do order ... that no trade or intercourse whatsoever shall be carried on between this province and the United States of America, 1809. Nova Scotia. Lieutenant Governor (1808-1811: Prevost) **NS64**

The prosperity of the Church in troublous times, 1814. McCulloch, Thomas **NS106**

Province of Nova Scotia. Revenue laws in force in 1802, 1802. Nova Scotia [Laws, etc.] **NS17**

Public notice. Whereas His Royal Highness the Prince Regent has been graciously pleased to grant the following indulgence, 1818. Prince Edward Island. Receiver General of Quit Rent **PEI31**

The question respecting the right of the United States of America to the islands in Passamaquoddy-Bay, 1805. New Brunswick. Court of Vice-Admiralty **NB21**

Remarks on a pamphlet entitled Popery condemned, 1809. Burke, Edmund **NS60**

Remarks on Dr Burns's View of the principles and forms of the Presbyterian Kirk, 1818. Milne, James **NB72**

Remarks on the Rev Mr Stanser's Examination of the Rev Mr Burke's Letter of instruction, 1805 [1806]. Burke, Edmund **NS36**

Remarks upon the life and manners of the Rev John Jones, 1810. Violet, Edmund **Nfld6**

The report, 1820. Halifax Poor Man's Friend Society **NS173**

The report of a committee appointed by the synod, 1818. Presbyterian Church of Nova Scotia **NS152**

A report of the case of the Nabby, 1818. Uniacke, Richard John, Jr **NS154**

A report of the formation, 1817. Methodist Missionary Society (Nova Scotia District) **NS130**

A report of the members names, 1807. Benevolent Irish Society (St John's) **Nfld1**

Report of the trial of Edward Jordan and Margaret Jordan his wife for piracy & murder, 1810. Fairbanks, Charles Rufus **NS70**

Report on the projected canal across the istmus, 1820. Lockwood, Anthony **NB87**

Resolved that the proceedings of the legislature of this Island in passing the two acts ... were in direct conformity with His Majesty's royal pleasure, 1805. Prince Edward Island. Parliament. House of Assembly **PEI11**

Resolves of the delegates, 1801. St Peter's Church (Halifax) **NS11**

A review of Edmund J. Reis's Short account of Michael McComb, &c., 1814. Knowlan, James **NB49**

The rights and powers of captors and prize agents, 1808. Nova Scotia. Court of Vice-Admiralty **NS53**

Rules and articles, 1802. Hand in Hand Fire Company (Halifax) **NS15**

Rules and articles for the better government of the militia forces, 1812. Nova Scotia. Adjutant General of Militia **NS84**

Rules and constitution, 1807. Benevolent Irish Society (St John's) **Nfld2**

Rules and regulations for the establishment and government of a watch and patrol, 1818. Halifax **NS143**

Rules and regulations for the militia forces of Nova-Scotia, 1808. Nova Scotia. Adjutant General of Militia **NS52**

Rules for the Saint Georges' Society, 1820. St George's Society (Saint John) **NB95**

The rules of the Heart and Hand Fire-Company, 1817. Heart and Hand Fire-Company (Halifax) **NS128**

School act, 1811. Nova Scotia. [School Act] **NS74**

The second report, 1817. Nova Scotia Bible Society **NS135**

Select portions of the new version of psalms, 1818. Hay-Drummond, George William Auriol **NB71**

A sermon in commemoration of the benevolence of the citizens of Boston, 1818. Sabine, James **Nfld15**

A sermon occasioned by the lamented demise of His late Majesty George III, 1820. Priestley, James **NB93**

A sermon on confirmation, 1801. Inglis, Charles **NS6**

A sermon preached at Saint John before the Saint John's and Union Lodges of free and accepted ancient Masons, 1820. Burns, George **NB86**

A sermon preached at St Paul's Church in Halifax before the Provincial Grand Lodge of free and accepted ancient Masons, 1803. Shreve, Thomas **NS25**

A sermon preached in the Methodist Chapel, 1819. Knowlan, James **NS157**

A sermon preached in the parish church of Fredericton, 1816. Mountain, George Jehoshaphat **NB55**

A sermon preached in the parish church of St Paul at Halifax on Sunday the 11th of June 1815, 1815. Inglis, John **NS113**

Sermon preached in Trinity Church, Kingston, 1809. Andrews, Samuel **NB33**

A sermon preached on 10th August 1804, 1804. Gray, Archibald **NS31**
Signal orders and instructions, [1802] **NS19**
Special notice to the landholders and resident agents of landholders, 1818. Prince Edward Island. Receiver General of Quit Rent **PEI32**
Speech of His Excellency Lieut. Governor Charles Douglass Smith at the opening of the general assembly ... 8th July 1817, 1817. Prince Edward Island. Lieutenant Governor (1813-1824: Smith) **PEI27**
Speech of His Excellency Lt. Governor Des Barres, 1805. Prince Edward Island. Lieutenant Governor (1805-1812: DesBarres) **PEI10**
Speech of His Excellency Lt. Governor Charles Douglass Smith at the closing of the session, 1820. Prince Edward Island. Lieutenant Governor (1813-1824: Smith) **PEI43**
Speech of His Excellency Lt. Governor Charles Douglass Smith at the opening of the general assembly ... 3d November 1818, 1818. Prince Edward Island. Lieutenant Governor (1813-1824: Smith) **PEI29**
Speech of His Excellency Lt. Governor Charles Douglass Smith at the opening of the general assembly on the 9th May 1820, 1820. Prince Edward Island. Lieutenant Governor (1813-1824: Smith) **PEI40**
Speech of His Excellency Lt. Governor Charles Douglass Smith at the opening of the general assembly ... upon the 25th July 1820, 1820. Prince Edward Island. Lieutenant Governor (1813-1824: Smith) **PEI41**
A statement of facts relative to the proceedings of the House of Assembly, 1802. Creon **NB8**
A statement of facts relative to the standfasts and the runaways, 1802. Job Creon **NB11**
The statutes at large, 1805. Nova Scotia. Laws (1st Parliament, 1st session: 1758 to 8th Parliament, 5th session: 1804) **NS37**
The statutes at large, 1816. Nova Scotia. Laws (8th Parliament, 6th session: 1805 to 10th Parliament, 6th session: 1816) **NS123**
The statutes, rules, and ordinances, 1803. University of King's College (Windsor) **NS26**
The substance of a decision ... upon a petition from the deputy to the treasurer of Greenwich Hospital, 1811. Nova Scotia. Court of Vice-Admiralty **NS75**
The substance of a judgment in the case of the Little Joe, 1813. Nova Scotia. Court of Vice-Admiralty **NS96**
The substance of a judgment ... in the case of the schooner Nabby, 1818. Nova Scotia. Court of Vice-Admiralty **NS146**
The substance of a sermon delivered in the Wesleyan Chapel, 1820. Alder, Robert **PEI37**

The theological compendium, 1817. Priestley, James **NS139**
The third report, 1819. Halifax Methodist Female Benevolent Society **NS156**
The third report, 1818. Nova Scotia Bible Society, **NS150**
To His Excellency Sir John Wentworth, baronet, and the honourable commissioners appointed to examine into the practicability and expense of opening an inland navigable communication, [1815]. Hildrith, Isaac **NS112**
To the honorable Caesar Colclough ... the address of His Majesty's Council, 1813. Prince Edward Island. Executive Council **PEI17**
To the honorable Caesar Colclough ... the address of the grand jury, 1813. Prince Edward Island. Grand Jury **PEI18**
To the honourable William Townshend, 1812. Prince Edward Island. Parliament. House of Assembly **PEI16**
A treatise on baptism, 1811. Monro, James **NS73**
A treatise on the first principles of Christianity, 1808. Burke, Edmund **NS50**
The trial of John Wilson alias Jenkin Ratford, 1807. Wilson, John **NS47**
The triumphale, 1820 **NS182**
Two sermons preached in St Matthew's Church, Halifax, 1820. Temple, Isaac **NS181**

Uniacke's laws, 1805. Nova Scotia. Laws (1st Parliament, 1st session: 1758 to 8th Parliament, 5th session: 1804) **NS37**
Union harmony, 1816. **NB59**

A valedictory sermon, 1817. Mountain, George Jehoshaphat **NB62**
Vastator perditus, 1819. Alder, Robert **PEI33**
A view of the principles and forms of the Church of Scotland , 1817. Burns, George **NB61**

We His Majesty's most dutiful and loyal subjects ... humbly beg leave to approach Your Royal Highness, 1811 **Nfld10**
Whereas it has been found requisite that certain alterations should take place in the table of fees, 1810. Newfoundland. Governor (1810-1813: Duckworth) **Nfld5**
Whereas it is the intention of His Majesty's government that the wharf ... should be used for the general accommodation of the town, [1812]. Newfoundland. Governor (1810-1813: Duckworth) **Nfld12**
Whereas the great want of specie in this island is continuing to increase, 1811. Newfoundland. Governor (1810-1813: Duckworth) **Nfld9**
Words of peace. McCulloch, Thomas, 1817 **NS129**

GENRE/SUBJECT HEADINGS

Acts
Addresses
Agricultural societies
Agriculture
Almanacs
Benevolent societies
Bible and tract societies
Biography
Canals
Carrier's addresses
Catechism
Charity sermons
Circular letters
Courts
Economics
Education
Election notice
Fast day sermons
Fiction
Fire companies
Fisheries
Freemasons
Funeral
Funeral sermons
Health
Hymns
Illustrations
Journals of parliament
Land holding
Laws
Legal opinion
Liturgy
Loyalist claim
Military regulations
Militia
Municipal government
Music
National societies
Natives
Pastoral letters
Peace of Amiens
Periodical
Petition
Politics
Printers and printing
Prize cases
Proclamations
Public notices
Religion
Religious societies
Sailing directions
Satires
Sermons
Shipwreck
Signal books
Slavery
Textbook
Trials
Verse
War of 1812

Genre and Subject Index

ACTS

see Name Index headings
New Brunswick
Nova Scotia

ADDRESSES

NS92 Bromley, Walter, 1813
NS103 Bromley, Walter, 1814
NS129 McCulloch, Thomas, 1817
PEI1 Address to Lieutenant Governor Fanning (Acadians), 1804
PEI2 Address to Lieutenant Governor Fanning (Charlottetown and Queen's County), 1804
PEI3 Address to Lieutenant Governor Fanning (Great Rustico), 1804
PEI4 Address to Lieutenant Governor Fanning (King's County), 1804
PEI5 Address to Lieutenant Governor Fanning (Prince County), 1804
PEI6 Address to Lieutenant Governor Fanning (Tryon River), 1804
PEI7 Prince Edward Island. Executive Council, 1804
PEI8 Prince Edward Island. Grand Jury, 1805
PEI10 Prince Edward Island. Lieutenant Governor (1805-1812: DesBarres), 1805
PEI15 Prince Edward Island. Grand Jury, 1812
PEI16 Prince Edward Island. Parliament. House of Assembly, 1812
PEI17 Prince Edward Island. Executive Council, 1813
PEI18 Prince Edward Island. Grand Jury, 1813
PEI27 Prince Edward Island. Lieutenant Governor (1813-1824: Smith), 1817
PEI29 Prince Edward Island. Lieutenant Governor (1813-1824: Smith), 1818
PEI40 Prince Edward Island. Lieutenant Governor (1813-1824: Smith), 1820
PEI41 Prince Edward Island. Lieutenant Governor (1813-1824: Smith), 1820
PEI42 Prince Edward Island. Lieutenant Governor (1813-1824: Smith), 1820
PEI43 Prince Edward Island. Lieutenant Governor (1813-1824: Smith), 1820

AGRICULTURAL SOCIETIES

NB91 New Brunswick Central Society for Promoting the Rural Economy of the Province, 1820
NS158 Lunenburg Farmer Society, 1819
NS184 Young, John, 1820

AGRICULTURE

NB63 New Brunswick [Agricultural Export Prohibition Act], 1817
NS167 Young, John, 1819

ALMANACS

NB36 *An almanack for the year of Our Lord, 1812* [1811]
NB38 *An almanack for the year of Our Lord, 1813* [1812]
NB60 *An almanack for the year of Our Lord, 1818* [1817]
NB68 *An almanack for the year of Our Lord, 1819* [1818]
NB69 *An almanack for the year of Our Lord, 1819* [1818]
NB77 *An almanack for the year of Our Lord, 1820* [1819]
NB84 *An almanack for the year of Our Lord, 1821* [1820]

NS1 *An almanack for the year of Our Lord, 1801* [1800]
NS2 *Astronomical calculations for the year 1801* [1800]
NS3 *Der Neu-Schottländische calender, 1801* [1800]
NS4 *An almanack for the year of Our Lord, 1802* [1801]
NS5 *An almanack for the year of Our Lord, 1802* [1801]
NS12 *An almanack for the year of Our Lord, 1803* [1802]
NS13 *An almanack for the year of Our Lord, 1803* [1802]
NS20 *An almanack for the year of Our Lord, 1804* [1803]
NS21 *An almanack for the year of Our Lord, 1804* [1803]
NS27 *An almanack for the year of Our Lord, 1805* [1804]
NS28 *An almanack for the year of Our Lord, 1805* [1804]
NS34 *An almanack for the year of Our Lord, 1806* [1805]
NS35 *An almanack for the year of Our Lord, 1806* [1805]
NS38 *An almanack for the year of Our Lord, 1807* [1806]
NS42 *An almanack for the year of Our Lord, 1808* [1807]
NS48 *An almanack for the year of Our Lord, 1809* [1808]
NS49 *An almanack for the year of Our Lord, 1809* [1808]
NS59 *An almanack for the year of Our Lord, 1810* [1809]
NS68 *An almanack for the year of Our Lord, 1811* [1810]
NS72 *An almanack for the year of Our Lord, 1812* [1811]
NS79 *An almanack for the year of Our Lord, 1813* [1812]
NS91 *An almanack for the year of Our Lord, 1814* [1813]
NS102 *An almanack for the year of Our Lord, 1815* [1814]
NS109 *The Nova-Scotia calendar for 1814* [1814]
NS110 *The Nova-Scotia calendar for 1815* [1814]
NS111 *An almanack for the year of Our Lord, 1816* [1815]
NS118 *The Nova-Scotia calendar for 1816* [1815]
NS122 *The Nova-Scotia calendar for 1817* [1816]
NS126 *An almanack for the year of Our Lord, 1817* [1817]
NS127 *An almanack for the year of Our Lord, 1818* [1817]
NS133 *The Nova-Scotia almanack for the year of Our Lord, 1817*, [1817]
NS134 *The Nova-Scotia almanack for the year of Our Lord, 1818* [1817]
NS136 *The Nova-Scotia calendar for 1818* [1817]
NS141 *An almanack for the year of Our Lord, 1819* [1818]
NS142 *An almanack for the year of Our Lord, 1819* [1818]
NS149 *The Nova-Scotia almanack for 1819* [1818]
NS151 *The Nova-Scotia calendar for 1819* [1818]
NS164 *The Nova-Scotia almanack for 1820* [1819]
NS166 *The Nova-Scotia calendar for 1820* [1819]
NS168 *An almanack for the year of Our Lord, 1821* [1820]
NS169 *An almanack for the year of Our Lord, 1821* [1820]
NS178 *The Nova-Scotia almanack for the year of Our Lord, 1821* [1820]
NS180 *The Nova-Scotia calendar for 1821* [1820]

BENEVOLENT SOCIETIES

see Name Index headings:
Benevolent Irish Society (St John's)
Halifax Methodist Female Benevolent Society
Halifax Poor Man's Friend Society
Society for Improving the Condition of the Poor (St John's)

BIBLE AND TRACT SOCIETIES

see Name Index headings:
Nova Scotia Bible Society
Society for Promoting Christian Knowledge. Halifax Diocesan Committee

BIOGRAPHY

Nfld6 Violet, Edmund, 1810

CANALS

NB87 Lockwood, Anthony, 1820
NS112 Hildrith, Isaac, [1815]

CARRIER'S ADDRESSES

NB18 The news-carrier's address, 1803
NB25 The news-carrier's address, 1805
NB31 The news-carrier's address, 1808
NB32 Address of the carrier, 1809

CATECHISM

NS93 Church of England, 1813

CHARITY SERMONS

NB55 Mountain, George Jehoshaphat, 1816
NB78 Burns, George, 1819
NB86 Burns, George, 1820
NS153 Priestley, James, 1818

CIRCULAR LETTERS

NS9 Nova Scotia. Legislature. Joint Committee on the Indians, 1801
NS56 Nova Scotia. Lieutenant Governor (1792-1808: Wentworth), 1808

COURTS

Nfld5 Newfoundland. Governor (1810-1813: Duckworth), 1810
PEI14 Letters on the DesBarres-Colclough controversy, 1812

ECONOMICS

Nfld9 Newfoundland. Governor (1810-1813: Duckworth), 1811
NS17 Nova Scotia [Laws, etc.], 1802
NS160 Native of the Province, 1819
NS162 Nova Scotia. Legislature. Joint Committee Appointed to Consider the Convention Lately Concluded between his Majesty and the Government of the United States of America, 1819

EDUCATION

Nfld4 Society for Improving the Condition of the Poor (St John's), 1808
NB88 Madras School, 1820
NS26 University of King's College (Windsor), 1803
NS74 Nova Scotia. [School Act], 1811
NS159 McCulloch, Thomas, 1819

ELECTION NOTICE

NB6 Chipman, Ward, 1802

FAST DAY SERMONS

NS31 Gray, Archibald, 1804
NS101 Parish, Elijah, 1813
NS106 McCulloch, Thomas, 1814

FICTION

NS172 Cleland, John, 1820

FIRE COMPANIES

NS15 Hand in Hand Fire Company (Halifax), 1802
NS128 Heart and Hand Fire-Company (Halifax), 1817

FISHERIES

NS94 Halifax Committee of Trade, 1813
NS144 Halifax Committee of Trade, 1818
NS162 Nova Scotia. Legislature. Joint Committee Appointed to Consider the Convention Lately Concluded between his Majesty and the Government of the United States of America, 1819

FREEMASONS

NB79 Freemasons. Solomon's Lodge, No XXII (Fredericton), 1819
NB86 Burns, George, 1820
NS25 Shreve, Thomas, 1803
NS155 Freemasons. United Grand Lodge (Nova Scotia), 1819

FUNERAL

NB76 Order of procession, 1818

FUNERAL SERMONS

NS113 Inglis, John, 1815
NS157 Knowlan, James, 1819

HEALTH

NS115 Nova Scotia. Lieutenant Governor (1811-1816: Sherbrooke), 1815

HYMNS

NB59 *Union harmony*, 1816
NB71 Hay-Drummond, George William Auriol, 1818

ILLUSTRATIONS

NS4 *An almanack for the year of Our Lord, 1802*, [1801]

NS20 *An almanack for the year of Our Lord, 1804,* [1803]
NS34 *An almanack for the year of Our Lord, 1806,* [1805]
NS121 James, William, 1816
NS170 Barrow, George, 1820
NS172 Cleland, John, 1820

JOURNALS OF PARLIAMENT

see Name Index headings:
New Brunswick
Nova Scotia
Prince Edward Island

LAND HOLDING

Nfld7 Newfoundland. Governor (1810-1813: Duckworth), 1811
PEI11 Prince Edward Island. Parliament. House of Assembly, 1805
PEI24 Prince Edward Island. Lieutenant Governor (1813-1824: Smith), 1816
PEI30 Prince Edward Island. Lieutenant Governor (1813-1824: Smith), 1818
PEI31 Prince Edward Island. Receiver General of Quit Rent, 1818
PEI32 Prince Edward Island. Receiver General of Quit Rent, 1818
PEI35 Prince Edward Island. Lieutenant Governor (1813-1824: Smith), 1819

LAWS

see Name Index headings:
New Brunswick
Nova Scotia
Prince Edward Island
Saint John

LEGAL OPINION

NB14 *Opinions of several gentlemen of the law,* 1802

LITURGY

NB7 Church of England, 1802
NB20 Church of England, 1804
NB43 Church of England, 1813
NB48 Church of England, 1814
NB71 Hay-Drummond, George William Auriol, 1818
NS14 Church of England, [1802]
NS43 Church of England, 1807
NS82 Church of England, 1812
NS104 Church of England, 1814

LOYALIST CLAIM

PEI9 Prince Edward Island. Lieutenant Governor (1787-1805: Fanning), 1805

MILITARY REGULATIONS

NS100 Nova Scotia and New Brunswick. Commander in Chief (1794-1800: Edward Augustus, Duke of Kent and Strathern), [1813]
NS51 Nova Scotia. [Billeting Act], 1808
PEI23 Prince Edward Island. Lieutenant Governor (1813-1824: Smith), 1815

MILITIA

NS52 Nova Scotia. Adjutant General of Militia, 1808
NS81 British North America. Commander of British Forces (1811-1815: Prevost), 1812
NS84 Nova Scotia. Adjutant General of Militia, 1812
NS85 Nova Scotia. Deputy Commissary General, 1812
NS97 Nova Scotia [Laws, etc.], 1813
PEI21 Prince Edward Island. Lieutenant Governor (1813-1824: Smith), 1814

MUNICIPAL GOVERNMENT

NB37 Saint John [Charter], 1811
NB47 Saint John. Town Major, 1813
NB67 Saint John, 1817
NB94 Saint John, 1820
Nfld10 Petition of inhabitants of St John's, 1811
Nfld11 Newfoundland. Governor (1810-1813: Duckworth), 1812
Nfld12 Newfoundland. Governor (1810-1813: Duckworth), [1812]
NS105 Halifax [Draft of Charter], 1814
NS143 Halifax, 1818
NS183 Wilkie, William, 1820

MUSIC

NB59 *Union harmony,* 1816

NATIONAL SOCIETIES

see Name Index headings:
Benevolent Irish Society (St John's)
St George's Society (Saint John)

NATIVES

NB40 New Brunswick. Executive Council, 1812

NS9 Nova Scotia. Legislature. Joint Committee on the Indians, 1801
NS92 Bromley, Walter, 1813
NS103 Bromley, Walter, 1814
NS171 Bromley, Walter, 1820

PASTORAL LETTERS

NB61 Burns, George, 1817
NS29 Catholic Church. Diocese of Quebec. Vicar General of Nova Scotia (1801-1817: Burke), 1804
NS30 Church of England. Diocese of Nova Scotia. Bishop (1787-1816: Inglis), 1804

PEACE OF AMIENS

NB7 Church of England, 1802
NS14 Church of England, [1802]

PERIODICAL

NS41 *The Nova-Scotia and New-Brunswick magazine,* 1806

PETITION

Nfld8 At a general meeting (St John's), 1811
Nfld10 Petition of Inhabitants of St John's, 1811

POLITICS

NB8 Creon, 1802
NB10 *The elector's mirror,* 1802
NB11 Job Creon, 1802
NB15 Spectator, 1802
NB15 Chipman, Ward, 1802
NS183 Wilkie, William, 1820

PRINTERS AND PRINTING

NS182 *The triumphale,* 1820

PRIZE CASES

NB21 New Brunswick. Court of Vice-Admiralty, 1804
NS53 Nova Scotia. Court of Vice-Admiralty, 1808
NS75 Croke, Alexander, 1811
NS96 Nova Scotia. Court of Vice-Admiralty, 1813
NS146 Nova Scotia. Court of Vice-Admiralty, 1818
NS154 Uniacke, Richard John, Jr, 1818

PROCLAMATIONS

NB39 New Brunswick. Administrator (1812-1813: Smyth), 1812
NS64 Nova Scotia. Lieutenant Governor (1808-1811: Prevost), 1809
NS87 Nova Scotia. Lieutenant Governor (1811-1816: Sherbrooke), 1812
PEI22 Prince Edward Island. Lieutenant Governor (1813-1824: Smith), 1815
PEI23 Prince Edward Island. Lieutenant Governor (1813-1824: Smith), 1815
PEI24 Prince Edward Island. Lieutenant Governor (1813-1824: Smith), 1816
PEI30 Prince Edward Island. Lieutenant Governor (1813-1824: Smith), 1818
PEI35 Prince Edward Island. Lieutenant Governor (1813-1824: Smith), 1819

PUBLIC NOTICES

NB47 Saint John. Town Major, 1813
PEI31 Prince Edward Island. Receiver General of Quit Rent, 1818
PEI32 Prince Edward Island. Receiver General of Quit Rent, 1818

RELIGION

NB9 *A dissertation on the thirteenth and seventeenth chapters of the book of St John's Revelation,* 1802
NB26 Norris, Robert, 1806
NB49 Knowlan, James, 1814
NB61 Burns, George, 1817
NB70 Burns, George, 1818
NB72 Milne, James, 1818
NB85 Burns, George, 1820
NS11 St Peter's Church (Halifax), 1801
NS33 Stanser, Robert, 1804
NS36 Burke, Edmund, 1805 [1806]
NS50 Burke, Edmund, 1808
NS60 Burke, Edmund, 1809
NS69 Burke, Edmund, 1810
NS73 Monro, James, 1811
NS139 Priestley, James, 1817
NS152 Presbyterian Church of Nova Scotia, 1818

RELIGIOUS SOCIETIES

see also Bible and tract societies
see Name Index headings:
Halifax Methodist Female Benovelent Society
Methodist Missionary Society (Nova Scotia District)
Nova Scotia and New Brunswick Baptist Association

SAILING DIRECTIONS

NS83 Directions for avoiding the Sambro ledges, [1812]
NS120 Directions for avoiding the Sambro ledges, [1816]

SATIRES

NB11 Job Creon, 1802
NS182 *The triumphale*, 1820

SERMONS

see also Charity sermons
Fast day sermons
Funeral sermons

NB1 Andrews, Samuel, 1801
NB33 Andrews, Samuel, 1809
NB62 Mountain, George Jehoshaphat, 1817
NB80 Milne, James, 1819
NB85 Burns, George, 1820
NB93 Priestley, James, 1820
Nfld13 Cubit, George, 1818
Nfld14 Cubit, George, 1818
Nfld15 Sabine, James, 1818
NS6 Inglis, Charles, 1801
NS25 Shreve, Thomas, 1803
NS181 Temple, Isaac, 1820
PEI33 Alder, Robert, 1819
PEI37 Alder, Robert, 1820

SHIPWRECK

NS95 Inglefield, John Nicholson, 1813

SIGNAL BOOKS

NS19 *Signal orders and instructions*, [1802]
NS137 *Orders and instructions for the signal duty at Halifax*, 1817

SLAVERY

NB14 *Opinions of several gentlemen of the law*, 1802

TEXTBOOK

NS138 Perro, B, 1817

TRIALS

NS47 Wilson, John, 1807
NS70 Fairbanks, Charles Rufus, 1810
NS170 Barrow, George, 1820
NS174 Hall, William Henry, 1820
NS175 Hall, William Henry, 1820

VERSE

NB18 The news-carrier's address, 1803
NB19 Odell, Jonathan, [1803]
NB25 The news-carrier's address, 1805
NB31 The news-carrier's address, 1808
NB32 Address of the carrier, 1809
NB50 Loyal British Hero, 1814
NS119 *A poetical account of the American campaigns*, 1815

WAR OF 1812

NB39 New Brunswick. Administrator (1812-1813: Smyth), 1812
NB40 New Brunswick. Executive Council, 1812
NB43 Church of England, 1813
NB47 Saint John. Town Major, 1813
NB48 Church of England, 1814
NB50 Loyal British Hero, 1814
NS81 British North America. Commander of British Forces (1811-1815: Prevost), 1812
NS87 Nova Scotia. Lieutenant Governor (1811-1816: Sherbrooke), 1812
NS101 Parish, Elijah, 1813
NS119 *A poetical account of the American campaigns*, 1815
NS121 James, William, 1816

Language Index

FRENCH

Perro, B. *Abécédaire religieux, moral, instructif, et amusant*, 1817 **NS138**

GERMAN

Der Neu-Schottländische Calender, 1800 **NS3**

Trades Index

BOOKBINDERS

Howe, David. Halifax **NS123**
Morrison, Alexander. Halifax **NS37**

PRINTERS, PUBLISHERS, ETC.

Acadian Recorder Office. Halifax **NS93, NS121, NS122, NS136, NS151, NS166, NS180**
Bagnall, James. Charlottetown **PEI1 to PEI44**
Bagnall, James. Halifax **NS49, NS70**
Chronicle Printing Office (Weekly Chronicle). Halifax **NS162, NS169**
Chubb, Henry. Saint John **NB54, NB60, NB61, NB69, NB70, NB77, NB83, NB84, NB86, NB92, NB93, NB95**
Chubb, Henry & Co. Saint John **NB48, NB49, NB52, NB53**
Cowdell, Thomas Daniel. Halifax **NS101**
Durant, William. Saint John **NB58, NB67, NB71, NB72, NB75, NB88**
Durant, William & Co. Saint John **NB37, NB46**
Fendon, G. **NS172**
Fillman, W.H.S. **NS172**
Free Press Office. Halifax **NS149, NS164, NS178**
Gay, Archibald. Halifax **NS4, NS13, NS20, NS25, NS27, NS28, NS29, NS33, NS36**
Gay, Elizabeth. Halifax **NS34, NS41**
Gay and Merlin. Halifax **NS11**
Gazette Office (Royal Gazette). Halifax **NS141**
Henrich, Anthon. Halifax **NS3**
Henry, Anthony. Halifax **NS2**
Holland, Anthony H. Halifax **NS92, NS96, NS101, NS103, NS118, NS121, NS125, NS136, NS139, NS144, NS145, NS151, NS153, NS159, NS160, NS166, NS183**
Holland & Co. Halifax **NS179, NS180**
Howe, David. Halifax **NS111, NS126, NS127**
Howe, John. Halifax **NS1, NS5, NS6, NS7, NS8, NS10, NS12, NS14, NS15, NS16, NS18, NS21, NS22, NS23, NS24, NS26, NS30**
Howe, John and Son. Halifax **NS31, NS32, NS35, NS37, NS38, NS39, NS40, NS42, NS43, NS44, NS46, NS47, NS48, NS50, NS52, NS53, NS54, NS55, NS57, NS58, NS59, NS60, NS61, NS62, NS63, NS65, NS66, NS67, NS68, NS69, NS71, NS72, NS73, NS75, NS76, NS77, NS78, NS79, NS80, NS82, NS84, NS86, NS88, NS89, NS90, NS91, NS95, NS97, NS98, NS99, NS100, NS102, NS104, NS105, NS106, NS107, NS108, NS141, NS147, NS148, NS150, NS152, NS161, NS163, NS165, NS176, NS177**
Howe, John Junior. Halifax **NS119**
Howe, John, Son & Co. Halifax **NS113, NS114, NS116, NS117, NS123, NS124, NS128, NS131, NS132**
Humbert, Stephen. Saint John **NB59**
Journal Office (Halifax Journal). Halifax **NS142, NS168**
Lugrin, George K. Fredericton **NB55, NB56, NB57, NB62, NB63, NB64, NB65, NB66, NB73, NB74, NB79, NB80, NB81, NB82, NB87, NB89, NB90**
Lugrin, George K. Saint John **NB51**
Member of the Congregation. Halifax **NS129**
Minns, William. Halifax **NS169**
Mott, Ann. Saint John **NB52**
Mott, Jacob S. Saint John **NB17, NB24, NB26, NB28, NB29, NB30, NB33, NB34, NB35, NB36, NB38, NB41, NB42, NB43, NB44, NB45, NB47, NB52**
Munro, John. Halifax **NS142, NS168, NS181**
Norris, C. & Co. Exeter, NH **NB59**
Novator Office. Halifax **NS70**
Recorder Office (Acadian Recorder). Halifax **NS101, NS103, NS109, NS110, NS118, NS174, NS182**

Reynolds, William and Company. Saint John **NB68, NB78, NB85**
Royal Gazette. Saint John **NB18, NB25, NB31**
Royal Gazette Office. Halifax **NS74**
Ryan, John. Saint John **NB1, NB2, NB3, NB4, NB5, NB7, NB9, NB12, NB13, NB14, NB16, NB20, NB21, NB22, NB23, NB27,**
Ryan, John. St John's **Nfld9, Nfld13, Nfld14, Nfld15**
Ryan, John & Son. **Nfld1, Nfld2, Nfld3, Nfld4**
Ryan, Michael. St John's **Nfld6**
Star Office. Saint John **NB85**
Times; or, True Briton. Saint John **NB32**
Ward, Edmund. Halifax **NS129, NS130, NS133, NS134, NS135, NS138, NS140, NS143, NS146, NS149, NS154, NS155, NS156, NS157, NS164, NS171, NS173, NS175, NS178**

Place of Publication Index

Charlottetown **PEI1 to PEI44**
Exeter, NH **NB59**
Fredericton **NB55, NB56, NB57, NB62, NB63, NB64, NB65, NB66, NB73, NB74, NB76, NB79, NB80, NB81, NB82, NB87, NB89, NB90**
Halifax **NS1 to NS171, NS173 to NS184**
Saint John **NB1, NB2, NB3, NB4, NB5, NB6, NB7, NB8, NB9, NB10, NB11, NB12, NB13, NB14, NB15, NB16, NB17, NB18, NB19, NB20, NB21, NB22, NB23, NB24, NB25, NB25, NB26, NB27, NB28, NB29, NB30, NB31, NB32, NB33, NB34, NB35, NB36, NB37, NB38, NB39, NB40, NB41, NB42, NB43, NB44, NB45, NB46, NB47, NB48, NB49, NB50, NB51, NB52, NB53, NB54, NB58, NB59, NB60, NB61, NB67, NB68, NB69, NB70, NB71, NB72, NB75, NB77, NB78, NB83, NB84, NB85, NB86, NB88, NB92, NB93, NB94, NB95**
St John's **Nfld1 to Nfld15**

www.ingramcontent.com/pod-product-compliance
Lightning Source LLC
LaVergne TN
LVHW082004060826
844660LV00031B/1275